BEING VICTORIAN

How It Felt Then,
Why It Matters Now

Jamie Camplin

UNICORN

For my children and grandchildren

Frontispiece: The names of the young couple are lost to history, though we do know that the man studied at Corpus Christi College, Cambridge during the 1860s.

Published in 2025 by
Unicorn, an imprint of Unicorn Publishing Group
Charleston Studio
Meadow Business Centre
Lewes BN8 5RW
www.unicornpublishing.org

ISBN 978 1 917458 28 3
10 9 8 7 6 5 4 3 2 1

Design by newtonworks.uk
Printed in Latvia for Finetone

BEING VICTORIAN

CONTENTS

'A WEEKEND BY THE SEA'   1
Prologue

1. 'WONDERFUL DISCOVERIES OF A WONDERFUL AGE'   10
Introduction

2. 'THE PECULIAR PRIDE OF THE PRESENT AGE'   26
Ideas of Progress

3. 'TRIUMPHS OVER ALL INANIMATE MATTER'   44
Global Economic Dominance

4. 'A NEW WORLD UNDER SCRUTINY'   84
The Press, the Books, the Debates

5. 'NOBODY DARES RESIST IT'   108
Who Should Govern – and How?

6. 'THE SOUND COMMON SENSE OF THE COUNTRY'   142
The Professionalization of Everything

7. 'THE MARCH OF INTELLECT'   172
Communicating Reason and Faith

8. 'ONE HALF OF ENGLISH SOULS THIS DAY'   193
The Condition of England Question

9. 'EDUCATION FOR ALL'   225
Even Women and the Poor?

10. 'WHO OWNS PROGRESS?'   249
Great Britain and the World

11. 'WHAT HAPPENED NEXT?'   288
Connecting Victorians to Us

Notes p. 305 • List of Illustrations p. 315 • Index p. 316

'A WEEKEND BY THE SEA'

PROLOGUE

Late one July weekend in the 1870s, when – it was said – the London Season was 'fast dying of the dust', Laurence Oliphant invited what the *Morning Post* called 'a select circle of friends' to his seaside villa, a house of porticoes and pillars and statues very much in the Classical style. It was typical of the extent to which the Victorians appropriated the Classical world for their own purposes (in a way that might not convince our more sceptical eyes) that it should be seen – at least through the eyes of a fashionable female novelist of the time – as the sort of house in which the gormandizing Lucullus might have feasted, or the oversexed Clodius wreathed the brows of the super-accomplished Greek courtesan Aspasia with rose petals.[1]

Oliphant was 33, some way past the days of his twenties, when his considerable talents suggested that he was likely to do something of note. An unkind observer might have hinted that he was heading for the time, though not just yet, when the consensus would be that he might have done anything if he had chosen to do so. He tells Isy Froude, whom we will meet during the weekend, that we are haunted with the power of imagining that there might be something worth living for, 'and are pursued with the knowledge that there never is'. He so wants one great cause, but politics is just a petty, weary game, while religion post-Darwin is dead and replaced by Humanity (a poor deity). What should he labour for? He hates wasted moments: 'I could do something…. I feel I have powers.'

Everyone had arrived by dinner on Saturday evening. One of the guests, who looks very like William Hardinge – an aesthete, a wryly romantic writer and, less charitably, nicknamed the 'Balliol bugger' in Oxford, where he had a troublesome relationship with the art historian Walter Pater – found Laurence in the library contemplating a pile of menu cards in front of him.

These cards were not concerned with matters of cuisine; the cook had that matter fully worked out. Instead, a different kind of fare was at issue: a menu for conversation. There would be tongues for tasting, and there would be tongues for talking. The two men discussed the matter. What would be appropriate for soup – 'the first vernal breath of discussion that is to open the buds of the shy and strange souls' gathered at the table? 'Love' proposes Hardinge. Too 'strong' at the beginning, too 'real' counters his host. 'Religion' was surely more suitable. But Hardinge suggests that, too, would be 'rather strong meat for some'.

The ice broken, they then make rapid progress. The 'Aim of Life' is decided upon for the soup, then 'Town and Country' – where best to achieve an objective – with 'Society' a natural sequel. For entrées there would be 'Art and Literature', 'Love and Money', 'Riches and Civilisation'. 'The Present' would be 'solid and satisfying', as indeed it was, leaving mere dalliance of an insubstantial kind for the *entremets*, focused on 'The Future'.

Who was to be present at this 'feast of reason'? It was soon to become clear that the company included many figures of distinction. Here was Darwin's bulldog, T.H. Huxley, with a formidable-looking face, copious black whiskers and bushy eyebrows, but by no means Darwin's poodle when it came to popularizing his ideas, rather using them as a vehicle to support the importance of science and scientific education for all. Like many of those among the company, his public profile and changes of mood could easily mislead; as he had written to Kate Amberley – mother of the philosopher Bertrand Russell – some years earlier, his protoplasm was 'by no means the unstable and semifluid character you imagine', but alas he was unable to take up her invitation because his excitable family would object to his absence on his birthday. That at least gave him the chance to offer evidence that he did, after all, have 'the ordinary natural affections'.[2]

Here, too, John Ruskin, who writes so divinely that God should surely not feel threatened by scientific discovery, 'a prophet for his age' because he teaches realism, rather than the vagueness that comes from 'the mists of feeling', according to the young George Eliot – rather misleadingly – in 1856; and Walter Pater, who found Ruskin's *Modern Painters* inspirational when he read it as a schoolboy, but had been rather crushed when another undergraduate at Oxford (allegedly W.H. Mallock) passed his correspondence with William Hardinge to the formidable Master of Balliol, Benjamin Jowett. Jowett sent Hardinge down for 'keeping and reciting immoral poetry', sonnets for a male lover.[3] Pater, depicted in the house as a 'pale creature, with large moustache, looking out of the window at the sunset', was nevertheless to become an important influence on the modern evolution of art criticism and literature, even if he did have to remove the Conclusion to his 1873 major work, *The Renaissance*, after an outcry against its amoral hedonism. The ever witty G.K. Chesterton summed up: 'In Pater we have Ruskin without the prejudices, that is, without the funny parts.'[4]

Pater, whether on academic matters or life itself, was all for a subjective, relativist approach, unlike another key Victorian figure present that evening, Matthew Arnold, with his hard, moralistic and – as he thought – objective mode of instruction. There was something very Victorian about the way he combined the roles of very considerable poet and man of letters with the direct experience of earning his living as a School Inspector, enabling him to experience new ways of life for an employment that involved using the railways, reading while waiting for trains, reading in diverse hotel rooms, as well as putting him in touch on the ground with one of the great issues of the age: how to educate the rapidly growing population and who was to fund that – church, philanthropist, state? In the end, he asked too much, a point made less kindly by his contemporary, Sir Joshua Girling Fitch (himself a brilliant educationist), when he described him as a 'man who held a moral smelling-bottle at his nose, and exacted an impossible standard of life from a busy and strenuous people who had a living to get.'[5]

Arnold, son of the celebrated headmaster of Rugby, was another Balliol man, though it was many years after his time that a further member of the house party, Benjamin Jowett, became Master of the College and acquired the tag, 'All there is to know I know it.' Jowett was certainly a considerable theologian, university reformer and Platonist, though not surprisingly, his suggestion that platonic love eschewed sex was not Pater's conclusion.[6] Not

1 Benjamin Jowett. Behind the gentle and unworldly demeanour of *Spy*'s 1876 caricature lay a man with a subtle yet steely determination, used to create a small army of pupils destined for public service at home and across the globe. In a letter to a friend two years earlier, Jowett had called for the working classes to be 'taught to demand a free education – free and compulsory'.

much liked by some of those present, Jowett was nevertheless an outstanding Victorian: not just a brilliant Greek scholar, but wonderfully skilful in trying to navigate the church through difficult challenges raised by the many discoveries of modern science by arguing for 'the spirit of inquiry into historical facts', thereby 'bringing to light…inconsistencies' in the ancient testimony that underpinned accepted theology, and above all by helping to foster a new class of public servants and other kinds of leader with the integrity and skills to contribute wisely to the needs of a society facing any number of changes. Moreover, as a young man, after being made a Fellow of Balliol as an undergraduate, he made a series of expeditions to France and especially to Germany in order to be fully informed about Continental scholars and their involvement in shaping the future through a better understanding of the past. The modern assumption that leaders of British thought were parochial is one of the many myths about Victorian Britain.

It would be unfair to describe such luminaries as mere observers – on the contrary, we shall see how they helped to mould the future – but there was certainly something distinctively different about the representatives of the scientists at the gathering. John Tyndall, who did so much to bring experimental physics to a receptive wider audience, succeeded Michael Faraday, pioneer of our understanding of electricity, at the Royal Institution, which had been founded in 1799 to introduce new technology and science to the general public. Tyndall had recently, in 1874, stridently told the Belfast gathering of the British Association for the Advancement of Science, founded in 1831, that science's position was now impregnable and that it would take from theology 'the entire domain of cosmological theory. All schemes and systems which thus infringe upon the domain of science must, in so far as they do this, submit to its control, and relinquish all thought of controlling it.' And W.K. Clifford, also a member of Laurence Oliphant's weekend party, whose work has been increasingly seen as important to geometry, mathematical physics and computing, was a fervent atheist, who was scathing a few years later in *The Ethics of Belief* (1877) about conviction based on 'insufficient evidence'.

Another guest, George Herbert, Disraeli's Under-Secretary for War (albeit briefly, 1874–75) and the 13th Earl of Pembroke – a peerage going back to 1339 – was a literal reminder that aristocracy still had a voice and seemed to be skilfully exploiting that in new circumstances. At a dinner in Salisbury in April 1874, he accepted that 'everybody, or nearly everybody' now believed in progress of different kinds, some of which was produced by scientific understanding. But while he was sure that John Bull was 'willing to consent to really necessary reforms', when it came to a mere following of theories, 'he showed that he had no notion of doing anything of the kind'.[7] To the annoyance of radicals, he was broadly correct. Also present was the beautiful Mary Singleton, later Baroness Currie, better known under her novelist's pen name Violet Fane, from a character in Disraeli's early novel *Vivian Grey* (1826) who dies tragically before the end. Her social skills enlivened any gathering; her poetry tended to focus autobiographically on illicit love affairs, of which she had many. At one point, she was empathetically to provide comfort to a depressed Oscar Wilde when he found the 'sunless, loveless winter' left him unable to write.

And yet all was not quite what this description has suggested. These real and significant – most, but not all – figures from Victorian England in fact appeared in a book by W.H. Mallock titled *The New Republic*, which the *Saturday Review* was to call 'a thinly veiled parody of the opinions, manners and personal appearance of a number of living persons famous in the world of science and letters', first published in volume form in 1877 and dedicated to Violet Fane.[8] They appeared under other names, and their weekend retreat recalled William Froude's house at Chelston Cross, near Torquay, a focus for a stream of English, Continental European and American visitors of note. William was Mallock's uncle and a noted engineer and naval architect; his brother J.A. Froude was perhaps the best-known historian in England after Macaulay's death in 1859 and had introduced Mallock to Britain's greatest polemicist, Thomas Carlyle.[9] In his Chelsea drawing room, Carlyle, dressed

2 Millais's portrait of Carlyle had a turbulent history, attacked by the Suffragette Anne Hunt with a meat cleaver in 1913 because Mrs Pankhurst had been rearrested. The subject himself, by then (1877) aged 81, seemed to have lost his 'passionate vehement face of middle age', now with hints of his peasant origins, of tenderness and sorrow, according to the painting's commissioner, J.A. Froude.

in 'a long, shapeless and extravagantly dirty dressing gown, offered a grunt as a greeting and crossed the room to the fireplace, lighting a pipe by sticking its head between the bars.' Mallock noted the decrepit slippers close by with distaste, accentuated when they went for a walk and the great man 'blew his nose in a pair of old woollen gloves.' 'If you represent fame, let me represent obscurity,' thought Mallock (and that is what history decided, supported by Carlyle, who expressed his own opinion when Mallock was leaving: 'Oh, man! But ye're a poor creature'[10]). Benjamin Jowett (Dr Jenkinson), who had a sister in Torquay, lunched at Chelston Cross. Mallock remembered him with blinking eyes, fresh pink cheeks, snow-white hair and a birdlike treble voice, coming 'to inspect me and see how I should pass muster as one of his own disciples.' Evidently, he did pass muster, and at Balliol Jowett introduced him to the poets Browning and Swinburne, resulting in such an effervescent meeting that Jowett eventually had to throw them all out.

Mallock's book was the work of a conservative thinker, though he insisted in his memoirs that his characters were 'drawn without any disguise' and that 'a definite fidelity of portraiture' was essential to his plan. It reflected its period in underestimating the role that women were playing, both in contributing to progress and making their own progress against heavy odds. Violet Fane, as Mrs Singleton, is given an attractive personality as a social animal, with quick discernment of the foibles of her friends but with gentle skill in pointing them out, but she was still in the end a male caricature. Less so Francis Pattison (female, but from childhood favouring the male spelling of her first name) as Lady Grace, whose multiple brilliances – as art historian, writer on French politics, campaigner for female work and trade unionism – were expressed as optimism by Mallock: society was growing more cultivated in the broad definition of that word used by Matthew Arnold (though not nearly cultivated enough for the latter). In various ways, whether a slow but sure retreat from the way women had always been treated, a new care for animals, a movement away from dogma or voices speaking against war, the future was looking an exciting place.

The real Miss Merton, Isy Froude – like her mother in thrall to Cardinal Newman and his impressive revival of Catholicism, and also cousin to Mallock, daughter of William – is treated kindly by Jowett, who tells her that in an age of change there are many things that will 'pain and puzzle us' – if they are allowed to – but that there have been many such ages before and will be many more in the future. 'Our age is not peculiar.' Miss Merton makes the acute point that their age was surely peculiar because of the extraordinary rapidity of the changes, not that Jowett takes the least notice.

Mallock's depiction may have been influenced not only by conventional male attitudes, but the possibility that Isy was the love of his life, though she was to refuse him.

Because so much of the political and intellectual discourse in the 19th century focused on male views, we will need to dig deeper just to find the creative and determined ways so many women contributed to an evolving society without being given the authority to do so. Isy Froude was to move to Cambridge with her husband, Anatole von Hügel, in 1880. She campaigned for undergraduate admission for Roman Catholics; at home, she was at the centre of an intellectual powerhouse with her friends from the newly created colleges of Newnham and Girton; in the university, she donated much of her own money to found the Museum of Archaeology and Anthropology. She worked tirelessly on improving living conditions for the poor and was quick to organize the taking in of Belgian refugees during the First World War. Was *The Tablet* being patronising in describing her as 'minute in stature and delicately made'? It was, but at least it acknowledged her seriousness of purpose when exploring her many interests.

Gender matters apart, figures in Mallock's life who debated that fictional weekend, together with the subjects they explored and the assertions they made, will weave in and out of the pages that follow. What he does so cleverly, despite his own conservative position, is to make clear the range of opinions, albeit satirized, exhibited in the century's great debates. Most of his protagonists – the aristocrats apart – were from the middle class. They set the agendas in a highly articulate and often dominant way, but they were not just preoccupied with themselves, conscious both of a still-powerful aristocracy and many voices from below that add different perspectives and who will be explored in this book not just for their intrinsic interest, but for their own role in making the future.

Mallock's book was for a while much commented upon, which isn't to say everyone approved. Jowett observed that 99 men out of 100 could have written the book, but the hundredth was too much of a gentleman to have had it printed. Violet Fane was supportive of Mallock. Disraeli hastened to tell her that he would lose no time 'in perusing the bright creations of your young friend's pencil'. The Prime Minister ranked it highly for originality with his own *The Voyage of Captain Popanilla* (1827) – Disraeli silenced his immodesty with his charm – and with Laurence Oliphant's *Piccadilly* (1870). Disraeli glanced at Oliphant, present at the time, when he said this; Victorian elites were close-knit.[11] Oliphant shared some of the characteristics of the host, called Otho Laurence, in Mallock's party; although he was in his forties

7

at the time *The New Republic* was published (not the 33 of Otho Laurence), his character was, as we shall see, well drawn.

The New Republic is significant for two reasons. With hindsight, it served as a significant bellwether for the way Victorian dreams and Victorian confidence had begun to go wrong, with consequences carrying through to the present day. On the other side of the world, many years later, when Mallock died in the 1920s, New Zealand's South Island newspaper, *The Press*, put it bluntly: 'He has seen plainly enough the clap-trap that is associated with the word and idea of Progress.' But back in the several decades immediately after 1850, before *The New Republic* was published, the belief in Progress had become the dominant view, even though it had a long history in the evolution of ideas before that. Its heyday – unique in many ways this book will describe – was brief. Whatever else, *The New Republic* showed what a can of worms had been opened up both by literal progress in many areas of material endeavour and discovery and by the widespread adoption of the concept as a mantra. Mallock himself, in his later book on *Socialism* (1907), made plain that he wanted to maintain society as it was, though he did acknowledge that it is 'capable of improvement' – improvement being a safer word for him than progress.[12]

In the country house, the participants get to the subject early on, when T.H. Huxley (Mr Storks) asks gruffly whether anyone has found out the aim of life: 'As he said this he looked about him defiantly, as though all the others were butterflies, that he could break, if he chose, upon his wheel.' Undeterred, the mathematician W.K. Clifford (Mr Saunders) adjusts his spectacles and declares,

3 T.H. Huxley in *Vanity Fair*, 28 January 1871. For him, science was simple common sense; it proceeded via accurate observation and was merciless when logic was fallacious. In the human ocean of inexplicability, we could in each generation reclaim a little more land.

'The aim of life…is progress.' Benjamin Jowett (Dr Jenkinson) interrupts coldly, as if he was stabbing Clifford with an icicle: 'What is progress?'

Clifford admits that, like poetry, progress has been 'somewhat hard to define', but confidently ventures that 'progress is such improvement as can be verified by statistics, just as education is such knowledge as can be tested by examinations'. He makes the controversial proposition that a man is superior to a gorilla not because of the former's belief in God (in freedom from superstition, the gorilla is the superior), but 'in the hard and verifiable fact' that man can build houses and cotton mills.

In a lengthy debate with Ruskin (Mr Herbert), Clifford asserts that a good sewer is a far nobler and holier thing than the most admired Madonna ever painted, 'for holy in reality does but mean healthy'. Were railways, telegraphs, gas lamps, the projected Channel Tunnel nothing? A generation that travels 60 mph was at least five times as civilized as one travelling 12 mph. Tyndall (Mr Stockton) objects that science 'does not deal with moral right and wrong'; Clifford is quick with the answer: no, it shows that we are just 'clockwork machines, wound up by meat and drink'. Huxley (Mr Storks) is happy to report that progress is there not to be rejected, but systematically investigated by using 'firm, solid, verifiable knowledge'. His explicit implication, however, was that the word 'sin' retarded moral and social progress; science would establish 'an entirely new basis for morality', using 'the sunlight of rational approbation'. Ruskin, voice of humanism, complains that all of importance to humans is banished or buried by the things now absurdly called 'civilization'. He hopes there will be 'a stop to this progress'. A debate had been opened up that would continue for ever. In our own time, we would perhaps describe it as 'what best supports our "right to happiness"'; before the 19th century opened up the possibility, there was no 'right to happiness', or even prospect.

The restless, troubled spirit of the host at the country house, Otho Laurence – so like the real-life Laurence Oliphant – is a prescient symbol of the modern world then being created.

Twenty-five years before *The New Republic* was published, the prevailing atmosphere did not reflect these troubles: the idea of progress – like all ideas that sweep everything before them – was largely unquestioned, except by those found in every generation emotionally attached to the past and unable to remember its faults. Once there were calls for definitions and voices of doubt, a window of optimism perhaps unequalled in the history of the world began to falter.

How all this came about, and its consequences for our lives today, is the theme of this book.

CHAPTER 1

'WONDERFUL DISCOVERIES OF A WONDERFUL AGE'

INTRODUCTION

Charles Dickens's *A Tale of Two Cities* was published in weekly instalments from April to November 1859 in Dickens's new literary periodical, *All the Year Round*. The focus of *Being Victorian* is the period in which *A Tale of Two Cities* was written, rather than the period that it depicts (namely the French Revolution). I want to explore what it felt like to experience 'the best of times', and why it might have felt so, and whether those simultaneously experiencing something close to 'the worst of times' – especially as a consequence of the Industrial Revolution, or of discrimination by gender or race – had grounds for believing in progress towards a better future for them.

Is the past a foreign country? It always will be if we want to view it through the eyes, the values and the aspirations of the present. To get closer, we need first to get to know these people who lived before we were born. What was it like for them 150 years ago? How did people drawn from all sections of society feel about their own past? For some, it was much worse if they looked back; for others, there was no past, just a grim present. In a different context, but much to the point, one of the 20th century's greatest philosophers, Walter Benjamin, explained that a reproduction of a work of art lacked a defining feature of the artist's creation: 'its presence in time and space, its unique existence at the place where it happens to be.'[1] The same applies to human beings themselves.

When, in each age, children and grandchildren make their parents feel, in Caitlin Moran's discerning phrase, like immigrants 'from another time', the loss of understanding of the past has already begun.[2] If we want to comprehend a context and how it might have shaped our present, we can legitimately identify underlying trends, impersonal forces as we have tended to think of them in modern times. But a people-centred narrative – listening to what they said, observing what they did – often provides essential clues to beginning understanding.

There are many things that *Being Victorian* is not: not another survey of the whole age, of which there are so many; not an account built around the name of the monarch who gave the era its name. Rather, I want to discover what it felt like to be alive when an idea of 'Progress' – social, economic, political, technological, scientific, medical, cultural –was so deeply ingrained that it was found in the consciousness even of those makers of events normally suspicious of reflection; where that sense of progress came from; what justification there was for it; who believed in it and who didn't. But also – despite strictures about hindsight – how its legacy played out in every area of life, with consequences through to the present day.

The word 'Victorian' was very quickly applied to the monarch's time after Queen Victoria succeeded to the throne in 1837. By 1860, an irritated art critic in the literary magazine *The Athenaeum* complained that the Queen's name was being applied to 'everything from a colony to a new science'.[3] The entrenchment of the word made it easier for post-Victorians to characterize it.

Perhaps the most exuberantly expansive and animated decades in all history, radiating out from the mid-19th century, have become associated – for reasons to be defined – with an uncomfortable stuffiness, with exaggerated formality and priggishness, and above all by hypocritical values that today we firmly reject. In fact, while *The Times* might be accused of smugness when it summed up the period in January 1859, it accurately described how many people felt, and in many respects how it was. Comparing one age with another is notoriously difficult, it argued, if you set out to be just: 'We of the 19th century are accused of praising ourselves.' That self-flattery might be true, but isn't it odd, the article argued, at least to the extent that 'we do not think it has ever been done before'.

The pattern for all ages, as a matter of course, is to praise what came before and consider themselves degenerate; that has always been considered the proper thing to say. Yet today, old people 'do not now praise the days of their youth...they say "Things are improved since those days"'.[4] Fast forward to the 2020s and we have long since stopped believing that Mrs Beeton's *Book of Household Management* was an innovative guide to sound, let alone adventurous, cooking, but that is because we think Victorians were fuddy-duddy, when in fact, in 1861, Beeton was offering recipes for coconut soup, sea kale and saffron curry.[5]

Queen Victoria herself is not the presiding genius in the pages that follow, though her husband, Prince Albert, was intimately involved in helping to make

4 Queen Victoria and Prince Albert were both twenty at the time this photograph was taken in 1840, their marriage year. History remembers her for many reasons, but the father of her nine children (in sixteen years) might well have been called 'the best king Britain never had'.

some of the most exciting changes as mid-century was reached. Nor are any historical periods capable of rigid chronological definition: Jeremy Bentham, William Wilberforce, Samuel Taylor Coleridge and William Cobbett, all of whom influenced parts of the Victorian psyche, had all died by the time the young queen had come to the throne.[6]

It may be that the essence of Victorian times, certainly for two decades after 1850, is better defined as the 'Age of Progress', for 'Progress' permeated society both as an idea and as a largely visible reality, which is not to say that it was uniform in its achievements, or always successful in its consequences, or accepted either as a reality, or even a desirable objective, by everyone.

The *Annual Register* for 1851, looking back on 1850, painted a reasonably accurate picture of the everyday life of the nation. In January, on the East Lancashire Railway, a passenger train of only one carriage left Preston at 8 o'clock in the evening. Many joined it at Ormskirk (only recently reached by rail, giving its famous gingerbread sellers a whole new market), so at Maghull an attempt was made to add an empty carriage standing in a siding. In the darkness, the sound of the approaching, fast-moving Liverpool train led several passengers to jump out onto the main line. Three were killed. Railways provided good lessons that new technology was not without its dangers.

In the same month, chloroform – newly introduced as an anaesthetic in operations – was used in Thrall Street, Spitalfields, by 'Fat Beth' Smith, later transported to the colonies for fifteen years, to rob Frederick Jewett, a solicitor, who was left 'in a wretched apartment, and in a complete state of nudity' except for an old piece of rag carelessly thrown over him. Chloroform crime, like railway accidents, was another warning that progress – in fact, all the defining features of a modern world – needed to be approached with care.

There was a riot at a Protectionist meeting in Stafford (the freeing up of trade from tariffs aroused strong passions); a Chinese pirate fleet was destroyed (the global reach of the British naval power was increasingly apparent); on the Tibetan frontier of Bengal, the Rajah of Sikkim temporarily seized the British resident in Darjeeling, Dr Campbell, as well as the English naturalist Dr Hooker (Dr Campbell could probably be criticized for lack of subtlety or sensitivity, but Dr Hooker represented a passion for scientific investigation, not British hegemony; both were typical); Buchanan House, Scottish seat of the Duke of Montrose, was destroyed by fire after all the water in the cisterns and pipes had frozen (asbestos was widely used as insulation in factories as a by-product of the Industrial Revolution, and when the newspaper industry began at this time to generate large amounts of waste newsprint, many people used it *ad hoc* to fill cavities, in effect the precursor to cellulose insulation; scientific progress usually brought mixed benefits). The last entry for the year 1850 referred to the explosion of a Portuguese frigate in Macao. That had been long before on 29 September. News travelled slowly. But not for much longer; the era of the electric telegraph was shortly to begin.

Certainly, and especially in the 1850s, Great Britain had progressed to a unique world position: commander of the seas and occupying the role later adopted by the US as the global power broker; the world's dominant banker, financier and trader; investor, too, on a scale that no rival nation matched. Britain led the race to make a world on the back of technological progress and of a considered, if flawed and to many today objectionable, belief in a moral, civilizing mission. It managed also to modernize the state without recourse to revolution or authoritarianism.

The young John Stuart Mill had succinctly set the agenda – though anonymously – in *The Spirit of the Age* (1831), first published in the radical magazine *The Examiner*: 'mankind have outgrown old institutions and old doctrines – and have not yet acquired new ones'. Unlike our own times, especially since the dawn of the digital era, in which change happens largely in a historical vacuum, or where history is muddled into a general sense of 'the past', the 19th century in the years after Mill's statement not only knew

5 If Canary Wharf is today the financial capital of London, the London docks that preceded it (here warehouse and transit sheds on North Quay, c.1890) were a perfect symbol of Britain's global trading dominance: a huge spectacle of power from a distance, though the home of appalling poverty close up.

where it had come from, but was confident in its trajectory. If the steam trains that were so quickly to transform the ease and speed of travel began to outstrip the stagecoaches, then you could be sure that was just a beginning. If the ultimate truths of religion or ethics came under question through the increase of knowledge, reason in tune with intuition would take us forward. In matters of the economy, of politics, of science or even of aesthetics, there was the certainty of progress, energetically pursued.

In our own time, much of this is dismissed. In Michael Ignatieff's striking phrase, Progress 'sits in the attic of our minds like a glorious Victorian antique, as magnificent as a stuffed moose head and just as useless'.[7] But it felt very different in 1850, which isn't to say that everyone was unquestioning. The barrister William Johnston, who tried to sum up *England As It Is* in 1851, explained that while there was a consensus that 'the present century, and especially the last thirty years, had been an era of great "progress"', there were different views about 'the nature of that progress'. Across society, 'activity' had 'accelerated' to 'a prodigious degree', and some argued that 'improvement' could be related directly to 'the quickened movement of society'. Others argued that the beneficiaries were the upper and middle classes, with doubt about 'the masses', even to the extent that 'the great bulk of the people' were worse off.[8]

As we shall see, this last suggestion was not correct, and improvement in the quality of life of the poor and all the working classes provides a key, if complex, theme of this book. It would be more difficult to contest that there were abundant signs of a kinder society developing in Victorian times – not 'kind' in our absolutist definition of the word, but a large leap forward from any previous era in history, partly fuelled by Evangelical religion and a new sensitivity to suffering expressed in philanthropy, accompanied by a 'seriousness' that encouraged questioning of the social status quo.

The Times, in 1859, was again helpful in providing perspective. In the past, it suggested 'human want and misery' were regarded 'simply as facts, they were necessary, unavoidable, and so on'. Except for a few philanthropists, people stood by 'with folded arms, and saw the ravages of wholesale disease and want'. Half a century before, a soldier might be given a thousand lashes 'for the merest trifle'. Society saw not 'the slightest severity in it': judges, comrades, bystanders felt no obligation, much less horror. It was not that people were 'exactly cruel', the writer suggested; it was just law and custom: 'They never reasoned, they took the world as they found it'. But now there was 'an active, inquiring, busy, penetrating intellectual spirit of benevolence' in which people 'question themselves, then others, then ferret out cases, then bring people together, systematize efforts and combine forces'. For the first time in history, misery could not just be called 'an insoluble problem, as if that was all to be said or thought about it'.

At its simplest, a sense of 'Progress' became embedded because the 19th century demonstrated that Enlightenment ideas of applying reason could be seen in practice in multiple ways. Writers like Thackeray and Dickens had rivalries, but were clear-headed in expressing their observations. If you lived in what Thackeray called 'the age of steam', you could see the gulf between the new and the old world. Yesterday was defined by 'stage-coaches...riding horses, pack-horses, highway-men, knights in armour, Norman invaders, Roman legions, Druids, Ancient Britons painted blue'. Gunpowder and printing, he conceded, 'tended to modernise the world', but the railroad in itself had started a new era.[9] Ideas that people can see and feel are usually genuine and the more powerful for that.

The excitement was given frequent expression. In George Eliot's first reputation-making novel, *Adam Bede* (1859), 'even idleness is eager now – eager for amusement; prone to excursion-trains, art museums, periodical literature, and exciting novels; prone even to scientific theorizing, and cursory peeps through microscopes. Old Leisure was quite a different personage.'[10] The very sounds of the new age were exciting: Thomas Carlyle, in his essay on *Chartism* (1839), described Manchester waking up on a Monday morning: 'Hast thou heard…at half-past five by the clock; the rushing off of its thousand mills, like the boom of an Atlantic tide, ten-thousand times ten-thousand spools and spindles all set humming there as sublime as a Niagara, or more so.'[11]

Of course, there was no ducking the problem of working-class discontent that occasioned Carlyle's tract or its political expression, Chartism, a challenge that all Europe had been grappling with since the French Revolution, expressed – as he wrote to his friend Thomas Story Spedding in 1839 – by 'revenge begotten of ignorance and hunger'. But while the challenges raised by the 'Condition of England Question', the division between the rich and the poor summarized by Carlyle's widely influential phrase, were intractable, that was not to say there were no solutions or no expectation of making progress.

Carlyle had figured in the original text of Mallock's book, published in the magazine *Belgravia*, as Mr Rokeby, but was expunged from the book. He needs to be approached with caution as a witness. Ruskin, in awe of him as a young man and into middle age, calling him 'Papa', wrote to J.A. Froude that 'he was born in the clouds and struck by the lightning'; Froude himself suggested he was 'not meant for happiness'.[12] In *Past and Present* (1843), Carlyle provided an introduction to what became an accelerating process: was materialism the only kind of Progress that mattered? Who exactly was 'the wealth of England' blessing, or making happier, or wiser, or 'beautifuller',

6 Victorians were great letter-writers, but just seven years after the public unveiling of the daguerreotype, Carlyle was able to give a new dimension to what was to become a 40-year correspondence with the man Nietzsche thought of as the most gifted of the Americans, Ralph Waldo Emerson: he sent this image of himself to his friend in April 1846.

or 'in any way better?' Earlier, his 1829 essay 'Signs of the Times' did admit to the idea of his age advancing. For one thing, it had 'ceaseless activity', knowledge and education were advancing, even the existence of discontent was a sign of promise. There was no going back – but it would be a struggle.[13]

Carlyle's conclusion that industrialization and utilitarianism were not the answer to social progress became deeply influential. Dickens used Bounderby and Gradgrind to spread that view in *Hard Times* (1854), which he dedicated to Carlyle.[14] Yet Carlyle himself was not opposed to hard work, even factory work. To the contrary, it defined him. When as a poor man's son he forms a relationship with Jane Welsh, he insists (in December 1824) that 'It is no part of my plan to eat the bread of idleness so long as I have the force of a sparrow left in me to procure the honest bread of industry'.[15] But he was distracted, both in his impatience with the problems created by industrialization and by his idea that only 'great men' could ward off anarchy and chaos. In a sense, the extent of change did require great men (and women) to set about painstakingly, bit by bit, making reforms of all kinds. That was not 'the great' that Carlyle meant, but – all too slowly, perhaps – the Victorians did eventually make progress for all. When Carlyle died in 1881, Matthew Arnold nevertheless admitted that he had never much liked him; he had preached earnestness to a nation that already had plenty of it by nature, but was lacking 'in several other useful things'.

What didn't get destroyed by a new focus on working-class conditions, or even the slow pace at which amelioration of their state continued, was a sense of excitement about the extent of changes made. Even those who did not believe in progress by the application of reason and scientific method were caught up in the enthusiasm. Benjamin Kidd, self-educated and in

7 Jane and Thomas Carlyle began their marriage in shy awkwardness and quarrelled frequently, but – as he said – she had the ability to see through all that was pretentious and fabricated; she also proved over a lifetime that letter-writing can qualify as great literature.

thrall to the role of Christianity in fostering human progress, looked back in his bestselling and widely translated *Social Evolution* (1893) to what had happened. In the beginning, man was 'a brute, feebly holding his own against many fierce competitors', with no wants above those of the beast. Then – so quickly! – he has 'obtained mastery over the whole earth. He has organized the face of continents. The earth produces at his will; all its resources are his. The secrets of the past have been plumbed, and with the knowledge obtained he has turned the world into a vast workshop where all the powers of nature work submissively in bondage to supply his wants. His power at length appears illimitable.'[16] Today, we have at last learned differently, but that is how it felt then.

While it would be an absurdity to suggest that there was a uniformity of opinion in the 19th century (to the contrary, there was a ferment of different opinions, not least because of the spotlight that 'progress' put on poverty and so many other social ills), the pragmatic English, ever suspicious of abstraction and eager to use what they viewed as common sense to make ideas useful, were able to apply thinking about progress that was first developed during the Enlightenment to the visible progress of the following century. Viewed through today's eyes, Kidd's enthusiasm for 'progress' easily turns him into an apologist for white imperialism (which he was). Yet first we should fully explore what the context suggested to him, and why.

In our own time, whether behaviour is expressed by thinkers or doers, almost everything is interpreted psychologically. Are we by nature optimists or pessimists? Is pessimism a weakness or even a failure induced by a lack of positive thinking? Do we need an ideas-based theoretical foundation for human optimism? Such questions would have been thought quaint in the Victorian heyday. After all, 'the workshop of the world' was deriving vast benefits from its advanced machine production of textiles, iron and, later, steel. No one yet fully realized what the effects were going to be either on the environment or the less-developed parts of the world.

The positive news of these things, and the positive ideas they encouraged, were accelerated in dissemination by the growth of cities and accompanying improvements in transport and communications of all kinds. Isolation – the product of both low-tech and high-tech societies – was not an issue. 'Various questions', Charlotte Riddell's novel *Far Above Rubies* (1867) noted, 'go the round of families, little communities, large masses, the bulk of the population, the inhabitants of countries, all about the same time.'[17] Social media, we might say, is just a feeble approximation of that process, diluted by reversing the command structure of human being and machine.

The past was slow; the exciting present was fast, easily satirized, but secure enough to survive that. Sir Edward Hamley's *Lady Lee's Widowhood* (1854) recorded it so: 'We have fast speculators, fast statesmen, fast clergymen who have left the slow Church of England far behind – even history is written today by fast historians, only to show how incomparably superior the fast present time is to the past, and their works are lauded by fast readers and fast reviewers accordingly.'[18]

To be captivated in these ways was a peculiarly Victorian experience. H.G. Wells, as so often, got to the heart of the matter in his 'A Story of the Days to Come', first serialized in *Pall Mall Magazine* in 1899, when he suggested that in the future 'we have almost abolished wonder'.[19] Of course, the discoveries of the present day far outmatch anything in the 19th century, but Victorians lived in the moment when the world moved on from the societies described by Sebastian Faulks's Professor Putnam in his 2018 novel *Paris Echo*, in which the focus was not 'progress and enlightenment, just that there should be no net loss of knowledge'.[20] Neither a comforting sense that everything would remain the same, nor a sense of fast change that could easily finish up with the destruction of the planet and all its life forms could have the same appeal as the Victorian belief that Progress would continue into a brighter future.

There was, nevertheless, a paradox at the core of living with Progress. Victorians wrestled with it, gave it a platform and endowed all succeeding generations with the challenge: how to reconcile materialism with morality.

First, materialism and the associated prosperity – relative, of course (there were economic crises in 1857 and 1864, for example). In industry, in trade and control of shipping, in the creation of modern banking, in acting as the world's clearing house, in investment in infrastructure, for a brief period Britain was the globally dominant nation. Some of the changes became apparent in the beginnings of the Industrial Revolution in the second half of the 18th century, but by the 1850s and 1860s, a modern world could be seen to be taking shape: in transport and other forms of communication, press and telegraph; in houses and hospitals and schools; or sanitation and other necessities of a fast-urbanizing country. Invention and discovery could be seen in every direction, both on the farm as well as in the town.

Nevertheless, revelling in triumphalism omitted the key question attached to Progress: if there were winners, were there losers, too? And worse, those who had been exploited to achieve success and prosperity? The answer was undoubtedly 'yes', something that will be examined throughout this book. For the moment, the interesting question is how and why the social and political reform (from which many benefited) that accompanied prosperity (for more than a minority, but not for all) and which was part of the 'Age of Progress' took such a distinctive form. In 19th-century Britain, there were many continuities and many fundamental changes, but the remarkable thing is how the changes allowed, or even embraced on occasion, so many of the continuities.

There is a clue to this odd inconsistency, in which opposing forces cohabit, in a book entitled *The History of Progress*, first published in 6d weekly parts from June 1859 to July 1860. Its writer, best known for the many editions of his *Enquire Within Upon Everything*, was Robert Kemp Philip (sometimes spelled Philp), a former Chartist who campaigned for reform and working-class rights. He is credited with drawing up the second of the three Chartist Petitions addressed to the House of Commons – this second document gathering over three million signatures and presented to the House in May 1842 (though Philip fell out with Feargus O'Connor and the more radical Chartists, a familiar story in later Labour politics). In his *History*, Philip is careful to say that 'The work of the future is to perfect Progress, and to diffuse its benefits, since no power can resist its outward course, and its blessings are too many to be held in the group of monopoly.'[21]

History loves revolutions for their apparent clarity. Yet here was a man who managed to be both part of what seemed like a revolutionary movement to the elites of his time and yet was in thrall to Progress, noting that 'the hundreds and thousands of people who, in present days, visit our museums and galleries, or the Crystal Palace at Sydenham, are being schooled in the humanizing art of refinement, and trained to fitness for a higher standard of civilization'. There were lessons in 'our very streets' – modern shop windows packed with works of value and beauty, from all over the world and resulting from 'every description of human skill and industry'. He exaggerates progress in mass education, but he can recognize that 'the lamp of knowledge' was enabling new generations to 'see their way into the broad avenues of the Future'.[22] By the century's end, that really was becoming true.

'Revolution' is most usefully defined – and most emotionally satisfying – when it destroys the past in search of a perfect society. That isn't what happened in Britain. The French historian and statesman François Guizot recognized the situation perfectly. Marx and Engels published their *Communist Manifesto*, in which Guizot was damned (together, and with more justice, with the Pope, the Tsar and the Austrian Chancellor Metternich) as a reactionary just before this conservatively liberal French Prime Minister was toppled in the 1848 Revolution. In Britain, the Tory *Quarterly Review* commented on Guizot's 'Pourquoi la Révolution d'Angleterre a-t-elle réussi' of 1850. Guizot's position was that the French Revolution had been 'blind, wanton and sweeping'; England's Revolution – referring to what happened in 1688 – succeeded because it was 'as little as could be of a revolution', 'the least possible deviation from the existing system'. Endearingly, the anonymous reviewer admitted that he didn't quite have Guizot's confidence in Britain's constitutional system.[23] Still, Guizot's view was reinforced by the admittedly more conservative French historian and critic Hippolyte Taine two decades later, when he compared France forcibly overturning and remodelling its governance every few decades to England lending itself 'without perturbations to continued improvements'. In practice, this meant a tendency to make 'good government, that which pays the most respect to individual initiative, and confides power to the most worthy'. Besides, he said, no press in the world was as well informed, nor assemblies as competent.[24]

Thus, in trying to reconcile materialism with morality and individual freedom – yet another vital ingredient of Progress – we will find well-founded, if slow and often muddled, reform, not revolution. Slow reform, like everything else in the Age of Progress, did not mean that it was half-hearted. There were many like Tom in William Pickersgill's *The Belle of the Ball* (1865): 'Reform was Tom's creed – his Bible – his whole political lexicon. He had written it as a copyhead at school, and since then it had been perpetually present in his mind. All the institutions of the country were lost for want of reform. He advocated parliamentary reform – municipal reform – educational reform – reform of the administration of mechanics' institutes, teetotal and temperance societies, and public companies of every description.'[25]

Given the Victorians' reputation for pomposity and dullness, they could be very wry and funny about themselves. George Eliot, herself part of a new progressive elite, drew upon her experiences of provincial religion whilst growing up for the stories that became, after magazine publication, her first novel, *Scenes of Clerical Life* (1858), in which 'well-regulated minds' were not prepared to see 'dear old brown, crumbling inefficiency' make way for 'spick-and-spam, new-varnished efficiency' and all its diagrams, plans, elevations and sections.[26] Progress took many forms, and there was no Victorian voice, but a cacophony of voices operating – as Taine also observed – in the same way as English boxing matches: the combatants mauled and knocked each other down, shook hands and bore no malice.[27] That was not always true, and women in particular had to box hard in all circumstances to be heard. Even so, we are a very long way from the grim conflicts of the 'Age of Social Media'.

Consequently, the apparently destabilizing force of material and technological progress could be received as something reassuring, or at least less worrying, when it was accompanied by a social and political evolution that seemed to be going in the right direction. 'Progress' was specific when exhibiting an actual reform, but it was also highly practical because it was never an ideology (except in the hands of its arch-propagandists). It came out of experience – although all too slowly, because industrializing and urbanizing the country created casualties. At its best, it was wonderfully adaptable and pragmatic, enabling a transformation that was in many respects fast – just a few decades were decisive – but avoided authoritarianism.

In our own time, we have guilt or anger about the past, worry or anger in the present, and fear of the future. In the 1850s and 1860s, many people across society (obviously, there are many exceptions, from the poorest to those struggling to reconcile their faith with evolution and scientific discovery) were happy to live in the present, not least because as a character in Charles Kingsley's *Yeast*, first published in *Fraser's Magazine* in 1848, puts it, 'Your very costermonger trolls out his belief that "there's a good time coming"'.[28] Although the novel by this Christian Socialist reformer dwells on poverty, it also signals Progress. Moreover, while conformity, social conventions and doubt were built into Victorian society, that gave the prospect of testing the boundaries an edginess that it is difficult – given that everything has now been transgressed – to replicate today. Ironically, when Francis Fukuyama announced 'the end of history' in his 1992 book – inevitable progress into a peaceful and prosperous liberal democratic order – it was a lot less plausible than it might have felt in 1850, not least because there were abundant opportunities for you and you and you to 'progress' in the 'Age of Progress'.

There remains a book to be written that does not whitewash or gloss over the many Victorian imperfections, but which tries to take us a little closer to why it might have been an energizing, bold, exciting time to be alive, with an overall spirit that, as we shall see, cannot now be repeated despite all that we have learned in well over a century since Queen Victoria died in 1901.

Not everything was complicated, however. Invention and discovery at every turn could be an exhilarating thing. The works of popular novelists spread the word. Mrs Henry Wood received the huge sum of a thousand guineas for her tale of the fall of the Godolphin banking family in *The Shadow of Ashlydyat* (1863). 'Monkeys are discovered to be men – or men monkeys, which is it? [Darwin's ideas had already entered popular culture.] A shirt is advertised to be made complete in four minutes (buttons, warranted fast, included) by the new sewing-machine; we send ourselves in photograph to make morning calls; the opposite sides of the world are brought together by electric telegraph; chloroform has rendered the surgeon's knife something rather agreeable than otherwise; we are made quite at home with "spirits", and ghosts are reduced to a theory. Not to speak of these other discoveries connected with the air, earth, and water, which it would require an F.R.S. to descant upon. Wonderful discoveries of a wonderful age.'[29]

Were the discoveries wonderful? Was there reform? Was it 'the best of times' and, if so, for whom? In the pages that follow, we will first see why the idea that they were living in an era that was the apotheosis of progress touched so many people, before testing the validity of that assumption in every aspect of life and action – intellectual, economic and environmental, professional, political and governmental, social, moral and religious.

There was a high point. Then much of it went wrong, leaving the very different assumptions by which the world lives today. In considering the latter, at least, there is a role for hindsight, for what began as a straightforward and largely pragmatic observation of progress turned into something very different.

Progress first encouraged a blind optimism about the beneficial effects of technology, which quickly became questionable. There were, and have been ever since, many beneficial consequences, but it is apparent that we are unable or unwilling to predict the consequences of what we discover, especially the destructive consequences – as the misery of the First World War soon demonstrated. Continuing 'progress' has left us with the military capacity to destroy the planet many times over, but also with a (mostly) non-deliberate tendency to destroy the planet by other means, especially environmental. The lifestyle that goes with 'progress' – mobile, urban populations – mixed with ever more powerful medicines and medical techniques of an unpredictable kind raise the possibility of global plague. When Horace wisely suggested, over two thousand years ago, that Nature had the skill and inclination to fight back, he spoke of unwisely trying to expel it with a pitchfork. Our 'pitchforks' are the more powerful – and thus the more powerful in their consequences. Covid is not the end of the story.

Second, what began as a cautious, pragmatic, worthy process – the development of liberal democracy – soon morphed into something much more ideological: a belief in the possibility of the perfectibility of our social, economic and political institutions and – by extension – of human beings themselves. During the 19th century, the great questions that were to frame politics throughout the modern period (never more so than today) were fully apparent for the first time. Capitalism and freedom were revealed as the twin engines of Progress, but not as an absolute good. Both needed moderating and questioning and clever regulation to protect the individual. As a battleground of competing interests, modern, urban societies need leadership that benevolently melds them together with something coherent and acceptable to the majority. In practice, leaders have not satisfied the feelings of their electorates; liberal democracy has been unable to sweep all before it. It was no easier in the 19th century. Some disappointed Victorians had exhibited eccentric utopian ideas; some others took Romantic comfort in an idealised past; and still more urged restraint in the progress towards democracy, conscious of the dangers of a manipulated mob or because of their selfish interests.

From early in the 20th century, Progress was hijacked and fully transformed from pragmatic description to ideology, ideology that encouraged popular support for extreme political ideologies and their ruthless leaders, resulting in dictatorships, repression and violence, ostensibly to further the greater good on a scale that had never been seen before. There was also a more insidious consequence of a blind belief in perfection. We depend on our social, economic and political institutions for our welfare (in every sense of the word), but once they were assumed to be perfectible, the emotional pull of 'the right to paradise' displaced the reason that slowly and patiently made tomorrow better than today, albeit in a flawed fashion. The polarization of political discourse in Western democracies today, accompanied by an apathy induced by failed utopian promises that could never be realized, is traceable directly to an evolutionary process that began in the 19th century.

Third, a combination of scientific discovery and the elevation of material values threatened to destroy belief systems, just as they were making some headway in reconciling the divine with the human-created within a tolerant framework. The effects of twentieth-century alienation, in response to the apparent reality of humans being no more than an aggregation of molecules in a meaningless universe, were compounded by the loss of many of the moral values previously accepted by moderate people and their replacement by a rampant materialism of a startlingly meaningless kind within greed culture. For the same reasons, those who refused to join the secular parade became easy prey for fundamentalists, able to disrupt societies of all political complexions (as we see so clearly today with the rise of radical Islam and multiple populist 'beliefs' that deny free speech to others).

Fourth, the creation of a global economy and the accompanying imperialism led to the exploitation of innumerable people and bitter legacies. It is right that we examine that in detail, but we also need to apply a historical lens in a different way. H.G. Wells, whose life took in 35 years of Victorian Britain and 45 of the new century, put it convincingly in his *Short History*: in the 19th century, 'energetic men grabbed the gifts of power and plenty that science gave them, with little gratitude and no suspicion of the price that might presently have to be paid for them. Now the bill is being presented. The scale of distances has been so altered, the physical power available has become so vast, that the separate sovereignty of existing states has become impossible. Yet we cling to it obstinately.'[30] The tribe and the nation, together with technology, remain the most potent of forces. Imperialism threatened and damaged multiple tribes. Nationalism, expressed as imperialism, created clashes of civilizations. And the undiminished record of competing nationalisms which – with the possibility of economic gain – fuelled imperialism shows the full force of nationalism's self-destructive character. No supranational alliance, save for helping trade, has yet come close to finding a way of protecting national, tribal or individual feelings.

All of these things now feed into the new digital universe. Human beings have always had difficulty in distinguishing reality (there was plenty of fake news in the 1850s). But now, as we ponder the long-term effects of digitalization, any brave, if imperfect, attempts to identify 'the truth' or even 'a truth' – as many Victorians did – are hampered by the fact that, in many essentials, 'reality' has been replaced by 'the screen' and the propaganda of AI sludge and hallucination; free speech cannot operate when social media allows narcissism to substitute for reasoned debate; and 'authenticity' has become a mere game of Internet influencers and brands. Tech companies have become the new imperialists, colonizing not territory but people's minds.

The result is a very long way from the world of 180 years ago. We can trace the path from the one world to the other, but we need first to understand – and feel – what it felt to be alive in the first modern 'Age of Progress'. In successive chapters, we join Victorians in making the globally dominant economy; in creating a free press; in hesitantly but surely creating something close to liberal democracy; in professionalizing all the country's institutions and using modern science to develop new ones; in debating everything about their society armed with new and sometimes troubling knowledge; in making a start on tackling poverty and discrimination; in finally beginning to free women from their historically subservient role and developing education for all; in taking the notion of progress around the world, with many disastrous consequences. The issues arising from pursuing 'the modern' have shaped the history of the world ever since.

Does this matter? As Prime Minister, Tony Blair – a man so very unlike his immediate successor, Gordon Brown – told the US Congress in 2003 that there had never been a time when a study of history provided so little instruction for the present day.[31] How wrong he was.

CHAPTER 2

'THE PECULIAR PRIDE OF THE PRESENT AGE'

IDEAS OF PROGRESS

Here is an odd thing. In an Age of Progress, of change and flux, the structure of society remained stable. The rise and rise of the middle classes and the new voices of the working classes did not lead to the demise of the British aristocracy. They received deference: the radical Richard Cobden reported the dismal news that merchants and manufacturers seemed to want riches just to prostrate themselves at the feet of feudalism.[1] Aristocrats increased in number: in the House of Lords, from 366 in 1833 to 551 in 1900, especially because of the peerages given to businessmen and industrialists after 1870.[2] They could be forward-looking (always 'carefully on the side of what is called "Progress"', as G.K. Chesterton put it).[3]

Just before Christmas 1865, Lord Stanley, son of a three-time Prime Minister and soon to be the 15th Earl of Derby, told the Liverpool Chamber of Commerce that there was a union, a fusion of the mercantile and manufacturing classes and the landowners: 'if we were to measure time, not by the lapse of years, but by the progress of ideas, we are essentially removed from the days when speakers could get up at public meetings and talk about being governed by a half-feudalised aristocracy, which looked down with contempt on trade, which was always ready to drag the country into quarrels, and multiplied military appointments for the sake of their relations and connections. If any man were to hold that language now, one would be tempted to ask him if he had fallen from the moon.' Everyone now was interested in 'the progress of the industrial enterprise' and 'the war upon our greatest national enemy – pauperism'.[4]

Aristocrats invested in coal mines, in docks, in stocks and shares. They continued to be Prime Ministers and Cabinet Ministers (not, according to the Frenchman Hippolyte Taine, like the French aristocrats, 'ornamental parasites' with 'antiquated minds', but for 50 years governing not in the interests of their class but the nation, yielding to opinion, directing reforms).[5] They were active in local government. The Duke of Norfolk, Premier Duke of England, was Mayor of Sheffield; Lord Rosebery, first chairman of the London County Council, only resigned when he became Prime Minister.[6] They appeared to have reformed. Caroline Norton, granddaughter of the playwright Richard Brinsley Sheridan, wrote letters as 'Libertas' to the *Morning Chronicle* in 1848, at a time of working-class discontent, to demonstrate that the aristocracy had presided over 'measures of improvement'; they had disputes, but were 'honest pioneers of progress'; they are 'workmen of intelligence, as you are workmen of production'.[7]

This last would be seen today as patronising and *parti pris*, and all generalizations about class attitudes suffer, of course, because they are generalizations. There were many exceptions. Superficially, everything seemed to be about class in Victorian times, but the key point is something different: the social structure remained solid – an enormous help when everything else was changing. Understanding comes from exploring shifting patterns and relationships, not class or race slogans. Many people were self-consciously determined to rise within society; such characters fill the pages of novels, like the followers of 'Marion's code' in Charles James's *The Bramleighs of Bishops Folly* (1868): to establish a family in three generations, make money; unite money and an ability to attain 'a certain station' of power and social influence; lastly, fortify these with marriage. Time would do the rest.[8] Others were more discerning and showed a rational pathway of progress to the future. John Saunders, in *Hirrell* (1869), dedicated to Gladstone, suggested that society was just 'so many individual men and women'. If 'wise, prudent, and beneficent legislation' could help people to be born healthy, properly trained, given 'the power to labour for adequate reward in a suitable occupation', the power to marry, to become a citizen and to have a say in securing that the next generation should have the same, then there was no need to be concerned about 'the fate of society'.[9] The failure of Saunders's magazines, *The People's Journal* (1846) and *The National Magazine* (1856–57), was a sign that the destination was not yet reached. But it was on the right road.

The middle classes effectively controlled the dominant narrative of the Victorian period, so we might not be surprised that, as Esmé Wingfield-Stratford observed – looking back in 1930 – a 'robust optimism' was 'the prevailing sentiment', expressed in the belief that the effect of all the great changes taking place 'would be to make the world, and everybody in it, unimaginably better'.[10] If this seemed to be too good to be true, it is perhaps best compared with the overall situation in the many millennia before the 19th century – for most people, a particular kind of equality: an equality of poverty and no prospects. You could not convincingly describe Victorian Britain like that.

Who were the middle classes? They were themselves divided (but never precisely, however much they might want that) by income, by occupation, by lifestyle, by location. There were more of them in London and the southeast. With exceptions, the bankers and the merchants were richer than the manufacturers, even in Manchester. As nonconformists, encouraged to a moral lifestyle and abstinence from alcohol, the manufacturers tended not to make for country estates – at least not immediately – and many had homes not far from their factories and workers. Not all were as heartless as the novelists depicted them, but nor were they all like Titus Salt, the largest employer in Bradford and creator of the model village of Saltaire in the 1850s, with houses, almshouses, library, chapel, and an infirmary.

We don't much hear the voices of the manufacturers, mostly happily inarticulate and instead focused on their businesses; it is surely significant

8 The middle-class home in 1856. Three generations of the Frith family celebrate Alice (within the wreath) on her birthday. This was not quite 'home, sweet home', but it became so by the end of the century for many working-class people, too. The artist William Powell Frith in fact had a turbulent domestic life, but the image of home as a special place was enduring.

that Dickens's much-loved heroes, where they found riches, did not make them from business and trade. Pride in being self-made probably spoke more powerfully to the working classes than the middle classes; increasingly, education counted for more. Matthew Arnold declared that the British middle classes were badly educated. To an extent, that related to his distaste for materialism encouraging social mobility: his Mr Bottles, in his 1871 *Friendship's Garland*, who is 'something in the bottle way' and ignorant of everything except the infernal bottles, is a believer in Progress, the Manchester School of Liberals and the *Daily Telegraph*. But that was perhaps less significant than Arnold's earlier assertion, when writing about Continental education, that the professional middle classes, unlike in any other country, were educated in aristocratic values.

In 1850, *The Gentleman's Magazine* avowed that it wanted to encourage 'whatever is kind or generous, whatever is fairly meant and diligently pursued'. The 'lofty arrogance of mere pretenders' would receive 'the test of a just and manly criticism'.[11] In practical terms, this became expressed in a broad liberal humanitarianism, but it was also accompanied by a strong work ethic and an increasingly energetic reform or creation of professional institutions, though politically no espousal of taxation: the income tax rate of 1875–76 was just 2d in the pound, and though it had reached 7d when Peel reintroduced it in 1842, it applied only to incomes over £150 and enabled him to remove duties on perhaps 750 items. Aristocrats and the middle classes, whether professionals or manufacturers, were hostile to income tax; the working classes were unaffected by it and also benefited as tariffs were removed in the era of free trade. All classes could unite around what was projected as a national success story – Britain's adoption of ideas of social progress (albeit with a very long way to go), individual liberty (a world leader) and a democratic government (with equivocation – how far should the country go in allowing everyone a vote?).

Without a big state budget, how were the working classes to make progress? We will see that in detail when examining what happened to the deprived sections of society in Chapter 8, but while the fragile – of whom there were a multitude – continued to experience many of the wretched circumstances that they had known since the beginning of time, there were also many who took Samuel Smiles's *Self-Help* (1859) and made it a reality, albeit sometimes with some help. Smiles himself has been almost wilfully misunderstood in our own time. Involved in Radical politics in the 1840s, he pushed for local action on education and sanitary improvements, as well as campaigning against money and power ostentatiously displayed. At the time, he supported universal suffrage, though later became disillusioned about political action as the key to change. His books *Self-Help* and *Thrift* (1875) are too often seen as equating their prescriptions with cruel self-righteousness. In fact, though he might well have derived his approach from being one of eleven surviving children of very strict Scottish Presbyterian parents, eking out a medical study only because his mother worked so hard to keep the family shop going after his father died of cholera in 1832, the connection is too simplistic.

The origins of *Self-Help* lay with the invitation to give lectures that he received from the working men of a Leeds self-improvement society intent on making their own way, rather than relying on middle-class philanthropy (and, in some sense, control). Smiles himself didn't quite see it like that; he emphasized 'character', 'moral worth' and 'public spirit', important for all sections of society and much more important than 'manners' or 'fashion'. Progress depended on contributions from artisans, yes, but also manufacturers, politicians, philosophers, even poets. That had always been so; the 'fortunate Great' were remembered by biography, but many unwritten lives had also contributed to civilization. That was because they felt the need to act within a moral framework, applying themselves, paying attention to accuracy and method and punctuality.

Did this just create a myth? If so, it was certainly a powerful one. Novelists got the point – endlessly. Some became famous, such as Dinah Craik's *John Halifax, Gentleman*, which pre-dated by a few years Smiles's book and was written by a female author herself determined to succeed, and in which the poor orphan is encouraged to try – 'you can do anything you try' – and duly becomes powerful and wealthy.[12] In the forgotten *How a Farthing Made a Fortune* by Charlotte Bowen, Dick is born in a cellar in a London backstreet haunt of iniquity and misery, survives poverty, finds a benefactor and acquires 'a considerable income' as a landscape gardener.[13]

But what about real life? First, there are many individual tales. Joseph Johnson, in *Living to Purpose; or Making the Best of Life* (1868) mentions several, including Dr Samuel Lee (1783–1852), born in poverty in Shropshire and starting work as a carpenter's apprentice, impressing the Church Missionary Society with his linguistic skills, eventually becoming both Professor of Arabic and Professor of Hebrew at Cambridge, as well as playing a key role in a dictionary of the Māori language; and Samuel Drew (1765–1833), son of a Cornish farm labourer, beginning as an apprentice shoemaker, but on becoming a theologian and through adopting Methodism eventually acquired the nickname of 'the Cornish metaphysican'.[14] But second, as an impressed Taine noted, there were non-state-funded societies

– for everything: houses for working men, protecting animals, emigration, studying economics, encouraging female teachers, advancing science, saving lives from drowning, helping savings banks. A German coalminer called Dükershoff, when writing about Northumberland later in the century, even suggested that, as a result of clubs and religious organizations, the middle and working classes are 'on very friendly terms'.[15] The most important institutions for the working classes were the Mechanics' Institutes, providing books, lectures and discussion in the absence of adequate state-funded education. Education, to be discussed later, was itself the most concrete route for the poor and the wage-earners to progress.

Smiles's 'character' did not help the many that were more vulnerable. Even more needed a little help. Presciently, we might think today, the much-maligned future Edward VII suggested in a speech in June 1883 to inaugurate a new scholarship programme at the Royal College of Music, that 'the tendency of increased wealth and increased civilization' to widen social differences made it essential to work 'most earnestly in bridging over the gulf between different classes'.[16] Among the new scholars was a mill girl, a bricklayer's daughter, sons of a blacksmith and a farm labourer. Similarly, Henry Swan, born in the West Country in Devizes in 1829 and apprenticed to a copper-plate engraver in London, was inspired by Ruskin at the Working Men's College, Great Ormond Street, where he learned manuscript illumination. Ruskin asked him to engrave some of the plates for his *Modern Painters*: 'Mr Swan,' his obituary read, 'was exceedingly in sympathy with all ideas of progress and reform.' He had gone on to engrave many plates for the inventor of phonography, Isaac Pitman. Swan invented a system of musical notation and a system of writing English phonetically to be used in teaching children to read, and had had Louis Napoleon, the exiled Napoleon III, among his sitters, with a technique to replicate the effect of a stereoscope, but without the instrument itself, for viewing an image. As curator, eventually, of the Ruskin Museum, he taught 'helpfulness, and beauty, and joy in life'.[17]

It took a revolutionary, rather than a proselytizer for Victorian social values or bourgeois ideas of progress, to express – with huge frustration – the social change that gathered pace from the 1850s: 'the English proletariat', Engels wrote in a letter to Marx in October 1858, 'is actually becoming more and more bourgeois, so that the ultimate aim of this most bourgeois of all nations would appear to be the possession, alongside the bourgeoisie, of a bourgeois aristocracy and a bourgeois proletariat.'[18] From Marx and Engels to today's social media algorithms, it has been a defining feature of 'the modern' to believe that society and social behaviour can be studied scientifically. It was

9 Herbert Spencer at 38 in 1858. That was the year he outlined an extraordinary work, eventually to encompass ten volumes, seeking to show how evolution could be applied to morality, psychology, sociology and biology. Benjamin Jowett was to write to his friend Robert Morier in March 1875 that 'the scientific men...worship him [Spencer] as a god'. Jowett hoped 'some day' to 'put a spoke in his wheel at Oxford'. For now, 'he is rather swaggering and triumphant'.

a short step from scientific knowledge enormously enhancing understanding of the natural world – as it did with ever-increasing force in the 19th century – to apply the same thinking to human beings. George Eliot, in a letter at the end of September 1851, describes meeting 'a Mr Herbert Spencer, who has just brought out a large work on "Social Statics", which Lewes pronounces the best book he has seen on the subject'.[19] Eliot and Spencer were to be close, though in the event it was George Henry Lewes, philosopher and critic, with whom she lived – unmarried – for 25 years. The effect of scientific progress on the economy was matched by a corresponding ferment of ideas about the study of society – in effect, the birth, if not the close definition, of sociology. Eliot, as Marian Evans, had come to London in 1850 and was staying with, and became the mistress of, the publisher John Chapman, who published Spencer's book. Spencer worked across the street in the Strand as a sub-editor for *The Economist*; the social circle that developed also included T.H. Huxley and John Tyndall from Mallock's country house.

For Spencer, Eliot was 'the most admirable woman, mentally, I have ever met'. In *Social Statics*, he was concerned with studying social structure and order, a starting point for studying progress within society; he argued, among many other things, for equality of treatment for women (though his views on political rights for them were to evolve). The two of them would walk on the terrace at Somerset House, overlooking the Thames, and talk and talk and talk.[20] Many years later, at the time of his 70th birthday in 1890, the *Pall Mall Gazette* called him 'the profoundest intellect of our generation', 'the first [among other things] to apply evolutionary method to the facts of society – to political organizations, ecclesiastical organizations, ceremonial institutions, domestic relations, and the rise and progress of moral ideas in humanity'.[21] He was a voice for gradualism, slow modification, the pursuit of equilibrium, but only after endless minute changes of structure and function. So, no drugs that 'act like magic'. It took another century to adopt a different idea of progress: instant gratification.

Spencer, much misunderstood by the 20th century and accused at one time or another of being responsible for almost all the pernicious consequences arising from what came to be called Social Darwinism, suffered in his own time because of his over-confident dogmatism. Ruskin wrote to Frederic Harrison, another controversial but in his way brilliant intellectual, in 1884: 'I was so furious at your praising Herbert Spencer that I couldn't speak…I can't think why you don't go on steadily in social reform, instead of writing Theology – or neology – or me-ology, for what is Positivism but the Everlasting Me.'[22]

Away from his ideas, Herbert Spencer could behave kindly and genially, a man with a hearty laugh. He was not a Social Darwinist or a Positivist (the philosophy that recognizes only what can be scientifically verified), but he did want to systematize, to organize everything in order to further human progress. At a dinner, John Stuart Mill said to Spencer that the radical and Classical historian George Grote would love his views on 'the equilibrium of molecules in some relation or another'. After a short pause, Spencer then spoke 'with unbroken fluency' for a quarter of an hour or more. Grote was convinced; Mill thought it wonderfully lucid.[23] But the sales of Spencer's books, way beyond the elite – over a million copies in his lifetime, completely unprecedented for a philosopher – show his influence over Victorian debates about every aspect of progress.

Spencer invented the phrase 'survival of the fittest' in his book *Principles of Biology* (1864). Yet he was anti-imperialist and anti-militarist, and certainly had no wish to (in some way) act to remove weaker members of society, or to see natural selection as the centrepiece of progress. Instead, if there was a struggle, it was an entirely positive and rational method of making things better; individual action rather than natural law. His own book on *Progress* (1857) emphasized how we had learned from mistakes that concern for others worked better than selfishness, that industrialization was better than making war; rational progress underpinned by scientific method. Just as organisms had evolved from simple to complex, so tribes had become industrializing, liberal and individualistic societies. Barbarian nomads had become urban but militarily expansive states; now we had to take another step forward.

Nevertheless, because Spencer was a fierce believer in laissez-faire, his ideas were not a specific programme for action, but an aid to understanding.

Reformers were abundant in Victorian society. In 1857, the National Association for the Promotion of Social Science was specifically founded to link the words of experts to the world of politics on such matters as public health, female education and local government. Its first secretary, Isa Knox, the mostly self-educated daughter of an Edinburgh hosier, overcame a great deal of prejudice against her appointment, was a significant campaigner for women's rights and against slavery, and was to join the enormously talented women we shall meet in Chapter 9 at the Langham Place Group. Over twenty years later, when Lord Norton gave the presidential address at the Association's annual congress, the overall momentum was as strong as ever. The 'rapid progress of ideas', argued Norton, had brought about the 'general demand for improvement' in all that concerns 'our social well-being', and 'no one can fail to see that the progress is still more rapidly advancing.... The requirements of civilised life, and inventions to meet them, increase in geometric ratio.'[24] That phrase, 'geometric ratio', would have been inconceivable before scientific method was favoured as a method of making progress. Idiosyncratic human beings, being idiosyncratic, can be delusional, just as they are today in their over-dependence on algorithms. But Victorians, understandably, were excited by it all: 'Who can imagine', asked Lord Norton, 'the condition of things 30 years hence?'

The Idea of Progress had a long intellectual tradition. J.B. Bury, who came to adulthood in the 1880s, by which time the manifold discoveries of geology, astronomy and a host of other scientific disciplines had transformed our understanding of the planet, was specific in his inaugural lecture as Regius Professor of History at Cambridge in 1902 that history 'is herself simply a science, no less and no more'. In his famous book on *The Idea of Progress* (1920), he summed up progress as a synthesis of the past and a prophecy of the future. From beginning as primitive and barbaric, mankind had gradually, if unevenly, improved knowledge and understanding, had found moral and spiritual value systems, and had thrown off many of the problems arising both from uncontrolled nature and from tyrannical governance. In fact, Bury's book, coming out not long after the destruction of the First World War, marked the end of an easy acceptance of progress.

While Francis Bacon, back in the 16th century, had argued that new knowledge enabled each generation to benefit – to progress – it was the Enlightenment that made the decisive step: applying reason, knowledge and the human will to the overall human environment; with it, government, education, the law, social structure and nature would result in improvement. Many politically active thinkers – certainly Turgot, Louis

XVI's Controller-General, and Condorcet, to some extent his protégé and often called the discoverer of the 'law of progress' – linked knowledge, well-being, economic growth and political liberty together. Gibbon's *Decline and Fall of the Roman Empire* (1766–88) addressed the question of whether civilization could collapse again, as it had done – in his view – because of the German barbarians. He is pleased to conclude that 'every age of the world has increased, and still increases, the real wealth, the happiness, the knowledge, and perhaps the virtue of the human race'.[25] That 'perhaps' was to be important. Turgot, unable to overcome aristocratic resistance to reform, was dismissed; Condorcet spent the last part of his life completing his posthumously published historical sketch of the *Progress of the Human Mind* (1795) while dodging the Jacobins, dying mysteriously after being imprisoned in the Bourg de l'Egalité (the equality borough).

The idea of progress needed to be born, but it was the visibility of progress that finally captured to the full the attention of all classes of society in Victorian Britain at mid-century. By that time, 'feeling' the good life, itself now projected by an array of 'facts' derived from empirical observations, had gained considerable momentum. The analysis of the economic data showed that Providence was no longer in charge, though – in later chapters – we will need to ask whether 'progress' was achieved only on the backs of the deprived and the colonized. It was humans who had conquered the winds and distance with their steam-driven boats, smashed tunnels through mountains and placed giant structures across previously unbridgeable voids; it was humans who could use the same skills of applying their will to what reason and empirically derived knowledge revealed to improve society. 'Improvement' was what accelerated 'progress'. The original meaning of the former, after the Norman Conquest, related to profitable land cultivation and, for the monarch, tax collection; it evolved to encompass any profitable investment. During the first half of the 19th century, it became essential to emphasize that mere change in every area of life did not signify progress; there needed to be – as the Radical manufacturer, politician and abolitionist Samuel Morley (1809–86) insisted – 'improvement'.

As the Victorian era developed, the chief problem was finding a consensus on the question of 'progress for whom?' For everyone? The Great Exhibition seemed to be one answer. 'Unsurpassable, indescribable, unique, amazing, real!' So said the London publisher and mapmaker John Tallis (1817–76). 'Indescribable' was perhaps the only inaccuracy in this summing up: few things have been so copiously described as the Great Exhibition in Hyde Park, held between May and October 1851. It was memorialized both by

10 In the Machine Court at the Great Exhibition, William Fairburn's innovative crane, patented in 1850, is in the foreground, with the hydraulic press used to raise the tubular sections of Robert Stephenson's Britannia Bridge across the Menai Strait in Wales, completed the year before, in the background.

its progenitors and by newspapers, magazines, books, diaries and letters, within families and within whole communities, in Great Britain and across the world, as an icon of global progress – domestic progress, too, since this was not just a spectacle for Londoners: 'Not a village, a hamlet, a borough, a township, or a wick', according to Henry Mayhew's novel *1851*, but each had its shilling club, for providing their inhabitants with a three-day journey to London, a mattress under the dry arches of the Adelphi, and tickets for soup *ad libitum*. Even the horrors revealed in Mayhew's *London Labour and the London Poor*, first published in book form and later expanded in the year of the Exhibition, could be mildly mitigated by the opportunities it provided. The milk-seller did not 'understand about this Great Exhibition, but, no doubt, more milk will be sold when it's opened, and that's all I care about.'[26]

Nearly 800,000 square feet of glass, thousands of girders and iron columns – four times the size of St Peter's in Rome – in which (if you used your imagination, as the Cambridge polymath William Whewell proposed) it was like a photograph of the surface of the whole globe, with all its workshops and markets, in one instantaneous, permanent picture.[27] Abundance! National wealth! Power! Prestige! Fun! Aged hedgers and ditchers, scarcely familiar with the high street of their own country town, were seen in their clean smock-frocks, alongside gentlemen who had fallen in love at first sight, not in three-volume novels, but in reality, 'actual reality', with young ladies they had met in railway carriages on the way.[28] A place that might herald peace – as Margaret Oliphant, biographer and at least distantly related to Laurence Oliphant, noted: surely 'it was impossible, in the face of civilisation, steamboats, and the electric telegraph, to entertain the faintest idea of a war.'[29] Politically, though Britain was unthreatened by revolution in practice, so soon after the 1848 Revolutions in Europe, it was psychologically helpful for Lord John Russell's Liberal Government to have a completely undivisive event, free from all party influence, as the *Manchester Guardian* asserted, controlled by a Royal Commission with Prince Albert's enthusiastic participation, and even – eventually – persuading Disraeli, previously an exponent of protectionism, that 'The spirit of the age tends to free intercourse.' If anyone knew that 'no statesman can disregard with impunity the genius of the epoch in which he lives', it was Disraeli in his practical politics. Prince Albert was brilliantly well informed, thorough, enthusiastic, able to be cogent when talking about architecture, or engineering, or chemistry, or fine art, as well as seeking to encourage his not easily encouraged Coburg family of the value of political liberalism and supporting industry.[30]

Victorian success! And there was a specific symbol of it: the Exhibition's late choice for architect, Joseph Paxton, leading the opening-day procession in top hat and tails, the runaway seventh son of a farmer, whose first job was as a garden boy, about to be knighted, soon to become a Liberal MP, an affluent railway investor. It is often said that Victorians replaced reality with myth; if so, Joseph Paxton turned that myth into reality. Did no one object to the whole enterprise? They always do. Years later, after the Crystal Palace had been moved from Hyde Park to Sydenham Hill, Upper Norwood, Ruskin compared entering a room in the Louvre ('an education in itself') to taking 'two steps on the filthy floor and under the iron forks, half-scaffold, half gallows, of the big Norwood glass bazaar'. The result? That debased 'mind and eye at once below possibility of looking at anything with profit all the day afterwards.'[31] Others complained about girders giving way, panes of glass being broken by the wind, birds getting into the building, imported goods not getting into the building but stuck in the docks. Moreover, any building that was effectively a giant greenhouse got hot in the summer, though Paxton did experiment with cooling ideas. Still, it was perhaps no tragedy that, as *The Times* reported on 30 June 1851, many visitors 'spent the greater part of the afternoon in eating ices and drinking lemonade and soda-water'.

Once accepted, the point about 'the idea of progress' was that it knew no limits, in grand matters or mundane, from politics and the evolution of democracy to cut-price tailoring. James Webster, of 86–88 Argyll Street, Glasgow, used the new power of advertising to complain about London tailors who targeted only the wealthy, while the only way of forming a correct idea of 'the progress of civilisation' was to make sure 'the Dress, Language and Manners of the People' were not neglected, the first to be achieved by his Scotch Tweed Trouser Scheme (with the trousers under a pound), the others to come about via educational support reaching beyond the rich.[32]

Were there dissenters? Some. But there were many to rebuff them. James Sully, an underrated contributor to the Victorian development of modern psychology, gave them short thrift in *Pessimism* (1872). Social progress was also individual progress, for 'society is merely a congeries of individuals'. The progress that had been made defeated the main premise of pessimism, which argued that the world was bad and incapable of amendment except by self-destruction, in the manner of Schopenhauer's and von Hartmann's prescription of the renunciation of the will to live as the only remedy for the malady of the universe. Look at the evidence, suggested Sully: since the first dawn of social life, the world had gone in the opposite direction, 'multiplying pleasures and mitigating pains'. Pessimism is 'contrary to experience'. Yet he did also provide a warning, which came home to roost in the modern world: optimism that depended on 'an indolent and unworthy habit of over-estimating the blessings of civilization and progress' wasn't any better.[33]

There was also the conservative view. Catherine Gore, a prolific novelist unconvincingly labelled 'the wittiest woman of her age' in her obituary in *The Times* in 1861, spelled it out in her *Progress and Prejudice* (1854). Once, we were 'happy and sociable', 'no disproportion, no envy, no jealousy'; now, 'we are grown more locomotive, more enlightened, more grand, and more selfish'.[34] Of course, as in any age, there were many who feared change was the same as making things worse, including those with vested interests. Even more were just uneasy about the scale of disruption and were perhaps trying to combat that by making monumental buildings, adorned with statues, and making use of long-abandoned styles: a search for stability. Romanticized conservatism, seen in Coleridge's poetry, or Carlyle's *Past and Present* (1843), in which monastic life in medieval times was uncorrupted by river pollution or the ravages of giant coal and iron industries, was a variant.

Anti-industrialization continued to be expressed by highly able writers, from Ruskin to William Morris.

'What is Progress?' – the question posed in Mallock's country house – impinged on class, social reform, politics, religion, morality, economics, everything. An attempt to make a rational economic case for it was expressed in the *Aberdeen Weekly Journal* in 1884. True line fishermen had to face new trawlers damaging their lines and their livelihoods. But to try to ban trawlers 'would be absurd, and against all ideas of progress'. There was a similar problem for sailing vessels engaged in trade and facing competition from steamboats, just as the railways had destroyed the jobs of stage-coachmen and country carriers. Yet there were new jobs and also remedies – off the coast of Banffshire, there were fishers who were taking to trawling in their sailing boats and earning more money. Progress could be creative: 'we see the changes that are taking place, and were trying to keep up with the times'.[35]

Even so, that was disguising the moral issues attached to money-making on a grand scale and the extent to which it corrupted and encouraged all the worst characteristics of greed. All the great novelists, from George Eliot to Dickens, filled their books with stories built around that view and its consequences. Laurence Oliphant's *Piccadilly* spoke of 'the commercial effluvium of Plutocracy', with expediency replacing principle, conscience crushed out of consideration in 'the lust of gain'.[36] Ruskin complained that Nelson's 'England expects every man to do his duty' was replaced by every man to do 'the best he can do for himself'.[37] Not everyone agreed. Trollope, in his *Autobiography* (1883), published shortly after his death, deplored 'the wailing and gnashing of teeth' from Carlyle and Ruskin when material comfort, health and education had improved nationally.

There were implications of this debate for political liberty and rights, for the self-appointed guardians of morality, the churches, for social and educational reform. In a sense, the differences of opinion were less important than the fact that, for the first time in history, there could be a peaceful national debate about the question that underpins everything involved in the organization of a modern society: the balance between materialism, morality and liberty. Middle-class voices were the most heard, precisely because their numbers grew fast through access to wider affluence and education. But it would be a mistake to write them off because their own lives were much freer from want than those of the ever-increasing working-class population. Robert Kemp Philip, who, as we have seen, played a key role in the Chartist movement, was very clear in his *History of Progress in Great Britain* that 'the perfection of our manufactures and the universality of our trade' would lead to the ultimate diffusion of 'intelligence, morality, and peace among all mankind'.[38]

In fact, while the political battles to extend the franchise and to bring about social reform were mostly conducted paternalistically by the middle and upper classes, throughout the Victorian era the working classes became more and more engaged in a constructive way. Even in 1848, when there was considerable hysteria about social disorder, *The Midland Progressionist*, a periodical 'for the People, devoted to popular enfranchisement and progress', was full of well-mannered debate in its first volume. Its mission statement, in this year of revolutions, referred to 'the unparalleled advantages of our age'; its concern was with 'Opportunity', not destruction. 'The lower orders' made no claim to educational accomplishments or Classical refinement, but they were clear-headedly anti-fraud and injustice, anti-slavery, pro-peace, pro-female influence, and with 'the march of the intellect', 'our countrymen are beginning to think *en masse*', with 'multitudes' beginning 'the work of self-culture' (an interesting variant on 'self-help').[39] These editors and their correspondents had no illusions about how much needed to be done, but the road they were taking was plainly never going to intersect with that of Karl Marx, finding safety in London for the next 34 years and dreaming up the dictatorship of the proletariat. Within a year, he and Engels had written their 'Address of the Central Committee to the Communist League', rejecting any collaboration with bourgeois parties and advocating 'revolutionary workers' governments'. It might be said that this was the moment when the two political propositions for the modern world were set out: seven decades passed and Lenin was being chauffeured in a Rolls-Royce while in process of banning all opposition parties, closing any press that was unsupportive and executing anyone who stood in his way; in Britain, by contrast, the first Labour Party Government would shortly be in power.

Nevertheless, there were plenty of reasons why Progress could be troublesome for the Established Church and religion in general. Many centuries of faith in the Bible story were shattered by geological and other scientific discoveries about how and when the earth was formed and the human place in evolution. Bury's *Idea of Progress* was to argue that humans had to become independent of divine Providence in order to 'organize a theory of Progress' and make it the 'animating and controlling' idea of Western civilization. Still, the Church of England, despite many internal disputes, managed up to a point to accommodate itself to change.

When the Rev. Canon Barry spoke to the winter session of the YMCA in Worcester in 1874, he noted the great increase in material progress, in

11 Bishop Samuel Wilberforce, later a vigorous opponent of T.H. Huxley's support for Darwin, began the Church's failed attempt to halt new ideas during the meeting of the British Association for the Advancement of Science in Oxford in May 1847 by preaching his Sunday sermon on 'the wrong way of doing science'. Like his father, William, he was a prominent anti-slavery campaigner, but that was about Christian values – science seemed to be threatening Christianity itself.

science and knowledge, in the growth of freedom, with moral progress as well (at least in terms of a lessening of brutality and violence, though not of deceit and hypocrisy). There was spiritual progress, too, but 'a certain haziness as to spiritual truth'.[40] It was easier – if not easy – for the Church of England to accept the beautiful ambivalence of this last phrase than it had been for John Henry Newman, who had wanted to return the Church to the purity of its Catholic past and encouraged troubled believers to convert to Roman Catholicism. But even he acknowledged, if negatively, the dominance of progress by remarking, in 1873, 'Whatever be the national excellence of the Turks, progress they are not'.[41] In the long run, notwithstanding a cross correspondence in the *Morning Post* in March 1852 complaining that 'Christians…who are taught to pray for their daily bread do not look to universal suffrage, vote by ballot, and all the rest of that stuff, as the forerunner of their return to the Garden of Eden',[42] the modern Western world did embrace the secularism that gathered force in Victorian times, but evidently retains a desire for spiritual connection or, less positively, what the *Glasgow Herald* called in 1864 'the bonds of superstition'.[43]

It was the nonconformist chapels that were most comfortable with combining belief with a moral structure, a motivation to make material progress and a political liberalism. They, together with 'low-church' Evangelical Anglicans, provided support for the poorer sections of society. The help they gave was conditional in the sense that it depended on accepting

12 Anthony Trollope's mother, Fanny, was herself a prolific writer. Her 1840 novel, *Michael Armstrong: Factory Boy*, based on first-hand research in the Manchester textile mills, provided an early example of novels encouraging philanthropy and support for the industrial poor. In this illustration from the book, the pupils look in no shape to benefit from their Evangelical Sunday School.

the sort of lifestyle, behaviour and belief drummed into generations of children in Sunday School, but it did help many to learn to read, reduced crime, encouraged a sense of community and, through philanthropy, to experience more tangible benefits.

So long as laissez-faire predominated in government (with an emphasis on minimum expenditure), fundamental social reform was bound to be limited, but the very focus on poverty, ignorance and hardship at a time of 'progress' itself helped to create a climate making the arguments for a bigger state unanswerable. And that, as we shall see, is what slowly happened. The debate continues today, but the vital steps forward in understanding that not everything could be left to the free play of the market happened during the Victorian era and was touchingly summed up by leading economists and social thinkers in a 'Complimentary Address' presented to Ruskin on his recovery from illness in Christmas 1885. They praised him for teaching that 'the use of wealth, in developing a complete human life, is of incomparably greater moment both to men and actions than its production or accumulation'.[44] Even Matthew Arnold, so preoccupied by what materialism was doing to civilization and expressing his concerns in his poetry, turned to social reform focused on state education and the necessity of strong organization for it, as well as using it to provide a source of authority to underpin social and cultural values.

Herbert Asquith, Prime Minster for eight years from April 1908, had been middle-aged by the time Queen Victoria died in 1901. Looking back, he observed that 'revolt' was not a Victorian characteristic. But nor was complacency: 'the Victorians were not allowed to wax fat, and to bask in the sunshine of their prosperity, and content, without reproof, exhortation, and even denunciation'.[45] We tend to remember the critics – Carlyle, Ruskin, Dickens – who so powerfully expressed the horrors attached to industrialization. But creating a prototype for a modern world in which slavery was abolished, privilege curtailed, liberty and press freedom protected, education provided free, support provided for the vulnerable – all of which involved abandoning all past history, anywhere in the world, and all of which continued to provide challenges through to today – wasn't going to happen like a consultant's PowerPoint presentation. Victorians agonized over these things, moving from muddle to clarity and back to muddle. As Matthew Arnold said, 'Freedom is a very good horse to ride, but to ride somewhere.'[46]

Next, we find out how the prosperity and economic growth that underpinned ideas of progress was created. But first an apology to Scotland, Ireland and Wales. Each has its own distinct national history; each suffered and benefited from being part of the United Kingdom in proportions only the individual can decide. In this book, 'the English' are often mentioned (they, too, have some characteristics of their own). More times than not, Europeans, Americans, Asians and Africans, as well as the English themselves, referred to 'the English' when they should have said 'the British'. At the same time, by being the centre of Government and the centre of world finance, England had a special role to play in shaping an 'Age of Progress'. Resolving the issues created by the English conquests of Scotland, Ireland and Wales – a worthy project – is for another book.

CHAPTER 3

'TRIUMPH OVER ALL INANIMATE MATTER'

GLOBAL ECONOMIC DOMINANCE

In the summer of 1857, Queen Victoria arrived in Manchester in the rain. Theodor Fontane, a German writer most remembered now for his novels, sought shelter next to a man who comments that the Queen always brings good weather – Lancashire needs rain and, look, the Queen brings it: 'God bless our gracious Queen.'[1] It would be hard to imagine, less than a decade after the 1848 Revolutions in Europe, any other monarch being quietly applauded in this way. The first country to industrialize could, apparently, accommodate economic revolution without political revolution.

Even taking into account 'the festive attire' the city had been given for the occasion, Fontane found that 'it is not quite the comfortless place' he had been told about. The suburbs – interminable uniformity – were depressing; only the factory chimneys headed heavenwards, for the nonconformist chapels were steepleless. The River Irwell flowing through Manchester and its twin sister Salford seemed like a grey, colourless Venice, coal boats substituted for gondolas, innumerable bridges springing from one bank to the other with gutters and pipes instead of ornament, the water itself of indescribable colours, like a glass of water in which a boy had tried out his new paint box. Yet there was also a contrasting Manchester, especially where Market Street and the Piccadilly of the north met and widened into a spacious square with a newly built, stately and domed hospital.

Hippolyte Taine, who visited from France a few years later, agreed about the suburbs: rows of cheap houses erected fast and profitably in a speculation. He gave a more troubling picture of fog and soot in air and soil. At six in the evening, a noisy crowd pours from the mills into the streets, men, women and children, many of them barefoot, with pinched, gloomy faces. Some stopped at gin palaces. He follows the rest to their wretched streets and their foul air.[2]

There had been perhaps 17,000 people in Manchester a century or a little more before; by 1850, there were more than 300,000 in 'Cottonopolis'.[3] Something fundamental had happened and we need to explain it – whether it benefited the great mass of this fast-growing population waits for Chapter 8, though some Continental European workers, so completely mired in poverty, appeared to think they wanted it, too. In 1851, 48 Sardinian workers had been invited to visit Manchester. In a thank-you letter, they were delighted to express their appreciation 'for the liberality with which the industrial treasures of the first manufacturing city of the world were freely opened for their inspection'. Especial thanks were given to the Mayor 'for having addressed them by the ideas of industrial progress which it [Manchester] expressed', with suggestions of hope for their own unhappy country.[4]

When the Irish journalist W. Cooke Taylor had reflected just under ten years earlier on his experiences of touring the manufacturing districts of Lancashire, he noted the extreme change after the steam engine, the spinning jenny, the mule and the power-loom had 'sprung into sudden existence like Minerva from the brain of Jupiter'.[5] It was not many years after the Sardinians' visit that the *Quarterly Review* could conclude that it was just a fact that South Lancashire had gone from 'a howling wilderness' to being 'one of the most remarkable illustrations of the force of industrial energy to be met with in the history of the world'.[6] Contemporaries were perhaps less concerned to explain why these changes had taken place than we are. Many reasons have subsequently been identified as to why industrialization came to Great Britain first and why this small country achieved, for a while, global economic dominance.

A single cause, so satisfying, so neat, will never ultimately convince. We can say that the context was more favourable than it was in most countries: the strength of the rule of law, the relative political and social stability, at least by comparison to the increasingly outdated – and increasingly threatened – caste-like aristocracies of continental Europe. But in the end, it is as well to observe that it began as a happily tangled affair, coming – as the Radical political economist Thomas Hodgskin was to argue – from individuals, from (largely) artisanal workshops and gentlemen scientists. Hodgskin emphasized the artisans in *Mechanics Magazine*, founded in 1823; Charles Babbage, polymath and now seen as the inventor of the first mechanical computer, proselytised for the scientists. Both were right and both were engaged in transforming the world in ways that in retrospect define the word 'modern'. Some recent research suggests that the number of inventors grew a bit like social media on a much-reduced scale: the inventors liked to talk about their empirical experiments to others, who caught their enthusiasm.

While there were many great inventors and businessmen in the 19th century in America, their early focus on scale and mass-manufacturing was effectively an ideology, or at least a way of life, almost from the beginning. America always thought big. In Britain, in the beginning, an equivalent emphasis on progress and self-improvement came out of the facts. This was, at the start, a quiet revolution.

The starting point has to be what the Liverpool *Statesman* called in 1812 'the machinery and mechanical inventions of this country',[7] especially since the consequences of the discoveries – not limited to industry and manufacturing – infused wider culture: Byron, who befriended Humphry Davy, inventor of the miner's safety lamp and key figure in establishing the prestige of science, presciently observed that not all the consequences were peaceful:

> This is the patent age of new inventions
> For killing bodies, and for saving souls,
> All propagated with the best intentions…

He compares the technology of killing with Davy's constructive inventions.[8] By the time Queen Victoria died, invention had become part of the professionalized 'applied science' that we would recognize, but the inventors of the Industrial Revolution took on the characteristics of heroes – partly because what changed economic life was not accompanied by the destructive effect of a political revolution, partly because they reinforced the idea that self-help and the character of the individual did not entirely depend on social status. Samuel Smiles's biography of the 'Father of the Railways', George Stephenson, created a model: for ever-quoting Stephenson, 'Do as I have done – persevere.' Those who received it as a prize at the Mechanics' Institutes and similar places furthering working-class education – through evening courses, accessible libraries and exhibitions – took note. In Bolton, in 1860, it was a group of workers who campaigned to ensure Samuel Crompton, hugely determined pioneer of the spinning industry, was commemorated. By that time, a school textbook such as *Outlines of English History* could sell hundreds of thousands of copies giving greater accolades to the inventors as 'benefactors of mankind' than the traditional military heroes.[9] Long before this, you could have visited the National Gallery of Practical Science, opened in 1832 in Adelaide Street, London. That wasn't free, but it did show another aspect of invention; it wasn't all solemn. You would have Instruction, but also Amusement as you viewed a Jacquard loom or a model steamboat.

In the early stages of these transformations, skilled artisans, toolmakers or millwrights used their skills empirically to design waterwheels or new tools. George Stephenson (and his son Robert), James Watt (and his 1766 steam engine), Richard Arkwright (entrepreneur, as well as inventor, in mass-producing yarn from the 1760s) and James Hargreaves (and his spinning jenny in the 1760s and 70s) had varied social origins, but none of them had something we would recognize as a formal scientific or engineering education. Many inventions came out of pragmatic need. We owe the rail ticket, provided with serial number by machine and replacing handwritten documents, to Thomas Edmundson, a clerk with the Lancashire and Yorkshire Railway Company, in 1839.[10] He had been a cabinetmaker. His system spread through the world, from France to Russia, Paraguay to Japan. When Victoria came to the throne in 1837, there were only just over 250 patent applications; there were a hundred times more when she died in 1901.[11]

Despite the individualism and rivalries in the activities of these competitive inventors, there was also a powerful impetus towards communication. Charles Darwin's grandfather, Erasmus, Matthew Boulton, Josiah Wedgwood, James Watt and other inventors, entrepreneurs, natural philosophers and intellectuals met informally at the Lunar Society in Birmingham from the 1760s. These were people from different backgrounds. Sometimes, there were quarrels (Humphry Davy was especially rude about George Stephenson's rival miner's safety lamp, patented in 1815, coming from 'a mere enginewright', as his biographer called Stephenson). Yet talking, letter-writing, enthusing, both casually but also in clubs and institutions, helped to accelerate innovation. With it came a sense of remaking the world. These social networks and webs of co-operation seem to have been a distinctively British attribute at the time.[12] Men of action and men of ideas both became in thrall to 'improvement', which spelled 'Progress'.

John Wilson Croker, MP, Secretary of the Admiralty and founder of the Athenaeum Club, was shrewd enough to see that invention was an ongoing

13 Medallion for those campaigning against slavery, designed by Josiah Wedgwood. His friend Erasmus Darwin, fellow member of the Lunar Society and grandfather of Charles, attacked slavery in his *The Botanic Garden* (1789–91) and insisted that scientific progress was and should be linked to political progress.

process. Lobbying Sir Robert Peel in March 1823, he wrote 'Mr Babbage's invention is at first sight incredible.' For now, it was more of 'curiosity than use'. But 'when I consider...the infinite and undiscovered variety of what may be called the mechanical powers of numbers, I cannot but admit the possibility, nay the probability, that important consequences may be ultimately derived from Mr. Babbage's principle.'[13] Babbage's 'Difference Engine' was less significant than his later 'Analytical Engine', never built but ultimately influencing Harold Atkin and his Harvard Mark 1, produced for IBM in 1943. Another portent for the future was Babbage's up-and-down relationship with Byron's daughter, Ada Lovelace; up and down because Babbage was often tactlessly self-destructive, while the brilliant Lovelace built up gambling debts and engaged in extra-marital affairs in the 1840s. Ada's key contribution to the confused development of the 'Analytical Engine' was an important sign that invention was not just a male matter, despite the obstacles put in the way of women. Croker, incidentally but significantly, refused to continue as an MP after the 1832 Reform Act. It appeared that supporter of economic progress did not mean automatic supporter of political progress.

It was perhaps George Stephenson who best illustrates the way in which Industrial Revolution innovation came about, as well as how inventors became synonymous with Progress and took on the aura of heroes. Stephenson, born

14 A woven silk picture of George Stephenson's early inventions (first locomotive and the Rocket, top) and how they were evolving (bottom). Cheap energy, efficiently distributed with steam power, was fundamental to British manufacturing success; today, British manufacturers pay almost four times as much for their energy as their American counterparts.

in 1781, began working in Wylam Colliery, near Newcastle, and was educated to the extent of taking himself to night classes in arithmetic, reading and writing. At his own request, he was able to strip down machines at another colliery, an empirical way of seeing how they were constructed. Others, too, were experimenting with how steam power might be applied to locomotion. Stephenson's experience of developing railways for steam haulage was that it was much easier to attract support from other people who saw the future than it was from the Government. Edward Pease, eldest son of a Darlington woollen merchant, could see what a difference it would make if you could transport coal or raw materials or manufactured goods efficiently from Durham to London, or other places. With his cousin, the Darlington banker and Quaker Edward Backhouse, they backed Stephenson as engineer in what became the Stockton and Darlington Railway. Stephenson himself suffered badly from the lawyer Edward Allison in a parliamentary committee in London (parliamentary approval was necessary for compulsory purchase of land); Allison focused on Stevenson's lack of formal qualifications. Inventors were not yet heroes among power brokers in the capital, or for that matter among the old rulers of the countryside: the Earl of Darlington, upset by railway disruption to his way of life, had tried to bankrupt Backhouse's bank.

An interesting pointer to the multiple sources of progress made in every area of life in Victorian times came from Backhouse's later life, in which he abandoned banking and became a key supporter of the first World Anti-Slavery Convention, which took place in London in 1840 (see Chapter 10). What did distinguish British politics, however, was the way that it slowly succumbed to the necessities – usually the desirabilities – of change. Far from fomenting revolution, its instinct was often to resist change, then – responding to practical needs – turn it into a virtue. Enough was achieved in the 1820s that the opening of the Liverpool and Manchester Railway in 1830, featuring the perfect collaboration between George and Robert Stephenson in building their steam train the Rocket, was attended by the Prime Minister, the Duke of Wellington. In the confusing way that history proceeds, the accidental death of the former Cabinet Minister William Huskisson in the path of the Rocket generated worldwide publicity for the reality of low-priced, fast, long-distance travel.

The Stephensons, by their own account, had used imagination to consider the parts of the Rocket; they came up with possible sizes of parts and possible combinations; they experimented. Steam power was the transformative key to much that happened. First, it powered factory machines; now, by applying it to transport, an inexpensive source of energy (coal) could be transported long distances and products could be brought to market. A future with apparently unlimited potential was opened up. A nation in which over half of the population lived in cities (as was the case in Britain by 1850) provided a different living experience – different both from all past history and from any other country at the time. Mrs Gaskell, in *North and South*, provided a brilliant description of the manufacturers, with their disregard for any limits on what was possible, and a 'fine intoxication' because of their achievements and what was still to be achieved. The prospect was of 'triumphs over all inanimate matter', beyond their lifetimes, certainly, but by implication the progress was assured.[14]

Hero status for both Stephensons became assured in less than a generation. Today, you can visit George Stephenson's cottage, where Robert was born, near Wylam, only because of the uproar from all classes in the Newcastle area when it was proposed to demolish it in 1857. There remains one thing that this rightful emphasis on those who made the creative leaps to create a new economy omits: the men that failed. When Samuel Smiles's publisher issued a revised edition of his biography of the Stephensons, he also included a short note, though 'probably more complete than any which has appeared', of Robert Trevithick.[15] Trevithick, born into the community of Cornish tin and copper miners in 1771, used observation, rather than formal education, to understand the workings of steam-driven engines, and became convinced of the potential of steam-powered road and rail transport. His ideas were solid (they influenced pioneers of the other side of the country, including at Wylam, in turn influencing George Stephenson), but it seems he lacked negotiation skills, could not support his family, and further failed when in search of new income from gold and silver mines in Peru. He only escaped from there, after being conscripted into Bolivar's rebel army, by designing and making guns for it, and then returning to England via a loan from Robert Stephenson, himself on a South American trip, having quickly grasped the potential need for railways and steam transport across the world. Trevithick died in poverty in 1833.[16]

What were the fundamentals of the economy that inventors and entrepreneurs were creating? The British were late to define their Industrial Revolution, a concept used earlier in the 19th century in France and Germany – where it had not properly happened – but only widely popularized in English by Arnold Toynbee's posthumously published *Lectures on the Industrial Revolution* (1884). The features of the new economy are simply stated: they include using science to mechanize production, with division of labour in a factory system; populations moving from rural to urban living (though with agriculture becoming mechanized also); engaging in national and international trade, rather than just having a local or domestic focus; and mobilizing capital to generate investment in natural resources, production, transport, as well as building a consumer market. The statistics showed the effects ever accelerating. In the twenty years after 1850, coal output doubled, using a workforce a third of its previous size and working shorter (though not short) hours. By 1890, Britain had 80 per cent of the world's trade in exported coal.

These changes – on a scale never before seen in the world – were not instant or uniform, but they were disruptive. Staffordshire and the Peak District, using water power, had dominated the cotton industry, but lost out at the end of the 18th century to steam and to Lancashire.[17] Nevertheless, if you were living in a cottage in 1850, as many were, your experience was still often working at home or in small-scale workshops. In some ways, the key point was that whether economics determined culture (as Marx argued) or not, in time, culture was more influential in shaping minds. It was something that the statue to James Watt, installed in Westminster Abbey only two years after the Great Reform Act in 1832, was way out of proportion to its space and the scale of the other statuary. However, it was a human symbol of what otherwise had been felt as an abstraction, human proof that Britain's inventors and scientists were, in the words of Lord Brougham's epitaph for the statue, 'the real benefactors of the world'. Later, the grand buildings and facilities of the new industrial cities obliterated the image of heavy industry and managed to show its use. In the case of the Foundation Stone of Birmingham Museum and Art Gallery, art experienced an almost alchemical transformation: 'By the gains of industry we promote art'.[18] Moreover, the same inventors and scientists were not only good at discovery, but emerged from their clubs and societies to make highly articulate arguments for memorializing the country's technological and scientific achievements.

We think of the factories resulting from industrialization as inhuman places with inhuman living conditions attached to them. They often were. But the more these conditions became visible, the more critics there emerged; the consequence was the beginning of the idea that prosperity created by industrialization needed to be accompanied by social and educational amelioration. There was a second characteristic of British industrialization that culturally might be seen to benefit Britain, but which economically did not (particularly in the future). The idea that the human hand and the human mind were the best controllers of machines was not a competitive advantage either against American skills using mass, simplified production to make uniform products for everyone, or against the rigour of German technical education. The German mechanical engineer Franz Reuleaux correctly predicted in 1876 that the English were being 'tossed out of the satchel' by the Americans and their methods.[19] His own focus on machines, so very different from that of George Stephenson, was to analyse them abstractly into chains of elementary links called 'kinetic pairs'. These he saw as the key to systematization and successful exploitation of machine types. Each of these three cultures – the British, the American and the German – represented a valid approach. The British one – wherein innovation threatened, but never quite lost, its human face – would be less commercially successful even in the medium term, but it helped to give the heyday of the Victorian Age of Progress a distinctive character.

There was no doubt about it. 'In these days', *The Athenaeum* declared in January 1852, 'the world runs fast'. The periodical was not just talking about transport, but we can safely say that without all the new forms of Victorian communication – railway, steamship, post, photograph, telegraph, eventually automobile, moving image, phone and (just out of sight in the new century) aeroplane – the modern world could not exist.[20] For the first time in history, as Seeley's famous book *The Expansion of England* observed, distance had very much lost its effect.[21]

It would be easy to paint a negative picture of the railways; some contemporaries did. The early trains were freezing in winter, smelly, dirty, noisy, crime- and class-ridden, too expensive for workers, food-less, suffering from lack of standardization of track, signalling, classification of goods and even time (the Great Western was four decades ahead of the Government in deciding to follow Greenwich Mean Time in 1840; many places preferred to continue their ownership of their local time). Yet instead of negativity, the most remarkable thing about the fundamental changes to national life brought by the railway was first that they were oh-so-quickly received with almost out-of-control enthusiasm, and second that almost all the problems were solved during the Victorian era. It took the observant William Johnston, writing in 1851, to make the provocation that came home to roost a century later: people who breakfast in York, he said, and dine in London, who may be summoned from Liverpool to the metropolis in minutes by electric telegraph and answer the summons in person in 6–7 hours by express train, 'acquire a habit of pressure and velocity in all that they do'. He suggested that, as a result, thoughtfulness and prudence became less valued.[22] Our world finds that analysis unconvincing, as did most Victorians: for the latter, it was exciting; for us, it seems, merely a danger to mental health.

The Honourable Mrs Jamieson, in Mrs Gaskell's *Cranford*, mostly set in the 1830s, but published in 1853, still uses a sedan chair ('Don't you find it very unpleasant walking?'). She also had her own carriage, but the principal form of long-distance travel, the stagecoach, died quickly. Lord William Lennox's novel *Percy Hamilton* summed up: 'whenever we hear – which we often do – unreasonable grumblings about the absence of trifling luxuries on railways, we are tempted to wish the parties consigned to a good long ride in an old stage coach.'[23] The aristocracy – even Lord Prima Donna, as Lennox was depicted in Disraeli's *Vivian Grey* – saw the advantages of the railways.

After Stephenson's Rocket had its inaugural journey in 1830, 6,000 miles of track were laid in just two decades; by 1896, there were nearly a billion journeys in a year.[24] As Stephenson said, 'The country made the railways, and in return the railways made the country.' The conservative *Morning Post* was happy to note in February 1842 that 'the Queen never travels by

15 An 1845 railway map of England, with 'floating' lines across the Channel. *Punch* observed that, while England would never be in chains, it would be 'pretty soon' in irons.

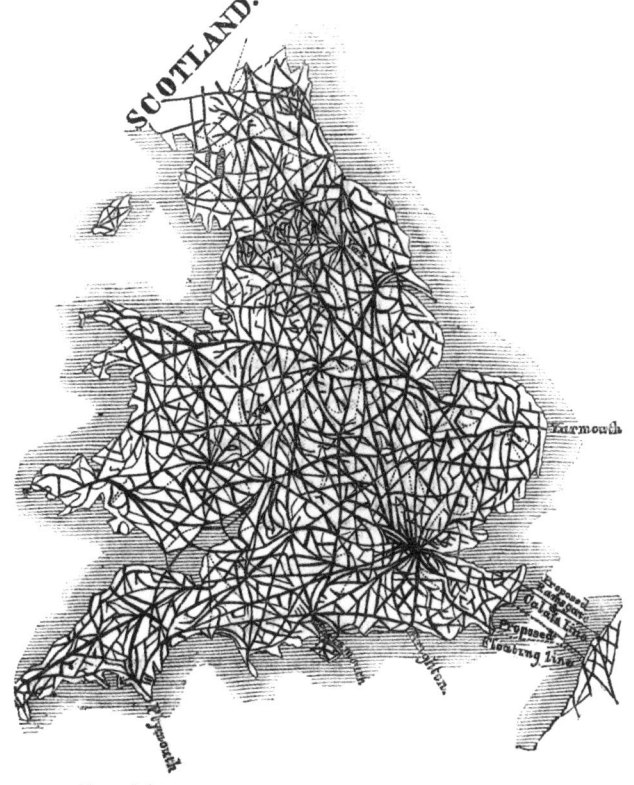

A RAILWAY MAP OF ENGLAND.

Proposed lines............

railways.'[25] She changed her mind. Matthew Arnold, no fan of materialism and technology, could not have been an effective School Inspector without them. Robert Lowe, the politician, had early experience in the Long Vacation at Oxford in 1831 of the Liverpool and Manchester railway a few months after it opened; he recorded 'the wonder, delight, and astonishment that such a journey occasioned; it was as if the Arabian nights had suddenly become true'.[26] One of the many hazards of considering the Victorians purely from the perspectives of today is a failure to comprehend how it felt to them. Tennyson's *Locksley Hall*, written in 1835, speaks of the great world spinning 'for ever down the ringing grooves of change'; he, like others new to rail track, at first thought the rails were grooves cut in the ground.[27]

The experiments of a few people created riches for investors (though big losses for some) and those with goods or raw materials to sell; its lines spawned new cities from nowhere, and employment with them. Middlesbrough was 25 people on a farm in 1801, no more than 40 in 1821. After an extension of the Stockton and Darlington Railway reached it in 1830, the population was 7,631 by 1851, 99,705 by 1871.[28] The world did not have to wait for computers to experience a source of change to patterns and type of work, lifestyle, diet, travel, perceptions of existence, though there was perhaps one negative consequence they both shared: Macaulay was wrong to suggest that rail and steamships would 'remove national and provincial antipathies' and 'bind together all the branches of the great human family'.

Many Victorians thought they were civilizing the world by building railways across the globe; in many countries, the labourers who literally built them – the Irish, as much as Africans or South Americans – were poverty-stricken before the process, and – if they survived – poverty-stricken after. In Europe, because Britain led the way, there was often an invitation, as in the case of the King of Belgium to the Stephensons in the 1830s. Rail could also be important strategically: the war that led to Italian unification in 1859–60 made considerable use of the lines Thomas Brassey built. Born to a Cheshire landowner, he was eventually responsible for perhaps 90 major construction projects. He operated in Canada and Australia, Argentina and India. Outside Britain, he also began with the French railway system in 1841, and he was active in Austria and Denmark.

All this, of course, required capital, and Britain, as the world financial centre, was often the place to get it. In Continental Europe, unlike Britain, the state often played a decisive role. Because the stakes were high, railways often acted as pioneers of modern financial crime. The Irish-born James McHenry, involved in the US with the Atlantic and Great Western Railway Company, first chartered in 1853, managed to get security from the Spanish royal family so as to get credit from London and Liverpool banks. His method, a common one, was not to use his own money, but to acquire construction contracts and own as much as possible of the stock. Things did not evolve smoothly in this and other giant ventures; litigation, bankruptcy, back-stabbing and bad faith were often accompaniments. There were many unhappy endings, but no stopping what had begun so modestly with small-scale, amateur, empirical, determined experiment.

The incentive and the frenzy to invest showed itself very quickly; 157 MPs and 257 clergymen had railroad shares by 1844; by the following year, 20,000 British people had subscribed £2,000 or more, with initial payment just a deposit.[29] Many wise people were drawn in – Darwin and John Stuart Mill among them – despite the fact that demand for rail travel had not yet found a match with costs and anticipated profits. The heavy losses that resulted anticipated the modern world's enthusiasm for whatever seemed most immediately appealing (steamships, almost as important in their own way, sometimes struggled for capital; any return looked as distant as the ships' destinations). Rail prices rose and dropped precipitously in the late 1840s. The hugely positive role the railways were going to play in economic development was not in doubt; how to organize their financial underpinning would trouble economic commentators and governments through to the present day.

George Hudson, dubbed 'The Railway King' by Sydney Smith in 1844, MP for Sunderland and three-time Mayor of York, was exposed by a pamphlet,

16 By this time (a cartoon attributed to Richard ('Dicky') Doyle, 1845), George Hudson had become a Tory MP and controlled perhaps a third of the entire rail network. After his disgrace, the reputation of this 'big swollen gambler', as Carlyle called him, never recovered.

'The Bubble of the Age', and formally by a series of enquiries in 1849 about paying shareholders out of capital; he was bankrupted. Such scandals were naturals to play out in semi-public in the press, but also in a boom of a different kind: the novel. Hudson had some of the characteristics of Mr Merdle in Dickens' *Little Dorrit*, published in serial form between 1855 and 1857, or Vigo in Disraeli's *Endymion* (1880), or Emma Robinson's *The Gold-Worshippers* (1850), where the fat, plebeian 'Napoleon of Steam', Mr Humson, is characterized by Mrs Skinflintz: 'He may well be worth a million of money, if he buys everything, and pays for nuffin!'; anyone dealing with him is 'thoroughly done'.[30]

For those who lost money, of course the experience was unpleasant, but in a way that just contributed to the British sense that railways were a definer of the age. We might join the opening of the Worcester, Bromyard and Leominster Railway in June 1864. We are in a field a few miles from Worcester, on a bank leading up to the Malvern Hills. Five or six years of vicissitudes have led to a marquee with sumptuous luncheon, while Lady Charles Hastings, invited by

17 Railway mania did not escape notice on the Continent. In this cartoon from the *Leipziger Illustrierte Zeitung* (1844), English promoters are desperate to present their schemes, which required approval by Parliamentary committee before a company could be formed.

the engineer, Mr Lewis, and despite 'suffering from an indisposition', cuts the first sod with an elegant silver spade. The Established Church is supportive, for the Reverend J. Pearson is at hand, toasting this railway and all railways for the way in which they are 'animating the people with the idea of progress, and making them all wish to be locomotives'.[31]

The challenges of large-scale finance continued. Sir Edward Watkin, called the 'Last of the Railway Kings', was not like Hudson, though – like many entrepreneurs – he knew how to employ self-righteousness. Brought before the Chief Justice, Sir John Coleridge, and a jury in a case that turned on whether a company director could be held liable for a prospectus, he declined arbitration through his brief and eventually won (see Chapter 6). Much was genuinely 'heroic' about Victorian entrepreneurs, but that didn't mean there were not times in which only humour was appropriate, or the many more times when inventions were dangerous. Watkin was involved in the development of the Metropolitan line, today part of the London Underground. A journey on the line was described in a letter to *The Times* in 1879: the atmosphere was so poisonous that 'I almost suffocated', the writer complained, and had to be assisted from the train at the next station. Some years later, a deadpan driver told a parliamentary committee that only rarely was tunnel smoke so thick that he was unable to see the signals.[32] Not untypical was the experience of Scottish novelist Lucy Walford, who heard a friend speak of being approached by 'a respectable old woman', perhaps a laundress, asking shakily whether the Underground Railway was 'very dreadful'. They share the journey together and the nervous woman has a panic attack in the tunnel and feels faint.[33] Behind the undoubted excitement generated by Victorian technology and grand statements about Progress, we need also to note that the changes, taking the country into a completely new place, were often disturbing and sometimes dangerous.

In the early stages of the Industrial Revolution – often overlooked – were improvements to old technology, notably canals and roads, that continued so long as rail freight times were relatively slow. Certainly, improvements to waterway infrastructure, such as warehousing or easier loading, as well as better road surfaces and drainage, were significant. Culturally, however, the drama inherent in the most ambitious works of the Victorian engineers was much more powerful in shaping both opinion and imagination. There was a decidedly missionary zeal in which the first editorial of *Engineering*, published in 1866 and funded by Henry Bessemer, the inventor of the Bessemer steel process, announced that 'our profession is working out a ground plan of our civilization...fifty years have made a new nation'. In that time, it suggested, practical sense, genuine Christian feeling and natural happiness had increased tenfold. Similarly, the president of the newly created Institute of Mining Engineers declared in 1868 that it was 'an Englishman's pride' to achieve what other countries relied on governments to do.[34] So often everything in society was linked together, but reflected in individual effort: Samuel Smiles' *Lives of the Engineers* stressed that we are 'an old people' but moving forward: engineering was young, trade was young, the civilisation of 'the masses' was only just beginning.[35] 'Just beginning' was of limited comfort to the poor, but it was a whole lot better than all past history.

The most effective rhetoric always has a basis in reality. There were opportunities: Sir William Arrol went from cotton worker (at 9 years old) to blacksmith's apprentice, to foreman in a boiler works, to independent boiler-maker, with night-school technical education along the way, to become head of the civil engineering company that built the Forth Bridge, finally completed in 1890. He would be memorialized inside the North Tower of Tower Bridge, opened in 1894. Arrol also played a key role in creating Tower Bridge, a bridge like no other, even today. There was high visibility for Victorian engineering feats, and even where there was not – the sewers – the transformation of lives that resulted spoke powerfully of Progress. Taine, a keen observer from a French perspective, also noted the absence of polytechnic schools – instead, engineers learned in engineers' offices. 'This,' he wrote, 'is thoroughly English.'[36]

Taine's account was perhaps misleading. There were many kinds of engineers – chemical, manufacturing, civil, electrical, mining – all of which, professionalized or not, played a vital role in Victorian international economic dominance. In fact, as early as 1818, the young engineers who founded the Institution of Civil Engineers had created the world's first professional engineering body. As the century progressed, unlike the manufacturers, they often had a central London base, a role in the most prestigious scientific body – the Royal Society – and sometimes a qualification in law. Being close to the centre of political power and the centre of finance was highly relevant. As the Baron Emile d'Erlanger noted, in presiding over a meeting of the Channel Tunnel Company at the Charing Cross Hotel in January 1897, it needed not more inventive engineering, but Anglo-French relations to improve (both countries, he felt sure, had innate 'ideas of progress' and would eventually join together for 'progress and civilisation').[37]

Isambard Kingdom Brunel's father, Marc, had been involved in the early years of the Institution of Civil Engineers. So, both Brunel and Robert Stephenson had able engineers as fathers. They were also friends and rivals

18 'I alone am hung in chains,' said Brunel of this 1857 photograph in front of the *Great Eastern*. Mr Lenox, of the company that made chains and anchors for the great vessel in its Pontypridd ironworks, had decided not to join the photograph. Those who wanted to be remembered by history embraced the new medium.

(and both suffered from Bright's disease, and both died in 1859). Both were also versatile, but they had different strengths as engineers: Stephenson with his profound common sense, Brunel with his bold, experimental, wild brilliance. Of Brunel's many projects, his steamships were perfect symbols of the most effective way to reinforce British dominance of world trade. Within less than a generation of the effective harnessing of steam power for transport, his *Great Western* reached New York from Bristol in fifteen days in April 1838. This and the *Great Britain* (1843) and the *Great Eastern* (1859) were each the largest ship in any yard in the world at the time. Brunel was dead by the time the *Great Eastern* – a vessel of extraordinary virtuosity in concept and multiple flaws in practice – had its maiden voyage, but when, in 1866, it achieved the laying of the first submarine telegraph cable between England and America, it was contributing to another piece of technology revolutionary in its effect.

Communications were not just a matter of moving people and goods faster and in greater quantity than ever before. Now, as Kipling's poem 'The Deep-Sea Cables' was to put it, 'in the womb of the world... / Men talk to-day o'er the waste of the ultimate slime'. After the *Great Eastern* carried 2,375 miles of cable, with four other ships carrying a further 1,225 miles of cable, the total weighing 7,000–8,000 tons,[38] the telegraphic cable from Bombay to Suez was laid within two months of the vessel arriving off Bombay in January

1870. By the 1870s, there were cables across the globe – not all British, but the British (and their 'cable king', the Liberal MP John Pender, originally a textile merchant) had a dominant role, thus cementing their worldwide soft power. *Le Temps*, the serious and respected Paris daily newspaper, unequivocally related the laying of an Atlantic cable 'to the tenacity of the English character', with Saxon perseverance to be honoured. If the fury of the ocean currents could be resisted by the human will, it was an excellent portent for 'peace, progress, and liberty'.[39]

These successes nevertheless disguised the financial turbulence and national rivalries embedded in the whole story. The practical effects were clearcut. Before there was a cable, when Abraham Lincoln was assassinated on 14 April 1865, the American Legation in London did not know until the 26th. In August 1857, Benjamin Moran at the Legation had blamed a snapped cable, with 300 miles lost, entirely on 'the stupidity of the opinionated English engineers'.[40] His mood briefly changed a year later when Queen Victoria was able to send a congratulatory telegram to President Buchanan, and the English started calling Americans neighbours, natural allies, proper friends. Alas, the cable stopped working and eight more years were needed.

How was progress made? Not, essentially, by the Government, though that wasn't wholly true. The Galton Report – Captain Douglas Galton at the Board of Trade had a background in the Royal Engineers – after the transatlantic cable failed was the last word in thorough; it wasn't published until July 1863, partly because it allegedly had more words than the Bible, but it did bring together some very impressive scientific minds. Nevertheless, successive Governments were (for good reason) most interested in strategic considerations; the emergency request to London for troops at the time of the Indian uprising in 1857 had taken 40 days to arrive.[41] The Government could be – and was – useful in the background, but the compensation it had to pay to shareholders for half a century after underwriting a Red Sea cable suggested that it had some way to go in learning negotiating skills.

In Britain, Robert Stephenson had been looking on in the shabby, cheerless room from which Charles Wheatstone sent a message the short distance from Euston to Camden Town station in London, in September 1837, and received a reply from his partner, William Cooke. The latter was entirely self-taught, while Wheatstone had only achieved a reputation by similar methods. When they fell out over who had made the invention, the wise arbitration committee, conscious of the speed at which it was being acknowledged that the telegraph had a big future, made a careful distinction between the roles of the two incompatible partners. Once the commercial potential was clearer – quickly so – the Liberal MP John Lewis Ricardo led a group of businessmen who bought the patent rights in 1845. The vital role played by finance in creating a substantial business tends to make us neglect the disorderly journey – a mix of scientific brilliance, crackpot enthusiasm, institutional conservatism, human rivalry, business ruthlessness and luck that preceded it and marked the progress of all the great Victorian inventions. Such participants as the medically trained but amateur electrical experimenter Edward 'Wildman' Whitehouse, fecund with ideas in many different fields, more or less disappears from history after being given a large share of the responsibility for the 1850s failure of the Atlantic cable. The man who showed Wildman's errors, William Thomson, later Baron Kelvin – the first to determine the temperature of absolute zero – was the opposite of amateur, but he was on the *Great Eastern* when the transatlantic cable was again lost in July 1865. He nevertheless received much of the applause when it was finally successful. That was just. But both men demonstrated that the 'Age of Progress' was not an abstract ideology, with clear consequences, but a human drama of absorbing intensity for the participants and the society in which they lived.

The shrewd William Johnston was probably correct in 1851 when he acknowledged that steamboat and railway were of more utility, but the electric telegraph beat them for 'triumph over natural difficulty...mastery over time and space...novelty and marvellousness'.[42] Less lyrically, among its benefits was instant news for financial and commodity markets just as a truly global economy was coming into being (Julius Reuter set up his news service in the Royal Exchange Buildings in 1851); world news for newspapers just as they were being transformed by new printing technologies and much bigger markets as more people learned to read; fast information in time of war, or threat of war (though local officials sometimes exaggerated said threat); even female employment (the six operatives at the Electric Telegraph Company, formed by Ricardo and Cooke in 1846, had become 200 at its London headquarters by 1870[43]).

To understand how far Victorians knew they had come from all previous history, Herbert Spencer's retrospect in the *Nineteenth Century* in 1884 provides a good clue when describing the telegraph: 'the ability of a mere iron plate to take up the complicated aerial vibrations produced by articulate speech, which, translated into multitudinous and varied electric pulses, are retranslated a thousand miles off by another iron plate and again heard as articulate speech'.[44] Of course, the potential of electricity was far wider than the telegraph – soon the world would no longer be such a literally dark place – and for once *The Times* was being prescient some decades earlier in predicting 'the result of a few more years of progress on the electric science and the discovery of its applicability to a number of uses now only dimly foreshadowed, will soon make our present attainments appear as nothing'.[45]

Then, as now, the results of urbanization have been differently interpreted. For the Congregationalist minister Robert Vaughan, in his *The Age of Great Cities* (1843), it was clear that 'Our metropolis has come such as the world has not seen. Our leading towns in the provinces equal the capitals of ordinary kingdoms'. More than that, 'the labours of science and the refinements of taste' owed 'their origins and progress so manifestly to the association of men in cities'. Even he, however, allowed a caveat dressed up as a blessing: 'and it may be that progress is only the more safe from not being speedy'.[46] Engels, at more or less the same time, was emphatic that the working classes were worse off. There were more people – so many more people – living in urban locations without the infrastructure – yet – to cope, so whatever the definition of 'poor', more individuals suffered. In the frenzy of growth and development, the battles between vested interests – new money and no money – did not allow for much in the way of town planning. Towns and cities were combat zones engaged in high theatre. Nevertheless, this strange form of progress, in which everything seemed to become much worse fast, then immeasurably better slower, had produced fundamental change by the end of the century, most notably increases in real working-class income, with education and living conditions to match. We will see how the poor fared in detail in Chapter 8, but – as the *Daily Mail* noted as it looked back from 31 December 1900 – it couldn't be too bad if bread was costing about a fifth of its price in January 1801; beef and mutton were no longer just for the rich; and a pair of boots had replaced bare feet for many.

In the quaint way the British make revolutions, the new often paraded its newness on the back of what it was replacing. When Crewe – about 70 people in the 1830s, then a 'railway colony' of 40,000 in 1871 – became a borough in 1877, and members of the new corporation subscribed to present a chain and badge of office for the Mayor, it was made as a golden spectacle, with shields surmounted by civic crowns for future mayors, and a larger shield supported at each side by a civic mace, with the initials of the first mayor in raised gold letters on an enamelled ground. The shield, crest and motto of the borough, surrounded by wreaths, formed another badge. The arms of the town – observed the *Leeds Mercury* – were 'distinctly modern' and appropriate to the railway 'enterprise' that had been the 'the making' of Crewe. The crest was an exact model of a recent locomotive engine and tender invented by Mr Webb of the London and North-Western Railway;

the shield, with elaborate enamel work, conveyed 'the idea of progress' of the town from the times of pillion and pack-saddle to those of stagecoach and canal boat, the locomotive completing 'the record of progress in its latest development'. An ornamental riband bore in gold the motto: 'Never behind'.[47] Civic pride's certainty that it was 'progress' was celebrated not with the boiler suits of the Russian Revolution just 40 years later, but a conscious aping of an aristocratic past.

Behind the ceremony, 'improvement' underpinned 'progress'. If you had gone to a meeting of the Commissioners discussing 'Bingley improvement' – Bingley, near and now part of Bradford, flourished during the Industrial Revolution – in January 1871, you would have heard their views on the control of gas prices, the authorization of costs for laying water pipes in Church Street, investigation of problems with cess pools and insufficient drainage in side streets off Hill Street. Central government was involved in such matters through the long-standing system of petitioning and private bills discussed by parliamentary committees. Typical was a message 'brought from the House of Commons by Mr Bernal and others' agreeing to the House of Lords' amendments to 'An Act for better paving, lighting, watching, cleansing and otherwise improving the City of Exeter and County of the same City'. The *Liverpool Mercury* reported 'The Town Council and the Improvement Bill', the *Birmingham Daily Post* the 'Walsall Improvement Bill', the *Manchester Times* the 'Manchester City Improvement Bill' – all in January 1871.[48]

Behind these changes, public virtue was certainly not the whole story – too many vested interests had strong lobbies, too much money was involved for competition to be a civilized process – but it would be easy to forgive the self-congratulatory celebrations that were often involved. In Framlingham, Suffolk, in February 1871, the Mutual Improvement Society enjoyed their annual soirée in the People's Hall. Their library had issued 4,482 books over the previous year – something that would have been inconceivable without improved reading skills. We might scoff to know that Miss Clodd's rendition of 'Home they brought her Warrior dead' was well received, but that would be a failure of imagination: the Victorians often enjoyed the creation of a community spirit, based on a shrewd sense of progress rather than mired in our world of fragmented digital distress.[49]

Sentiment usually mixed with Victorian practicality, reinforced by the power of nonconformist morality. In the half-century from 1820 to 1870, government expenditure remained almost out of sight, some 3 per cent of GNP; it then doubled as a percentage, more as a sum of money, over the next 35 years. At the same time, local government took a much greater share than hitherto, reaching 51 per cent in 1905 (a percentage never subsequently exceeded).[50] Cities were big enough – with ever-larger numbers of rate-payers – to get good long-term loans from the London money market. Buying up new local monopolies with some of this money – from transport to heating and water – enabled them to be run for local needs, reinforcing fast-developing civic pride. In the difficult – and still unsolved – matter of ensuring public efficiency, devolution was often more effectively deployed than it is today. Amidst the obvious reflection that philanthropy was no longer close to being sufficient for urban needs, the powerful social cohesion created in nonconformist towns and cities, in chapel and community organizations alike, motivated many of the most successful people to use their organizational and other skills.

Was 'self-help' just a cruel method of ensuring continued deprivation? Sidney Webb's *Socialism in England* (1890) made some observations. Town councillors abhorred anything other than individualism. Yet, if an imaginary one took a walk, it would be on a municipal pavement. The gaslight was municipal, the pavement cleaned with municipal water (by municipal broom). The councillor knows the time from the municipal clock in the municipal market so that he can pick up his children from the municipal school, near the municipal hospital. He can use the national telegraph to tell the children not to walk through the municipal park, but to take the municipal tram and meet him in the municipal reading room. He can be working there on his next speech in the municipal town hall; the reading room is close to the municipal art gallery, museum and library.[51]

The *Charity Organization Review*, formed via an 1885 report on charity organizations, complained that Mr Webb was attempting to convince Americans that the English were all becoming socialists (the book was derived from a lecture at the American Economic Association in 1889).[52] If so, it was highly misleading. The brilliantly thorough investigations of Sidney and Beatrice Webb correctly demonstrated that the British way was evolutionary and not revolutionary, and there was to be a greatly increasing voice for working-class opinion in the 20th century. But, ironically, Sidney's playful picture of the municipal councillor demonstrated what had already been achieved from effectively nothing before the end of the Victorian era – albeit far too slow for those with a taste for the instant, equally far too painful for the many before the urban death rate began declining from 1870. Even the fact that middle-class people – the Webbs – could call themselves 'Socialists' (merely suffering from H.G. Wells's 1911 satire of them in *The New Machiavelli*) was in fact progress.

Nothing about the British economy was ever uniform. There were industrial towns in the south, not just the north; population increased fast in the first half of the 19th century in Brighton and Bournemouth, seaside towns, not just inland industrial towns and major ports. Bury, in Suffolk, sometimes called 'Dull Bury', admitted in 1886 that it had been 'rather slow – that is, in conforming to modern ideas of progress and improvement', even though Charles Dickens had called it 'a bright little town'.[53] Now it was waking up, mending roads, making street improvements, with a sewage scheme 'and the like'. Meantime, no one had better shown that individuals could win against rate-payer resistance than Joseph Chamberlain in Birmingham, with an influential improvement scheme beginning in 1875, with a 'Parisian boulevard'-type Corporation Street. 'True economy', argued Chamberlain, followed from investment in homes, schools and environment; it would increase productivity, create urban civilization and increase prosperity. He wasn't being ideological, just practical – and it worked.[54]

19 Joseph Chamberlain began his political career as a brilliant and popular creator of Birmingham civic pride. Later, in the 1890s, he was thin-skinned enough as a famous national politician to send a photograph to the caricaturist Francis Carruthers Gould inscribed 'from the real Chamberlain' to the author of the fictitious one.

The 50 years after the Victorian era ended gradually saw the genuine parts of the civic pride the Victorians had created sapping away, while accentuating their worst environmental failure: pollution. There was a Disraeli-appointed Royal Commission on Noxious Vapours in 1876: 14,000 questions and inspections of 'alkali works, cement works, chemical manure works, coke ovens' and much more. Many of its recommendations were accepted, but the Commission itself placed limits to avoid affecting local and national prosperity; the courts often took the same view. Shephard Taylor, a trainee doctor, had noted in his diary in January 1861 that the fog from the Thames was so intense that he had to give up dissection; over 90 years later, in 1952, the London killer smog killed 12,000 people. Much the same applied to pollution of rivers from manufacturing residues. Again, Disraeli legislated (in 1876), but governments then (and even more governments today) paid insufficient thought to, and provided insufficient funds for, effective enforcement of statute and regulation.

In the second half of the 19th century, city streets became animated by commerce as never before. In London, if you negotiated successfully the confused bustle of too many horse-drawn vehicles and too many pedestrians, you could clamber up the staircase of a double-decker and pass the advertisement for 'Cadbury's Cocoa Absolutely Pure Therefore Best'. Outside boardmen might show irresistible ads for the winsome Bella Pateman ('For This Night Only'), or on any available space ads could encourage 'Dancing to MARRIOTTS BAND of 60' at the Highbury Barn, Islington; across the street was the entrance in Ludgate Hill to Goodman's Dentists, promising 'Painless Gas Extractions for 5s'. However, you might think twice about stopping for lunch. Dr Taylor, in December 1860, noted that the college puddings at Upton's were not 'all that could be desired', though the macaroni puddings at Browne's, near Temple Bar, were 'decidedly worse'. Still, when he went later in the month with his father to Islington Cattle Market (where 9,000 bullocks were to be slaughtered), the farmers were observed enjoying their hearty breakfasts. Something was happening everywhere: one evening, he went to see an accident at the Metropolitan railway, when water irrupted from the Fleet ditch or sewer into the deep railway cutting. It reminded him of Niagara.[55]

This was the city Henry James called in 1881 'the biggest aggregation of human life – the most complete compendium of the world'.[56] It had long been a world city and was already the largest as the Victorian period began. That, it could be argued, was more, or as important, as anything in giving Britain an early dominance in the world economy. It did develop, or could already provide, banking, insurance, legal services and all that was necessary for trade, not just for Britain but for the world. Its population in 1860 was greater than the largest nine cities in America combined; and it was not one but many cities contained within one. Despite higher property and other costs, it remained not just a great manufacturing city (giving employment to one in three Londoners in 1871), but a versatile one, not dependent, as many of the new cities were, on a single raw material or product. It was the seat of a government that, as the decades passed, had ultimate responsibility for large parts of the globe and great influence in the rest of it. Its railways linked its disparate parts, enabling expansion not just to St John's Wood, or Kensington, or Chelsea, but further afield to Ealing, 'Queen of the Suburbs', where the extended Metropolitan District Railway provided several stations. The suburbs, much satirized then (*Punch* invented 'Kensington Railway' in the 1840s as 'a road leading from a place nobody ever was, to a place nobody

20 London's transport network was built by private enterprise – effectively beginning with the Metropolitan line linking Paddington and King's Cross in 1867 – but eventually nationalized by the second Labour Government in 1933. Here, the Lord Mayor, Sir John Ellis, marks the beginning of the inner circle of the London Underground, 17 September 1881.

was ever going') and ever since were in fact a new kind of urban living that offered a loveable, safe home: for the army of newly prosperous working-class and lower middle-class office workers, dullness was certainly progress, an end to the slum.

London was also a magnet for persecuted Continental intellectuals and political exiles, numbered in British records at over 4,000 in 1853: Marx, Mazzini from Italy, the French feminist Jeanne Deroin, Kossuth from Hungary, Worcell from Poland, Herzen from Russia, but also others such as Karl Schapper and August Willich, with actual experience of manning barricades and a comfortable engagement with the British working class rather than intellectual life. Turgenev, an admirer of the British political system and the prevailing moderation and tolerance, made multiple visits to see Herzen in 1862 when Dostoevsky, whose relationship with Herzen was complex, also came to London and discussed education and the abolition of serfdom. Dostoevsky's observations exactly described the dilemmas of an increasingly prosperous modern urban civilization: apparent disorder, clamour on all sides, the brutality of life in Whitechapel, removed from any glimpses of prosperity, the poisoned Thames and the poisoned air, but behind these

21 Constructing sewers in Tottenham Court Road, London, in 1845. A drawing by
George Scharf, later founding Director of the National Portrait Gallery.

things a disciplined bourgeoisie engaged in making a more orderly future
for everyone. When he saw either the Great London Exposition, in South
Kensington from May to November 1862, or the Crystal Palace in Sydenham
(he seems to conflate the two), he found it overwhelming – 'amazing', 'the
grandeur of the idea', 'victory and triumph'. But London also made him
nervous. Was this where history stopped? Was it the end? He describes the
experience as a biblical sight, something to do with Babylon: 'some prophecy
out of the Apocalypse being fulfilled' – and in front of his own eyes.[57] No one
showed better than Dostoevsky on his one visit how it must have felt to live
through it – the Shock of the New on a giant scale.

There remained many things that did not work in this dominant city.
Time and again, the uniqueness and ancient conventions of governance
resisted attempts at reform. London, for example, was excepted from a town
improvement Act in 1847. There were reckoned to be some 300 bodies with
some authority in 1855. The Metropolitan Board of Works, an unelected
body, was given some powers in that year, but some decades of scandal and
incompetence followed. The City Corporation was perhaps the worst in
wanting to go its own way. There was progress, but its focus was money-making;
not so much taking account of the public good as manipulating opportunity
and particular needs, with access to newly professionalized services in an
explosively growing environment. Even when the London County Council
was created in 1889, the City was little touched by it. Still, the Victorians did
finally reach a solution of sorts when 28 metropolitan boroughs replaced the
many local vestries and boards in 1900, assuming some of the LCC powers
while sharing others. The whole story pointed up the essential problem of
planning modern urban society: the pace of change makes it impossible to

consider either greenfield thinking (there are no green fields or their urban equivalent) or regulation that will be effective amidst flux.[58]

Did that mean most things had been out of control? If you encountered what William Farr, Victorian pioneer of medical statistics, called the 'highly agglutinative compound' (derived from roughly 40,000 tons of manure dumped in the streets in the 1850s), you might have thought so. But Joseph Bazalgette, chief engineer of the Metropolitan Board of Works, showed after his appointment just what might be achieved in a city whose great river, the Thames, was effectively an open sewer. It did take 30 years, but over 50 acres of land was reclaimed from the river, over a thousand miles of street sewers and over 80 miles of brick underground main sewers were built to control overflows and divert the raw sewage to treatment plants. All this owed an enormous amount to Bazalgette himself, his remarkable analytical skills, his punctiliousness and his single-mindedness. Progress became a social gospel – but its underpinning always leads to individuals.

To give a perspective on all these developments, from Industrial Revolution to urbanization, we might turn to the unlikely source of 'Mr Hole of Leeds'. Actually born in Manchester, son of a tailor, in 1820, and brought up there, James Hole moved to Leeds in his twenties, but always paraded the virtues of the Manchester Mechanics' Institute and his local Mutual Improvement Society. In his analysis of Victorian society in 1851, he combined practicality with idealism, but rejected theory: 'No conclave of philosophers and engineers could have pre-arranged the railway system.' He expressed confidence in people to find the right solutions to social issues, making progress by bringing them together. There would always be 'some misfortune to amend, some wrong to amend, some right to defend – for progress is as infinite as man's nature is limitless'. The imperfect proceeded the highly developed. His many ideas – in 1852, he proposed sending boxes of books to Yorkshire village communities without access to them, and bringing paupers to employment – were sound, just not instantly achievable. Only in one respect was he naïve: he thought the best form of meeting objectives 'may be safely left to time'.[59] This was true of the evolution of British political parties, but it was not universally true – as Marxist and other authoritarian 'communities' offering the perfect society were to show.

Mr Hole, in his dislike of theory, might have pointed to many new realities. We might compare the experience of the foreign traveller arriving at Heathrow today with a tawdry motorway journey to London to follow, with what happened when François Wey, president of the Societé des gens de lettres, went aboard the steam packet *Cité du Boulogne* one summer evening

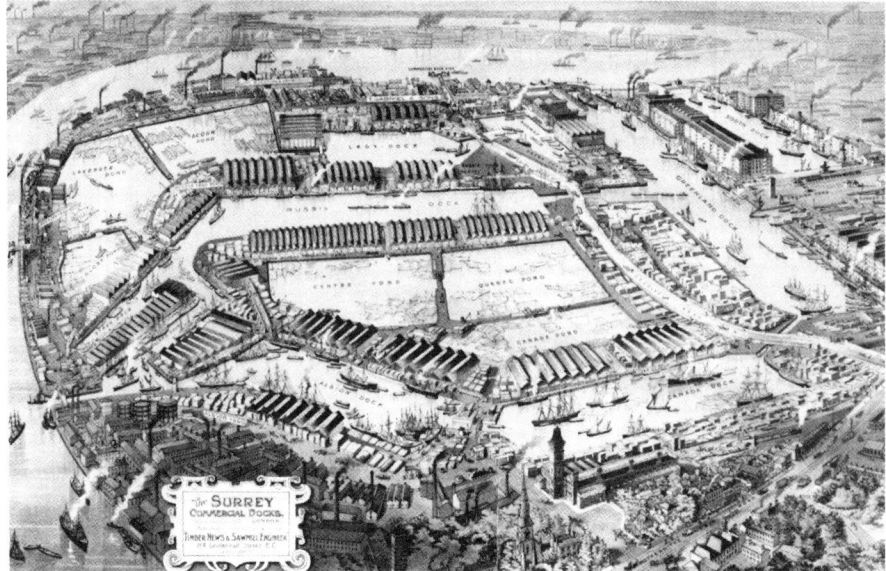

22 Surrey docks, seen here not long after Queen Victoria died, were the only docks south of the river. By then they were almost a century old and had come about in a frenzy of acquisition, takeovers, amalgamations and a desire to monopolize certain trades. After the Great Dock Strike in 1889, dockers had an hourly pay of 6d, 8d for overtime, but nothing for meal breaks.

in 1856, his destination the London docks, the anchorage for 'the opulent fleets of this modern Tyre'.

St Katharine's, opened in 1828, or the giant East India Company docks, begun at the beginning of the 19th century, or the West India docks, built at a cost of £35 million (all from public subscription) – these were set in an unbroken landscape of warehouses containing vaults as underground storehouses, the whole stretching for 5–6 miles. M. Wey suggested that it would be easy to imagine 'the fecundity of the whole earth had been exhausted' in this place, in which you would find yourself ankle-deep in sugar, with an unforgettable honey-like smell of molasses; there were preserved fruits, spices, spirits, cottons, perfumes, logwood in vast quantity. And what was the prevailing sense? 'This commercial cave of Aladdin gives one an idea of the splendour and the preponderating wealth of this nation... [a] monstrous octopus whose tentacles reach out and drain the substance of the whole world.' When he returned to Paris, it seemed like a quiet provincial town, the Seine a modest stream.[60] Novelists like Charles Collins expressed similar thoughts: in the London docks were 'piles of hemp that might suffice to weave a net to encompass the whole earth.'[61] And it wasn't just London:

Joseph Hatton described Liverpool as 'a city of ships' on which the world's eye was focused, with people coming and going to and from everywhere.[62]

Britain's lead in maritime technology and investment in factory production fuelled exports, sometimes accompanied by raw materials that could be sold on through the reach of the merchant marine. Robert Kemp Philip analysed the growth of tonnage of British shipping from roughly 1.8 million in 1800 to over 4.3 million 50 years later. The big increase in foreign trade, once the technical possibilities had been enhanced, resulted – according to Leone Levi's 1872 examination of commerce and economic progress – from one thing: free trade, the political battle for which had been won, with difficulty, in the 1840s. 'So manifest and unmistakeable has been the prosperity during the period of Free Trade, and so directly is this prosperity traceable to the policy in question,' said *The Times* in March 1852, 'that to dispute the matter is a perfect absurdity.' Did we want plenty or penury, comfort or misery, progress or stagnation?[63] Whatever else, the change was certainly a big one: for five centuries, there had been tariffs and an evolving landscape of regulation, whether Corn Laws, or restrictions on ships from outside Britain, or monopolies given to chartered companies. Britain became a powerful proselytizer for free trade, making commercial treaties with France in 1860, followed by key countries across Europe (though not Russia). It wasn't to last: before the 19th century was over, at a time of ever-increasing nationalism, Germany and France reverted to tariffs, while America's soared upwards. Georg Friedrich List (1789–1846), a German economist who also spent time in America, had already made the case for linking political economy to nationalism and – like much of Continental Europe – specifically not linking political liberalism to liberal economic ideas. He was an inspiration to his fellow countryman, Dr C.J. Fuchs, later in the century, who straightforwardly dismissed British trade policy as masquerading as a philanthropic promotion of globalization when in fact it was entirely in the interests of Britain.[64]

It is true that the fervent free traders in Britain sounded, at times, almost messianic. Richard Cobden, who negotiated with John Bright the trade treaty with France despite the habitual distrust of the two countries, though with the help of the free market liberal statesman Michel Chevalier, used the word 'missionaries' in relation to exports. The *Caledonian Mercury and Daily Express* in Edinburgh happily quoted from John Stuart Mill in December 1859, explicitly seeing the rapid increase in international trade as 'the principal guarantee of the peace of the world' and 'the great permanent security for the uninterrupted progress' of human ideas, institutions and character.[65] The same sentiment – international, not (yet) explicitly imperialistic – had already found its way into popular culture. For James Grant, in *The Highlanders of Glen Ora* (1857), railroads and steamships brought the opposite ends of the world together in bonds of friendship and commerce; the freer the intercourse between nations, the more certain peace was.

We may call this naïve (as subsequent history showed, the market was not as efficient as Adam Smith's *Wealth of Nations*, in 1776, had suggested, and individual self-interest and nationalism could only be stretched into imperfect regionalism) as well as retrospectively deeply hypocritical (the indigenous peoples of the world were not invited to participate), but for many Victorians the link between political and economic liberalism was genuine. When neither Britain nor France nor Austria provided military help to the troubled Ottoman Empire, facing revolt in Egypt from Mohammed Ali in 1833, Russia and the Sultan agreed to support each other's defensive security. But that just reflected the uneasy relationship between the two, going back to 1492 and continuing until the end of the Empire and the Communist era. Britain used a different weapon to the giant Russian army's long-lasting push towards Persia, Afghanistan and India; it sought influence in Turkey by negotiating – effectively imposing – the Treaty of Balta Liman in 1838. That certainly increased trade, though disastrously to the disadvantage of the pre-industrialized Turkish textile looms. It could not be argued that the many wider Ottoman reforms in the following decades in the Tanzinat ('Reorganization') – to protect life, property and belief for all, with provincial representative assemblies, new commercial and criminal codes and standardized taxation – were enacted perfectly or owed their origins entirely to the British (they embodied a mix of European ideas). And British diplomacy was not coy about using British power, at least privately. But the links between 'modernizing' trade and 'modernizing' administration, institutions and moral values all came out of British ideas of progress, albeit sometimes precariously perched on an uneasy world 'balance of power'.

At home, the Great Exhibition was one giant signal for another defining feature of this Victorian progress: modern consumerism. It wasn't 21st-century consumerism, both because thrift was a central Victorian value and because choice wasn't remotely unlimited. It was still where our world began. First, consumers needed to be in the know: the first advertisement on a building is believed to have been on Ludgate Hill, where Charles Sharp's 'most excellent and superb razors' were sold.[66] When *Nicholas Nickleby* was sold in monthly parts (1838–39), it incorporated 'The Nickleby Advertiser' for both products and services. But it was after the tax on newspaper advertisements was repealed in 1853 that the second half of the century introduced the sense that there was

– for the first time – 'much more of everything' for many more people. The professionalization of advertising helped. The first agencies dated from 1845, but the awareness was much more visible by 1870 in Trollope's *The Struggles of Brown, Jones, and Robinson*, set in the world of lower-middle-class urban shopkeepers in which Robinson not only says, 'Advertise, advertise, advertise. And I say it again and again – advertise, advertise, advertise!', but also explains how to make it effective.[67] As it happens, Robinson's extravagance (in part) results in bankruptcy for the would-be haberdashers, but in the real world, professional guidance gathers pace, from William Smith (manager of the Adelphi Theatre) and his *Advertise: How? When? Where?* (1863) to the barrister Thomas Smith's *Successful Advertising* (1886). The latter, with gusto, explains the twenty stages that lead to a sale, comparing the impact of advertising to James Nasmyth's steam hammer, first invented to forge the paddle shafts for SS *Great Britain*.[68] His assumption that his readers would know about and have been impressed by an engineering analogy regardless of their own particular interests was a good indicator of the way Victorian progress became culturally all of a piece. Cultural fragmentation waited for the 20th century.

To sell all the new products, the landscape of shopping was transformed by Victorian department stores, with origins in the 18th century, but an all-encompassing symbol of metropolitan modernity by the end of the 19th. From 1863, Whiteley's, once a modest drapery store, acquired 6,000 staff in 30 years, many of them in live-in accommodation. The 'Earl of Oxford Street', the American Harry Gordon Selfridge, whose London store opened in 1909, had summed up the transformation in *The Romance of Commerce* (1918). He thought advertising was a parasite, but in the newly created consumer society, both skilled advertising and skilled retailing had plentiful opportunities to flourish.

The economy's key financial engine, the City of London, seemed by comparison more concentrated on its function than courting publicity. For a decades-long brief moment, global supremacy does not clothe itself in plutocratic excess and conspicuous consumption. Perhaps that is because the throng in a small area of the City of London in 1850, within the confines of the Poultry, Cornhill, Threadneedle Street, Lombard Street, Lothbury and Broad Street, is too busy financing the world. In the day, all is hubbub. Visit the City before 9am or after 7pm and it has the stillness of death, quiet even in the labyrinth of little lanes and alleys and courts that adjoin the better-known streets.[69]

Nevertheless, some, evidently, still live there, or did: in Lombard Street, where the merchants of Lombardy had settled in the twelfth century, the banker George Beadnell lived with his brother John at No. 2, next door to Messrs Smith, Payne and Smith's, which George managed. Twenty years before mid-century, you might have seen a moody Charles Dickens pass by, hoping for a glimpse of his first great love, George's daughter Maria, then nineteen. The senior Beadnell did not approve, however, and the match went nowhere, though some say that Maria is memorialized as Dora in *David Copperfield*. Everything seems to connect, if not always consequentially, in Victorian London. Macaulay's cheque for £10,000 for his bestselling *History of England* – no larger amount had ever been paid to an author – was drawn on his publisher's account at Smith, Payne and Smith's. His publisher was Longmans, today the educational giant Pearson.

Most of those who worked in the City, especially as London mushroomed rapidly outwards, with better transport links part of the expansionary process, went home to the West End and to the new suburbs. Bankers' anonymity was not universal. The sons and grandsons of Nathan Mayer Rothschild, who had founded the British branch of the famous banking family early in the 19th century, became considerable social figures. But the largest fortune to be valued for probate before 1870, nearly £3 million plus property, was that of a man who did not even figure in the original edition of the *Dictionary of National Biography*: Richard Thornton, who died in 1865. The Thornton drama was mainly overseas; its financial exploitation at home. Richard's brother had been in the Baltic when he caught wind of Napoleon's retreat from Moscow and got word back to him three days earlier than anyone else, including the Government. Wholesale prices inflated by the now-lifted blockade dropped immediately, with huge profits to be made by anyone snapping up goods at bargain prices. By mid-century, he was operating everywhere, but quietly, next to Rothschilds and Barings.

What might you see, and what exactly went on in the City? For a while, banking self-esteem was high. Many bankers – of course, not all – might at least seem to exhibit the truth of Samuel Smiles's suggestion that being 'gentlemanly' was a set of values that was not owned by the gentry: values of honesty, truthfulness, self-respect, self-help, being polite. Bankers could distance themselves from the antagonistic stance taken by early industrialists against aristocracy (and vice-versa). They operated functionally and professionally without threatening the social status quo – or so many thought. The grandest of them seemed like aristocrats (and some became members of the House of Lords). In the 19th century, that appeared to spell stability.

The Bank of England – both its presence in the City and its role – gave it a special place. The respect given to it was not entirely based on rationality; as a joint-stock company, it continued to have a contradiction at its heart until it was finally nationalized in 1946. Did it owe its obligations to its shareholders or was it a lender of the last resort that could maintain stability? In 1850, we are on the cusp of the modern and there is everything to play for; in that year, all banknotes from this issuer bank still needed a cashier to fill in the name of the payee and provide a signature for each note, though the first printed notes came just three years later. The interior of the room in which the 24 directors met was spatially magnificent, but otherwise meanly furnished. There were long mahogany settles, covered with faded crimson merino wool, and a few scattered chairs. The walls were entirely devoid of any decoration. Much, or most, business was conducted standing.

Even so, by 1850 we are a long way from the beginning of the century. From the 1770s, stockbrokers could be found in a coffee room at the end of Sweetings Alley (known for obscure reasons as Sweetings Rents), but the new century was to add a galaxy of new opportunities to the market – railway shares, mining shares, foreign securities. The clearinghouse in Lombard Street was dealing in big money even by 1839, when London's 25 or so clearing banks were responsible for clearing £100,000,000 in a single year. Each day in Lombard Street, private bankers settled accounts with each other, and a committee with inspectors authenticated each day's business. The private banks, some 60 in London at mid-century – perhaps half in the City and half in the West End – kept the joint-stock banks out. There was a pronounced difference in style. The cashiers and clerks in the former were retiring, formal figures, courteous to their customers and inquiring politely of the weather or perhaps the prospects for business. Their flashier, though not yet flashy, rivals, the inheritors of the future, dressed with less reticence and might, almost extrovertly, took time to discuss current opera or other amusements in London with their clients. All this changed in the 19th century: at the beginning of Victoria's reign, there were perhaps 600 banks in England; just before the First World War, there were just seventeen, and only five of these were dominant.

Change was well symbolised by generational change. In the early 1840s, you might see Levi Salomons, with a benevolent air, a close-cut grey beard and a bent back, walking with his crutch down Bartholomew Lane to his offices in Shorter's Court, Throgmorton Street. Not a grand figure. His politically interested son David became the first Jewish Lord Mayor of London and, as a campaigner for Jewish emancipation, was first elected to Parliament as a Liberal, standing in Greenwich, in 1851. He was several times forced to withdraw, though not without pointing out his large majority; when change finally came in an Act of 1858, it was Lionel de Rothschild the following year who was the first person of Jewish faith to be able to take his seat.

David Salomons was also a founder of the London and Westminster Bank. Everything was getting grander, but it was to be a long time before banking was to reach the megalomaniac narcissism exhibited by 21st-century ideas of global expansion as evidenced by Fred Goodwin's takeover in 2000 – the biggest in UK history – of NatWest (which, after many changes and additions, the London and Westminster had become). Even so, as the journalist David Morier Evans noted in 1864, the London and Westminster had already 'swelled its proportions' into such a conspicuous building that it seemed to rival the Bank of England. Evans warned that this new 'love of show' could lead to excess and 'sometimes to embarrassment'. That was exactly what happened. Yet, if you had visited some of the coffeehouses in the City of London in the 1850s, by comparison, you would certainly have become instantly aware of global expansion, some of it highly risky, but its primary characteristic was the excited shock of the new, rather than self-regard or megalomania.

23 Forward-looking city planners (the railway bridge across Ludgate Hill, 1863, was built with a span to accommodate a widening of the road) or vandals (it ruined the majestic view to St Paul's; *Punch*, 8 August 1863, spoke ironically of 'the great improvement which the march of intellect and the progress of commerce' were creating)?

A perpetual challenge of fast-modernizing societies is how to deal with everything. In a way, it made the activities involved in making a new world more exhilarating, if at times exasperating, because the necessary building of infrastructure – domestic and office housing; roads; sewers; public lighting; new forms of heating – did not keep up with the activities themselves. If you had gate-crashed a meeting of the City Commissioners of Sewers at the Guildhall on 26 January 1870, you would have heard a report of the Finance and Improvement Committee on a proposal to widen Gresham Street to help traffic flow. This street in the City, named after the Elizabethan financier and merchant Sir Thomas Gresham, founder of the Royal Exchange, had only been created in 1845 by widening and amalgamating other streets. Twenty-five years later, the Committee saw the need, but decided against the 'vast expense' for a gain of a few feet.[70] Evidently, the focus on successful trading won against the wish to create a state-of-the-art environment. It wasn't exactly back-of-the-envelope behaviour (this was also the first age of modern statistics), but it did create many lasting businesses and reputations. Even today, when the priority of the two things (ostentatious display or the detailed mechanics of the business) are easily reversed, Gresham Street is home to Lloyds Bank, Alliance Trust, Investec and other financial institutions.

Meantime, in the mid-19th century, City coffeehouses were where sea captains and traders met to conduct business. Lloyd's Coffee House focused on shipping and the underwriting of risk for the mercantile marine. A set of rooms in the Royal Exchange opened its doors when the clock struck 10am. In the Captain's room, in the 1840s, you would probably find Joseph Somes, one of the originators of Lloyd's Register of Shipping and briefly an MP for Dartmouth, a plain dresser, a steady persevering man. With his friend Thomas Ward – a small man, habitually in a shabby blue coat, and frequently fumbling his only visible sign of wealth, an old gold chain and seals to which, possibly, a watch was attached – you would have been looking at major capital investors in everything connected to the Port of London. Around were those who depended on them – brokers, agents, sea captains. From every part of the world, agents provided for Lloyd's information on departures, arrivals of vessels, accidents, wrecks, sailings, sales of effects, proceeds to be collected for underwriters.

Everything had its place in the City. In the North and South American Coffee House, there was a subscription room for traders – news of the day and other papers from across the globe, all related to the Americas. 'No quotation for United States Bank shares. Ohio Sixes are up 2 per cent. Little movement on anything else': a rare dull moment. Similarly, there was the

Jerusalem Coffee House in Cowper's Court, Cornhill, for China, India and Australia, as well as others for the Baltic or for Jamaica.

The Royal Exchange itself operated to help City traders conduct their business. On Tuesdays and Fridays, in particular, Rothschilds showed its dominance in foreign bills after arriving mid-afternoon to take contracts from or with other exchange brokers. Barings was prominent in America and also advancing its reputation for large loans elsewhere; £5,000,000 advanced to Russia was not untypical. The stockbrokers, in the course of the century, never lost their practical desire to make things happen, but if you had visited towards 1900, their success had become much more visibly represented – just not in public: the entrance in Capel Court to the first stock exchange in the world (from 1801) and the six other doorways into the building were unassuming and gloomy. The doormen were less noticeable for their dark-blue uniforms, scarlet collars and gold-braided hats than for their knowledge of perhaps 4,000 brokers and jobbers, as well as thousands of clerks. Inside, the Exchange was a vast, 16,000 square feet oblong hall, rather like the gaming rooms at Monte Carlo, but much, much noisier. A gilt dome and vaulted roof of glass, supported by huge columns of red-brown granite and with bare marble walls like polished glass, radiated importance. Electric arc lights and the telephone room spoke of the modern. Yet, despite the tumult and loud voices bidding, much significant business was calmly conducted on the steps of the Stock Exchange or in Throgmorton Street after it had closed. Despite millions of pounds being involved, there were no contracts (yet repudiation was almost unknown – here Progress spelled optimism), no proper records, perhaps a hasty entry in a pocketbook. Here you might meet Sidney Brimstowe, rooted to one spot: nicknamed John Bull, a staid, respectable, unostentatious figure who departed quietly at 4pm sharp. Or perhaps Tommy 'Our Tommy' Marks, probably less than 5 feet, a bag of energy, but a kind man, maker (and loser) of fortunes.[71]

Why was the City of London the world centre for this activity? Continental Europe of course contributed, but was frequently politically unstable. In the 1850s, Germany and Italy were not yet nations, and were to that extent inward-looking, focused precisely on nationhood and regional rivals. The French, throughout the 19th century, struggled in the wake of the French Revolution and the ongoing legacies both of the Ancien Régime and of the Napoleonic era to find out how they wanted to be governed. Protectionism took a long time to wane in Continental Europe, and tariffs and other barriers to trade were not dislodged until the success of the British espousal of free trade could no longer be ignored. Britain's longtime devotion to the sea acquired a huge extra boost from steam-powered vessels, manufactured at home, eating up distance. For confident adventurers, whose confidence grew the greater as British dominance became the more apparent, the world had become a trading emporium on a scale that earlier generations could barely have imagined. Besides, the Royal Navy provided comfort as self-appointed world peacekeeper. Peaceful political reform and the rule of law at home, combined with maintaining peace abroad (if tainted, we would now say, by imperialism), were powerful prerequisites for prosperity.

As important, in just three decades from around 1840 to 1870, a modern world of finance began to take recognizable form. In this first true age of globalization, using the gold standard (except during the American Civil War, the pound sterling and the US dollar kept within a 1 per cent variation from 1840 right through to the outbreak of the First World War), the Bank of England operated as the world's central bank, the 'conductor of the international orchestra', as John Maynard Keynes put it in the 1930s. The UK was the leading foreign lender; its financial market was generally more liquid than anywhere else; and the Bank of England managed international interest rates, ensuring that gold would flow out of any country with an overvalued currency.

None of this happened with a controlled ease. The story could be told through a series of banking collapses and company failures stretching over decades. Given the sheer scale of reform needed to ensure finance could support infrastructure at home, followed by a credit system that would create and conquer, all at a time of laissez-faire in the Government, large numbers of inconsistencies and anomalies, as well as endless consolidating legislation, are less significant than the fact that, in the end, Britain had created the modern world of finance. Robert Peel's Bank Charter Act (1844) gave the exclusive power to issue new banknotes to the Bank of England. What we would now call 'quantitative easing' – the central bank introducing new money into the money supply – was not allowed because a limit was placed on the number of new notes that could be issued in excess of what was backed by gold reserves. The pace of growth ensured that the Act was not without its critics and that same growth showed it to be too inflexible in a crash, especially in a newly linked world economy. An export boom in the 1850s – fuelled by railway building, fast steam-shipping and fast telegraph communication – was undermined by the sudden collapse of the Ohio State Life and Trust Co. on 24 August 1857. By October, the panic induced had brought down no less than 1,415 American banks.

Who better to explain what had happened than Karl Marx, in his role as European Correspondent of the *New York Daily Tribune*, a 2 cents paper founded by Horace Greeley in 1841 and designed to have blue-collar appeal? Marx related the problem to the need for the Bank of England to beg its aristocratic leaders in the Government to allow the printing of more notes, as they had already had to do ten years before. British manufacturers, he said, were vulnerable to contractions in foreign markets. Too many goods had gone to turbulent places (in which he included both America and India), and so many goods had been exported elsewhere that you could find them cheaper in Adelaide, Sydney and Melbourne than in London, Manchester and Glasgow.[72] He was not wrong, but failed to see that what was happening – a phenomenal period of growth needed empirical, pragmatic responses. In this case, Liverpool and Glasgow felt some economic pain; some more notes were printed, but not in the sort of wild additions to money supply that encouraged asset appreciation, rather than productive investment, in the years since the 2007 banking crisis. Before the end of 1857, stability had returned to the UK and a solid beginning made to bring down the temporarily very high Bank Rate.

Ironically, Marx himself suffered. The *Tribune*'s advertising revenue and circulation went down; one of Greeley's backers went bankrupt. Marx got fewer commissions. Never one to value understatement, he wrote to Engels that he thought he had 'tasted the bitterest dregs of life. *Mais non!*' Disraeli's criticisms in the House of Commons were more cogent: what was the point of an Act regulating the currency if we are perpetually in a state in which it needed to be suspended? Gladstone differed, suggesting separation of the issuing part of the Bank from the lending. Walter Bagehot, who leaves traces all over Victorian life and thought, and at this point is part-editing the magazine he had recently founded, the *National Review*, disagreed with both and proposed discretionary power for the Bank and a larger reserve to be called upon as needed. That was the essence of the matter: Britain was in a position of strength. As Bagehot said, 'there may not be in the world at this moment a single large and adventurous speculation in which there is not some sum of Anglo-Saxon capital.' He might have said – halcyon days – that Britain really was too big to fail.

Other changes to company law and regulation were also imperfect, frequently in need of updating, but generally sensible ways forward. Robert Lowe, who takes on both Gladstone and Disraeli in Chapter 5 at the time of the 1867 Reform Act, provides an interesting symbol of modernization; on the one hand, well able to use Classical references and similar comparisons found in high culture, he was also in some ways a forerunner of the technocrat, a keen believer both in scientific education and in excellence. As Vice-President of the Board of Trade, he presided over a hugely significant consolidation of change in his Joint Stock Companies Act in 1856, following on from the Limited Liability Act of the previous year. Here was the legislative invention of the suffix 'Ltd' applied to a company, one of a number of reforms that, as Lowe said in private, were 'too hard or too dangerous for aristocratic hands'.

There were certainly those who took the view that limited liability – investors putting at risk only what had been invested, not the total debt of the company in which they invested – would encourage fraud. Lowe's view was that it would promote growth through democratising capitalism and encouraging an aspiring meritocracy. Bagehot was in favour on the original grounds that it would actually encourage speculation. Bankers weren't meant to be cautious property owners.[73] Remarkably, at this time we are only a generation from a widespread view that bankruptcy was divine punishment. We have wrestled with the dilemma ever since: do we legislate to encourage enterprise, or do we protect society from greed? A curious commentary was to come as the 19th century entered its last decade in one of Gilbert and Sullivan's least-known operas, *Utopia, Limited, or, The Flowers of Progress* (1893), which made a mockery of what had happened in finance and limited liability in the Age of Progress.

'Black Friday' – possibly the earliest use of the phrase, in *The Times* – referred to 3pm, 10 May 1866, when Overend Gurney suspended payments;[74] it seemed salutary, though ultimately misleadingly so. Robert Cecil, Viscount Cranborne, Disraeli's second great adversary in 1867, though unlike the Liberal Robert Lowe from his own Conservative Party, wrote sheepishly to his father a week after the crash that he stood to lose £18,000 or more. He was one of many. But had the problem arisen as a result of reckless instability created by limited liability? Not really. As so often in the financial world, now and then, there were human causes, not technical.

Under the sound leadership of Samuel Gurney, the company in the first half of the 19th century flourished as a bill broker – intermediary between lender and merchant – to the extent that by 1850, Overend Gurney was turning over bills equivalent to half the UK's total national debt in that year. The danger was that it had also developed as a lender, as well as an intermediary, thus greatly increasing the risk. That risk could be contained, but after Samuel's death in 1856, the company rapidly got into trouble through the influence on one of the partners of an accountant called Edward Watkin Edwards, the feckless, high-living David Chapman. Edwards encouraged expansion into high-risk loans in a wide variety of businesses. The bill broking continued to be profitable, but there were overall losses averaging half a million pounds a year after 1860. Conversion to limited liability in July 1865, only three years after the legislation was extended to include banks and discount houses, took place when Overend Gurney was technically insolvent.[75]

The investors were not to know this, though already the new power of the press, explored in the next chapter, encouraged corruption. It emerged (albeit long after the event in both cases) that two one-time City Editors of *The Times*, David Morier Evans and Marmaduke Sampson, had taken bribes from the rascally Baron Albert Grant. Another journalist, Malcolm Meason, after the collapse, examined the role of 'bears' in *The Profit of Panics* (1866) and suggested a simpler explanation: not corruption as such, just the spread of misinformation. Besides, *The Bankers' Magazine and Journal of the Money Market* had declared the Overend Gurney conversion 'the greatest triumph which limited liability ever achieved' – this on the basis of a prospectus that contained just five paragraphs.[76] In *Fun* – a competitor to *Punch* – a few weeks after the collapse, the cartoon Old Lady of Threadneedle Street lectures her young friends, 'Let this be a warning to you against rash speculation. What would you have done but for my little savings?' It had not been limited liability that had brought Overend Gurney down, but greed. While the financial systems were being modernized, the effects of collapses tended to be exaggerated and that, in turn, tended to produce reasonable and pragmatic reform or evolution. The Catch-22 for the 21st century has been that, after 150 years of modernization, the sheer scale and the spider's web of links between the constituent parts of the global financial system have created an environment so vulnerable to technology-enabled greed that collapse of a kind that might appropriately be called 'cosmic intensity' is a built-in risk – something very different from the infinite promise of the Victorian Age of Progress. Viscount Goschen, Chancellor of the Exchequer (1887–92), was optimistically incorrect – in the long term – when he suggested that limited liability had a democratic effect: instead of private cabals, there was open scrutiny and a chance to participate.[77]

Today, we behave over-confidently without excuse in financial matters. In Victorian Britain, some people behaved over-confidently with some excuse. A new world was in construction. For example, before the creation of the Greenwich Meridian in 1884, there was no standardized global time. Over a period, every country, every continent, related to this prime meridian – zero degrees longitude – on which the world's time zones are based. There were practical reasons for basing it in Britain: more people in more locations around the world would immediately find it valuable for trading, finance, travel, the conduct of business. It also, as a concept, oozed confidence.

While the reference points for time were stabilized, time itself seemed to have speeded up. Financial markets, in particular, needed capital to move quickly across the world. Britain's national telegraph network was effectively completed when Glasgow joined in 1847. London was linked with Paris in 1851; only the day before – well, earlier in the century – Rothschild's use of secret carrier pigeons to carry messages seemed as fast as it could get in joining the capitals. In 1866, the transatlantic cable reduced the relay of price information to perhaps twenty minutes; it was down to ten by 1914; so, as we have seen, while the cable had many false starts – it covered 2,000 miles at great depths – it had finally been achieved by the Brunel-designed *Great Eastern*, a ship so strong that when it was finally scrapped, several hundred men spent two years in taking it apart. From the 1870s, ticker-tape machines – Thomas Edison's American invention – gave price information simultaneously to anywhere that could receive it. The phone room arrived at the City of London Stock Exchange in 1883. By then, the last UK banking collapse of the 19th century, the City of Glasgow Bank, had happened – another tale of loans with poor security and speculative investments far away in America and Australia, this time without limited liability. Most of the shareholders became bankrupt. The directors received prison sentences, itself an important step forward.

A global economy had become a reality, rooted in using borrowed capital. When Bagehot described what he called 'by far the greatest combination of economical power and economical delicacy that the world had ever seen' in *Lombard Street* (1873), he was clear that it had been the development of the British banking system that had enabled the vast expansion of international trade.[78] If you could get 15 per cent for helping to service Turkish debts, having borrowed at 3 per cent, even if Turkey defaulted (as it did), you would find new opportunities. Disraeli did just that, investing in the Suez Canal in 1875; with an advantageous loan from Lionel de Rothschild,[79] on the security of the Government, he purchased the Khedive's shares for £4 million. Wildly ill-judged, and often patently fraudulent, schemes trapped the unwary across the planet, but the elation induced by wide horizons – and plenty of profit – seemed good reason for believing in progress.

CHAPTER 4

'A NEW WORLD UNDER SCRUTINY'

THE PRESS, THE BOOKS, THE DEBATES

'There she is – the great engine – she never sleeps. She has her ambassadors in every quarter of the world – her couriers upon every road. Her officers march along with armies, and her envoys walk into statesmen's cabinets. They are ubiquitous. Yonder Journal has an agent at this minute giving bribes at Madrid; and another inspecting the price of potatoes at Covent Garden.' Thackeray's *Pendennis*, written at the end of the 1840s, provided a timely title-page quote for Frederick Knight Hunt's *The Fourth Estate* (1850). Hunt started as a night boy in a printer's office and died of typhus in 1854 while successfully editing the *Daily News*. There is a respectable case to be argued that the creation of the modern world of journalism, and of the modern world of books, matched or surpassed economic revolution as an agent of social change in Victorian Britain. By the 1880s, W.T. Stead, at the centre of the 'new journalism' and viewed with great distaste by Matthew Arnold, could even argue that Parliament had been made irrelevant, the servant of the people expressing their will through the press. The resulting creation of celebrity culture and other expressions of media power transformed innumerable patterns of life and continue to do so.

It all happened so very quickly. While *The Times*, the 'Jupiter of the Press', remained dominant for much of the first half of the 19th century, by 1876 an article in the *Daily Review* identified 1,754 newspapers and 746 periodicals, even one in the Lancashire dialect of English.[1] Much happened in printing technology that vastly speeded up both preparing the type and printing speeds. Repeals of newspaper taxes and of those on paper set up the possibility of the mass-market Victorian penny press and encouraged the continuing investment in more efficient printing. News arrived faster because of the telegraph. The railways not only allowed comfortable reading of what Robert Surtees's *Ask Mamma* (1858) called 'the huge avalanche of papers that have broken upon the country within the last twenty years,'[2] but also distribution of the papers themselves, especially after W.H. Smith, the

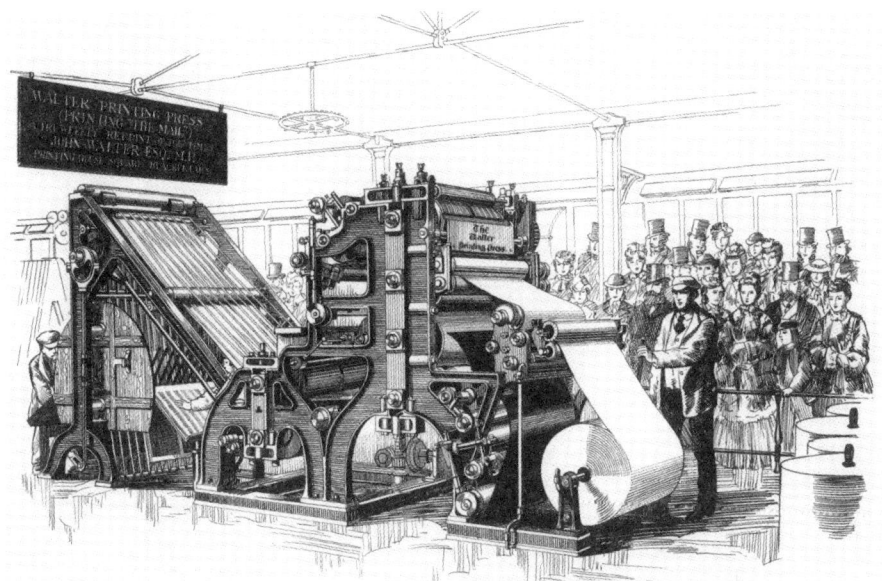

24 When John Walter founded *The Times* in the 18th century, there was no shortage of good writers, but it was the Victorians who transformed the press via revolutionizing production and distribution. 'The John Walter Printing Press', under the proprietorship of the scholarly John Walter III, was a rotary printer turning out 10,500 copies an hour in the 1860s. By the death of Queen Victoria that output had itself increased by at least five times.

MP for Westminster, gave the country what neither the USA or any European country had: newspaper stands and bookstalls on every platform.

In West Africa, where British trading and imperial strategies frequently brought them into conflict with the Ashanti Empire, itself an embodiment of centuries of African imperialism ('Asante' means 'war'), a bizarre byway resulted in 1874. Heading inland in order to reach the Ashanti capital of Kumasi, the British made their way through thick, dark, jungle forest, a perfect incubator for malaria and only punctuated by occasional villages protected symbolically by human sacrifices on the pathway. On arrival, they found scattered in the King's abandoned palace numerous copies of...the *Illustrated London News*.[3] While the resulting treaty, which called for an end to human sacrifice and aggression towards neighbouring tribes, but was otherwise highly punitive, has been a major concern for historians for other reasons (namely looted gold treasures), the speed with which the magazine had achieved such wide distribution, domestically and globally, showed that the power of the press would be a key element in making the future.

Herbert Ingram, a Nottinghamshire newsagent who founded the *Illustrated London News* in 1842 and was greeted with heavy scepticism, eventually experienced astonishing success. The King of Siam subscribed. Polar explorers looking for Sir John Franklin found copies in Eskimo huts. 'Special artists' were present to record Garibaldi's conquests, the American Civil War and the Franco-Prussian War, but also the opening of the Suez Canal or the Emperor of China's marriage. As the Prussians closed in on Paris, artist sketches and photographic prints were sent off by balloon. A modern world of illustrated press had begun.

The technology and distribution networks were the enablers. But why the big new audience? The short answer is population increase, urbanization, literacy and prosperity. For the first time, workers could be targeted; as early as 1832, the Chambers brothers launched the *Edinburgh Journal* 'to present knowledge under its most cheering and captivating aspect': literature, history, science. Looking back in 1877, William Chambers suggested that a cheap (but respectable) periodical acted as an engine of 'social improvement'.[4] The Government itself pointed out that 'the calm forbearance' of Manchester cotton workers suffering as a result of the cotton famine in the American Civil War was connected to 'the excellent information' they had received. It would be wrong to see this as middle-class smugness (the press was mostly middle-class-owned, and the middle class provided the education), though some worried that knowledge was taking on the character of the factory: mass-manufactured blandness. That was hardly the point when John Cassell gave prizes, sometimes as much as £5, for essays by working-class men – and women – on 'Sanitary Reform'.[5] Even the 'penny dreadfuls', such as *The Boy Detective*, played a positive role in a young population; their texts, when presented as serials over a period, could contain tens and sometimes hundred of thousands of words. Anyone would acquire a reading habit from that.

In the last few decades of the century, the huge growth in numbers of office workers, clerks and other semi-skilled tradespeople created an enthusiasm for knowledge – and entertainment. The *Newcastle Daily Chronicle* noted in March 1882 that there was now a journal for everything: *The Hairdressers' Chronicle*, or the *Journal of Gas Lighting*, or *The Athlete*, *The Cyclist* and *The Matrimonial News*. These were also a reminder that the provincial press played an ever-bigger role in people's lives. London papers arrived safely and speedily by rail; lack of copyright restrictions allowed international news to be found where people wanted it – in their local press. Reductions in price helped immeasurably: the *Manchester Guardian*, founded in 1819, was typical of many in becoming a penny daily in 1855. At the beginning of the 18th century, you would have found just one provincial paper; by 1854, there were 289. Lives were changed as a result. The businessman Joseph Cowen, who would eventually follow in his father's footsteps to become MP for Newcastle, with his Tyneside accent (and, as some thought unfairly, uncouth manners) not only transformed the *Newcastle Daily Chronicle* and formed friendships with radicals across Europe (Garibaldi and Kossuth visited him in his birthplace, Blaydon-on-Tyne), but provided books, an educational fund and sporting facilities for miners and other workers, as well as engaging otherwise in town improvements and social reform. Progress created a palpable sense of excitement – and the press spread the word. *The Budget*, very little known in London but 'a household word' in Lancashire, provided Saturday night and Sunday reading for the working class. Sometimes, too, the northern press was more reflective than London's 'first with the news' mentality.

A sure sign of audience demand were the evening newspapers that also proliferated – *The Express* (the evening edition of the *Daily News*) and the *Evening Chronicle*, for example.[6] Both were in London and – in the end – London was dominant in all things. Its journalistic tradition stretched back centuries; you might have met Caxton's assistant, Wynkyn de Worde, 'Father of Fleet Street', Walter Raleigh, or Dryden, or Dr Johnson or Thackeray in Fleet Street over the centuries; even in the 1880s, the Cock Tavern had not changed much since Pepys ate a lobster there with Mrs Pierce and Mrs Knipp (though it was soon to disappear and become the new offices of the *Daily Telegraph*).[7]

London was not just the seat of the Government, but a place of world papers that brought news of the latest intrigues in Constantinople, or what the Emperor of China felt about San Francisco Chinese emigrants, or the price of bacon in Chicago.[8] Increasingly, it wasn't second-hand news either. Papers needed representatives in Paris, with an additional one for the Chamber, paid correspondents in Montreal and Jamaica and China and New York and Bombay, agents across Europe in Berlin or Lisbon or Naples. Special correspondents were needed to report on Kossuth fleeing across the Turkish border, or Sooloo pirates (in the troubled Sulu Sea, where James Brooke, the White Rajah of Sarawak, battled them in the 1840s), or what was happening in California.[9]

J.T. Delane, Editor of *The Times* for 39 years from 1841, was a good symbol of how far journalism had progressed from Grub Street. A neat and compact figure, though perhaps more with the air of a country gentleman than of the modern world, he had a great deal of power and influence. 'I think', said Disraeli to the Liberal statesman, Lord Granville, 'I had better postpone giving you my view of Delane until he is dead.'[10] Delane wasn't quick in adapting either to the professionalization of politics from the 1860s, or to making use of technology, but *The Times* was able to hold a price of 3d against its penny rivals in that decade. The *Daily Telegraph*, founded in 1855, halved its price to 1d when tax was abolished. It had a difficult start, but flourished following the principles of Leigh Hunt as Editor – keep the intelligent public informed about science, fashion, changes in business, all the things that were revealing of daily life, but also signposts for the future. The proprietor, Moses Levy, launched the slogan, 'the largest, best, and cheapest newspaper in the world'. Marx, himself Jewish, made an unquotable antisemitic attack on Levy, as Marx tended to do with anyone Jewish who criticized him, but under the ambitious guidance of Levy's son, Edward Levy Lawson, the newspaper took on the world. When the journalist Edwin Arnold asked about his budget, Lawson told him that it was anything he liked. Arnold went off to discover 'the beginnings of the Bible', resulting in some remarkable material.[11]

Less dramatic, and with limited circulations but wide readerships, were the weeklies, monthlies and quarterlies that expressed and shaped opinion both for the powerful and those who were learning about their world, some themselves on the road to power. The *Edinburgh Review* (1802–1929) was strongly Whig, the *Quarterly Review* (1809–67) Tory. At first, the monthlies, such as *Blackwood's* and *Fraser's*, were too expensive, but in 1859 *Macmillan's* (1859–1921) became the first shilling monthly and, with such weeklies as *The Athenaeum* for books (1828–1907) and the *Saturday Review* (1855–1938), as well as all the newspapers, a parade of ideas and information reached many minds simultaneously. The press, as Frederick Knight Hunt observed in 1850, had become 'a positive necessity of civilized existence – a portion, indeed, of modern civilization'.[12] That was a new experience, and one that jaded palettes today – awash with disinformation, social media detritus and AI hallucinations – are denied. One of the challenges of understanding the Victorians today is an unwillingness to engage with the values defined by *The Economist* in its review of Thomas Escott's *England: Its People* (1879): Escott was Editor of the *Fortnightly Review* in the 1880s and is described as 'conservative, without being reactionary, liberal yet not subversive'. That formula was often the key to Victorian progress, in his case manifested in his help in writing Joseph Chamberlain's Radical Programme in the 1880s (an attempt to modernize the Liberal Party to meet the challenges of a new world), but also in having intense discussions with Matthew Arnold about working-class education, engaging with the ungovernable passions of the young Lord Randolph Churchill, or impressing Robert Browning with his ideas about poetry.[13] As Taine said, the press could be frank to the point of rudeness; it used cold and prolonged irony; it contained concentrated and reflective passion – but no one in England, unlike France, was going to fight 'about a sheet of inked paper'.[14]

One of the reasons this was important related to the symbiotic relationship between press and politics. For one thing, there were journalist MPs. The Liberal MP John Walter III (1818–94) was the son of an Editor of *The Times* and became its manager. Henry Labouchere, MP variously for Middlesex and for Northampton (1831–1912), became famous for his dispatches from the siege of Paris for the *Daily News* in the Franco-Prussian War. A Liberal who became Radical, he founded *Truth*, which exposed frauds of all kinds in a new form of investigative journalism. When Labouchere wrote City articles for *The World*, he got wind that *The Times* was dismissing its City Editor, Mr Sampson, for fraud and outed him in the journal. Journalists – like politicians – were competitive and drawn to scandal. It had only been just before the Victorian era began that the *OED* finds the first reference to 'journalism' in the *Westminster Review*.[15] The press had come a long way fast.

Of course, this brought its own dangers. Disraeli criticised the influence of 'the gilded salons' of Ministers' wives on editors; Palmerston went out of his way to praise Mr Delane (a frequenter of his wife's parties) for his high honour. But Disraeli himself had been 'Runnymede' of *The Times*. Sir Algernon Borthwick, long-time Editor of the *Morning Post* and son of the MP for Evesham, was close to both Disraeli and Palmerston. When the ex-Empress of France, Napoleon III's widow, first heard of her son's death in 1879 in the Zulu War, the news of this 'saddest intelligence' was conveyed by Disraeli's specially selected envoy, Borthwick.[16] Already in 1857, the German observer Theodor Fontane noted that the press support for party was imperilling objectivity: 'Arrogance increases'.[17]

In fact, Napoleon III had directly tried to influence the British press. In 1854, he made a financial arrangement with the then owner of the *Morning Chronicle*, Sergeant Glover, to be his advocate. This turned out to be not so much the power of the press, but a failure of the power of the press: circulation plummeted, for – after all – France was Britain's traditional enemy. Glover sued in the French courts for non-fulfilment, but this did not stop Napoleon from using an American called De Lille, from Charleston, to try to buy the paper when Glover was forced to sell in 1859.[18] It did sell, but this distinguished journal, first to give Dickens regular work and publisher of Henry Mayhew's articles on the London poor, died in 1865.

Nothing better symbolized what was beginning here – the modern debate about media integrity and politics – than the reporting of House of

Commons debates. No notes were allowed before 1783 in the Commons. Dr Johnson wrote Commons speeches from scanty details supplied to him in his garret in Exeter Street, often improving them; his publisher, Edward Cave, told him he had 'exceeded Demosthenes himself'. But again, everything developed very fast in the 19th century; Dickens and Coleridge were early parliamentary reporters at the time Macaulay made his famous assertion in the *Edinburgh Review* that 'the gallery in which the reporters sit has become a fourth estate of the realm'. Still, when we speak of progress or integrity or power, we need also to be reminded of how humans actually conduct their affairs. Angus Roach, one of the reporters, described the scene in about 1850. The little door opened, and they stood in the Reporter's Gallery, 'the back of the Speaker's ugly gothic [chair] below us'. The MPs, hats on, were variously sitting, standing, walking, lolling. The clerk sat with the shiningly bound volumes of the statutes around him. After its rebuild, the House replaced candles with the bright oil lamps – later gas – named after its inventor's home town, Bude in Cornwall, and recommended by Faraday for lighthouses. The luminous remarks of the Hon. Member for Fortywinks had distractions from more than a hundred private conversations. *The Times* sharpened his pencils; the *Morning Post* drew caricatures; the *Morning Advertiser* mused on what was for supper. The general view was that literally reported debates 'would infallibly disgust the nation with representative government'. All arguments, good, bad, indifferent, were recorded; facts, too, certain or dubious.

If you read Hansard in Victorian Britain, you will know that this was satirical. Many debates were astonishingly well informed and impressively conducted. The most important thing was the new social acknowledgment of the importance of the press in a country embodying Progress. Frederick Knight Hunt, in his *The Fourth Estate*, concluded: in Russia, newspapers are comparatively unknown 'and we see the people sold with the earth they are compelled to till'. There were no serfs in Britain: 'in proportion to the freedom of the press is the freedom and prosperity of the people'.[19]

Charles Dickens provides a link between journalism and perhaps the most powerful force for shaping society ever invented: the book. Not everyone approved of Mr Popular Sentiment, the name he was given in Trollope's clever Dickensian satire (in his first literary success, *The Warden*, in 1855). 'It is incredible the number of evil practices he has put down'; 'his good poor people are so very good; his hard rich people so very hard'; 'when he has made the working classes comfortable, and got bitter beer into proper-sized pint bottles', will there be anything further for him to do? One thing is clear:

Mr Sentiment is 'a very powerful man.'[20] Bagehot summed up what Dickens wrote as 'sentimental radicalism'.[21]

There are different opinions about when the word 'celebrity' took on its full, modern meaning. Its use as 'well-known or famous person' is dated to 1831 in the *OED*, a timely signal as the world began to enter the age of fast mass communication. Apparently, the British continued to be relatively unskilled celebrating fame in the old way – by public sculpture. When Theodor Fontane caught the omnibus from Charing Cross to the Bank, he found the new statue of Robert Peel at the entrance to Cheapside 'ridiculous'. 'He stands there as though he was wearing rubber pants instead of trousers.'[22] When the US diplomat Benjamin Moran went to hear Dickens read *A Christmas Carol* in St Martin's Hall, Longacre, the ungrand entrance was long, crooked, narrow and 'in every way irregular'. After struggling to get in, he recorded Dickens reading 'tolerably and that is all'.[23] Dickens himself took the view that his many readings in the country did open up a new public. Where did his advocacy of social reform put him in relation to believing in Progress? Ruskin's skill with words probably lays as many traps as Dickens's own, not least when he described Dickens on his death as 'a pure modernist – a leader of the steam whistle party par excellence'.[24] There seems no reason to doubt the genuineness of Dickens's wish to right wrongs and, as a fiction writer, it is his brilliant word-pictures that most people continue to use to define Victorian England through to, or even more so in, the present day. We should argue that in some sense they are caricatures, but cannot match his literary skills.

As the austere James Fitzjames Stephen, Virginia Wolf's uncle, suggested, Dickens – but also Elizabeth Gaskell or Charles Kingsley – mass-produced 'stern and somewhat terrible working men who are always embodying profound observations in studiously bad grammar.'[25] It is true that the *Daily News*, founded in 1846 with Dickens as its first Editor, claimed in its first editorial to advance the 'Principles of Progress and Improvement, of Education, Civil and Religious Liberty, and Equal Legislation', but the brief tenure of Dickens was chaotic and evidently profligate, with a Railway Editor on a dumbfounding £2,000 a year (perhaps Ruskin was right about 'the steam whistle party', after all). Of the two essentials of modern democratic parties – shaping opinion and understanding how to construct and manage effective reform – Dickens was master of the first only.

There were countless influential books before the Victorian era, but – viewed from G.K. Chesterton's perspective – even Jane Austen 'belongs to a vanished world before the great progressive world'.[26] The largely self-educated Sir Edward Clarke, Oscar Wilde's barrister in 1895, left a record of books prominent as he was growing up in the 1850s. They included *The Tale of Two Cities*, Spencer's *Psychology*, Darwin's *Origin of Species*, several volumes of Macaulay's *History of England*, George Eliot's *Adam Bede*, Tennyson's *Idylls of the King*, and many more.[27] It would be easy to add to the list: Mill's *On Liberty*, Ruskin's *Stones of Venice*, the first published poems of Matthew Arnold. It was a good time to learn to read – such great books, ever-cheaper prices and also access to Mudie's Select Library, run on a subscriber basis, with nearly 400,000 volumes since 1858, with history, biography, travel, adventure, fiction, science and religion all being popular. When Charles Mudie was seven, he could just reach 'S' in his father's bookshop; Charles Lamb found him sitting on the floor behind the counter reading Shakespeare. Later, inspired to start a circulating library, with books on loan for a small fee, after finding students at the new London University were too poor to buy but desperate to read in a way lost by some of today's students, he built a substantial business. Yet it was not just the middle class that enthused about reading, and Mudie's selections were beyond the reach of those further down the social scale.[28]

It was technological progress that helped to democratise books. New cheap reprints of both fiction and non-fiction, sometimes in 'board' bindings (precursor to the paperback), proliferated on railway bookstalls. Printing had changed little since Gutenberg until steam-driven printing machines began to be used for newspapers and, in the 1840s, for books. Through the century, innovation continued, with rotary printing, hot-metal typesetting and, eventually, lithography and the substitution of electricity for steam.

The pure passion with which so many working-class people took to books in Victorian times is one of history's great stories. Robert Collyer (born 1823), a child labourer in a linen factory in Fewston, Yorkshire, never looked back after buying his first book, a history of Dick Whittington and his cat; his library grew to 3,000 volumes; he read, he said, 'for dear life'. Edwin Waugh (born 1817) lived in a cellar after his father died when he was eight, but finished up as 'the Lancashire Burns', better known in some parts of the country than Dickens. It took him until 39 to get payment for his poetry – one can imagine the excitement when the *Manchester Examiner* paid a guinea for the copyright in 'Come Whoam to thi' Childer an' Me'. Joseph Ashby (born 1859), also fatherless from a young age, and a farm labourer from the age of eleven, became enthused by Mill's *On Liberty* and studied Tom Paine's ideas for a progressive income tax. The great joy of such stories is that the appeal and the value of books overcame the sluggish pace of educational reform. And while we are used to people being captivated by literature, or by politics, the workers turned to both. You could find Charlotte Brontë or Fenimore

Cooper in the Chartist paper, the *Northern Star*. The 30-year-old John Stuart Mill's essay on *The State of Society in America* neatly – and far-sightedly – argued that the route to democracy was the combination of universal reading and high wages.[29]

Not everyone made the same automatic conclusion, and many middle-class moralizers were propagandists in their own cause. Charles Kingsley criticised Dickens for 'a false ethical theorem': that faults were a product of circumstances, not failed responsibility. Tom, the chimney sweep in Kingsley's *The Water Babies* (1864), is appallingly treated by Mr Grimes and denied any moral compass, but – in an evolutionary fable – eventually becomes a 'a great man of science'. In the end, Kingsley – full of moral tests – was nevertheless more successful than Dickens in achieving practical results; the 1864 Act regulating chimney sweeps was certainly influenced by his book. It also helped that what Leslie Stephen, in his book on George Eliot, called 'the elaborate panorama of the manners and customs' and 'the minuteness and psychological analysis' included in the novels of Eliot and other writers, provided an accessible guide for anyone socially aspirant (though social climbing was also satirized). As the century progressed, there were even novels that served as introductions to consumerism, a point noted disapprovingly by *The Athenaeum* in 1887 in connection with Rider Haggard's *She*: an epic tale that also read like an advertisement for the Army and Navy Stores.[30]

When criticised by a subscriber to the same magazine in 1860, Charles Mudie said, yes, he had excluded books on moral grounds from his collection. Benjamin Jowett made clear his disapproval of the gushing romance of Rhoda Broughton's *Red as a Rose is She* (1870) when she asked him what he thought. Women's struggles, let alone their desires, were not for public consumption. But he had read it – and so did Gladstone.[31] Books made a modern world; they didn't and couldn't destroy inconsistency and confusion (Broughton was herself the daughter of a clergyman). They taught people of all classes more than they had ever known about human nature and a particular society. And even an undistinguished novel like Frederick Chichester's *Masters and Workmen* (1851) was correct to point to workers' subscriptions, readings of and circulation among themselves of serious penny pamphlets on philosophy and religion. Moreover, the vast amounts of knowledge made available by the proliferation of Government Blue Books of Statistics and reports prepared by Royal Commissions and Parliament were read by novelists, as well as working class and middle class alike. Disraeli's often quoted *Sybil, or The Two Nations* (1845), about rich and poor, was influenced by talking to Edwin Chadwick, famous for his *Sanitary Conditions of the Labouring Population* (1842).

Was there a simple correlation between prosperity and social well-being? Charles Bray's *Philosophy of Necessity* (1841) suggested a statistical connection between marriage, corn prices and workers' pay. Victorians taught us the value of data, but now we have big data: a collaboration between the Alan Turing Institute and several universities analysed many millions of books and articles since 1820, with the results revealing almost two centuries later that Britons were happiest in the 1880s, the period around Queen Victoria's Golden Jubilee, despite being much richer now. This produced an outcry from many people, whose frequent response was to say, 'read Dickens and you will know this is a lie'. A more balanced view might be that a 'sentiment analysis algorithm' is likely to offer at best a partial truth, with inherent distortions, but it is unquestionably more fruitful than the social media assumption that Charles Dickens was an unbiased social commentator in his novels.[32] The Victorian 'evidence' from innumerable newspapers, memoirs, letters, books of all kinds, official publications and other documents points in many directions, but it seems clear that a very large number of people, spread across the classes, felt a sense of progress by comparing everything that had happened to them with their own past and everyone's past; and they expressed that sense with delight and pride during the Victorian period.

Libraries have lost their lustre in the 21st century. The Victorian experience was completely different. George Birkbeck established early Mechanics' Institutes in Edinburgh, Liverpool, Glasgow and London in the early 1820s. 'Mechanics' did not have a narrow meaning; education for the working class was the essence of the idea (the London one eventually became Birkbeck College in the University of London). Although there were more than 700 of the institutes in the United Kingdom by 1850, only three libraries – in Warrington, Salford and Canterbury – were supported by public tax revenues at that time. Against conservative opposition (why should the upper and middle classes pay for something of main benefit to the working class?), the estimable social reformer William Ewart carried the Public Libraries Act of 1850, allowing for rates to be levied. It was in some ways weak and flawed legislation, like so much Victorian social legislation, but equally began a sea change. Not long after, Dickens, so brilliant as a communicator, made an inspiring speech at the opening of the Manchester Public Library in 1852, making the case for the mutual interdependence of capital and labour. His 'earnest hope' was for freely available books to be 'a source of pleasure and improvement in the cottages, the garrets, and the cellars of the poorest of our people'.

Dickens was using hyperbole, but by 1900 – despite the evident failure of the Government to give sufficient impetus to local authorities to support public libraries through the rates, and with help on a phenomenal scale from such philanthropists as Andrew Carnegie and John Passmore Edwards – libraries had begun to be associated with civic pride. When Thomas Escott visited a Chelsea library in the 1890s, books asked for three times that day included Mill's *Logic*, Smith's *Wealth of Nations*, Spencer's *First Principles*, Todhunter's *Euclid*, Spinoza's *Ethics*: not a sufficient sample to provide evidence, but a good sign that the population had not been corrupted (as opponents of democratising reading had argued) by just reading popular novelists. All but the most reactionary were beginning to discover that books were versatile enough to encompass entertainment and education. And for writers themselves, the premises were acquired in 1840 for what became the London Library, which would lend books but was also become a place where Thackeray could discover the exact hues of Washington's waistcoat by 373 consultations with the then librarian, Robert Harrison.[33]

The press and the book created a (mostly) different kind of celebrity than we know today, one often connected to exciting discoveries and new knowledge being passionately communicated by their celebrity pioneers

25 Scientists learned from each other. From left to right (in 1876): Michael Faraday, T.H. Huxley, Charles Wheatstone, David Brewster, John Tyndall. Brewster, dubbed 'father of modern experimental optics' in the 1859 edition of William Whewell's famous *History of the Inductive Sciences*, like many of his generation's scientists, was also a learned theologian. Of course, there were rivalries, too: some said Wheatstone became involved in disputes because he purloined others' ideas.

themselves. All this was consolidated in the rapid development of museums. The museums visit was itself a new experience; and anyone who suggests that children groaned at the prospect of a visit should be challenged to find evidence. Legislation – again inadequate, but a beginning – authorized rates to be used for maintaining museums. They became an effective method, in addition to their original role as places for study, for spreading ideas (such as evolution), and for giving self-help an aid via organized education, with visible artifacts and clear descriptions to help the imagination. In particular, Natural History, once part of the British Museum, was given a new home in 1881, shortly followed by the Science Museum in 1885. The phenomenon was by no means confined to London, with civic pride creating a wide range of institutions whose physical solidity was not so much intimidating, but a reliable welcome to a new world in which inspiring knowledge, like the new electric current, came into the lives of more people than previous generations could ever have dreamed.

One way and another, the press, books and museums informed about everything, but perhaps above all they were revealing of a gigantic turmoil in the human mind: how would religion fare in an age of rapid scientific and technological discovery? Today, technological progress is commonplace. It excites many, but it is also the kind of consumer excitement that the commonplace engenders. New versions of the iPhone are almost as common as the daily cycle of dawn to dusk. Who needs understanding? For Victorians, there was a different kind of delight: the understanding of the science was felt to be enthralling to the extent that it also felt magical. Today, scientists tend not to shout with joy and dance round the room, as Humphry Davy did. In 1851, the barrister William Johnston described the new theatres – the lecture rooms of scientific institutes, 'where gay bonnets are ranged opposite galvanic batteries, and the natural electric light of ladies' eyes is brought into rivalship with the artificial light of electro-magnetism'. Johnson himself was unpersuaded, but not so those who were fascinated by the ways science impinged on their daily lives and who thronged to Faraday's lectures at the Royal Institution in May–June 1850, in which this great scientist (who was also a celebrity) focused on all the knowledge we have about 'a fire, a candle, a lamp, a chimney, a kettle, ashes'. Here was a window in which science could provide the comfort of understanding to replace the comfort of religious belief (under challenge from the same science). The as-yet-unleashed genie – a meaningless universe of incomprehensibly small particles, accompanied by destructive technology, destructive to body and increasingly mind – lay largely in waiting for the next century. But for now, who could fail to be

26 Faraday exemplified the characteristics of the modern celebrity scientist. He had studied the art of convincing communication, and his lectures were theatrical in style. Here, at the Royal Institution in February 1856, he throws an object in the air as Prince Albert (*left*) looks on.

excited by seeing life-size reproductions of the Megalosaurus at the Great Exhibition in Sydenham? Wonder and education have never been such close allies as they were to the Victorians; the Progress they encouraged inspired confidence in the railways, the telegraph, the printing presses, not to mention the prosperity that were the accompaniment.[34]

Key scientific discoveries often came from unlikely sources. William Whewell (1794–1866) – an Anglican priest and theologian; a mathematician; a translator of Goethe and Plato among others; expert on German Gothic churches; polymath; later Master of Trinity College, Cambridge (1841–66) – published a three-volume *History of the Inductive Sciences* in 1837. This not only dealt with history but the chemistry, astronomy and mechanics of 'modern times', acknowledging that – by comparison – writing essays on Greek philosophy produced 'acute' results, but 'fruitless' ones. It was Whewell who encouraged Darwin, back from his voyage on the *Beagle*, to take on the secretaryship of the Geological Society (1838–41). But he continued to oppose university reform, and in finding a definition of 'scientist' (while acknowledging that that might encompass 'Physicist', or 'Mathematician', or 'Naturalist'), had no desire to embrace the fragmentation that comes naturally to us from specialization.[35] Many Victorians wanted to change the world – and did – by understanding it, but most did not want to destroy the structural underpinnings of society and culture.

Many able (though not of the same brilliance) Victorians just wanted to get on with their chosen profession: the medical student Shephard Taylor, made to go to Professor Miller's electricity lectures in 1860 and witnessing the annoyance of the professor when foggy weather sabotaged his planned electric flash, declared that he had quite enough of electricity at the end of the class.[36] By contrast, Charles Lyell, famous for exploring the natural causes explaining the natural evolution of the earth in his *Principles of Geology* (1830–33), was fulsome in his praise of Poulett Scrope, Professor of Geology at Oxford in the 1820s, for his 'most active intellectual mind' – Scrope was also a political economist of great note.[37] Whewell's position on such matters involved having many specialisms, but being expert in all, while recognizing the temptation to push chemistry, geology, physiology 'and the like' into a system in which the principles of each were violated 'at every step' by superficial acquaintance.[38] We are at a moment in the creation of a modern world that posed an unanswerable question. On the one hand, when another polymath – statesman and man of letters George Cornewall Lewis – mused on 'authority' in an 1849 essay and wisely observed that no 'body of persons' could competently judge all subjects, or guide all opinions, he was just showing common sense. On the other, so great was the ferment of discovery in Victorian times that it was only out of an avalanche of conflicting opinions that positive change could be, and was, made. The new methodologies of science could result in pseudoscience, from phrenology to mesmerism, but in the end, Victorians found a practical way forward – if only just. In 1862, Bagehot pointed out that scientists 'differ on every practical question'; on a complex point of engineering, a dozen engineers would give evidence on oath with perfect sincerity, while twelve more would give 'opposing testimony'. That was why 'a blind following of science' didn't work.[39] He was particularly focused on controlling costs and expenditure, and he was right. Today, a much, much bigger version of the same challenge demands better scrutiny of technological advice.

Whether or not scientists disagreed (and they did), one way or another, in the press, by education, or by the formation or development of professional societies, the Victorian embrace of all kinds of communication influenced everyone, both elites and wider society. Towards the end of the century, Thomas Escott noted that, while there were plenty of Classicists in

27 John Tyndall was one of the greatest of the Victorian educators, conveying an understanding of the enormous strides being taken by experimental physics both to general public audiences in his lectures and through such books as his trilogy *Heat* (1863), *Sound* (1867) and *Light* (1873), widely translated in Continental Europe. His genius was to combine all this with multiple discoveries of his own.

Parliament, when looking for the clinching metaphor or epigram, MPs went for their tropes and ideas not to the library, but to the laboratory.[40] In 1865, George Eliot advised Miss Sara Hennell – with her sisters generally believed to have been the Meyrick family in *Daniel Deronda* – to send for the last *Fortnightly* to read Professor Tyndall 'On the Constitution of the Universe': 'It is a splendid piece of writing on the higher physics, which I know will interest you.' Since many Victorians were preoccupied with seriousness and moral worth, there were counter-voices. A *Saturday Review* article in 1875 expressed concern that fashion dictated science, so that it just became a vehicle for gossip about the latest ideas of Huxley or Tyndall. Money-making activities – another Victorian skill – were also apparent: an advertisement in *The Athenaeum* in 1852, accompanied by others for furthering education, invited a visit to 149 Strand, London to become informed about 'GEOLOGY' through purchasing collections at 2, 5, 10, 20, or 50 guineas each. Practitioners themselves, such as David Ansted, 'rendered science to commerce in every part of the world', according to *The Times*. One moment in Algeria, the next advising on the California gold-rush, he gave his name to Ansted, Virginia, because of his work finding rich seams of coal.[41]

Not all the scientists were great popularisers. Sir Humphry Davy, despite being fathered by an often-unemployed woodcarver in Penzance and being mentor to Faraday, himself son of a blacksmith, became much more comfortable as first chairman of the Athenaeum or president of the Royal Society. He was enormously influential in demonstrating through his own work how empirical science could and would transform the world, but other scientists, such as Faraday and Huxley, used press, lectures and education to reach beyond the expert. In 1862, Huxley began a series of lectures to working men on natural phenomena. He was paid nothing (which, it is true, annoyed him when they were subsequently published in low-priced weekly parts), but Darwin congratulated him on spreading 'a taste for the Natural Sciences'. Huxley was in fact always concerned about what came in the 20th century to be called *haute vulgarisation*, but he pushed hard for the *Saturday Review* to publish regular articles by specialists – Tyndall on physics, for example – on every aspect of science. In his mind, science communication was connected to education, certainly, but also the reform of society as a whole and – as we shall see – the demolition of the authority of Anglicans and other elites. Victorians tended to be preoccupied by the idea that knowledge should not be a trivial matter – one of the reasons why they were so successful. Even in 1852, *The Athenaeum* was warning about over-popularization, false knowledge, bad science, looseness of thinking, carelessness. 'The railway system of speed has extended itself to the mind.'[42]

Faraday was partly so successful as a celebrity scientist because as a young man he and some friends supplemented their chemical experiments with 'the mutual improvement plan', which involved studying English grammar and syntax, as well as having lessons on 'oratory'. Formal education was slow to improve. *The Athenaeum* noted in 1855 the importance of giving science a properly acknowledged place in education. In the elementary schools, it was often seen as detrimental to religion; in the colleges, 'the cudgels are taken up on behalf of Classical attainments'. A modern press, a modern book publishing industry gradually helped against prejudice and state inaction: Routledge's natural history handbooks (from 1857), Macmillan's Science Primers (from 1872) and Chambers's Science Manuals (from 1875) were some antidote to Matthew Arnold's assertion that 'The sciences have been abominably taught, and by untrained people.' But something far-reaching was in train: in his letter in 1866 to Mrs Forster about her daughter Florence's education, Arnold suggested that Latin grammar was a much less fruitful stimulus of 'powers of observation and comparison than the verification of the laws of science like botany'.[43] As in all areas of life, women continued to battle against powerful odds (Huxley did his best to keep them out of professional societies), but at least sometimes showed how they could take care of themselves. Mary Ward, who had eleven pregnancies in fifteen years after marriage in 1854, embarked on the first of her many books with *A World of Wonders Revealed by the Microscope* (1858).

In a unique moment in world history, the arts, science and religious belief often came joyously together before falling deeply apart. Constable expressed his enthusiasm for geology in 1835; Arnold dined at the Geological Society at Huxley's invitation in 1868 and found Tyndall 'very pleasant'; Tyndall himself found that reading Tennyson inspired him to invigorate his scientific researches; and Tennyson's reading crossed numbers of scientific fields of study.[44] It remained true that, in the fever of scientific transformation of economic life and ways of living, along with the public and private discussions of it, perhaps the most momentous challenge to nearly 2,000 years of history focused on the challenge to religion. To understand it, we need to enter into the minds of a population for whom 'history' simply meant the story of Classical civilization, the progress to Christian civilization and the taking of European Christian civilization to the barbarians elsewhere.

At the simplest level – defined by Herbert Spencer in an article on 'Religion: A Retrospect and Prospect' in 1894 – 'the heavens declare the glory of God'. But now biologists had their own sense of wonder at 'a speck of protoplasm under the microscope', geologists theirs as they examined the weathering of the glacier-rounded rock on which they were sitting, or astronomers theirs as they used telescopes to look beyond the sun to 'a multitude of such suns'.[45]

What was the state, and the status, of the church from the mid-19th century? Laurence Oliphant's *Piccadilly* explained to an American that it was essential to grasp that the Church of England 'is founded chiefly upon Acts of Parliament'; 'the clergy are only a paid branch of the Civil Service, exercising police functions of a very lofty and important character'; '"the Articles" are interpreted by the Privy Council' and 'England expects every clergyman to do his duty'.[46] Darwin's furious opponent, Bishop Wilberforce, had a greater enemy than evolution: 'Everything Romish stinks in my nostrils,' he said. The Pope was a foreign potentate expelled for ever 300 years before to enable the country to be a sovereign nation. Gladstone had gone too far when, as a young High Tory, he had argued that propagating religious truth was one of the chief aims of government; his critic at the time, Macaulay, shared the common view of Parliamentary sovereignty, with the Queen as Head of State (with limited powers) and Head of the Church. Gladstone remained a very religious man, but (as he recorded in 1868) his allegiance was 'to God's truth in England's Church', not 'the vile harlotry of the Papacy'. Cardinal Newman, long since a convert to Roman Catholicism, more or less expressed it accurately when he described the Reformation as something in which England 'affected' to take on the spiritualities of the Church of Rome, but 'actually' stepped into the temporalities. Gladstone's own Minister Robert Lowe, when debating the 1870 Education Act as Chancellor of the Exchequer, made it clear that he did not sit in the House to discuss religious questions, nor to inflame sectarian differences, but to try to deal with 'the pressing want of the people of England'; it was 'the undoubted duty of the Government to provide for the education of the people'.[47]

The key questions of 1850 were not 'who rules – Church or State?', but the abandonment of Elizabeth I's vision of a particular English blend of uniformity and conformity, tempered – unless the State was threatened, as it was from the Catholic monarchies – by limited tolerance, and the impact of science and social change on belief itself. Those two issues had a strange context: immediately preceding modern secularism, there was in some sense more religion, or at least more religious institutions. In Dickens's *Hard Times* (1854), there were nearly twenty rival denominations in Coketown. Many of them, including the Church of England, had their own splits, formal and informal. A census of church attendance in England and Wales on a Sunday in March 1851 revealed that just under 61 per cent of the population attended, but somewhat under half of those were Church of England. In England and Wales as a whole, 37 denominations were identified, partly the result of half a century of building new places of worship outside the Established Church. Although Scotland was not included and had its own census, it also had massive fragmentation, accompanied by doctrinal division so extreme that it was very distinct from the English experience (not that that was always well-mannered). Meantime, the Irish also had their own census, and their predominant Roman Catholicism was perhaps less of a problem (except to some Anglican clerics) on matters of faith than English disdain for them as 'very little advanced from barbarism', as Peel once said. Whether their poverty and destitution were their own fault, a result of God's judgment, or long-term exploitation by the English was, and is, widely debated.

The subsequent march of secularization, and its association in the West with modernization, consistently underestimates the continuing significance of belief to Victorians. Equally, both secularization and the growth of nonconformist denominations, with their close association to social and political reform, were played out in public because of the new power of the press, all fuelled in the latter by scientific progress. There were many reasons why the Age of Progress put faith centre-stage. Toleration – allowing not only freedom of worship, but the ability of non-Anglicans to hold political, university or other offices in a country whose national church was identified with the nation – came slowly, but was still a characteristic of the 19th century (at least in retrospect). While Disraeli's Jewish father converted to Church of England, in part because it made life easier, it is surely impossible to imagine that Benjamin would ever have become a political leader among the Russian pogroms or in the Catholic France of the Dreyfus affair. Urbanization and regionalism also played a key role: Trollopeland – Barsetshire in his novels, but in practice much of the land occupied by rural and county towns of southern England and its extension into the middle of the country – was mostly solidly Anglican. Even without the industrial towns, the Rev. John Atkinson could go to a parish in North Yorkshire in 1850 and find his experiences similar to those of a missionary in the far reaches of Charlemagne's Saxon frontier.[48] Nevertheless, for a long time, there were no new Anglican churches or church schools in the populous towns and cities of the Industrial Revolution. Religion, like politics, finds a vacuum a perfect recruiting tool.

The Church of England did reform – but slowly. Charlotte Brontë's *Shirley*, published in 1849 but set in Yorkshire in 1811–12, at a time when there were Luddite disturbances in the textile industry, included the shrill cry: 'Britain would miss her church, if that church fell. God save it! God also reform it!' Through the century, there was progress in the Church being more helpful to parish communities and in becoming a serviceable choice for religious denomination in a society whose belief systems, like its marketplaces, had become more competitive than ever before. Nevertheless, Catherine Spence, brought up in the Church of Scotland and, after much agonizing – a strength of so many earnest Victorians – took Britain's religious debates, as well as the battle for women's education and suffrage, with her when the family emigrated to Australia. She converted to Unitarianism, and in her *The Author's Daughter* (1868) described an Anglican church where 'the rector was neither High Church nor Broad Church nor distressingly Low Church, but it is probable that if he had been either, he would not have been so absolutely useless in the Church as he was, for any kind of view would have been better than his indifference and inactivity'.[49]

The nonconformists themselves benefited from, and to some extent were the makers of, a climate of laissez-faire economics, individualism and deep suspicion of state interference (whether in belief, business or anything else), the sense that self-help could lead both to moral perfectibility and riches. An impetus came from the belief that the Church of England always opposed progress.[50] That was a strong message to mill-owners and their workers alike. Before John Bright, son of a Quaker textile manufacturer, joined Gladstone's Cabinet in 1868 – no nonconformist had ever been a member of the Government – lay a long history which, in Bright's case, began with a meeting in St Chad's churchyard, Rochdale, in 1840 in which his 'tombstone' speech railed against church rates and called for disestablishment. The speech was

28 The greatest orator of them all – John Bright: no gushing, no foaming, powerful, resonant, clear, according to his fellow Liberal Justin McCarthy. When a defeated and depressed Gladstone spoke of retirement after Disraeli won the 1874 election, McCarthy judged Bright and Robert Lowe to be intellectually above all the others as a successor. But in politics, stamina and health count for more: Gladstone was to be Prime Minister three more times; Bright achieved respect, but not power.

reprinted from the *Manchester Times* for distribution, an early sign of the power of the press to campaign.

The press, another powerhouse of the Age of Progress, gradually became freer than it had ever been to criticise establishment narratives. A very hostile review of Thomas Hughes's *Alfred the Great* (1869)[51] – Hughes the author of *Tom Brown's Schooldays* – was unable to accept that just because the great king always carried the Psalms of David in his pocket, his victory over the Danes at Ashdown in 871 was assured. The Psalms certainly didn't save him from his subsequent defeat, expulsion from the throne and fleeing to the marshes. Plainly, the medieval testimony of ecclesiastical writers was increasingly being challenged – in books, in newspapers, magazines – by what a more scientific history was revealing.

First, there had been geology. In 1800, you were born into a society in which many people still believed in a literal Creation moment. The trouble was that the geologists, even when they themselves remained believers, now created uncertainty. As Shirley Brooks's *Sooner or Later* (1868) put it, the Christian narrative had always been presented as literal truth; if scientists could now prove 'a good deal of it' wasn't, 'we lose faith in the rest, you see'. Brooks was one of those journalists and writers who were getting closer to the realities of the world they were helping to change and was one of the team at the *Morning Chronicle* who worked on Henry Mayhew's account of the London poor at the end of the 1840s. For the moment, though geology and the beginnings of modern archaeology made a literal reading of Genesis untenable, religion was not about to die. In some respects, support for biblical events came from research. George Smith, of the British Museum, for example, was able to show in his decipherment of a clay tablet from Ninevah – published as a book in 1876 – that there was evidence in a Chaldean account of Noah's Flood.[52]

Finding out about the planet was one thing, but Darwin and ideas of evolution raised even bigger questions about human beings and divine purpose. When the 22-year-old Charles Darwin joined a surveying expedition in the South Atlantic on HMS *Beagle* in 1831, one that, unintended, was to go on for nearly five years and take him around the world, he was diffidently expecting that it would be an opportunity to improve himself – another idea that gathered pace as Queen Victoria's reign began. His father saw it as an interim stage before his son entered the Church of England. Ironically, it was a priest, John Stevens Henslow, Darwin's mentor at Cambridge, who gave up his own place on the *Beagle* (but he was also a botanist and geologist; multifaceted theologians paved the way for scientific discoveries that would later threaten their faith).

Evolutionary theory was simultaneously developed by a number of people, and Darwin had himself arrived at a fairly complete view fifteen years before the publication of *On the Origin of Species* in November 1859; it proved to be perfect timing, not because of God's design or even particularly because of human design, but at least in part because scientific discovery and increased literacy had created an appetite, met by newspapers, magazines and books, that now had an infrastructure for mass distribution. The anonymously published *Vestiges of the Natural History of Creation* (1844), significantly, was in fact the work of the publisher Robert Chambers wanting to show that social progress was just a continuation of a natural process found in the development of life on earth. Darwin thought its geology bad and its zoology worse, but ideas attached to progress could now be seized upon by larger and larger audiences.[53]

Victorian Britain coped very well with Darwin on the whole, especially since popularization on such a scale had never been known. At the same time, Darwinism had its crude form: men came from monkeys, or were seen as part of the struggle for existence (no benevolent deity in evidence) and survival of the fittest (plainly amoral), with no decisive moment of creation (just random mutations of species over time). If so, that was bound to put a bomb under the moral foundation of the state – its church – going back twelve and a half centuries to St Augustine's arrival in Britain.

It could not be said that this was Darwin's intention. In the 1866 edition of *Origin*, he said there was no good reason why his views should shock anyone's religious feelings. Besides, his views – like any great, or not so great, scientist and thinker – were not always consistent and themselves evolved. In a letter in May 1860 to Asa Gray, perhaps the most important American botanist of the 19th century, whom he had consulted for *Origin*, he was pleased that Gray agreed his views were 'not at all naturally atheistical', but also that the more he thought, the more bewildered he became. Even when, in November 1880, he replied to a man requesting a straight 'yes or no' answer on his belief in Christianity, his reply remained ambiguous: that he was sorry that he did not believe in the Bible as divine revelation and therefore not in Jesus Christ as the son of God. The distinction made between thinkers and doers is often simplistic; Darwin's research changed the world, but he himself was no more interested in political, educational or social matters than in upsetting religious opinions. When Emma, his wife and first cousin, asked the cook if she could find a way of increasing his appetite, she suggested – after observing him in the garden the previous day staring at a leaf for two hours – that having something to do would be a solution.[54]

Darwin, in his way humble and certainly full of humanity, was plainly in thrall to 'this wonderful universe'. He found, as in the last sentence of *Origin*, 'grandeur in this view of life', one that involved chance, death, time, altering forms producing an organic unity of nature. The long-term challenge that created – still unresolved today – was to destabilize reason, order, meaning and perhaps humanism, but in the 19th century, it turned into a fissure between science and religion, what the American John William Draper called the *History of the Conflict between Religion and Science* (1874), though

29 Of very few people could it be said that nothing in the world seemed the same after they died. However much he was misunderstood, misquoted, beaten down by critics, or merely acting as a catalyst in a period of multiple, overlapping discoveries, Darwin was a great man. Who else, a year after this cartoon in *Vanity Fair* in 1871, would have thought of tickling chimpanzees for his comparative *The Expression of Emotions in Man and Animals* (1872)?

Draper's indictment of the way the human intellect was limited by traditional religion was mainly directed against Roman Catholics and not, for example, Islam (which had given early support to science) or Protestantism (which had no papal infallibility).

You need to be bold to make the future in any era. The makers of Progress didn't have it easy. Bringers of radical change were often socially ostracized; conservatives saw their world disappear. It remained Britain's peculiarity – so peculiar that it might seem that only divine intervention made it possible – to experience turmoil and upheaval, given great scrutiny by a newly modern media, while remaining socially stable. It seems probable that more people than acknowledged it became quietly sceptical about faith, while the noisy, articulate believers and unbelievers fought their battles under the magnifying gaze of the press. It seems equally likely that more people than we might suppose quietly retained their faith and enjoyed the social, as well as the spiritual, context it provided. At the same time, a more visible social change, the product of believers, unbelievers and sceptics, took place: the expression of moral values, especially of fairness and of improving the lot of society as a whole, through political means. In the chapters that follow, we will follow the political debates, the reforming skills of the professional modernizers, the intense battle of ideas within the intellectual elites, the perspectives and experiences of the poor, the working classes and women of all classes, and the consequences of Empire.

CHAPTER 5

'NOBODY DARES RESIST IT'

WHO SHOULD GOVERN – AND HOW?

15 August 1867. Today is the occasion of the final reading of the second of the great Reform Bills that extended the franchise. The Houses of Parliament stand resplendent, radiating the feeling that they must have been present here by the Thames for a thousand years, as surely you would expect from 'the mother of Parliaments'.

In fact, these august buildings had been completed just fifteen years before. Time and again, when we imagine how lasting change and reform are made, our reaction to symbols, our own preoccupations and the assumptions of the age in which we live mislead us. The old Houses of Parliament, destroyed by fire in 1834, were truly old. From the time of William the Conqueror until 1826, hazel or willow tally-sticks, notched to show payment to the Exchequer, were split, one part to provide the Treasury record, one a receipt. These 'pillars of the constitution', as Dickens, a parliamentary reporter in his early twenties, described them, were stored in large quantities. What do you do with (Dickens again) 'worm-eaten rotten old bits of wood'?[1] If you are the Clerk of Works, better not to tell anyone, but quietly start burning them in the basement stoves of the House of Lords. The resulting fire could be seen 20 miles or more away in Windsor Castle. Yet, should there be a need to leave the 'new' Parliament today for restoration, we might note that in 1834, William IV's offer of Buckingham Palace as temporary home was declined, and sufficient re-roofing and repairs were made until new buildings could be constructed for MPs and Lords to be back in just four months.

In the third decade of the 21st century, as the Parliament buildings literally crumble, many of us would be surprised to know that the making of them engaged a host of brilliant, modernizing scientists – themselves newly 'invented' because the word did not exist until its coinage, together with 'physicist', by the Cambridge polymath William Whewell not so long before. That was the moment when 'natural philosophers' could begin to think of themselves as 'scientists'. As it happens, Whewell also argued against basing

30 The chambers of both Houses of Parliament were destroyed by the Great Fire of 1834. Westminster Hall remained, helped both by a change of wind direction and the then Chancellor of the Exchequer, Viscount Althorp, who is said to have shouted: 'Damn the House of Commons…Save, O Save the Hall!' 'Honest Jack', known for his integrity, knew well the symbolism of a building that had stood since 1097. It remains revered today.

political economy on universal principles and using scientific observation and data in the real world: a political battleground for the next two centuries – empiricism or ideology?[2]

In the new Parliament, the ventilation, the lighting, the acoustics, the longevity of the stone used for the buildings – all received excited investigation. Even the quality of the air outside was measured by hanging meat and seeing how it decomposed.

In the decades before, scientific and engineering genius at work on making the future – and housed in new institutions or developing old ones – had given central London a particular air of intellectual passion, empirically and practically directed. The Royal Society and the Royal Institution, completed laboratories in 1846 at the new University College, the 1834 Chemical Laboratory at the new King's College, Isambard Kingdom Brunel and other engineers in Duke Street, the members of the Pall Mall clubs[3] – in such places discoveries were being made, discussed and debated and, as the century progressed, science also caught the public imagination in a way that our age, much more preoccupied by style than easily taken-for-granted scientific 'necessities', might find it difficult to understand.

The building of the Houses of Parliament was certainly not to be missed. From 1841 to 1844, some 200,000 cubic feet of stone a year appeared on the banks of the Thames. Did it all go smoothly and did the experts all agree? Not a bit. The Scottish physician David Boswell Reid was finally sacked after seventeen years of work. His ventilation system was scrapped after two years, except in the House of Commons, and yet his experiments combining physics, chemistry, physiology and experimental psychology had relevance for the future. Sir Edmund Beckett's great bell cracked shortly after casting, even though he – as Sir Benjamin Hall explained when answering questions in the House of Commons – 'probably knew more about bells than anyone in Europe'. The ferment of empirical experiment in what the anonymous author of *The New Palace of Westminster* called the place for settling not just the most important affairs of Britain but 'all the world' was a characteristic key to every aspect of Victorian 'progress'.[4]

Of course, it wasn't just the technology that proved troublesome. In May 1850, Mr Oborne, MP for Middlesex, noted in the Commons that Mr Barry (the architect Charles Barry) had estimated six years to completion in 1837, but now 'they were not near' the end. A harrumph from Sir Benjamin Hall, MP for Marylebone, was followed by the suggestion that if any honourable Member had been building a house and been told it would cost £20,000, then found after that the cost had risen to £60,000, 'he would have applied a rather strong epithet to the architect'. Mr Drummond, MP for Surrey Western, had a different perspective: why couldn't they have allowed enough space? All the commissioners had to do was 'take the fattest Member they could find, and multiply by 658'. There was much, much more; the Chancellor of the Exchequer commented drily that 'it was not easy to please so many masters'. A more discerning view came from France, from Taine. 'We admire the stability of the English Government,' he wrote; you would not be able to destroy it by blowing up Parliament because the solid rest, in each parish, was intact. Almost independent of suffrage, this was government by consent.[5]

Theodor Fontane observed the quietness of the scene in the 1850s while energies were happily concentrated on making Britain ever richer, or perhaps enjoying the summer weather; when the session closed on 28 August 1857, he noted that 'Not a soul took notice of the event.' Two policemen patrolled up and down; a dozen cabbies were parked in the middle of the square. Probably taking them for granted, Fontane did not mention the horses, a hidden influence on politicians; the former Prime Minister Robert Peel had died by being thrown from one on Constitution Hill in 1850; the Liberal MP Robert Lowe, a year after 1867, recorded in a letter that his new horse 'seems to have some views as to breaking my neck'. Outside Parliament, a dry-stone path, a few inches above the gravel, was used by Ministers and other Members to enter Parliament; the crossing sweeper, decades into the job, could give you any name for a shilling if you wanted to watch from a couple of yards away.[6]

Despite the fact that not everything worked in the new Parliament, this was nevertheless the moment from which governments began to subscribe to the mantra that was so often repeated during the Covid pandemic: 'Follow the science'. Government action and legislation increasingly needed the justification provided by what at least purported to be rigorous analysis, using scientific methods.

From this time onwards, there was also a growing recognition that the organization of the political process – of political parties and how they turned into governments through an electorate – required reasoned scrutiny. But it could not be said that science had been necessary to underpin parliamentary reform until then or was much in evidence at all; the issues were already clear enough. Could it be right that only a handful of voters could elect a Member of Parliament? Without a secret ballot, they could easily be bought. And what rationale justified a rural county like Cornwall sending 44 MPs to Westminster, while such towns as Manchester and Birmingham – growing immeasurably as a result of the Industrial Revolution – had no representation at all?

Nevertheless, logic doesn't necessarily dictate political development, and the first significant act of parliamentary reform, the Great Reform Act of 1832, did not become a statute by an easy process. Underpinning it was not so much giving a voice to the people as solving a prior challenge. How could you find a balance between the aspirations of a growing and increasingly prosperous middle class while still allowing those controlling the power strings, the upper class, not to feel that they were being displaced? In the decades to follow, politicians of all parties mastered the art of reforming to preserve. In the early 1830s, no major regime across Europe looked stable; the British ruling class, despite much complaining from some of them, preserved their own control. You could argue that Henry Maine's late-Victorian definition of democracy – 'the government of the Commonwealth by the Many' – was hypocritical, but it was a whole lot better than the tumbrils of the French Revolution or Lenin's 1917 'All Power to the Soviets'. Earl Grey, Prime Minister in 1832, looking back in Edinburgh a few years later, spoke of 'the great truth': that there was no possibility of liberty if 'extreme and violent changes' destroyed order, the rule of law and the ability to govern.[7]

Some sort of compromise – the 1832 Act – did not silence the calls (from many directions) for further reform, but a consensus about what 'further reform' should be became further complicated by huge economic growth and the attendant social changes, especially by the 1850s. Periodic Reform Bills failed; yet the general need for further reform became more and more apparent. Who could break the deadlock?

Politics was changing. Although Lord John Russell was a principal architect of the 1832 Bill, twice Prime Minister, with a ministerial career extending into four decades and described after his death by Lord Houghton as 'the chief political figure in fifty years of English history', it was a decisive time in the development of modern professional politics. Russell once joined the brilliant civil servant Edwin Chadwick – 'an animated calculating machine' and portent of the future – in a visit to Southall School. Chadwick expatiates upon figures, the cost per farthing of every child in the school, every item of maintenance and instruction. They visit a dormitory with floor to ceiling windows without shutters, curtains or blinds. Russell listens, hums and haws, and finally says, 'But what about the children's eyes?' The poet and writer Matilda Betham-Edwards saw the story as a symbol of 'the stone blindness of benevolent reformers'. In fact, it foretold the inability of elites ever since to reconcile technocratic data with human common sense.[8]

Despite residual fears of mob rule derived from mostly unfair characterizations of the Chartists and a different mood, apathy (called 'the prevailing temper of the times' by the *Quarterly Review* in 1860[9]), there had been a slow movement of opinion across Parliament to cautious extension of the franchise. That helped, but in the event, it took a peculiar kind of unscrupulous genius to put Britain on the right side of history.

How did 'progress' fare that August day in 1867? Surely, we suppose, parliamentary reform is carried out by radical or at least liberal political parties? Not always. This Reform Bill was introduced by a Conservative administration. It might seem odd that the leader of that administration, the Prime Minister, was not among the MPs making their way to the House of Commons, disembarking from their broughams or strolling from nearby homes through summer sunshine. The Prime Minister – hard and aquiline in face, blunt and masterful in manner, with tousled, shaggy hair – was not in the chamber for the simple reason that the 14th Earl of Derby sat in the House of Lords and, like his son, himself a considerable politician who had turned down the Greek throne earlier in the decade, was happiest with his popular designation as 'King of Lancashire', Stanley family territory since the 14th century. Both of them retained their Lancashire burr.

31 The Derby Cabinet. By the time this print was produced, Disraeli had replaced the 14th Earl (standing at the head of the table) as Prime Minister (in February 1868). Disraeli (with open papers) is left of the fireplace, Derby's son Stanley, later the 15th Earl, is at the other end of the table from his father. The man with the long beard (it was ginger) is Sir Stafford Northcote, who – as we shall see – had been a central figure in professionalizing the civil service in the 1850s and was later Chancellor of the Exchequer in Disraeli's second administration.

The Prime Minister was a considerable figure, tied to his desk all day, exerciseless, during the Crimean War before making for the House of Lords, but more importantly an accepter of reform – 'judicious changes', he called them in Parliament – when it was necessary for stable progress, the saviour of the Tories when they were in danger of becoming landed has-beens after the defection of the Peelites.[10]

Nevertheless, this was to be the Chancellor of the Exchequer's day. No one could have failed to recognize his figure, the man who also led the Conservative Party in the House of Commons, as he entered the Chamber: a presence with the aura of a potent wizard, olive in complexion, with coal-black eyes and a forehead in the form of a mighty dome. Benjamin Disraeli and his great rival William Gladstone could not have been more different, almost their only similarity that they stood out in a crowd. When Matthew Arnold met Disraeli for the first time some three years before at Aston Clinton, home of the banker Nathaniel de Rothschild, he described him sitting opposite at dinner: 'looking moody, black, and silent, but his head and face, when you see him near and for some time, are very striking.'[11] This was a man who was at his best in power; then he wasn't, now he was. His rival? Mr Gladstone, in dark frock coat, with buttonhole flower, and no longer fashionable brown trousers with a stripe running down them: a well-proportioned figure, on occasion perhaps like a Greek statue of an ideal body, though with a black finger stall where his finger had been amputated on the left hand. He somehow managed to combine scholastic brilliance with – as Bagehot said – the demeanour of an industrious Lancashire merchant.

Disraeli, seen by many as the 'Prince of Darkness', made progress seem feasible and salutary: an opportunism grounded in rationality and clothed in emotionally appealing romanticism. Mr Gladstone, enormously able though he was, treated Queen Victoria as a department of state; Disraeli had the emotional intelligence to discern that she was human and a woman. As Carlyle observed, they were both 'jugglers'; the latter consciously, the former in his deeper mind only.[12]

As it happened, Gladstone had been made very angry back in March, when after his two-hour speech he pointed to multiple inconsistencies in the Government's Reform Bill, in which he found 43 members of his own party voting with the Conservatives and his amendments rejected. For a moment, he had contemplated retirement, and took a conscious decision to lie low as the Bill reached its final reading some months later. As he had told Disraeli and the Conservatives at 3am in the House of Commons when speaking of his own Bill, 'You cannot fight the future. Time is on our side.'[13] The first sentence was correct.

The whole affair created its own mythology. The London Working Men's Association and other radical organizations saw extension of the franchise as a victory for their active populism. The Liberals claimed the policy as their own, unscrupulously stolen by the Conservatives. The Conservatives presented it as thoughtfully constructed measure that they had always planned.[14]

In fact, not all the boroughs created in the Great Reform Act of 1832 had produced electorates wanting further reform. Some large London constituencies did, but so did some small ones in the West Country and some of the longest established in the Midlands. Neatness is not much loved by history, though sometimes it is by historians reasonably searching for explanations. Gladstone had himself first obtained a seat through one of the unreformed rotten boroughs; Disraeli, the exemplar of the democratic idea of a career open to talent, was to become head of a conservative and aristocratic party. Everything seemed topsy-turvy, with plenty of what the Liberal John

Morley called 'blunder, caprice, chance, folly, craft' combining with 'reason' to create the 'tide of public opinion'.

Disraeli was in his element in such a situation. The most dangerous opposition in the House of Commons on 15 August came from one Liberal and one Conservative. Though both were implacable that extending a vote to uneducated working men was dangerous to wise and stable government and to society as a whole, both showed support for other reforms in their careers.

The Liberal was Robert Lowe. In the debates over the last, failed attempt at extension of the franchise – by his own party – the radical MP John Bright had compared Lowe and his followers to the forlorn figures David gathered around him in the Cave of Adullam. Lowe suggested – rather asserted – that the working class were the ultimate repository of venality, ignorance, drunkenness, impulsive and unreflecting violence. Gladstone hastened to defend 'our fellow-subjects, our fellow Christians, our own flesh and blood'. Robert Cecil, the Conservative who challenged Disraeli on 15 August, called that sentimental claptrap; after all, tramps, paupers and lunatics were also flesh and blood.[15]

Yet Robert Lowe, who was not against 'progress', but saw 'true progress' as something to be promoted 'by pure and clear intelligence alone', was the politician who by sheer single-mindedness managed to get an order in council to introduce competitive examinations across the Civil Service. He had not enjoyed elections: in Kidderminster in 1857, his appeal to 'rectitude and reason' didn't appeal to those no longer allowed bribes and beer. Stones were thrown; he was struck on the head by a brickbat and, streaming blood, only reached safety behind a high brick wall. Rioters were fined – moderately.[16] Here was the old world, but new, gentler penalties. Robert Cecil, later – as Marquess of Salisbury – Prime Minister, who was Secretary of State for India in Derby's Government, despite his illiberalism, made a devastating attack on officials who had failed to help during famine in Orissa – officials who were pathetically concerned with not wasting money or upsetting their superiors while forgetting 'that man did not subsist without food beyond a few days'. On that occasion, the Liberal John Stuart Mill – who in the context of extension of franchise pushed for female suffrage – crossed the floor of the House to applaud his political opponent.[17]

Though Mill failed to get female suffrage, he had put down an important marker in 1861 with his book *Representative Government*; he argued that 'difference of sex' was 'irrelevant to political rights'. Everyone had an interest in good government; the welfare of all was affected by it. If that seems obvious today, 'obvious' in retrospect is a very bad guide to how to make effective political change at a particular time. Mill's tract *The Subjection of Women* two years after 1867 was further helpful for the future, especially coming from a man. By this time, his brilliant wife Harriet was dead, but Mill acknowledged that she had in fact been joint author of many of his books. We are edging, painfully slowly, towards women at last acquiring their true status, as we shall see in Chapter 9.

A similar process was unfolding in extending the male franchise. That mysterious thing in politics – the moment when something becomes possible – came to Disraeli's aid. Matthew Arnold had written to his mother from the Athenaeum in March 1867 expressing his hope that Lord Derby and Disraeli would 'bring in a good measure, and let Cranborne [Robert Cecil] and others leave them if they like.... Quite a passionate desire to get the question done is springing up, and is gaining all the better conservatives themselves.' The motive? Well, as Derby's son later said, his father was 'bent on remaining in power at whatever cost, and ready to make the largest concessions with that object'. The Prime Minister told Tory peers in the House of Lords that he would resign if they rejected the Bill. Even so, things had not happened at lightning speed: Parliament had been prorogued on 10 August 1866; there was no new session until 5 February 1867. Gladstone had not resigned over the failure of his own Bill; but Robert Lowe knew the score: in autumn 1866, he had written to Henry Sherbrooke: 'What I am afraid of is your friends the Tories, and, above all, Dizzy, who, I verily believe, is concocting a very sweeping Bill.'[18]

Strong opinions, vigorously debated, were no bar to progress, as they are today, with debate replaced by people shouting over each other's heads on social media, often inducing paralysis. Expediency might rule, but good arguments could change minds. Disraeli could certainly change his own mind. Back in the previous decade, he used the power of words in a debate on the Naval Estimates.

'Two years ago' – his speech was on 18 February 1853 – the First Lord of the Admiralty had said, 'in a manner the most decided... "I take my stand upon Progress." Well, Sir, I thought at the time that progress was an odd thing to take one's stand upon. I thought at the time that a statesman who took his stand upon progress might find he had got a very slippery foundation.' This last phrase proved a gorgeous irony; it was fifteen years later, when Disraeli finally became Prime Minister, that he told his friends, in the sentence indelibly associated with him, that he had climbed to the top of the greasy pole. It was embracing selected aspects of 'Progress' that had got him there.

Back in 1853, he continued in satirical vein. Evidently, the First Lord was now speaking of a system perfectly matured and in action. 'For now we have a Ministry of "Progress" and everyone stands still. We never hear the word "reform" now; it is no longer a Ministry of Reform; it is a Ministry of Progress, every member of which agrees to do nothing.'[19] The observation was not entirely incorrect – much of the 1850s was spent in celebrating the progress that had been made, and enjoying that feeling, rather than continuing. A pause, but not an end.

By the end of the 1850s, Disraeli himself was sensing that, if the Conservatives adopted an attitude of irreconcilable antagonism to all popular demands, in a very fast-growing country, they ran the risk of dwindling into an impotent faction. The votes of the new urban populations were an enticing target, or, as he put it in 1859, avenues should be open to the mechanics – meaning the skilled working man – 'whose virtue, prudence, intelligence and frugality entitle him to enter the privileged pale of the constituent body of the country.'[20]

Some years later, when it came to the 1867 Reform Bill, he could be confident, at least in public, which was just as well. Robert Lowe, in particular, was not an easy opponent, though no one could accuse him of exploiting charisma. Lowe had been much bullied at Winchester: born an albino, he had eyes that reacted badly to light and suffered other imperfections; as a result, he was never able to identify his attackers. He was often churlish, combative, crusty and curt, but also dogged and tenacious. And, on occasion, witty. Disraeli's skill was to treat attacks with calm disdain, ridiculing Lowe's Classical allusions as 'the production of some inspired schoolboy'.

32 *Vanity Fair*, in 1869, offered a paradox in its caricature of Robert Lowe: 'An enemy to democracy, yet a professor of liberal principles, which tend to democracy: the combination will one day make him Prime Minister of England.' The last prediction was wrong. In fact, Lowe linked franchise extension to education, still not adequate for the masses. Is democracy a human right, as we would now argue, or is it a practical device, as he saw it, to ensure effective, liberal government?

Disraeli's speech in the final debate – how sad that his voice could not be recorded – was masterly. He wasn't there, he said, to defend or vindicate or even to mitigate every expression he may have made on the subject of reform over many years. Great constitutional principles must be dealt with and could not be approached as if duties on sugar were being settled. Another failure to carry a bill – the last one had effectively been defeated by Lowe, bringing down his own Government – would not just be bad for his party but dangerous for the country. His had been a deliberate policy to arrive at a settlement by united effort and frank exchange of views.

Disraeli had his eye on new voters. 'Progress' did not question political motive. In retrospect, doubling the size of the urban electorate and perhaps adding four times as many voters as the Great Reform Act of 1832 – the chief consequence of the 1867 Act – was part of the process by which localized patterns of influence and patronage were replaced by modern, professional political parties. Legislation on secret ballots and corrupt practices soon increased the momentum.

Behind the scenes, Queen Victoria was not at all sure she approved and had written to the Earl of Derby to seek amendments 'with a view to arrest the danger which may apprehend from the great increase of democratic power'. But despite the Prime Minister's absences from the House of Lords, when his gout got on top of him, and mumbles and rumbles from High Tory peers, little resulted. And, for those who like symbols, the whole story seemed to confirm that power was passing from monarch and lords, even if 'the people' in the House of Commons were by no means – yet – wholly representative.

Later, Disraeli would claim he had been 'educating' his party; an interesting claim, especially since this Conservative Act went further than the Liberal one Lowe had managed to thwart. Certainly, celebration seemed in order. Ever since the 17th century, 'the best whitebait in the world' had been caught at Greenwich and enjoyed at 'whitebait dinners'. At this one, the Lord Advocate sang a Scottish song, written for the occasion:

> *Now from this day the country's sway*
> *Belongs to no Whig fogie;*
> *And none can now of Tories say*
> *They scrimped the people's cogie* [a wooden drinking vessel,
> associated with pleasing alcoholic fillings].

The Scottish flavour continued, with Disraeli going north to Scotland for the first time in over 40 years. He had not endeared himself to the Scots – nor *The Scotsman* on this occasion – by using 'England' to mean 'the United

Kingdom of Great Britain and Ireland' (as, alas, most English and foreign people always did, but that's another story).

Near the close of a lengthy banquet, he made a key statement, some of which was repeating a passage earlier in the speech (always a sound rule for political oratory): 'In a progressive country, change is constant; and the great question is not whether you should resist change, but whether that change should be carried out in deference to the manner, the customs, the laws, the traditions of the people, or in deference to abstract principles and general doctrines.'[21]

Whatever Disraeli's motives, he had put his finger on why Britain was able to absorb multiple revolutions in the 19th century. Was the Reform Act a populist victory? No, at least not according to those who approached politics according to ideology – 'abstract principles', as Disraeli had called them. Karl Marx wrote to Engels complaining that, during demonstrations in Hyde Park, the campaigners for reform should have removed the iron park railings and murdered a score of policemen; then 'there would have been some fun'.[22] It was a good portent of what was to happen in the 20th century; the inevitable surge of the tides of history, Marxist style, needed a little violence to jolly it along. Later, Engels was to complain that 'the most repulsive thing here is the "respectability" bred into the bones of the workers'.

That had been what Disraeli realized. In the original March 1867 Bill, he first spoke of 'safeguards' and how the proposals were effectively conservative; in the months after, those were abandoned in the interests of keeping power.

But because this was English 'progress', in the first election called under the new electoral roll in 1868, it was the Conservatives who were defeated. It would be hard to find a better vindication of the English form of democratic progress than that.

What happened in 1867 provides a halfway point between the symbolic beginning of modern politics in the Great Reform Act and the end of the Victorian era in 1901. While it was true that 1832, for the prescient, was a signal that the future might not just be about interest groups, but also the power of public opinion expressed through an electorate, it is only in retrospect that the force of Robert Peel's 1834 Tamworth Manifesto, setting out the principles of Conservative reform – systematically organized taxation, acknowledgment of the significance of both landed interests and those of industry and commerce, stress on law and order, an end to abuses – can be appreciated. As it happened, his administration was to be short-lived, but – more important – it was no charter for populism and rejected more constitutional change. For that matter, popularity with the wider public

33 *Punch's Monument to Peel*: CHEAP BREAD, 1850. The repeal of the Corn Laws was a huge benefit for a hungry population, and after Robert Peel died in an accident four years later, 'the People...raised Monuments in many places' (so his children's memorial tablet in his parish church records). Many Conservatives, out of office for a generation after the repeal, took a different view.

(Peel was by far the most popular person in the country for abolishing the Protectionist legislation inflating the price of food) did not stop his second Government collapsing and his party splitting over the repeal of the Corn Laws in 1846. Politics is often confusing. Manchester and its Liberal cotton manufacturers provided the headquarters of the Anti-Corn Law League, which was able to send its campaign to a mass audience using the new Penny Post, but it was a Conservative who began the era of free trade, though in the process so destroyed his party that it could not command a majority for a generation.

Much of what happened politically for many decades was unexplicit conflict – gradually, oh so gradually resolved – between the new visibility and dissemination of public opinion and a political system that had previously only responded to the particular interest groups a limited franchise brought to Parliament. Even in 1874, Bagehot, in *The Economist*, explained that opposition leaders only 'occasionally' needed 'to find a programme'. 'The present Government' – this was Disraeli's second administration, to be in power for six years – 'has succeeded to office without any announced principles.' He advised a divided Liberal Party not to rush with any new manifesto. But Bagehot did make another point: 'The old questions have mostly been settled'; it was too early to see clearly what should happen next.[23]

This last observation is a key to understanding Victorian political life: cumulatively, enormous changes for the better were made by governments of both parties; but everywhere we look, everything seems to be the same old inertia. Tick boxes, PowerPoint presentations, spreadsheets and other revered tools of today's politics are a hopeless guide to how much was eventually achieved. Without them, in less than half a century, Victorians created recognizably modern political parties, and the role of the state changed for ever.

Why didn't it seem like that? First, the unexpected scale of changes brought by the Industrial Revolution, urbanization and global economic presence overwhelmed antiquated political and administrative institutions. Despite Chartist and other labour disturbances, the stability honed over centuries encouraged complacency (in some), while the instability of the rest of the world was bound to induce a sense of superiority by those who ruled. In an 1863 novel, Sir Frederick Wraxall, who spent more of his life in Continental Europe than Britain, looked back on a 'convulsed' Europe in 1848: 'old institutions collapsed like a child's house of cards, absolutism was found to be rotten at the core, and of the whole European family England alone rode out the storm without serious damage.' The 'ill-omened word "nationalities" became a household term.' Macaulay put British distinctiveness down to its constitution. We could purify it, amend it, 'but let us not destroy it'. We should shun extremes, because 'each extreme necessarily engenders its opposite'. Of course, he was providing a rationale for conservatism, but the many brutal Continental reactions to the events of 1848 supported his point for Victorians: in France alone, around 500 were killed at the barricades, roughly 3,000 were executed without due process, and up to 12,000 were imprisoned. In England, William Johnston acknowledged the grievances of the workers, but praised their common sense in perceiving that there were better ways than revolution to make progress. Continental opinions reinforced Britons' own views. Even back in 1833, the Baron d'Haussez, sentenced in his absence to life imprisonment after the July Revolution in France in 1830, was bemused to note that 'In France, a revolution is accomplished in three days. In England, the country deliberates many years before the work of reform is entered.' By then, passion had cooled.[24]

Passion was partly cooled from mid-century by something new: there was appalling poverty, but more people in society were enjoying the fruits of relative prosperity. Politics was plainly not yet democratic, since the electorate was not the mechanism for a political leader to be turned out of office from 1852 until Disraeli's resignation in the aftermath of the election in 1868. Modern political parties had not yet been created – when they were, as we shall see, they played a key role in progress towards democracy. Politics instead revolved around personalities – their collaborations, which might be a matter of friendship or common interest or evolving ideas, and their hostilities, often personal, sometimes disguised, sometimes overt. No great harm was done because this was a period in which the Progress, especially economic, that had been achieved encouraged belief in nothing more radical than what had been learned so far from the experience of the Industrial Revolution and technological change. There were difficult issues, of course: the Crimean War in 1854 was one, the Great Stink in 1858 another – the latter in which what *The Times* called 'proximity to the source of the stench', the Thames, finally resulted in an Act pushed through in eighteen days and eventually Bazelgette's utterly brilliant new sewerage system. But a blind and deaf person, not knowing whether a particular bill had been put forward by Lord Derby, Lord Aberdeen or Lord Palmerston – all very different characters, but all Prime Ministers in the period – would have been very unlikely to be sure about the initiator.

Lord Malmesbury, who served in the Government under both Lord Derby and Disraeli, received a letter from the former shortly before Christmas in 1856. The letter began with Derby's gout, but spoke of his surprise that Palmerston's Government had held together 'in the absence of any cry or leading question to serve as a broad line of demarcation between the two sides of the House'. Looking back from 1913, the barrister Horace Samuel noted that Gladstone, early in his career, had put it with a slightly different nuance: 'The great English parties differ no more in their general outlines than by a somewhat different distribution of the same elements in each.' Although governments did attempt to reduce the number of private bills, as well as the time spent on them, it could not be said in the 1850s and 1860s that the Government's programmes dominated the legislature.[25] Should we see this as massive complacency? By comparison, regimes across Europe were either tightening repression to sustain what still looked, from a British perspective, like liberty-less tyrannies, or being forged into new nations, amidst blood, battle or bitterness. That didn't seem appealing.

Of course, outside a Westminster which in this era had become much preoccupied by liberty, much less by equality, it was easy to be confirmed in the view that 'democracy' was best left to elites because of lack of sophistication in the electorates. J.A. Froude once questioned his landlord's agent about the difference between a Conservative and a Radical. Mr Emmot replied that he didn't know about 'the philosophy of the thing', but he did know that the Radical Jack Radford was 'the biggest blackguard in the parish'. He, Emmot, was Conservative. 'Now you know.'[26] Even at Westminster, John Stuart Mill famously asserted in 1861 that the Conservatives were 'by the law of their existence, the stupidest party'. That, he concluded, was the basis of their success, though it could hardly be said to be accurate, whether the party was led by new riches (Peel's brainpower was prodigious) or old aristocracy (Derby translated Homer when not otherwise occupied).

This was playing around at the edges. Was it really appropriate for a nation so pleased with its success, as Britain was, to create its Government in the manner so brilliantly satirized by Dickens? 'Then, giving the Home Department and the Leadership of the House of Commons to Joodle, the Exchequer to Koodle, the Colonies to Loodle, and the Foreign Office to Moodle, what are you to do with Noodle? You can't offer him the Presidency of the Council; that is reserved for Poodle. You can't put him in Woods and Forests; that is hardly good enough for Quoodle. What follows? That the country is shipwrecked, lost and gone to pieces...because you can't provide for Noodle!' In *Bleak House*, first serialized in 1852–53, Lord Boodle tells Sir Leicester Dedlock that he doesn't see 'to what the present age is tending'. If the Government was overthrown, 'you would have a choice between Lord Coodle and Sir Thomas Doodle (it would be impossible for the Duke of Foodle to act with Goodle after the Hoodle affair)'.[27]

What we are really observing, even if it doesn't seem like it, is something of world significance: the tortuously slow, difficult transition away from governments that just kept law and order, ensured the defence of the country and raised limited tax revenues for limited purposes. By the end of the Victorian era, it was completely clear that future Governments would be substantively more active in solving social ills and actively regulating many aspects of personal and social lives. But for a short period, Adam Smith's assumption that the nation dominant in world trade would benefit the most from free markets felt correct. If Britain's industrial, commercial and financial skills ushered in an era of ever-widening prosperity, it wasn't for the Government to threaten that by abandoning laissez-faire – to the contrary, it removed tariffs to many goods during the 1840s and 1850s – or by profligately increasing government budgets and expenditure.

Equally, it would be wrong to assume that nothing happened to help society as a whole. Palmerston, no fan of proactive domestic policies, had a period as Home Secretary in which there was consolidating and improving factory legislation, even a Vaccination Act, and a Smoke Nuisance Abatement Act, which resulted in hundreds of fines on London factories – all these Acts from 1853. As it happens, the radical *Manchester Times* suggested in 1857 that the apparent adoption of populist ideas by liberal conservatives as well as Liberals – dealing with smoking chimneys and unflushed sewers, or immigrants ('the crowds of orange women and German organ-grinders who infest our great cities') – were just about how to create a 'social organization better adapted for "spontaneous progress and self-elevation"'. That was no good; it was franchise extension that was needed, the paper argued.[28]

Franchise extension was 'progress'. But for progress properly to allow for political discourse to move on from 'ins and outs', there needed to be structures and memberships and discipline and organizations that were recognizable to electorates on a semi-permanent basis, a point especially important if working people were ever to have their own party. That would have seemed very distant when Victoria came to the throne; by the time she died, it had become a reality. By then, there were national issues and national policies encouraging people to vote. A third Reform Act in 1884 further increased the electorate. The process was by no means complete, as more and more women testily pointed out, but late Victorian elections, with 70–80 per cent turn out or more, showed an appetite for democracy.

The Liberals and Conservatives of that time tended to give themselves the somewhat bogus lustre of a historical heritage. Whig aristocratic control was a long time dying for the Liberal Party, but the increasing numbers of 19th-century believers in liberty – as a political value, in religious toleration, in the economics of unrestricted free trade – argued they were standing on the reforming shoulders of Magna Carta and 1688's Glorious Revolution. The Whiggish historian William Lecky pushed all this a bit far in his 1892 political essay *The Political Value of History* by suggesting that we are all Cavaliers or Roundheads before we are Conservatives or Liberals. Some say that for three decades before mid-century there were signs that a reforming Whig faction derived from the Foxites in the 18th century slowly attached itself to Liberal Toryism or – after Peel's repeal of the Corn Laws in 1846 – the Peelites who broke away from the Tory Party. If so, it had not been apparent immediately after the Great Reform Act, when *Dod's Parliamentary Companion* for 1833 did not identify 'liberals' at all, just reformers, radicals, repealers, anti-slavery supporters, as well as Whigs. The social fact was that a mix of manufacturers, nonconformists, aspirational professionals and middle-class intellectuals preoccupied by ideas of liberty coalesced sufficiently to be recognizable, especially once progress and (relative) prosperity were undeniable in the 1850s.[29]

The actual turning point came on 6 June 1859. Gladstone, as part of his journey from High Tory to Liberal Prime Minister, with other Peelites, agreed to join a mix of Whigs and radicals or reformers to form an administration after meeting in Willis's Tea Rooms in St James's Street, London. Curiously, their strongest policy ground for coming together was not about Great Britain at all, but the issue of Italian reunification. The British were often better at giving Europe a lead (though not by conquest) than governing themselves. Yet there were still plenty of Whigs left. In the decades that followed, there were far fewer of the old families in the House of Commons, but enough in both Houses to fill positions in Gladstone's Cabinets until an exodus in 1886 to the Conservatives as Unionists in reaction to their elderly leader's passion for Irish Home Rule.

It wasn't surprising that George Gleig, no-nonsense Scottish military man, writer and priest, could call the Liberals 'a heap of sand' in 1865.[30] After all, as the debates on the Second Reform Act had shown, the party contained both John Stuart Mill, trying to get the suffrage for women, and Robert Lowe, utterly opposed to extending the franchise at all. In so far as all political parties are coalitions, they can all fall apart; sometimes that might be because of social change, but often – despite attempts to rationalize it – it is because decisions made by individuals for multiple motives, as well as random happenings, cannot be forced into a logical framework. Neither Lord Melbourne nor Lord Palmerston, long-serving leaders of the Whigs in the early decades of Victoria's reign, were great reformers; both also served in Tory administrations.

Recognition that this was an Age of Progress was overwhelmingly helpful to the new Liberal Party. As Lord Rosebery, later Prime Minister, said in an address to the Liberals of Aberdeen in October 1878, 'It was the essence of the Liberal Party that it should adapt and assimilate new ideas of progress.' A Leicester newspaper, reviewing party history the next year, insisted that 'if England is blessed politically it must be with Liberal ideas of progress.' The 15th Earl of Derby, son of the Conservative Prime Minister, spoke after formally joining the Liberals at the Liverpool Reform Club. Even as a Tory, he said, he had learned of the uselessness of 'attempting to oppose the progress of popular ideas'. He had come to think more and more highly of the moderation, the fairness and the general justice with which masses of men, including all conditions of life, were disposed to use their power. The Liberals could also (and did) claim moral high ground. In Derby's short-lived administration in 1852 (this the father of the 15th Earl), Disraeli was Chancellor of the Exchequer for the first time. Two days before the Government fell, the night before the final debate on Disraeli's budget, the Chancellor sent a note asking John Bright and his supporters to remain neutral and promising some changes. Bright declined and recorded: 'He seems unable to comprehend the morality of our political course.' Bright's devotion to principle was as solid as his bulky body; it was a long time before he was given a government job in Gladstone's 1868 administration.[31]

Where did this leave the Tories? Well, the 15th Earl came back when the Liberal Unionists joined the Conservatives over Home Rule. But in the first instance, reform did not improve their fortunes; the irrevocable split between Robert Peel and his followers and the landed supporters, as well as the majority of Conservatives, thereafter led by the man who was to become the 14th Earl of Derby, pushed the Conservatives into opposition, at best unstable minority administrations, for a generation. Disraeli, who campaigned with fierce skill to bring down Peel, effectively delayed his own journey to the top of the greasy pole by over two decades. Nevertheless, the Conservatives, once they could find something approaching unity, did have one advantage: their dominance in England, always the most prosperous of the constituent countries, and becoming ever more so. Liberals, meanwhile, had to chase votes at the extremities.

Over a period, the Conservatives learned the basic rule of winning elections: take account of realities. Derby's minority administration in 1852 abandoned protection as its policy because free trade had become the orthodoxy for creating prosperity. Even back in the 1820s, when the right-wing 'Ultras' hated the very thought of Roman Catholic Emancipation, allowing Catholics to sit in Parliament and hold most public offices (enacted in 1829), some of them were to take the view in retrospect that some enlargement of the franchise in a very Protestant England would be the kind of measure that would have prevented it: up to a point, a pragmatic attitude to the franchise therefore, and – for the future – other reform. The Tory Prime Minister, the Duke of Wellington, did not unite his party, but he too acted pragmatically by introducing and fighting for the Emancipation Bill, taking into account a serious threat to law and order posed by Catholic Ireland and the inability of its Catholic representatives, notably Daniel O'Connell, to take their seats in the British Parliament. Robert Peel, who was against Emancipation, was persuaded to take the same view.[32] Later, when the Peelites left the Conservative Party, they tended to think that Parliament, if just expressing the popular will, was not behaving responsibly; thus it was natural, if not an explicit motive, for them eventually, in 1859, to merge with Liberals favouring an executive that would take the lead with both economic and moral reform. Here are the roots of today's unresolved challenges to democracy. Who rules: people, people in Parliament, or the executive? At least it was settled during Victorian times that it was not the monarch.

The Conservatives got better and better at attaching themselves to 'Progress'. When, in 1873, the *Spectator* suggested that the idea of progress was distasteful to them, the *Nottinghamshire Guardian* vigorously argued that fear of the people, paternalism or a wish to revert to a state of things out of the spirit of the age was not Conservative motivation, but also provided a let out: if the change was wanted, if the remedy worked, if the resulting good trumped the danger of bad, then it should be made. The Liberals, by contrast, just wanted change 'simply because it is change'. Their 'passion for progress' ignored whether the reform was beneficial. An address by an Edinburgh advocate to the Bute Conservative Association put it with a little more nuance: 'Mr Robertson argued that the Conservative was the party, on the whole', most in touch 'with sound ideas of progress'. The 'on the whole' and 'sound' were also let outs. The issue of who holds the reasonable centre ground, so much argued for and so often absent today, kept on coming up. At the Conservative Annual Conference in 1893, Mr Rankin MP referred to the dangers of 'extremists and faddists of all descriptions' against moderates 'capable of interpreting the best and noble national ideas of progress'. Use of the word 'national' had significance; except for a few issues, such as threats to the country, politics was often very local.[33]

For the first time, the press had given a sense of politics to a much wider range of people than ever before. Politicians did not always stand up to scrutiny. The Rector of Holy Trinity, Windsor, Arthur Robins – Mudie refused to stock one of his books for being too High Church – wrote an unflattering *The Present Position of the 'Liberal Party'* in 1862, in which 'the Proprietors of Progress' were savaged: Lord John Russell, self-seeking, incapable, dishonest; Palmerston an insincere placeholder; Bright a selfish demagogue; Gladstone subject to 'the hire of every agitator'; his brother Peelites 'inconsistent apostates'. The reviewer in the *Bristol Mercury* suggested that the Liberals had even pushed their opponents to advance the banner of progress, but had no faith in 'the Derby-Dizzy concern'. More than twenty years later, approaching an election, the view in Bristol was still arguing that the Tory 'conversion to ideas of progress' was not to be trusted.[34]

This was all about the invention of modern party politics, but it was accompanied by what we see in retrospect as mundane though was in fact highly exciting as a change from all past history: once the two main parties were more clearly defined, they needed formal organization. For the Liberals, this was the National Liberal Federation (at least for England and Wales), with its first conference held in Birmingham chaired by Joseph Chamberlain in 1877; it was Chamberlain who had paved the way a dozen years earlier by attracting substantial membership and electorally selling the party in his Birmingham Association. Of course, new organizations carried with them new risks, and Chamberlain himself did not take the National Federation with him when he left the party over Irish Home Rule. In general, the NLF kept pushing Gladstone for more radical social and franchise measures than he would entertain. In the new century, NLF pressures played an important role in persuading Asquith, as Prime Minister, that female suffrage should be supported, though that was further delayed by the First World War. Meantime, with aristocrats as Presidents throughout the Victorian era, it was Disraeli who established the roughly equivalent Conservative body in 1867, in a National Union of Conservative and Constitutional Associations, though its role and name changed a number of times subsequently.

While these organizations, essential for electioneering and at times important for policy, failed to capture the imagination of a wider public, that wasn't true of the Tories' extra-parliamentary Primrose League, all but forgotten now, but on the eve of the 1891 General Election with an astonishing one million members. After his death, Disraeli was given cult status; Queen Victoria sent a wreath of primroses, his favourite flower, to his funeral. The brilliant communicator and highly ambitious Lord Randolph Churchill used pride in the former leader's achievements and pride in Britain's status linked to a glorious past as an underpinning to the League. But he also harnessed the support both of the most confident generation of highly articulate women there had ever been – women on bicycles offering help to register for a vote proved a good catalyst – as well as newly enfranchised working-class voters across the country, happy – or happier – with better living conditions and enthused to a degree now lost at the prospect of having a political role denied them since the beginning of time. Here was an organization that not only gave subscription benefits to workers, but provided annuities for support in sickness or old age or other basic matters of well-being still unprovided for by the state. Added to that mix, social activities were well judged to appeal to the aspirant middle classes. While, as we shall see, a new Labour Party was also emerging as a counterpart, perhaps no political body at scale, before or since, has ever managed to make politics a matter of merry-making and camaraderie across classes and sexes while at the same time efficiently marshalling resources and organization to serious ends. The Primrose League did. That seemed like progress.

Party machines, supported not just by franchise extension but by such reforms as a secret ballot Act (1872) and control of candidate expenditure in a corrupt practices Act (1885), benefited both parties, though – in an imperfect world – they didn't expunge unfair influence and corruption and not everyone was in favour: the elitist *Pall Mall Gazette* complained that the Ballot Bill was 'somehow associated with the idea of progress'.[35] Sir Charles Dilke, Liberal and Radical (and the second husband of Francis Pattison, Lady Grace in Mallock's country house, despite his involvement in sexual scandal), made an additional point when addressing a crowded meeting of electors in Walham Green in January 1883 – that the new associations reached beyond 'the great centres of population', so that 'they now saw the whole of the Liberals inspired with ideas of rapid progress'. With the further extension of the franchise (which was to come the following year), the same could be expected with 'the country people'.[36] In fact, that proved an opportunity for the Conservatives, but General Elections had been fundamentally changed by the press, by party organizations, by more opportunity – and need – to proselytize for particular policies, rather than have the result artificially controlled by influence, social status and self-interest. Gladstone's speeches in his Midlothian constituency and in carefully targeted cities across the country, reached by fast train, in the several years before the 1880 Election, eventually covering every aspect of national and international policy – almost messianic, often many hours in length, but always brilliantly and rationally structured – were carefully organized to make national news through the press. The result was to bring his party together and defeat Disraeli for the last time.

Notwithstanding their role in the Primrose League and other social and political institutions, women continued to be scorned when it came to giving them a vote. When the second edition of *A Handbook of Political Questions of the Day* was published in 1880, it was recorded that there was support for the vote going to women with a sufficient property qualification in their own right. But the long list of reasons against would cause a riot today. They included that they were 'not fitted by nature' to 'exercise a calm judgment' on an exciting political question or to face 'the roughness of the polling booth'. It was contrary to 'the natural position of women to be entrusted with power'. 'Women questions' would be manufactured; they could influence their brothers or husbands. There was the 'latent fear' that franchise would be followed by displacing men from occupations which 'they now monopolize', thus diminishing their earnings. In any case, the 'majority' 'do not want, and would rather be without the suffrage'.[37]

As we shall see in Chapter 9, women by no means mutely accepted these shocking prejudices and while, like so many other things, they appeared not to have made progress by the time Queen Victoria died, in fact there was a decisive shift from unthinkable to the probability of decisive change to come. The same applied to the creation of a party to represent the working classes. While Chartist agitation fizzled out in the 1850s, more workers had glimpses of a better life, and for some decades it was meaningful for them to focus energies on the evolving trade unions. There were 'independent radicals' in Parliament in the 1850s before Liberals became a properly coherent party, but it was difficult to identify a convincing occupational or social basis for them; they were geographically scattered and not just a product of northern manufacturing cities. Many ex-Chartists did support the Liberal Party, but that party remained largely middle class and to an extent aristocratic even after the franchise was extended.

Yet opinions did change, as for women, especially towards the end of the century. James Hole, whom we met in Chapter 3, presciently pointed to what was happening and proposed what should happen in 1851, year of the Great Exhibition, in his book applying the social sciences to the organization of labour. He suggested that there was a recognition that concord, rather than conflict, combination rather than isolation, were the best methods to achieve social objectives. National education and free public libraries were a necessity; town councils needed to be subject to roused and informed public opinion, so that they focused on more beneficent social objectives. In effect, he was defining his own idea of workers' progress. Numbers in Mechanics' Institutes, Co-operative Stores, Freehold Land Societies were not huge, but they were 'the germ' of 'magnificent organizations the world will one day witness'. 'Growth is the law of Association, as of all Progress and Life' – the imperfect proceeding the highly developed. This was so utterly not the voice of Marx; instead, there would always be misfortunes to amend, wrongs to address, rights to defend, for 'progress is as infinite as man's nature is limitless'.[38] It was over 40 years before the Independent Labour Party was formed in 1893, to be followed by the Labour Party itself in 1906. And while we are best advised never to speak of historical inevitability, what happened in the Victorian era, inconsistently, intermittently, often opposed, foretold a different political story for working-class people in the 20th century.

Much was achieved by the Victorians simply by abolishing things, especially the Corn Laws and other protectionist taxes. Yet over time, cumulative change – to education, to social ills of many kinds, to the organization of local government and competitiveness in the Civil Service – set the state up to express the most radical transformation of its functions that has ever happened in the following century: a powerful central government, tempered by accountability to an electorate, but regulating in some way almost every aspect of life. The Victorian changes, if by no means imperceptible, often seemed against the odds. For Gladstone, responsible for thirteen budgets over nearly 30 years, abhorred waste not only as inefficiency, but a moral weakness; his first budget, in 1853, included the intention to reduce income tax from 7d to nil by the end of the decade (just as Pitt's invention of the tax in 1798 was temporary and Peel's reintroduction of it in 1842 was said by him also to be temporary).[39] In fact, both party leaders, Gladstone and Disraeli, proposed to repeal it in 1874; Disraeli failed to honour the pledge when he won. Realities trumped ideology, though it was not until Asquith's reforming Liberal administration before the First World War and then the huge costs of the war itself that income tax became truly a prominent feature of life.

Victorians had their own perspective, sometimes smug and complacent, but reminding today's unforgiving gaze on their era that change was occurring. Examining the budget in 1873, the *Morning Post* noted that 'quite independent of party questions', the great total of £76,617,000 was to be spent in the next financial year; it drew attention to the fact that 'the proportion of outlay on the social progress of the country is so large'. Half a century before, English statesmen had almost no place for 'internal progress' in their minds. There was no Education Department, no Science or Arts Department, no museum worth mentioning, no reformatories as Industrial Schools, no moral agencies of any account. Heavy taxes (that was an exaggeration) were now mostly spent on works of 'actual national improvement'.[40]

It cannot be said that George Eliot's political comments were usually cogent, but in the year of the 1848 Revolutions she got it exactly right in a letter to her clergyman friend John Sibree: 'There is nothing in our Constitution to obstruct the slow progress of political reform. That is all we are fit for at present.' On social reform, 'we English are slow crawlers'.[41]

In retrospect, the crawlers usually win the race. Combining material progress with political liberty and consent with social fairness should be a patient process not helped by the diktats of manifestos. A thoughtful letter in the *Morning Post* in March 1867 rejected Lord John Russell's assertion that Conservatives were not 'real reformers', as if 'a Reformer' was of a separate class, to occupy 'a place in Darwin's enumeration'. Necessities trump desires. The statesman must accept 'the necessity of progress'.

Though he might 'regret it'.[42]

When we think of Victorian political leaders, the description of the American Benjamin Moran of Lord Aberdeen in 1857 (when the former Peelite Prime Minister and leader of a coalition government from 1852 to 1855 was 73) might stand for many of them: 'He looks old, is wrinkled, somewhat sallow, grey, and stoops.... He is...rather stout but not corpulent.' It is true that Robert Peel first became Prime Minister (in 1834) when he was 46 and had first become an MP when only 21: a forerunner of today's technocrats, without the common touch, though much less like them in having a very Victorian focus on reconciling business with morality, understanding why essential reform was essential, and seeking effective solutions to social problems methodically, slowly and realistically, rather than glibly assuming that greater prosperity automatically meant greater prosperity for all. George Howard, Earl of Carlisle, confided to his diary that Peel was in fact 'the prominent type of an age whose great characteristic is the love of the useful in politics'. In fact, this became somewhat easier after Peel's death in 1850. As John Wade, who had so determinedly exposed corruption as a young man, observed in 1856, civil agitation was now 'paramount to physical force'. The emphasis was instead on 'gradual advancement, moderation in demands, and an equitable compromise of them if conflicting' – an over-rosy picture, but often how it worked out over a period in practice.[43]

While it is impossible to find the 'typical' Victorian politician, curiously a very 'untypical' figure gives very helpful clues. That is Robert Lowe, much more interesting than his adamantine approach to the franchise suggested. He is even a helpful guide to other politicians: in a speech at Romsey in 1876, he praised Palmerston – often derided for being a cynical games player, preoccupied by foreign affairs and the good life (involving a different kind of affair), but failing to get to grips with domestic reform. Palmerston remained popular in the country: for being always courteous, good tempered, dutiful, attending the House of Commons more than his Ministers, at 80 arriving at 4pm and for four nights a week prepared to stay until 2am, with nothing but a cup of tea. It may be that the nation benefited from having leaders guided, as the French President Thiers said, 'par la charactère, non par la raison' (though Palmerston's first English biographer called it 'strong natural common sense'), yet also leaders (like Lowe) insistent on reason and logic.[44]

Lowe, in life and career, displayed so very many Victorian values, skills and achievements, a man (according to his *Vanity Fair* portrait) 'whose talents will make him Prime Minister'. That was not to be. His sight was so bad that he could not tell what effect his speeches might have, or often recognize to whom he was speaking. Disraeli, while agreeing that Lowe was fond of his wife, unkindly suggested he could not see how plain she was. When he was 28, three leading authorities advised that he had perhaps seven years of sight remaining; they suggested out-of-doors employment, which took him to Australia – very bad advice, given the strength of the sun. Yet this was a man who could tell brilliantly funny or informed stories in company, leaving Gladstone – notoriously stiff and formal – with 'a long face' at dinner at Hatfield House in 1868.[45]

He was first a considerable scholar, reading maths papers in other languages, treating each new language as a riddle leading to power; a visit to Algiers in 1876 gave him Arabic, to the Pyrenees Spanish, to add to modern Greek, French, German and an interest in Sanskrit and hieroglyphs. At the Oxford Union, instead of talking about the rights of man, he presented a thought-through scheme for emancipation of West Indian slaves (and was described as 'an old gentleman with sugar-white hair' – he was eighteen). It was also at the Union that he moved for the abolition of taxes on knowledge, the measure that, eventually, was to revolutionize press and books. He met Darwin on a geological tour of Wales and recognized him as a special being; his proof, which he called 'somewhat canine', was that he followed him for 22 miles. He also criticised the unreformed Oxford for being 'a clerical gerontocracy'. This was a man who, when not yet eight years old, compiled a Code of Laws for the defence of society for the other children at Bingham Rectory, who was completely comfortable with Greek or Latin verse, but by observation came to the conclusion that 'all real progress must come from scientific research'. Much later, in 1876, he wrote to his brother Henry enthusiastically about the newly introduced typewriter – a robust machine, much faster than the pen, and usable with practice without sight of the keyboard. He delighted in mastery of 'our latter-day mechanical contrivances'.[46]

Jowett, then a young and rising scholar in Oxford, met Lowe as an undergraduate. Perhaps because he was the supreme manipulator himself, if usually for good ends, Jowett tended not to be unequivocally complimentary about anyone, and after Lowe's death referred to the rigidity of his principles. But it was Lowe who persuaded Gladstone to offer Robert Scott, the then Master of Balliol, the Deanery of Rochester to enable Jowett to take his place. Lowe got things done. Today, his elitist views would be rejected out of hand, but at the time he was not wholly wrong – when he argued in a speech in 1866 – that the 'half-educated' could easily influence the ignorant; both communism and fascism in the next century showed that democracy was not the automatic result of giving power to the people.

That apart, Lowe left his mark everywhere that 'progress' happened. With his eyesight too bad for him to become a lawyer, he first went to the new colony in New South Wales and became proactively involved in politics, with ideas, especially on finance and education, helpful to stable governance, sometimes expressed in the *Atlas* newspaper in Sydney. Interestingly, as a member of the Legislative Council, he argued for lowering the franchise property qualifications on the grounds that the present system had led to an unbalanced constitution with power too concentrated in the hands of the wealthy. He insisted that political power was not a right, but a means to good government. While his political judgments might be questioned, he was quintessentially Victorian in pushing what was practical and improving, not something abstract and metaphysical. For the same reason, back in England, he objected to the Church of England's temporal power, which – in education, for example – made for less efficiency.

In April 1851, Delane asked him to join *The Times*. A demanding editor met a willing commentator: newly arrived intelligence at the newspaper would be sent to Lowndes Square after midnight. His wife Georgina was speedily out of bed to take dictation while the messenger waited. Lowe continued contributing until 1868, long after he had entered Parliament in 1852. The breadth of his achievement in office exhibited the Victorian capacity to make reforming progress: as Vice-President of the Board of Trade, his Joint Stock Companies Act (1856) provided an essential structure for a fast-expanding economy; in charge of health and education in Palmerston's second government (1859–65), and despite his own suspicion of state interference, he made smallpox inoculation compulsory, policed by an inspectorate, and went into battle for a safe water supply and waste disposal. He regulated poisons and tried to ensure quality in elementary schools by relating achievement to teachers' pay, with heavy emphasis on reading, writing and arithmetic.[47]

There is not much to be learned from the insults that, in private and in public, Gladstone and Disraeli hurled at each other: Gladstone's view (in which he was hardly alone) that all the principles the Tories once had, 'Dizzy destroyed'; Disraeli's that his rival was an 'unprincipled maniac' (the latter a view almost echoed by Queen Victoria when speaking of 'that half-mad man', and more interestingly by her private secretary, Henry Ponsonby, in describing Gladstone as 'earnestly mad', so intense that truth was difficult to discern). The novelist and historian Edward Benson witnessed Gladstone dealing with a persistent heckler complaining of a U-turn by the Prime Minister by pointing at him, thrusting one arm as if stabbing, furious in face, fierce in imperious gesture. Three times 'there shot out that menacing hand, and the heckler could not stand against it'. Gladstone continued with indignant energy, his voice quivering. Oratory counted, reaching well beyond the audience; animated prints, press reports and reprints of a particular speech were widely disseminated. Here was a man who – playing backgammon for relaxation – rattled and threw the dice as if engaged in a war with the powers of darkness.[48]

There was not much 'moral' about Gladstone's early career: son of a Scottish merchant and well connected enough to obtain a seat in a pocket borough controlled by the Duke of Newcastle, defender of his father's slavery plantations, which, after emancipation, continued with Indian indentured labourers (effectively replacement slaves). When he first met Disraeli at a dinner with the Lord Chancellor, Lord Lyndhurst, in January 1835, he found him 'rather dull' and wearing foppish clothes, yet Disraeli – without Gladstone's connections – had already failed three times to gain election and had a tough fight to progress in the political world.[49]

Moral missions are often connected to self-deception and complexity. Newark, Gladstone's original constituency, may have been a rotten borough, but he would allow no bribery. He started, as Macaulay said in the *Edinburgh Review*, in a fierce criticism of Gladstone's youthful attempt to argue for a unity of moral purpose by State and Church of England, as the great hope 'of

34 This pen and ink drawing of the young Disraeli, possibly by Daniel Maclise (c.1833), bears out Gladstone's impression when he first met him that he was an inconsequential fop. He is even wearing a chain of a kind that 1970s fashion made *de rigueur* for vulgarity. Debt and dreams of his hero Byron, rather than political success, marked Disraeli's early years. Many years later, in December 1878, Benjamin Jowett gave a simple (and convincing) summary: he was 'a very great man with great faults'.

those stern and unbending tories'. However, in four periods as Prime Minister, he created reforms in many areas of life that may have needed further development, but would never be fundamentally abandoned. Presiding over a society in which Christianity was challenged as never before, he remained a High Anglican, said his prayers every morning and linked his moral mission to God. Although it took him decades to understand why the flourishing nonconformist churches were so appealing to so many Liberal leaders and to a much wider population, he could retain his own adherence to Anglicanism while infusing – at least in intention – Christian moral values into the conduct of the state. Whilst still a Peelite, he agreed to join Palmerston's Liberal administration in 1859, rationalizing it as both a duty and the will of God to support a government helping to further Italian independence and nationalism (whereas the Tories would just support the established order). Of course, the two most powerful members of that government, Palmerston himself and Lord John Russell, were old men. His decision was well judged to make him heir apparent. That was a convenient fact, not a matter of morality.

If the state was to be moral, that certainty didn't imply profligate expenditure. He was true to his own principles: a prolific letter writer, he paid for his own stationery; with his family, he travelled third class from Paris in 1850 and worked out that it was expensive at 13d a mile for a party of five. His period as President of the Board of Trade in the 1840s taught him the importance of free trade to commerce, and he followed Peel in supporting the abolition of the Corn Laws, as well as other restrictions making trade more difficult. The answer to social problems was to create prosperity by hard work and thrift (moral values) allied to free trade. That worked, but only up to a point, just as his policies when he became Chancellor of the Exchequer (seeing the virtue, as he put it, of saving the cost of candle-ends and cheese-parings, preventing waste) were inadequate for a population growing so fast in a rapidly changing environment. As Prime Minister, he had several spells in which he was Chancellor of the Exchequer also. But when he finally abandoned the second of these roles at the end of 1882, it was with the observation, which he did not welcome, that 'economy and retrenchment' were no longer tenable rules for the government. By then, the necessities of reform overruled the ideas that had underpinned the great leaps forward in economic progress.[50]

Gladstone was also, like so many Victorians, committed to the paternalism of rule by the best; when Ruskin visited him in December 1878, he denied that one man was as good as another. He changed his political view only because of the visible evidence that working men had moved on from the

35 Gladstone picnics on 16 September 1893, aged 84 and Prime Minister for the fourth time. His companions, other than his solicitous wife to his right, look slightly awkward and diffident. Gladstone himself stares almost fiercely at the camera: a man of account.

destabilizing protests of the first half of the century, that many of them were engaged in self-improvement by reading and study, or that the Lancashire cotton workers had followed a moral cause during the problems created in cotton supply during the American Civil War. Accepting an extension of the franchise was not because it was a human right, but an acknowledgment that many workers had demonstrated self-respect in their behaviour. The tortuous route by which in strange Britain the aristocracy began sharing power with the middle classes and the middle classes with the working classes, all without revolution, is one of the great – if decidedly unglamorous – wonders of history. *Punch* summed it up brilliantly in a cartoon not long before Christmas 1879: Gladstone, a towering presence with massive legs spread across two jetties, holding Finance as retrenchment and Foreign Policy as peace, while a tiny boat identified as REFORM passes through his legs.[51]

Gladstone's foreign policy was about peace in the sense that it was not one of imperial expansion, though it became so in practice in furtherance of free trade, economic interest and trying to maintain the balance of power among other European powers. It was especially activist in liberal causes: the Italian struggle for independence was a symbol of that, whereas Prussia and the unification of Germany was a different kind of nationalism. By comparison, Disraeli was more recklessly engaged in assuming the role of world statesman (it is a debating point as to whether he or Queen Victoria was the more delighted when the 1876 Royal Titles Act created her as Empress of India). Disraeli might have doubts, but he understood the manipulation of power; Gladstone was usually sure he had right on his side, so was less likely to feel the need to understand the art of persuasion.

This was also exhibited in their attitudes to their parties. Sir Thomas Acland, a friend of Gladstone, pointed out to him in 1868 that he needed to mingle in the Smoking Room at the House of Commons, and make himself agreeable to the powerful and the potentially powerful, but not to neglect those who would never be powerful. That didn't mean anything to a man who saw party as a collection of individuals sharing common views and values, his own views and values. He was a central participator in the creation of a modern party, but the importance of managing parties was largely lost on him; his way worked well, particularly when it won elections. Disraeli, by contrast, was a consummate charmer; he didn't even need a reinforcing smile. He could weave magic out of grand cries: 'liberty of the subject', the duty 'to secure the social welfare of the PEOPLE', 'strength to the Crown', all phrases from his novel *Sybil* (1845), which made the famous distinction between the 'Two Nations', the rich and the poor. The persuasive guile of the 'Primrose Sphinx' convinced his party, but Francis Hitchman's presentation of his career towards the end of his life as the 'disinterested and patriotic statesman' led to its author being described by Carlyle as 'one of the helpless, somnambulised cattle whom he led by the nose'.[52]

Carlyle, not being very practical, wasn't prepared to accept that reform was not possible without the leadership skill that would hold together an uneasy coalition of interests – as there was in the Conservative Party's MPs: old-fashioned Tories, patriotic country squires, some progressive thinkers, commercial and manufacturing businessmen who were not natural Tories or heavily political at all unless their interests were threatened, professionals with their own agendas. Winning helped – as it always does – so the unexpected passing of the 1867 Reform Act helped to restore or create some momentum for progress. No matter that when Disraeli proposed extending the franchise in February 1867, he had no clear idea of what 'reform' meant. If Disraeli had no master plan, he seemed to grasp that by giving votes to the skilled working class, there was the potential to catch them for the Conservatives through social reform, but also by appealing to national pride (a policy which Joseph Chamberlain was to take to an electorally disastrous consequence in the new century with his plans for a tariff wall around the British Empire: 'making the foreigner pay').

WHERE THE TREE GROWS AND WHERE THE FRUIT GOES.

36 The Tariff Reform League, founded in 1903: the Free Trade tree had been planted by Britain, but its fruits were picked by the USA, Germany, France, Holland, Russia and the East. Despite Chamberlain's charisma, his plan to make the British Empire a single trading bloc was an electoral disaster for the Tories. Ironically, he was more open to increasing government expenditure on social reform – with revenues from tariffs, not domestic tax – than many Conservatives and Liberals.

Disraeli had only two periods as Prime Minister: one very short one after Derby's retirement (February–December 1868) and one of over six years (1874–80). In April 1872, he brought public health centre-stage, bravely since his speech of over three hours, said to have been sustained with the help of two bottles of a white spirit, was in the home of Liberalism: Free Trade Hall, Manchester. Liberals scorned him for pushing the 'policy of sewage', but he returned to the theme two months later in the safer environment of the National Union of the Conservative and Constitutional Associations. For 'the labouring multitude of England', it was life or death, and one way and another affected every aspect of the quality of life. Disraeli was right.[53] Later, his 1875 Public Health Act created new local sanitary authorities with power to use the rates for hospital provision.

This – and much legislation in his second administration, ranging from the right to strike, protecting women and children from factory exploitation, helping the working class to save, protection against the adulteration of food and dangerous drugs, slum clearance and much more – had a lot to do with the skills of a banker and solicitor from Lancashire named Richard Cross, who became Home Secretary in 1874. Cross himself, in a private political memoir, pointed to Disraeli's reliance on other people's ideas, preferring to hold attention on the European political stage. But the practical point was that, while some of it was consolidating legislation, a Conservative administration had showed that it was just as important as the Liberals in making social progress through central government action. Identifying the party with progress, if only to an extent, gave it greater coherence than just relying on the majority faction for identity. Others, now forgotten – George Sclater-Booth, President of the Local Government Board; Viscount Sandon and his defining 1876 Act; Monty Corry, for fifteen years Disraeli's Private Secretary – contributed hugely. Disraeli got the credit, albeit not from J.A. Froude, whose 1890 biography of this 'not quite English character' made clear that he left behind nothing of permanent or enduring value.[54]

Time and again, what unites even Disraeli and Gladstone was what the great constitutional expert Erskine May described as a reform spirit that was not about a total break with the past, but a 'mission to improve and

37 Do Prime Ministers make successful writers? Disraeli did: his *Lothair* (his hero wrestling with faith and bewildered by love), in the year of this cartoon (1870), produced what his publisher, Thomas Longman, called 'mania'; the American edition sold out 25,000 in three days and 80,000 in a few months. Gladstone's most recent work, *Juventus Mundi* (1869), was just scholarly eccentricity, suggesting that Christ had been foreshadowed by the Greek Gods.

regenerate'. This was Victorian self-congratulation, but it could be applied both through Disraeli's brand of cynicism mixed with common sense and romanticism and through Gladstone's relentless moralism. Disraeli's Liberal opponent, Sir William Harcourt, graciously acknowledged that 'To the imagination of the younger generation your life will always have a special fascination. For them you have enlarged the horizon of the possibilities of the future'. The comment might equally apply to Gladstone, whose last address in his Midlothian constituency in 1895 referred to all the changes of his century 'in the direction of true and most beneficial progress'.[55]

CHAPTER 6

'THE SOUND COMMON SENSE OF THE COUNTRY'

THE PROFESSIONALIZATION OF EVERYTHING

One day towards the end of the 1840s, a very unlikely event takes place in western New York State in a place called Geneva. What an American medical journal patronisingly called 'A pretty little specimen of the female gender' begins going to lectures in medical college. She enters the first class entirely composed, removes her bonnet and places it under the seat. She seems to have a good and civilizing effect; when she is present, at least, there is 'a good decorum' in the lecture room.[1]

What is going on? It was only during the 19th century that married women were even allowed a separate legal identity, or the right to retain their own earnings and money. Although progress was made in giving access to professions in some American states earlier than in Britain, it could not be argued that this aspect of social reform proceeded anywhere in the world at the same pace as much else in this century of multiple transformations in life and environment.

The young woman in Geneva was called Elizabeth Blackwell. She had been born in England, in Bristol, in 1821. When her father's sugar refinery had been destroyed by fire in 1832, the family uprooted itself to New York and did not flourish. Exactly twenty years later, Elizabeth was the first – and for a while, the only – female doctor registered by the British (and newly created) General Medical Council in 1858. She only got in by a loophole – on which more below.

It's never much fun being ill, but you certainly would not want to have been ill in 1850. There had been a clue that things might get better (at least, as far as pain was concerned) when the young Humphry Davy noted in 1799 that inhalation of nitrous oxide, an Enlightenment discovery, could induce both euphoria ('laughing gas' was his coinage) and analgesia. But it was not until the 1840s that there were public demonstrations of operations using anaesthesia, and that coincided with some attempts to professionalize medical education (the alcoholic activities of Bob Sawyer and Ben Allen in *Pickwick Papers* [1837] would not have encouraged confidence), if not yet for nurses (Sarah Gamp, the dissolute nurse in *Martin Chuzzlewit* [serialized in 1843–44], was too close to reality). The waves and waves of people that descended on towns and cities as a result of the Industrial Revolution did lead to the opening of what later became famous hospitals: University College Hospital in 1833, or St Mary's in 1845. But the mortality rate came close to doubling in the period 1831–44. In London, drinking water came from the Thames in sight of outpipes from the sewers. Lack of knowledge about disease causation combined with lack of professional skills. The record of the first great census in 1841 suggests that up to a third of doctors were completely unqualified.

Meantime, the young Elizabeth Blackwell and her very talented sisters showed what enterprise could achieve. They campaigned against slavery; they campaigned for female education, even beginning a school when the home-educated Elizabeth was not yet eighteen.

In Geneva, before she was allowed entry, the faculty asked the student medics how they felt. They were unanimous in agreeing that 'one of the Radical principles of a Republican government is the universal education of both sexes; that to every branch of science education the door should be open equally to all.' That was quite a moment. Elizabeth had been rejected by the four medical schools in the then acknowledged American state-leader of medical education, Pennsylvania. Similarly, New York rejected her, as well as eleven of the 'county schools' in New York State. It was still tough in Geneva. Female townspeople decided that she was either 'a bad woman, whose designs would gradually become evident', or 'that, being insane, an outbreak of insanity would soon be apparent'. Even in college, she had to push hard to be allowed to go to anatomy lessons.

In the summer of 1848, Elizabeth sought to widen her experience in the hospital wards of the Blockley Almshouse in Philadelphia. In Ireland that year, the 'famine fever' – epidemic typhus – was raging. As emigrants crossed the ocean in search of a better life, they went down with it and many were carried off, on landing, to lie on the floor in the almshouse. The resourceful would-be doctor combined assistance with study and used the experience to write her graduation thesis on this form of typhoid. One of the most thrilling – and at the same time, awful – ways in which medical progress was made was at the front line against typhoid, relapsing fever (yellow fever), dysentery, dropsy, scurvy, cholera, ophthalmia, all of which were rife in Ireland. The doctors were not immune, almost 200 of them dying of 'fever' in less than five years in Ireland itself in the 1840s.

Miss Blackwell persisted, graduating in 1849. Weighing things up, she decided that the greatest opportunities would lie in her native England. Off the boat from America on 30 April 1849, she made for Portway Hall, Dudley, home of Charles Plevins, an old friend of her cousin. She made a key observation about him: he was representative, she said, of a class of Englishmen that was constantly increasing – reformers in spirit, but not destroyers; not necessarily with clear immediate plan of reform, so earnestly maintaining the present system until they could find a better one. That caught the mood precisely as England entered its greatest Age of Progress in the second half of the 19th century.

Charles arranged for her to visit Birmingham hospitals. Not everyone was completely unhelpful; even Dr McKay, of the Lying-in Hospital, who thought that God and Nature had indicated the unfitness of women for 'such a pursuit', showed her all he could. And at the 60-year-old General Hospital, Dr Heslop 'received me with the utmost deference, showed me every ward, male and female, pointed out every case of note, let me examine it, and detailed the treatment, particularly one operation for subclavian aneurysm [a weakness in an artery, just below the collarbone], which was so remarkable that they were going to publish the case'.

Next, a journey to London, much faster now that there were trains, but it stiffened her up, notwithstanding the champagne she drank ('the only wine I like; iced champagne is really good'). At St Thomas's, a complex of enormous buildings, as it struck her, the surgeon to whom she had sent her letter of introduction knew nothing about her and 'thought it a very indelicate undertaking'. She was handed on to a nurse with strict instructions not to enter men's wards, but saved by Mr South, the senior surgeon, who showed her everything, including many notable specimens. He allowed her to attend one of his clinical lectures, where a large body of students 'peeped at me in every direction'.

This was a time when Britain was about to enter a new decade in remarkable tranquillity. Much of Continental Europe continued to be engulfed in the turmoil resulting from the 1848 Revolutions. In Paris, which was not untypical in denying women roles in hospitals, dispensaries or practical *cliniques*, except as nurses or cleaners, cholera was threatening and politics reaching boiling point. Against all advice, and with what she called a slender purse, that was where she went in May 1849, quickly finding that 'the French made a point of cheating the English unmercifully thinking they are immensely wealthy'. She thought it 'amusing' how universally politics was discussed – the boy who arranged a room, the market-women at their stalls, everyone found time to read a journal and give an opinion.

She did get herself into La Maternité, the great state institution that trained midwives from every département in France. That was a vigorous training: no distraction of any kind allowed, no reading except from medical literature; lectures, ward work, drills, *cliniques* from morning to night, with no confusion, but no pause, and multiple tests. Along the way, she picked up a serious eye infection and lost the sight of an eye.

A year after arrival, she hurried back to England. Her cousin Kenyon Blackwell, a South Staffordshire ironmaster, lobbied Barts – not exactly a new hospital, originally founded by a favourite courtier of Henry I in 1123 – to allow a visit. It took a committee decision, and though she was allowed access in May 1850, she was immediately treated as an oddity. There were some who appeared to think that she must be an extraordinary intellect overflowing with knowledge, more who supposed that she was a queer, eccentric woman. No one, she regretted, seemed to perceive that she was 'a quiet, sensible person who had acquired a small amount of medical knowledge, and who wished by patient observation and study to acquire considerably more'. The dean, Mr Paget, was cordial and told her that more prejudice was likely to come from women than men. 'I think', he said, 'that English women seem wonderfully shut up in their habitual views. But a work of ages cannot be hindered by individual feeling. A hundred years hence women will not be what they are now.'

38 Elizabeth Blackwell gives us a chastening sense of just how difficult it was for a woman to make her way in a man's world: winning her doctor's degree was, she said, 'a great moral struggle' – that it was! – but then, as a female physician, she was isolated, patronised and mostly unable to obtain professional advice. From New York in the early 1850s, when she opened a clinic for poor women, to her appointment as Professor of Gynaecology in 1875 at the new London School of Medicine for Women, she blazed a trail through an almost impenetrable landscape.

That same year, 1850, Elizabeth met Florence Nightingale, another remarkable woman, notwithstanding her effete later persecutor, Lytton Strachey, in *Eminent Victorians*, who graciously allowed some of her heroism, but gives full display to the idea that she was a bitter, sardonic figure of ruthless determination. At first, the two women, who had been born just a few months apart, got on very well, but later in the decade, when Florence wanted Elizabeth to be superintendent of a nursing school built with the Nightingale Fund – donations from the general public – the latter would not contemplate attaching herself to an institution not willing to support female doctors.

39 Heroes have their detractors: Florence Nightingale and Miss Management, with a muddle of medical supplies, from leaches to bandages. Or is this image meant ironically? In fact, shocked to encounter total administrative incompetence when she reached Scutari in the Crimean War, she not only had the nursing skills to help the wounded, but applied what became modern management orthodoxy – control of supplies and their distribution; rational organization of labour; culpability and responsibility.

Florence accused her of focusing on educating just a few cultured women; Nightingale wanted to 'diffuse as much knowledge as possible' and privately told John Stuart Mill that Elizabeth was just preaching 'mischievous jargon'. Having an American female physician benefited no one. The future thought otherwise. In later life, the last two doctors to attend on Florence Nightingale were both women. And it was her letter of introduction to the President of the Medical Council that enabled Elizabeth to become the first woman to be included in the new British Medical Register in 1858, via an anomaly allowing doctors qualified overseas to practice in the UK, even if British women could not.

These two special people were both right. Education, in any area, had to take account of elites, but also of everybody – a lesson learned, if too slowly and too painfully, by the end of the 19th century. Elizabeth and Florence also demonstrated a different point: that, in the end, 'politics' (with a small 'p') underpins everything. Neither woman's chief achievement was medical as such: Elizabeth Blackwell left more mark as a political campaigner than as a medical innovator; Florence Nightingale's achievement was as a brilliant, visionary, organizer and strategist more than it was strictly as a virtuoso nurse.

Nightingale's driven personality was the root of her success and, like many such people, a cause of her own anguish, though some of it may have come from undiagnosed brucellosis. Benjamin Jowett, who tried to calm her (what Strachey unfairly called instilling 'his own particular suavity'), became close and encouraged her towards quietism, the active life, but 'a sort of passive life too', and was to persuade her not to take her own life when she was a patient in St Thomas's. However, she came to the conclusion that emotionally she was giving more to him than he was to her.[2] In no doubt is her adoration across Europe and in America, too, for her inspirational work on hospital design and management and her blueprint for nursing, as well as her iconic presence (in Derby, Calvert the grocer, Hulme the tobacconist and Byer the provision merchant all used paper bags with her portrait). Eventually, the thin, acerbic, rigid, haughty-eyed woman became plump and sometimes smiled. Until health prevented it, she remained active, unlike Elizabeth Blackwell, who retired before she was 60 and enjoyed a quiet retirement in Hastings.[3]

It was in Victorian England that most professions literally professionalized. The process was not inevitable, nor without opposition from established oligarchies. In the case of medicine, two things came together. The first was the increasingly consistent application of science to medical understanding; the second – of fundamental importance in this and other professional activities – was the spirit of empirical investigation and the desire to move mountains exhibited by numbers of single-minded individuals. Blackwell and Nightingale were among them.

On the science, Robert Brudenell Carter, who as a young man was a staff surgeon in the Crimean War and later a long-serving consulting ophthalmic surgeon at St George's, looked back in 1887 on 50 years of 'the application of science to the art of restoring health and promoting longevity'. Progress had focused on preventive, more than curative, medicine, above all the causes and processes of disease. Vaccination, patient isolation and water purification prevented countless deaths. He was a tad chauvinistic – a characteristic of late Victorian England, when too much pride in progress started to distract from the thing itself. His reflections were in fact part of Thomas Ward's celebratory survey of 'Fifty Years of Progress'; Huxley wrote about science, Arnold about schools. Carter suggests that the contribution of 'England and her people' (Scotland, Wales and Ireland unfairly missing – again) to 'the advancement of medical science had been greater, not only than that of any other country but that of all other countries together', though it was conceded that it was to Germany that we owe the ophthalmoscope, to France the stethoscope, and to the United States anaesthesia. But there was now a special school for women at the Royal Free Hospital, as a result of which some of the qualified women were working in Africa, China and India.[4]

In some senses, Britain could claim to be the 'workshop of the medical world'. A number of Continental countries had a more professional institutional structure by the end of the century, but it was Britain whose citizens were having longer lives and in better health.[5] Of course, the twentieth century was to make multiple advances, but the sense of progress, with excitement attached, in the decades after 1850 was palpable. The idea of specialized medicine (the Royal Marsden, the first in the world dedicated to cancer, was founded in 1851), of children as a special case (The Hospital for Sick Children, 1852), of the disadvantaged (The National Hospital for the Paralysed and Epileptic, 1860) came in quick succession. Even if the motive was sometimes to prove that this was not just an age of wealth and power, the effect of what Sir John Simon called in 1897 'the constantly increasing care of the community at large for the welfare of its individual parts' was visible.

Even so, quackery was encouraged by the very idea that there were at last answers. Moreover, a patient's eye view was less comforting. Peter King was admitted to St Thomas's, London, in the 1870s for a leg ulcer problem. There, the very eminent and advanced surgeon Sir William McCormac declared that 'This abscess must be opened'. At tea the following day, the ward sister told King that he would go without supper and have an operation under chloroform. In the event, the house surgeon said he would do it without chloroform. The cuts were deep, as the patient lay under a carbolic spray, and the sister gave him brandy and water. Next day, Good Friday, a ward service began with 'O Come and mourn with me a while'. Sir William returned after

Easter Monday with students and declared there was a diseased bone, which should be opened. King protested that he had come in for one operation: 'You must please yourself.' The patient decided against – but married a St Thomas's nurse and lived through to the Second World War.[6]

A role for the state in health was much debated in Victorian Britain. The conservative *Quarterly Review* at mid-century was opposed to 'central interference' that is 'premature and excessive' – actually a step forward from outright negativity.[7] *The Lancet* went further in 1858: 'The truth is, we do not like paternal governments.'[8] But whatever the opposition, national issues needed national policies, even if action had to be applied locally. Humanitarians, sentimental communicators (Dickens or Kingsley), professionals believing in social responsibility, supporters of civic pride, even Queen Victoria (who stopped off at the army hospital at Netley, whose creation she had suggested in 1856, en route to Osborne in the Isle of Wight) – all these provided a context and a catalyst for the many voices engaged in scientific improvement and for a new breed of civil servant. G.H. Lewes, George Eliot's longtime companion, provided *Popular Lectures on Physiology* for the first issue of *Nature* in 1870. He argued that we no longer looked on life as something 'essentially mysterious'; physiology just needed analysing like any other natural phenomenon. When it was, the results could be communicated to 'form an element in general culture'. Health was a concern for everyone.[9]

When cholera had arrived in autumn 1831, after a five-year journey from Bengal and bringing uncontrollable diarrhoea, fever, vomiting and, within days, death, there were many theories about its origin and its treatment – a Dr Quin dosed Lord Malmesbury with pints of wine as a remedy – but no doctor understood the disease. Sir Henry Halford, a court physician, was unwilling to attend victims, except when the bad-tempered Lord Chancellor, Lord Brougham, 'launched at him one of his diatribes'.[10] Harassing politicians clashed with hapless doctors. In the fifteen years from cholera's appearance, there were three violent assaults on public health from that source, but also typhus, typhoid and influenza. In that time, there were no solutions. The impact on the national psyche was immense, especially in relation to cholera. The novelist and historian of France, Annie Challice, was one of many to describe a typical scene: 'it was summer time, but the sky was often darkened by a leaden hue, usually portentous of a fresh outbreak of this dire disease. The bells tolled, the coffins were carried along the hot streets, the atmosphere reeked with revolting and retributive suffocation in that quarter of this great city.'[11]

The *Annual Register* for 1850, after more cholera outbreaks in 1848–49 and the creation for the first time of a General Board of Health by the Public Health Act, shows a country struggling with a disease – it was observed – that struck at night, producing a terror of going to bed. The Board declared that quarantine would be of no avail, and that overcrowding led skin and lungs to exhale poisonous gas and 'a certain amount of animal matter of a highly putrescent nature' that was deposited on walls and clung to clothes, beds and furniture. Apparently, only lunatic asylums, prisons (kept very clean, despite 'the evil condition of their class of inmates'), London hospitals (except for cholera patients) and model homes for the poor appeared to provide immunity.[12]

There were clues here, but it was (as ever) individual clearheadedness that won the day. The surgeon Robert Brudenell Carter looked back on the life of his friend John Snow, who 'rose Smiles-like' via education and effort from extreme poverty.[13] He was one of the pioneers of anaesthesia, against the opposition of many doctors and the Church of England, which saw it as unethical, and was to administer chloroform to Queen Victoria twice in the 1850s during childbirth. But it was also he who, by carefully mapping outbreaks of cholera in Soho in London, traced them to a single water pump in Broad (now Broadwick) Street and also carried out a wider study comparing water supply from contaminated parts of the Thames with that from further up the river. Sadly, it was only after his death, aged 45, in 1858, that there was a gradual acceptance of the importance of clean water and sanitation.

The Public Health Act failed; the Board was weakened, then disbanded in 1858. These steps backward – in the curious way humans make change – were made just as the facts and the principles that could have informed it were being established. It is also a common pattern of lasting change that what is begun for rational reasons – here, state interference in health – will not die; it just awaits its right human instruments and a tipping point in the *zeitgeist*. There were many Acts in the 1860s and 1870s, and a new Royal Commission in 1868. Yet again, an individual played a central role: the surgeon and public health reformer Sir John Simon was employed by the Government for over two decades, creating a different department to administer public health, involving the state in research, giving supervision to the medical profession and improving vaccination. Vested interests are not usually dislodged by bluster and rage; Simon persuaded, learned empirically, applied himself pragmatically and navigated gradualism. Robert Lowe, responsible for building up the medical department of the Privy Council after 1859, had a completely different character, but the two of them provided a perfect model for how politicians and public servants can work very effectively.

While these changes were occurring, medical students inhabited a world in which ancient and modern co-existed. When Shephard Taylor was training in the late 1850s in Norwich, translating Cicero's treatise on friendship was part of the University of London matriculation exams, but he was very soon in the thick of it, watching amputation of the penis for cancer, breast amputation (by a surgeon who read Odes of Horace with his wife in bed), and nearly suffocating himself and the surgery boy when making chlorine gas. There were many lectures (Dr Ende on 'Urinary Secretions' was 'very interesting'), but much learning on the job (including hitting a voyeuristic maid, illicitly watching surgery, on the nose via a glass pea shooter). Alongside what we might call medical student humour (at least, in days of male chauvinism – 'The new maid-servants arrived, neither of them very killing in appearance'), he displayed an engagement not just with medicine, but all the great issues of the day: he disapproved of 'Mr Disraeli's Reform Bill'; he found the judge Baron Pollock, in Norwich to preside, too deaf to do his job properly; he explored first-hand the different denominations of the churches; he blamed Napoleon III for manipulating Britain into the Crimean War, though derivatively so from Alexander Kinglake's history; and he engaged with the surgeon Peter Nichols and Professor Sedgewick as they entered into an animated discussion of Darwin 'in ward No. 4'. Medical life, 1850s-style.

All this is revealing of a pivotal moment. Taylor notes that Nichols seemed 'not to be well up on anatomy', though his operations were generally successful. Nichols had trained when there were no exams, just a seven-year apprenticeship. The early exams would need you to be 'intolerably stupid to fail'. Now professionalization was in train, a great deal of progress followed. Taylor watches Professor Ferguson perform a resection of the knee joint, the first surgeon to do this as an alternative to the norm: amputation. He goes to electricity lectures; and at his final *viva voce*, in 1862, he has to wait for seven hours in the anteroom, at the last moment managing to fill a gap in his knowledge from *Gray's Anatomy*, first published four years before, about the ovule. To his astonishment (luck rules the world), his examiner, 'the great Professor Huxley', quizzes him on this early stage of foetal development.[14]

As to luck, we might instead sum up everything that happened in society and medicine in the 19th century for what it tells us about Victorian optimism by noting the absurdly ponderous, but in its way rather wonderful, account in the *Quarterly Review* in 1850: 'It is as true of Sanitary improvement as of human progress in all kinds, that its successive steps are not fortunate but determinate; each real advance, however apparently independent, being in fact but the logical extension of improvements already achieved.[15] Perhaps that might help explain why diet could figure in the thinking of the medical student Taylor, worrying about the amount of oxalate of lime there might be in the stalks of the rhubarb he ate, and in Sir Henry Thompson's *Diet in Relation to Age and Activity* 25 years later. Thompson's father believed medicine was contrary to divine revelation. His own book was very clear about why half of the 'chronic complaints' that embittered many from middle age were the result of 'avoidable errors of diet'. Sir Henry, and those like him, led 19th-century lives, but felt sure they were making a modern world.[16]

Big changes usually excite or disturb; they get noticed. What happened to the government machine in the Victorian era represented a fundamental shift that would last for ever, yet prolific Victorian letter writers, diarists and even historians showed little interest in 'the Civil Service'; then, as now, it was politics that had the attention. The term itself only came into full use as a result of reforms in the 1850s, though it was used earlier. Peel spoke of 'the Civil Servants of the Crown', and after 1832, the distinctions between them and both MPs and Ministers were relatively clear. But what was the function of all these groups – what was government for? Very little. Even in 1843, the young Herbert Spencer argued that it was not to regulate commerce or to educate the people or to teach religion, administer charity or make roads or railways. It just had to administer justice by protecting its citizens and their property, and defend the country where necessary. Was that extreme? Well, in 1833, the Home Office had 29 officials (*The Times* reported in 1847 that the French Ministry of the Interior had almost 204,000 employees). The Treasury had 115 in the same year (it needed to collect taxes), the Foreign Office 39 (though supplemented by Ambassadors and Consuls). Approaching 90 per cent of all government employees (a little over 20,000 in 1829) were involved with Customs and Excise, Stamp Duty and the post, the last of which rapidly increased after another Victorian invention, the Penny Post, was introduced in 1840.[17]

Wasn't this odd for a country leading the world with its Industrial Revolution and progress towards liberal democratic freedoms? Curiously, the obstacles to reform of central administration were the same as the arguments for it; if much of it was incompetent, extravagant, nepotistic, that was not perhaps an argument for more state action and more of the same. Besides, who wanted it? Some decades later, the novelist Charlotte Riddell described government as being 'a good old house mother', sitting quietly at home while her sons 'have been delving, and digging, and mining, and boring, and blasting abroad'. We – 'the subjects' – were 'hundreds of miles ahead of government in everything'. We had made railways, stretched telegraphs, sent out ships, lit our streets with gas, explored other countries, all without government, which was just 'a useful drag on the wheel of our progress' stopping us from running off with democracy 'at once'.[18]

Nevertheless, the case for change lay in every practical direction. The new urban living of a much-increased population facing inadequate and insufficient housing, polluted water, industrial and trading waste, black, belching smoke and disease, the state of the poor – all of these coincided with the Victorian passion for assembling information systematically, especially by empirical research on the spot and using new methods of analysis adopted by the new science of studying society. Civil registration of births, marriages and deaths (from 1837) and the first full census (1841) were some of the starting points. The Treasury tried (in 1840) to make sure clerks understood double-entry bookkeeping (many still didn't, but the attempt at least looked forward).[19] It would be very hard to argue convincingly that the influence and ideas of Jeremy Bentham and his utilitarian disciples were more important than the facts of Victorian life, though some historians have taken that view, but prominent and practical Victorian politicians could applaud greater efficiency in the spending of government money and, in the case of Gladstone and others, the moral connection between that and the importance of private and public duty. Over a period, telegraph and steam transport led to a radical reduction in well-paid Foreign Office messengers, some earning over £1,000 a year in the early 1850s; and even before the full effects of that were seen, Lord John Russell, as Foreign Secretary, cut their pay in half and reduced their expenses.[20]

There were pressure groups everywhere in Victorian Britain – the prototypes of today's organizations – but often (as today) they did not have the decisive effect, though were usually well meaning and contributed to the climate of opinion. Samuel Morley (1809–86), textile manufacturer, devout nonconformist, philanthropist, part owner of the Liberal *Daily News*, Gladstonian MP, President of the Peace Society and abolitionist, added first chair of the Administrative Reform Association to his busy life in 1855. It was no surprise that he had support for Civil Service appointments to be meritocratic from Thackeray and Dickens, or to see his career as part of the values of the middle-class takeover of everything.

Some outstanding figures exhibited the growth of public service virtue before reform. Sir James Stephen (1789–1859), grandfather of Virginia Woolf and Vanessa Bell, dictated the elaborate Slavery Abolition Bill in two days in

1833, a bill with 66 complex sections – this despite having overcome smallpox (but not its effects on his eyes, though it did give him a breakdown). So, it could not be said that, by coming from a family of successful professionals, he abused the advantages life gave him. He had given up the Bar to join the Colonial Office and, as his friend Henry Taylor said, 'to get a hold upon the policy of the government in the matter of slavery'. In his role as permanent secretary in the Colonial Office for eleven years from 1836, it was not completely inaccurate to say that 'King Stephen' singlehandedly ruled the Empire.

In the succeeding decades, however, belief in meritocracy – but demonstrated by fair competition – strengthened, certainly with Robert Lowe, relentless in a speech in Kidderminster in 1855 about ensuring that 'any man, however poor and however devoid of interest' was 'able to vanquish by the force of his abilities' and 'get possession of an appointment'. In that speech, he went further in attacking the way MPs sold themselves to government for patronage. If merit wasn't 'the only avenue to public offices, we are fighting with a leaden sword against a man who uses a steel one'.[21] Fast-forward to today and we are still grappling with that problem – but it was the Victorians who first showed that there was a better way.

Some of the opposition to reform was plainly elitist. The Queen was opposed to public offices being filled with 'low people without the breeding or feeling of gentlemen'. The conservative *Quarterly Review* argued in 1860 that much of government was a practical matter and 'theorists' did not understand that 'men of moderate endowments are equally or more useful'. Mankind was capricious and complex, and that wasn't helped by 'symmetrical theories and logical formulae'. Nevertheless, the prelude to reform stretched over many decades. Henry Brougham (1778–1868), Lord Chancellor in 1830, had railed against sinecures long before that. In his memoirs, the long-serving Clerk to the Privy Council, Charles Greville, writing about 1830, recorded that 'A placeman is in these days an odious animal and as a double placeman I am doubly odious'. The recognition that the system was flawed was almost as decisive a change as actual reform.[22]

The climate for reform partly changed because of the 19th-century love of commissions of inquiry. Dickens's word pictures had their value, but the Poor Law Commission proved unquestionably that fetid streets, dirty water and overcrowded tenements were linked to the spread of disease and crime. Factory inspectors had been introduced in 1833, mining inspectors from 1842 (with Home Office exams for them from 1850). Was this perfect? Of course not. Simon Tremenheere (1804–93), in many ways a wonderful public servant involved in many Royal Commissions, himself able to get fourteen Acts of Parliament with socially improving objectives passed, became an inspector of mines who did not need to inspect mines, let alone venture below ground.[23]

If this was a time when individuals absolutely made a difference, that didn't mean they believed in empathy. Some reformers always had it but lacked – so Sir Edwin Chadwick thought – the impartiality that came from 'Reason' and the application of a 'uniform principle of administration'. Some criticised him for being 'essentially a despot and a bureaucrat', as *The Economist* put it in 1854, coercing people 'for their own good'.[24] Chadwick, who continued to devote his time *pro bono* to social and economic issues after retiring that year as commissioner of the General Board of Health, wasn't just a super-rational Benthamite supporter, but by personality a man whose belligerence, clear thinking and powers of organization got things done. If he would not acknowledge that he could not always be right, it remained true that his report on *The Sanitary Condition of the Labouring Population of Great Britain*, published in 1842, was to lead, in the Public Health Act of 1848, to a milestone in state responsibilities: for the first time, government was accepting a responsibility for the health of its citizens.

It was all this – a mix of much better information about society, the progress of liberal ideas, the reality that a country undergoing massive change was not the country of the past, the flawed but often brilliant contribution of individuals – that helped to make it possible to reform the mechanisms of government. Not that the past was ever dead: Sir Charles Trevelyan and Sir Stafford Northcote's 'Report on the Organisation of the Permanent Civil Service', published in 1854, owed at least something to Chinese Han Dynasty competitive examinations 2,000 years earlier. If so, there was at least one other, George Cornewall Lewis, the politician who notably managed to persuade the government to remain neutral in the American Civil War, to argue that Ancient Rome had done perfectly well without 'open competition'.[25]

Trevelyan had become permanent secretary in the Treasury in 1848. A man of extraordinary energy, clear-headed focus and a skilful understanding of the levers of power, he worked with Northcote, a younger MP who had greatly improved the Board of Trade when acting as Gladstone's Private Secretary. Northcote was more malleable than Trevelyan, but there were certainly advantages in a report (1853–54) under the name of two individuals, rather than a cumbersome Royal Commission. Jowett, who wrote a letter-attachment to the findings, linked, as Northcote did, university reform to government reform, as part of his educational mission to train suitable candidates to guide Britain in its enhanced global activities. The overall purpose was to arrive at merit in recruitment and in career development, reorganization of structure to distinguish between clerical work and research and analysis involving the intellect, introduction of methods to remove the incompetent – all 'in view of the great and increasing accumulation of public business'.[26]

Sometimes in government it is better to delay. Some of that is a practical matter – the 1850s, before the modern party system had been created, were marked by coalitions and consolidations of the economic gains and social reforms that had accompanied Britain's rise to world power, though the transparent mismanagement of the Crimean War was powerful propaganda for change. The pear was not quite ripe, as Macaulay – Trevelyan's brother-in-law – noted in his *Journal*; there was 'open-mouthed criticism of the Report at Brooks'.

Ironically, it was an extra-parliamentary instrument, an Order in Council, that was used to progress reform. There was considerable parliamentary debate (and disagreement), and Parliament still had right of scrutiny of costs, but constitutionally Royal Orders in Council had always regulated government administration. Even so, like so many Victorian reforms that changed the country forever, it took more than 50 years, part implementation, part experiment, with several commissions through to that of Lord MacDonnell just before the First World War, to cement the professionalization of administration. As the 1881 edition of Traill's *Central Government* declared, 'we are being indefinitely [sic] more "governed" in the current year than we were fifty, twenty, or even ten years ago; and we shall, in all human probability, be still more governed ten years hence than we are to-day'.[27] The era of big government that had been ushered in was also better government. The arguments about making it better still remain unresolved today; but it was in Victorian Britain that government programmes, instead of the individual policies of politicians, first became possible.

In the St John's Ward of Winchester, the death of a councillor in 1865 produced a competition between a Conservative, Mr Fielder (a rope factor), and a Liberal, Mr Jacobs (a jeweller), to replace him. Both had grown up in Winchester and both were respected. The crucial factor, according to the local newspaper, was that Mr Jacobs espoused 'ideas of general progress and improvement' and as a result was set fair to 'add to the number already in the council who are for improvement'.[28] 'Local government' is a modern term that begins to establish itself, like so much else, in the decades after 1850. For centuries, custom, charters and self-perpetuating elites controlled municipal corporations and parish vestries, which continued their relatively undefined roles without central government having much concern. The notion of representing the local community's interests through a democratically elected council with paid officials was not even on the horizon.[29]

The Industrial Revolution and the oh-so-rapid growth of towns and cities made this (lack of a) system untenable. Vested interests, corruption, lack of professional skills, disorganization would not deal with a much bigger population for whom increased prosperity and increased poverty and crime went hand in hand. Roads, lighting and new sources of energy, waste disposal, water supply, hospitals – all needed more and immediate attention. In the 60 years between the Municipal Corporation Act of 1835, the result of a Royal Commission whose findings were devastating (not least, the frequent expenditure of borough funds 'in feasting, and in paying the salaries of unimportant officers'), and two important Acts in 1888 and 1894 finally systematizing county, district and parish councils, the reform momentum was strong but not easily evidenced in practice. Like the state itself, the essential dilemma locally was at the heart of all public governance in a modernizing country. Those in power don't want to lose it; if they were made to, that was no guarantee that councils would perform better. If private enterprise was more effective, at least in some areas of activity, then self-interest kept trumping public interest.

And where should power lie? The Birmingham political theorist and lawyer Joshua Toulmin Smith (1816–69) gave an address to the new Social Science Association in 1857 in the form of a powerful plea not to centralize everything. Then, as now, the balance not just between private and public, but between national and local, was difficult to resolve. In December 1856, *The Times* argued that local government institutions should have legally defined limits; within those limits, they should have 'the freest and most unfettered discretion'. Less than a year later, contradicting itself, the paper argued that a town could not be left to 'spend money as it likes'; there needed to be a 'Central Power of enforcing improvement'. If *The Times* was inconsistent, so were all the political parties. Governments, said Toulmin Smith, used 'meddling, shifting, experimental legislation'. Like all those absolutely persuaded of their own veracity – in any era – he was unable to countenance the fact that the human process he had criticized had created what he himself called 'our enlightened age of Progress' and was improving a new world whose previous foundations were becoming less and less relevant. Moreover, central government could make possible local progress, as it did, for example, by allowing municipalities to buy up commercial tramways on viable terms in 1870, despite Treasury concerns about local borrowings.[30] There was also a constitutional allowance, as described by Erskine May and based on a 17th-century resolution, that 'every commoner in England' could 'prepare and present petitions to the House'; it was in part seen in the roughly 500 Acts brought forward by towns and cities between 1800 and 1840, with double that number in the next three decades to provide permission to invest in public infrastructure.

Ironically, in a geographically uneven process, the country's dominant city, London, with vested interests to match its power, was the slowest to reform (in Roy Porter's memorable description, ratepayer 'democracy' was manifested in 'parish-pump narrowness and acrimonious penny-pinching' except for the feasts and private abuse of 'public' property). There were at one point nineteen separate street-paving boards just in St Pancras. All these obstacles, many of them wilfully created, disguise the fact that a remarkable transformation took place. Taine certainly applauded Manchester administering its own affairs, paying and appointing its police, governing itself 'almost without intervention of the Government'. In his view, the revolutionary events in France of 1830, 1848 and 1852 would have been 'impossible' in England, where there was a stability of the social edifice through having many independent local powers, so different from French centralization. The asset value of utilities grew enormously after 1850, and by the end of the Victorian era, almost half of water, gas, electricity and train investment came from the public sector, and nearly three-quarters of that in schools and hospitals. The truth was that, even if it did not seem so, local and central government had an interdependence.[31]

To an extent, while the technical skills needed by council employees was recognized, we are still in an era in which amateurs were sometimes highly effective. Sir Joseph Heron, Manchester's first town clerk, in post for 40 years from 1838, got short thrift from the *British Medical Journal* when it criticized his evidence before the Royal Sanitary Commission. Heron said that there were very many great questions seriously affecting public health that would probably be 'better understood by a gentleman who is not a medical man'. It was 'difficult to perceive', was the response, 'how a knowledge of medicine can be a barrier to the comprehension of such questions'.[32] Here was the perennial dilemma of the modern world: follow a scientific expert, or follow someone who has practical experience of human behaviour within social structures? The common-sense answer – combine the strengths of both – comes up against the egos of those participating. Heron did achieve many remarkable things for Manchester with his single-mindedness. The construction of the chain of reservoirs that brought clean water to Manchester and Salford over 35 years was on a scale not matched at the time anywhere else in the world. In 1899, however, whether it was a good idea (other than being meritocratic) for Manchester's Treasurer to be a promoted clerk, rather than someone professionally qualified, was a legacy for the new century to resolve.[33]

One of the great strengths of many big cities later in the 19th century was genuine civic pride, today just a pale copy. Hospitals or libraries or public parks were not only needed, but reinforced that pride. Joseph Chamberlain's leadership in Birmingham – he became mayor in 1873 – in taking over utilities was part of a 'civic gospel' and provided a model for his later campaigns in Parliament to extend the powers of local authorities. By 1884, 24 of them were authorized to issue stock to pay for housing or sanitation or education or social welfare.[34] From small beginnings, lives were transformed. To have 'The People's Park' – the nickname of Victoria Park in East London – in 1845 represented a basic lifestyle change. In the very first report of the Registrar-General of Births, Marriages and Deaths in 1839, an appendix by the epidemiologist William Farr suggested that such an amenity would add years to the community's lives and reduce the annual deaths figure by several thousand. Today, according to the council's figures, its annual visitorship flourishes as never before. The initiative for creating it began with a mass petition to Queen Victoria. Campaigns marshalling the resource or authority of the state at its apex could be expressed locally and powerfully.

There was another area of activity that affected local and national life equally: the law. When Robert Lowe was writing for *The Times* at Delane's invitation, he did not spare the country's proud institutions. The Inns of Court were 'rigid about eating, careless about learning, strict about money, negligent about knowledge; lavish to the stomach, but niggards [the word had nothing to do with racial slurs and came out of the Middle English for 'stingy'] to the mind'. He suggested that if Oxford was abolished and degree-giving powers were given to landlords of pubs, 'they could not be less fitting depositories of the trust than the four Inns of Court have shown themselves to be'.[35] Lowe proposed a legal university, with lectures instead of dinners and exams instead of room-rents, all to further the primacy of merit. This British ability to be self-critical astonished other Europeans. The German Theodor Fontane, after seeing a play entitled *Judge and Jury* in October 1855, recorded in his diary that its importance lay 'in the fact that England can tolerate such a parody of its highest authorities and its oldest institutions'.[36]

The law, like so many institutions and customs that the Victorians inherited, certainly needed reform on practical grounds. As Sir William Anson's *The*

Law and Custom of the Constitution, which went through multiple editions after first publication in the 1880s, pointed out: 'Medieval legislation, where it was not simply declaratory of custom, was scanty. Modern legislation is restless, bold, and almost inquisitorial in its dealing with the daily concerns of life'. And though Anson didn't mention it, if the Empire at its greatest extent was four or more times larger than the Roman Empire, that made for a legal and governmental challenge on a completely different scale.[37]

If reform was essential, it was at least helped by a strong foundation. Respect for property, the rule of law and parliamentary sovereignty had been reinforced, despite vicissitudes and inadequacies, for centuries. On the brink of Victorian changes, William Blackstone's *Commentaries on the Laws of England* (1765–69) supported acclaim for common law against Continental European Roman law. Taine, a century later, noted that there was no codification based on philosophical principle, as there was in France; he observed jurors' 'concern with points of fact, distinguished from points of law'.[38]

Bentham criticized Blackstone for not acknowledging 'the futility and waste of having two different systems of jurisprudence' – law and equity – as well as 'the needless prolixity of all existing pleadings in proceedings of both systems'; he referred to 'codification' – a word that entered the language in the sense of enabling sound organization and efficiency – in a book of essays around the theme of public instruction in 1817. Under his influence, John Stuart Mill and other reformers used the word, but in practice it meant something different from its use in Roman law – instead, it simply (and for good reason) meant the systematization of the courts of law and their procedures.[39]

If the original purpose of 'equity' was expressed most simply as 'fairness', with the Court of Chancery as its principal instrument, it was not achieving that in the middle of the 19th century, and it did not help that Chancery and Common Law courts were hostile to each other, or that Chancery, far from simplifying the problem of there being so many precedents, had managed to acquire a cripplingly large number of its own. The upper classes had complained about Chancery for centuries, but the enormous growth in wealth and international trade made it a necessity for middle-class reformers to abolish sinecure offices, speed up procedures and otherwise improve efficiency. There was no inevitability about it – the inertia induced by time-sanctified customs and vested interests were an obstacle in this, as in other areas, of public life – so it is all the more remarkable that a series of piecemeal reforms culminated in the 1873 and 1875 Judicature Acts, creating a Supreme Court of Judicature with two sections: the High Court, bringing all courts under the same umbrella and creating some new ones, such as divorce; and the Court of Appeal, simplifying the process of appeal, though not yet allowing it in criminal cases. That was an achievement – the rules of common law and equity had been different; now there was a uniform system of pleading and procedure and a Supreme Court to have power of enforcement in case of conflict.

How to operate a legal system remains an ever-evolving debate today (just as legislators will never fully succeed in producing laws that can be called definitive or are fail-safe in operation; in Victorian times, the beginnings of claims for workplace injury could be judicially decided on the basis that the injured were not compelled to work in an unsafe workplace). Yet the Victorian reforms were a fundamental step forward, and the product of individuals with values that greatly improved public life. Lord Selborne, at Winchester for schooling with two other reformers – Robert Lowe and Lord Cardwell, the political brain behind reform of the armed forces – combined subtlety with single-mindedness and worked as a QC incessantly, on one occasion without sleep or rest from 2am on a Monday through to the following Saturday. It was he who was Lord Chancellor during the passage of the Judicature Acts. Unlike Lowe, he favoured 'household suffrage' and contributed to the popularization of the phrase.[40]

Memoirs are often an unreliable guide. As James Atlay, who wrote about the Victorian Chancellors shortly after the era ended, observed, Lord Brougham, despite his contributions to reform, if much criticized for his arrogance, had a 'recollection of events' in his autobiography that 'differed widely from the impression retained by other actors and eyewitnesses'. Nevertheless, we have a good window into *Life in the Law* from John Witt, the 'Sporting Lawyer', as *Vanity Fair* called him in its caricature (he did play football for Cambridge against Oxford in the 1850s, a sign of the popularization of sport, though not yet of its professionalization).[41]

Witt, made a Fellow of the prosperous King's College, Cambridge, in 1859, benefited from another Fellow being a member of Lincoln's Inn and getting him in. There was then no separate examination to pass; a student simply needed to have been in a barrister's or pleader's chambers for at least a year. The Victorian progress, in many areas of life, towards professionalization is even more remarkable because conventional ideas of 'professional' conflicted with the deeply ingrained belief in learning practical skills by observing – and as a solicitor friend of Witt's said – not by 'purely theoretical studies in pursuit of distinctions and prizes'. Lowe had told him that it was impossible to start in the English Bar without good connections with a solicitor. Was it nepotism, asked Witt, if your brother was a solicitor and gave you work? Patronage, then as now, could never be completely fair. Walking home with the Liberal politician W.E. Forster, Witt was told by him that 'If I had been at Eton, I should have been in the Cabinet ten years earlier'. Yet, if connections continued to be used, the Victorian work ethic was very powerful – Witt, self-described as having a constitution of iron and the digestion of an ostrich, rose at 5am for a working day of fourteen hours, seven days a week.[42]

That was essential. As Witt said, 'The abnormal complexity of modern affairs adds greatly to the judicial task.' Large companies, 'created and maintained by the tortuous brain of a financier', were constituted by contracts never intended to be intelligible, with volumes of minute books and correspondence that obscure. To add to the written word, there were messages by telegram and – before the century's end – telephone. Witt provides many examples of eccentricity or – as we would say today – abuse of power. Before Lord Esher in the Court of Appeal, quoting a judge who had asserted that a ruling in the Court of King's Bench 80 years before was an 'accurate and binding statement of the law', Witt was asked what use it could be to read out 'what those old men had got to say'. In response to Witt citing a passage from Roman law, Esher averred that if he was going to give us that 'we will go out to luncheon'. Evidently, the birth of modern law did not also signal a change in human behaviour by everyone in power.[43]

More seriously, we can see how the roots of the complexities of modern life would provide severe challenges to the possibility of fair, efficient and uncostly working for the law. In theory, Witt suggested, the Common Law of England, tempered by Equity, constituted a high – being *parti pris*, he said 'the highest' – expression of human reason and morality. He accepted that many Victorian statutes – for example, ending disabilities for Catholics, Jews, Quakers and nonconformists – were admirable. But liberal ideas provided no solution for insolvency law: 'Parliament proceeded to pile Ossa on Pelion and Olympus on Ossa in the shape of pages of statutory stuff, which it cost thousands and thousands of pounds to explain, and all of this cost came out of the pockets of the wretched creditors'. Was that progress? We wouldn't describe it with Classical allusions now, but evidently – taken to extremes, as today – it was not. When Joseph Chamberlain introduced his Bankruptcy Act in 1883, he was following at least a dozen others on banks and insolvency. It was laid down 'solemnly' from the Bench that the Act 'is a new code of law, and that its language is not to be governed by repeated decisions in older statutes'. That was never going to work: a 'modern world', created 150 years ago by Victorians, was already finding that it was very expensive 'to find out what Parliament meant'.[44]

Another legal view, from the perspective of a solicitor, was given by Sir John Hollams, who found the changes of the Victorian period, after he came to London in 1840, 'astounding'. Judges became much less reticent, while counsel was free to impress on jurors that it was for them to decide and not the judge. Now a Chancery judge, where the matter was of law rather than equity, would direct a case to a civil court for an opinion. For the provincial courts, the judges needed a Bradshaw (the railway timetable), but implied speed did not work in practice. When the Chief Justice left London for north Wales in July 1900, he began at Newtown – 'There was no business of any kind, and the judge received a pair of white gloves.' The same thing happened at Dolgellau and Beaumaris, or it might be that the court sat for only a few hours in the day. In London, at the Guildhall, different kinds of problem dogged the proceedings when Sir Edward Watkin (1819–1901; the same dates as Queen Victoria), MP, reformer, last of the railway kings and serial entrepreneur, was involved in a case that sought to make him liable as a director for statements in a prospectus. On the first day, Sir John Coleridge, for the plaintiff, asked for referral to arbitration because the case needed 21 days and the court could only sit for fourteen, as well as being too complicated for a jury trial. The defence declined. On the second day, there was a dense fog, and the jury interposed to say that they were in a fog about the case. The judge supported referral and crossly supposed that Sir Edward, who again declined, was being advised to take advantage of the fog to defeat justice. The jury found for the defendant.[45]

Despite all, from a 19th-century perspective, much had been achieved. Sir Henry Maine, one of the key proponents of applying ideas of evolution to social issues, suggested in his *Ancient Law* (1861) that we should look upon the past of the law in much the same way as geologists examining the primary crusts of the earth. Maine noted the way that in the past actions were controlled 'by a regimen not of law but of caprice'. He asserted that there had been few 'progressive societies' and many 'stationary'; the progressive moved to 'a phase of social order' in which there is 'the free agreement of individuals'. That produced a vital movement, exhibited in the legal system, 'from Status to Contract' in determining outcomes.[46]

Nothing better symbolized the fact that the law had entered a new era than when Temple Bar, the only surviving gate of the original medieval entrances to the City of London (albeit reconstructed after the Great Fire in 1666), was removed to help traffic congestion and to allow the Royal Courts of Justice to move from Westminster Hall to a new building, opened by Queen Victoria in 1882. The heads of two Jacobites who, after the 1745 rebellion, were put on a spike on top of the main arch of Temple Bar, miraculously remained there for 50 years. Now, justice was expressed differently: 450 houses were demolished, nearly £1.5 million paid for the site, and nearly £1 million spent on construction and fitting out. Portland stone bricks – 35 million of them – as well as other supplies had to be brought by tunnel; 3.5 miles of corridors resulted. The new courts, rightly or wrongly, became an icon of modernized British justice.

Yet Britain never throws away the past lightly. The bricks of Temple Bar were numbered, bought by the brewer Henry Meux and, after peregrinations, re-erected in Paternoster Square in 2004, by which time the 'new' Royal Courts were looking distinctly un-21st century.[47]

There would be little point in reforming the country's institutions if the government's historically most important function – defending the realm – was neglected. The optimistic surge of the 1850s was dented by the Crimean War against Russia (1853–56). What should be remembered about it – other than that Lord Cardigan, who led the Charge of the Light Brigade, had 'the worst face I ever saw on a human being' (according to Benjamin Moran in 1857), 'redolent of beastliness', and that the war, which Britain and its allies

40 Photography for the first time showed war as a human experience, rather than an abstract arena of glory for the victors. Here, Crimean wounded arrive back in London in 1855. Florence Nightingale's *Notes on Nursing* (1859) urged that more thought should be given to the effect on the minds, as well as the bodies, of the wounded: 'the ghosts of their troubles haunt their beds'.

ultimately won, did not go very well? *The Times*, separate from its criticism of aristocratic military men and government incompetence, thoughtfully noted that it was 'an affair of science and machinery, of accumulated capital and skilful combination'. Volunteers, many with previous experience of constructing Canadian railways, used 1,800 tons of rails and fastenings, 6,000 sleepers, 600 loads of timber, 3,000 tons of other materials and machines – from pile-engines to chain-falls, wire-rope to sawing-machines – to build, rapidly, a railway deep into enemy territory. The submarine electric telegraph was taken from the shores of Bulgaria to those of Crimea, linking with cables elsewhere in Europe, to produce what a contemporary account called the application of 'the most wonderful gift ever made by the arts of peace for the purposes of war'. Brunel sent what was effectively a prefabricated hospital, complete with drainage and air-conditioning.[48]

Motives for war are always more complex than they seem, but the main narrative is clear. Russia's almost unbelievably large armies were aggressively intent throughout the 19th century in driving towards influence or conquest in the Ottoman Empire, Persia, Afghanistan and India. Britain used its power to encourage modernizing social and political reform to the Ottoman Empire, but mostly to bring free trade, to Britain's advantage. Herbert Spencer's early work *The Proper Sphere of Government* (1843) argued that there was 'no such thing as a necessary war', except perhaps in defence against invasion. Britain did not acquire global dominance through its army. The contrast with Germany in 1914, by then well on its way to technological and industrial dominance in Europe, was stark: the Kaiser and his myopic generals equated power with military might. For Britain, strength was economic strength, neatly summed up by *The Times* in 1859: an abundance 'of employment, wages, material progress, increased population, and wealth'. That would cover the cost of 'several wars' – but only to prevent trade and its necessary accompaniment, peace, being threatened.[49] The great European powers of the 19th century – Russia, Prussia, Austria-Hungary, France – all had armies much larger than Britain's, but that, as many Britons observed, was partly because they were so intent on fighting each other.

The effects of Cromwell's rule by Major-Generals rang down the centuries in the British psyche. As the Duke of Wellington observed, 'Depend upon it, the only way to keep an army in this country is out of sight.' By the mid-19th century, while the case for reforming armed forces that often seemed just a social plaything for the upper classes was often noted, the 'almost certain' continuing economic growth and the continuous 'progress' suggested, according to the *Morning Post* in 1868, that 'the sound common sense of the country' would not be rousing public opinion in a time of peace to be more militaristic. As many as 71 MPs had been officers as the Crimean War began, but that was partly a consequence of the class from which they came. Lord Cardwell, for six years Secretary of State for War in Gladstone's first Cabinet (1868–74), was a barrister before embarking on a political career (there were 107 lawyer MPs in 1853), but conscientiously studied military matters and was respectful of those with military experience. If Parliament did experience some lobbies, it – and its military members – were far too individualistic to have much more than their own opinions. Apart from his religious beliefs, Gladstone was a politicians' politician, noting how Prussian professional soldiers crushed France and how a pragmatic protection of Britain's global interests could justify abolition of the purchase of officer commissions as a liberalizing, democratic reform. Cardwell engineered the reform, which also included the creation of British-based reserve forces with skills obtained in short-term service and a more efficient centre in the War Office.[50]

Moreover, the Queen's first cousin, the Duke of Cambridge, Commander-in-Chief of the Army for nearly 40 years from 1856, now became subordinate to the Secretary of State for War. As the *Leeds Mercury* noted towards the end of his career, 'No one will suspect the Duke of Cambridge of too much sympathy with our modern ideas of progress.' The Duke was explicit that he could not see why 'fine old institutions, which have done their duty well' should be changed just for 'new-fangled notions'. The fact that reform came at all reflected the wider change of subordinating the authority of the Crown to the authority of Parliament, and the even wider change involved in transition of power to the middle classes. Several decades before Cardwell's reforms, Thackeray's *Vanity Fair* (1848) showed us an army with the empty-headed Rawdon Crawley, son of a baronet, and George Osborne, self-loving vain son of a merchant, if one who was a fast learner of aristocratic ways, but also the admirable grocer's son William Dobbin, 'gentleman' in character, but poor. Britain was almost ready for what Cardwell was to call 'the aristocracy of merit and professional talent', 'the true aristocracy'.[51] And Cardwell was himself one of the first of Jowett's pupils to have the skills to run a global empire. The army was not quite like other professions, but it was no accident that change occurred in the decades in which solicitors and pharmacists, dentists, vets and patent agents all became professionalized.

Much still needed to be learned about modern warfare, soon to become war of whole populations in 1914; it was also expressed in a completely opposite experience than world war – Kitchener, in 1900, experienced defeat by a small force of 'stinking' Boers who, he said, hadn't stood up to a fair fight. Meantime, there is a strong sense that it was a small group of far-sighted individuals who acted as pioneers slowly gathering support against inertia by their visible achievements. The illegitimate Sir John Burgoyne (1782–1871), Director of the Royal Engineers, took his brilliant engineering skills to conflicts all over the world, along the way proposing a uniform system of Imperial weights and measures as early as 1834, or advising the government, who were faced with a decision about broad and narrow gauge railway companies in the 1840s. Fresh water supplies, roads through jungles, innumerable bridges, supply by sea and rail, telegraph communications – who could say that war was just about knowing your enemy when much of it was logistics and engineering. Those who were trained to arm themselves with technical and scientific skills at the Royal Military Academy at Woolwich had a substantial failure rate, but they did not need to purchase a commission.[52]

Sidney Herbert, who sent Florence Nightingale to Scutari and was father of George Herbert, whom we met in Mallock's country house, gave a brilliant speech in the House of Commons in June 1856, emphasizing that the engineers and artillery were 'the last corps upon which the hand of retrenchment ought to be placed'. We didn't need an army 'of the size of the great military nations of the continent'; we needed 'professional and practical knowledge'. Palmerston, in the same debate, while tactfully agreeing that the army was 'capable of great improvement', inadvertently pointed to that strange confection of Britishness in the period: it had world leaders in science and engineers, but also – as Palmerston casually pointed out – the Duke of Wellington, who liked to take his officers hunting because that enabled him to judge their 'quickness of eye, rapidity of decision-making and hardiness under difficulties'. Such a view, in Britain, somehow got reconciled with what Disraeli, three years earlier, had declared: war and defence, like everything else, needed to take account of 'the application of science to the business of life'.[53]

Thomas Escott, looking back in 1916, got carried away in describing the changes: 'Farewell, therefore, for ever the dashing leaders of foot and horse who learned how to lead their men to victory on the playing fields of Eton.' But there were for the first time senior British officers like Sir George Grove (1839–1920), a Balliol graduate with a Maths first, fluent in communication and with impressive plans for military training. Much remained unchanged, but in calibre we are a long way from the Duke of Wellington, untroubled by having enlisted men who tended to be the drunkest and worst villagers, by the time Lord Wolseley – Commander-in-Chief for five years after the Duke of Cambridge – visited Wellington Barracks on Christmas Day 1895, to 'taste the pudding and test the comforts'.[54]

What was the view from outside the elites? One of the few dangers of so many more people learning to read is that it gave them an unrealistic view of warfare. Creasey's *Fifteen Decisive Battles of the World* went through 31 editions in the three decades after 1852. While some military failures in Asia and Africa seemed shocking, the great growth of a popular press and the sense of adventure fostered by books about the Empire did encourage an unpleasant jingoism in the last decades of the 19th century. It helped that the army had been replaced by a professional police force in maintaining order at home and was usually engaged in distant parts of the world, an easy source of heroic myths and race prejudices (though there was some true heroism, too). Idealist voices, not so many, hoped for peace and often argued, as the *Midland Progressionist* had in the late 1840s, that it was the people who bore the burden of paying the war debt and maintaining the Army establishment.

If there remained a suspicion of military people in politics in Britain, in a global power they offered useful skills, not all in fighting. Mathematician, linguist and artist Major-General Sir John Ardagh (1840–1907) was involved in the judgments of frontier commissions – Bulgaria in the Balkans and also the Turko-Greek frontier; he also acted as private secretary to the Viceroy of India, Lord Lansdowne (1888–94). But there was also the reinforcement of numbers provided by the voluntary or non-voluntary support of indigenous peoples. When Victoria came to the throne, there were perhaps 26,500 Company troops in India; 50 years later, after she became Empress and in the year of her Diamond Jubilee in 1897, there were under 75,000 British troops, but nearly 130,000 Indian.[55] At the same time, money could sometimes be saved if colonies looked after their own security. Cardwell withdrew forces from Australia, New Zealand and Canada, save for one naval base.

The navy has been the missing part of our military story, yet it was fundamental for obvious reasons: there would have been no global trading dominance or Empire without it. Who else would protect the merchant fleet or stop ships carrying slaves? While the defeat of Napoleon had for a time led to the reduction of both army and naval forces, the Emperor had himself given the clue in St Helena: Britain should focus on its marine, 'the real force of your country'. It was even sufficient – or so Lord Esher argued, if not entirely convincingly, not long after the Victorian era ended – to 'deal with home defence, not the army's job'.[56] The crucial point was that through the 19th century, the navy could not be attacked either by submarines or from the air; that rapidly changed in the new century.

Along the way, though life at sea was never less than tough, new measures were introduced – to protect from scurvy by a better diet, find better ways to store water and, as early as 1838, to allow libraries. Reforms in the 1850s also gave more promotional opportunities for petty officers, even paid leave for some. In 1859–60, supplies for the navy were set approximately half as much again as they were for the army. Even if the Asquith Government, on the outbreak of the First World War, badly underestimated the number of soldiers that would be needed on the Continent, the Grand Fleet also provided the possibility for blockade of the enemy in a long war. As in every area of life, technology was transformative. A popular novel by Charles Lever, published in 1841, recalled how English troops en route to Portugal in the Peninsular War were becalmed and the sailing ships 'lay a mere log upon the water'.[57] Steam power spectacularly changed that, and all naval vessels effectively became obsolete, with steam or without, once *Warrior*, the first ironclad battleship, was launched in 1860.

It is not difficult to criticize Victorian reform and professionalization as inadequate or unfair to some sections of society. But taking everything together, a massive change, setting principles for the future, had defeated inertia and prejudice. What previous society had spoken, as *The Gentleman's Magazine* did in 1850, of keeping 'steadily in view the importance of presenting facts'? Thomas Gradgrind, in Dickens's *Hard Times* (1853), made fun of educating the assumption that 'Facts alone are wanted in life', ignoring the reality that they were an essential starting point in the social reform Dickens supported. The efflorescence of scientific discovery, with its glimpses of prediction and control, was accompanied by a proliferation of learned societies whose members much of the time bridged that difficult gap between loving knowledge for its own sake and applying it practically. Often the supporting 'facts' were misleading, but over time that just led to more sophisticated efforts to make data as neutral as possible. In addition, the reality faced by census-takers in tenement flats, full of large, disorganized families and many itinerant residents, was a challenge: 'John dear', as the mother in one cartoon, surrounded by children of all ages, says to her husband with the census-taker at the door, 'don't forget the two babies'. But that disguises what a revolutionary new step had been taken in the nation's understanding of its own population.[58]

Together with much more ordered information, there had been other foundations of professionalization. Mill's prediction that he could foresee the time that competition would be indispensable to progress became a reality in the second half of the 19th century. And there was something just as important that was cultural and lasted until its steep 21st-century decline: probity in public office and probity in business, 'my word is my bond'. Would any judge today repeat what Baron Alderson said of financial crime: 'A greater or more serious offence could hardly be imagined in a great commercial community like this'? For this was a society in which Samuel Smiles could acknowledge that possession of money was power of sorts, but assert that 'public spirit and moral virtue' were powers, too, enablers of success.[59] Did everyone accept that in their behaviour? Of course not – but then a professional police force was also a Victorian invention, and after its initiation in London in 1829, spread throughout the country.

The new or reformed professions were peopled by elites inculcated in common values in reformed (up to a point) public schools and universities. It is easy to clothe the professionals with the word 'privilege'; they found work and lived in London and other prosperous areas, usually far from the industrial landscape. Elitist they were, but in many cases not highly motivated by money-making. That came later. Their work also provided the essential support for the modernized economy to flourish, while their values and skills, eventually embodied in public education, were to revolutionize opportunity for the poorer sections of the community in a way that would have been inconceivable at any previous time.

There was a less solemn area in which progress was made: leisure. The opportunities before the Victorian period were few: harvest celebrations, fairs, hymn-singing, communal religious conversation. But from the 1850s, half-day working on Saturday was introduced for some, and the Bank Holiday was introduced by an Act of 1871. Edwin Beard Budding's lawnmower (1830) made cricket, tennis, football possible or immeasurably better. Railways enabled trips to the seaside (it is hard to imagine Blackpool in 1800, its population numbered in hundreds and essential supplies arriving

41 The first international cricket tour: the English team heading for America by steamship, 1859. John Wisden, first player on the left in the middle row and later to be famous for his annual almanac, advised applying the heavy roller to the Atlantic waves. The team returned unbeaten, with a crowd of thousands in Philadelphia. Modern sport was on its way.

42 Along with sewers and railways, bridges, hotels, houses, hospitals and schools – in the 1860s making London's building its biggest industry, a massive, chaos-creating, magnificently energetic activity – we have the visible signs of the creation of modern leisure: musical entertainment in the Philharmonic Hall, Islington. 'This is, indeed, the age of progress', declared the Sunday newspaper, the *Era*, when it opened in 1860.

by cart twice a week from Preston); sightseers could visit Hampton Court free, thanks to Queen Victoria; the Tower did charge, but there were free days later in the century and annual visitorship in the hundreds of thousands. That might be labelled 'rational recreation' and 'self-improvement', like visits to free libraries and museums, but many learned fun for the first time, as they did also when Prince Albert popularized Christmas and music halls proliferated after 1850. Thomas Cook began with excursions in England in 1841, but with the opening up of the world, travel provided a mix of adventure, pleasure and the pursuit of riches. As Theodor Fontane said in 1852: 'Anyone who wishes to be a travelled man in the present day must have drunk tea in China and have worn real Nanking trousers; he must have dug for gold in Australia and have taken part in a lynching in California, must recognize the difference in size between a Patagonian and a Laplander.'[60] That to start.

CHAPTER 7

'THE MARCH OF INTELLECT'

COMMUNICATING REASON AND FAITH

When Benjamin Jowett – Dr Jenkinson – was, to an extent, satirized in W.H. Mallock's house party, with which this book began, it was partly because Mallock was cross with him. He felt that, at Oxford, Jowett had treated him as a mere dilettante and idler who would bring disgrace on Balliol by coming to grief in the schools (he didn't, and won the coveted Newdigate prize for poetry, awarded at different times to John Ruskin, Matthew Arnold and Oscar Wilde). Mallock had already been working on *The New Republic* as an undergraduate, modelling the country house discussions on Plato's *Republic* and other books in which circles of friends discuss philosophy, religion, art, society. His desire for what he called 'polite antagonism' as a means of exploring had turned into the essential question at the heart of Victorian progress: 'the rational aim of life, and the manner in which a definite supernatural faith was essential, extraneous, or positively prejudicial to this.'[1]

There was at least a distinct chance that you would find the answer next to Victoria railway station in the 1870s. The station, to which access by trains was obtained on the first railway bridge to cross the Thames, was developed by the contractor Sir John Kelk, who more or less simultaneously worked on constructing the grandest hotel London had yet seen: a five-storey edifice of yellow brick and Bath stone with a French pavilion roof, with plenty of gold and grand marble archways internally. This was the Grosvenor Hotel, completed in 1862.

The architects, father and son of the same name, were James Knowles. The father had lost out to Sir Charles Barry when competing for the new Houses of Parliament; the son, not at all strange for the time in being torn between architecture and literary society, designed his friend Tennyson's home at Aldworth without a fee. He was also, for much of the 1870s, editor of the influential *Contemporary Review*.

During that decade, between the months of November and July – the dates during which Parliament sat – you might have encountered at the

43 The Grosvenor, the first hotel in Britain to have rooms with a separate bathroom, designed to be London's 'grandest hotel', a building like a Parisian palace next to a railway station that itself aspired to grandeur. The Grosvenor's design was shown at the Royal Academy Summer Exhibition in 1860. Was this perhaps the place where life's great issues would be resolved?

Grosvenor Hotel a number of Mallock's country-house guests, Mr Storks (T.H. Huxley), Mr Stockton (John Tyndall, the experimental scientist), Mr Herbert (John Ruskin), as well as Robert Lowe, another pupil of Jowett's, fresh from beating Walter Bagehot to become the first MP for the University of London (a constituency created by the Reform Bill he had so opposed in 1867) and installed as Gladstone's Chancellor of the Exchequer. You might also have seen Bagehot and Gladstone themselves; or Tennyson; or the formidable Catholic Archbishop of Westminster, Henry Edward Manning.

They were to debate what Henry Sidgwick – polymathic super-brain, Cambridge philosopher and earnest proponent of higher education for women – called 'the great questions that concern them as a rational being' via exchange between people of 'diverse positions'. As another member, the prominent Liberal John Morley, said of Sidgwick, 'If any Englishman ever belonged to the household of Socrates, Sidgwick was he.' The debates took place at dinners of the Metaphysical Society, founded in 1869 at the suggestion of the Grosvenor's architect, James Knowles.[2] Like so many earnest Victorian debates, however elevated by intellect, the Society had some strong grounding in the real world: the challenge to almost two thousand years of Christian faith – and the social, ethical, legal, institutional frameworks attached to that – by multiple scientific discoveries. Could the idea of Creation survive what geology was newly revealing? Where did a deity fit into Darwin's evidence of evolution? After all, as Morley said, Darwin was revealing his 'zoological conclusions' in his *The Descent of Man* (1871) at the very moment the Paris Commune was making the Paris sky red with flames.[3] Where now did authority lie? What would the moral principles – without which society would fragment – be based upon?

There was no single answer, as Metaphysical Society discussions were to demonstrate. You could ignore what science had discovered about the universe; perhaps reading Trollope and imagining a landscape of country parsonages might be a whole lot more comforting. You could retreat (or advance) into the world of Roman Catholicism, as Cardinal Newman did. You could try to remove 'incrustations' from Christianity, as Jowett and six other writers did in *Essays and Reviews* in 1860 and animate press, government, university and secular opinion, with 'hell' discussed in court by the Lord Chancellor, who wisely (though with the dissent of the Archbishops) decided that it was not for the tribunal over which he presided to adjudicate on its existence. 'Hell was dismissed, with costs,' as one wit put it. Or you could leave everything open for discussion by being an agnostic, a term coined by Mallock's Mr Storks (T.H. Huxley) at a dinner of the Metaphysical Society. The square-jawed Huxley, less simple than he imagined himself, greedy for debate but scornful of sophistry, would not allow anything that smacked of mysticism, but was very alive to morality. First, perhaps, you needed to decide what value to give to a science, a subject over which Huxley and Matthew Arnold, who politely declined membership of the Metaphysical Society, had long debates. They did not agree, and Arnold was no scientist, but – as a good Victorian – he saw the virtue of observation and experiment that could be verified: we 'can see that it is so.'

Matthew Arnold beautifully exemplified a range of voices that fundamentally rejected the idea that material progress was sufficient to stand for all progress. In the 1850s, his poetry gave plenty of clues to the challenges created by the clash of science and religion, what he saw as a lack of moral purpose and the unquestioning way 'middle-class man', as he later put it in *Friendship's Garland* (1871), 'thinks it is the highest pitch of development and civilisation when his letters are carried twelve times a day from Islington to Camberwell', with trains running every quarter of an hour from one 'illiberal, dismal life' to another.

44 A month after Matthew Arnold died in 1888 – this photograph sees him perhaps five years before that – Benjamin Jowett described him as 'The most sensible man of genius whom I have ever known.' He was, and he wasn't. Nobody so well expressed the idea that unless material progress was matched by an education grounded in morality and cultural understanding, the world was heading for disaster. But it was a message of too elitist a kind for the coming age of the masses.

He found himself, in *The Grande Chartreuse*, first published in *Fraser's Magazine* in 1855, 'Wandering between two worlds, one dead, / The other powerless to be born.' There is a sadness about Arnold: the saintly Cardinal Newman could lose his temper, Carlyle could rarely keep his, but Arnold, as G.K. Chesterton observed, kept 'a smile of heart-broken forbearance.'[4]

As he grew older, his focus on education helped to make him more practical, and even if his emphasis was on 'a cultured, liberalized, ennobled, transformed middle class', that could also be a model for working-class aspiration. His own reports on elementary schools in poverty-stricken neighbourhoods encouraged the importance of order, light, air and cleanliness as essentials for the environment in which education took place.[5]

Formative experiences count. In the wake of revolutionary disturbances in spring 1848 in Sicily, in Paris, in Germany, in mainland Italy and the fall of the mighty Chancellor Metternich in Austria, the 26-year-old Arnold travelled extensively in Europe that autumn and again in spring 1849. Disturbances over widening the franchise in Hyde Park reinforced the view later expressed in *Culture and Anarchy* (1869) that the 'rough' needed to learn the 'principle of authority' to avoid anarchy.[6] His fears were overdone, underestimating the desire of the lower classes – not brutalized by the system, but lacking enough of the good, value-full education Arnold supported – to take opportunities and not to threaten society instead. It was a general fault of many Victorian intellectuals to over-privilege elites: Carlyle supported 'the aristocracy of talent', and even John Stuart Mill had concerns about the 'tyranny of the majority'. But for Arnold, with characterizations of the aristocracy as Barbarians, the middle classes as complacent Philistines, and the Populace as a disorderly, untrained mess, social reforming zeal began with education. He noted often enough Marx's view that society would not change merely in response to enthusiasm for reform.

Arnold was right that when the once Radical MP John Roebuck kept declaring that 'every man in England' had the right of saying what he liked, that alone didn't get to the fundamentals: what was the moral structure underpinning that freedom? As we shall see in Chapter 9, by the time Arnold had completed his 35 years as a School Inspector in 1886, the acknowledgment that the whole of society must be educated changed all previous history. John Morley wisely observed of Arnold that 'He did not willingly talk about nothing, which might seem a peculiarly modest merit, if it was not so uncommon'. Morley was an uncommonly empathetic politician. There was not much room for that after the First World War devastated minds, as well as bodies and landscapes. Herbert Asquith, for more than eight years Prime Minister in the new century, misunderstood the important role for both thinkers and doers when, in 1919, he suggested Arnold was not motivated so much by 'moral resentment at the social paradoxes of his time [evidently, politicians had also learned to be mealie-mouthed] as intellectual irritation and impatience at the stupidity and sterility of contemporary life', as exemplified by the Philistine bourgeoisie: narrow in intellect and spiritual outlook, on a barren treadmill of routine, absorbed in the superficiality of goods, smug and sordidly complacent. Asquith could also see the agonizing doubt of Victorians, but neither their smugness, nor their paradoxical self-doubt, dented the basic Victorian zeitgeist of restlessly seeking progress.[7]

In the case of the youngest member of the Metaphysical Society, W.K. Clifford (Mallock's Mr Saunders) – proposed by Huxley in 1874, soon after he became Professor of Mathematics at University College London aged 29 – there had already been abundant evidence that he was one of the cleverest people who ever lived, with an extraordinary personality to match. Even Mallock, who hated him for his hostility to 'everything that in general the world calls religion', and could not resist describing him as 'uncouth and careless in manner and dress', with a laugh that 'knew no conventional restraints', had to admit that his moral behaviour would put many Christians to shame, a man who if he met his worst foe suddenly would have as first impulse the desire to shake hands with him.[8]

45 When W.K. Clifford died in 1879, *Popular Science Monthly* pointed to his imaginative ability to communicate 'ideas into forms of wonderful simplicity'. The appetite that was created by Clifford and his fellow scientists was reflected in the range of topics in that year in the same magazine, ranging from the development of the house fly to chloral and other narcotics, from dry rot to inherited disease.

Clifford told the long-serving Master of Trinity College, Cambridge, William Whewell, that his nature was to touch nothing without leaving some stamp of invention upon it. It helped that he had one of those mysterious qualities associated with genius: the ability to see abstractions as vivid pictures. His private tutor at Cambridge, the Rev. Percival Frost, had no success in persuading him to spend more time on his examination subjects; if he wanted to read mathematical papers in other languages, he just viewed an unfamiliar language as a riddle to be solved – in addition to French and German, Spanish was learned in a tour of the Pyrenees, Arabic was begun in Algiers in 1876; he was fluent in modern Greek and curious about Sanskrit and hieroglyphics.[9]

Frederick Pollock, later best known for his history of English law before Edward I, co-authored with the father of English legal history, Frederic Maitland, was wrestling in the Long Vacation of 1866 with Ivory's theorem concerning the attractions of an ellipsoid and how it relates to the analytical treatment of statics (a branch of mechanics when bodies are at rest, forces in equilibrium). He was finding it 'a grind': the chain of symbolic proof seemed artificial and dead, in that it compelled understanding but failed to satisfy the reason.[10]

Out for a walk with Clifford, the latter seemed able to explain merely by telling what he saw. Without diagram or symbolic aid, he described the geometrical conditions on which the solution depended. It only required to see them as real and evident facts, without need to deduce logical consequences. Was this intellectual games-playing? No. At root, it was arguing that science knew no limits; as Clifford put it in a lecture published in the *Fortnightly Review* in 1874, science under human control (that was important) was unbounded in the 'purifying and organising work' it could do – 'she ploughs up weed and briar; from her footsteps behind her grow up corn and healing flowers; and no corner is far enough to escape her furrow'. He did not see science as an accompaniment or condition of human progress; it was progress itself.[11]

Although Clifford was apolitical – beyond a youthful enthusiasm, shared with others, for Mazzini's republican nationalism and the unification of Italy, which made him the priest of evolution – his atheism takes us to the heart of the 19th-century debate (which became a 20th- and 21st-century debate): if religion was going to die, what moral structures could replace it? As Dostoevsky's *The Brothers Karamazov* was to ask: if God does not exist, is everything permitted?[12] Clifford's importance was that he showed there was, intellectually, a serious alternative. He had a High Church upbringing in Exeter, with a father who supplied devotional literature to churchmen. In Cambridge, he kept a crucifix on his bedroom wall when he first became a Fellow (though one morning – a possibly apocryphal but plausible story – the crucifix inverted, and a Phrygian cap of liberty was placed upon it). But Clifford came to believe that the full domain of science was 'all possible human knowledge', which could then rightly be used 'to guide human conduct'.

Mallock, who was bitterly opposed to him, suggested he was replacing the Bible with the Propositions of Euclid. In fact, Clifford was arguing that while the earth would eventually be destroyed (there was scientific evidence for that), in the meantime science could ameliorate the human condition, while history provided lessons for conduct. The long struggles of both Jews and Christians taught the weakness of solitary and selfish effort. They had given us the morality of the Sermon on the Mount. Now we could apply it consciously and, with the aid of science, improve the secular social organism, eventually encompassing the whole human race.[13]

Here was a kind of optimism denied both to those in the past (constrained by religious dogma and sanction) and in practice denied to those in the future (because Clifford's belief that scientific progress – free enquiry – would guide us in knowing the difference between truth and falsehood, right and wrong, was largely naïve). Clifford's statement of *The Ethics of Belief* was presented to the Metaphysical Society in 1876 and then published in January 1877 with modifications in the *Contemporary Review*. It was a dangerous document – even a questioning society would not easily abandon nearly 2,000 years of Christian belief – and the Editor of the magazine, James Knowles, lost his job.[14]

In an earlier essay, Clifford related human morality to the 'tribal self': Darwinian natural selection, 'in the long run', preserved those tribes that 'have approved the right things', which gave advantage in the struggle for existence. In *The Ethics of Belief*, he rooted part of the argument in scientific good sense. Why did Australians continue to tie their hatchets to the side of the handle when the Birmingham fitter had made a hole for the purpose? Call in question 'the authority of tradition', invent or learn something better, ask further questions. This was the moment in history when you could link optimism to progress, and 'the labours and questionings of honest and brave men' would build 'the fabric of known truth to a glory which we in this generation can neither hope for nor imagine'. The wry laugh, or the scorn, these ideas might receive from the perspective of the 2020s is understandable, but also a failure to engage with how it felt then.

This is not to say that, in a probing, changing, animating cockpit of ideas, everyone agreed. Ruskin, lecturing about Ezekiel, complained about education by 'mellifluous railroad whistles', developed by 'the equally mellifluous theology of Professor Clifford, and other cornerstones of recent science', which feed 'on the Petroleum truth of such oil as they strike among flinty rocks'. Matthew Arnold described himself half-sighing, half-smiling at what he called Clifford's hopeless inexperience of youth, irredeemable by any cleverness.[15]

In fact, this was in some sense an objection to what we would find strange, since we separate sciences and humanities. The sciences were becoming professionalized in Victorian Britain, but scientists engaged in the same debates as literary intellectuals about the effects of scientific materialism on society and belief. You would find Thomas Hardy and George Eliot at Clifford's home for Sunday gatherings. To many, Darwin's ideas of natural selection seemed deeply dehumanizing; Clifford was beguiled by evolution, but not if it took romance out of nature; he took it rather as an opportunity to make 'a more perfect cosmos'. Herbert Spencer, himself often accused today of dehumanizing by applying scientific method to the story of human society, actually suggested in *Principles of Psychology* (1855) that aesthetics and humane culture would result from moving on from sheer survival.[16]

Men of action, men of ideas also came together more naturally than they would do today, though Sidgwick, in an article on 'The Prophet of Culture' – Matthew Arnold – in 1867, while acknowledging that Arnold's criticisms of contemporary culture had value, suggested that 'culture' was 'uncomfortably eager to excuse its own evident incapacity for action'. Nevertheless, it was a distinctive feature of Victorian intellectual life that it was not just (as Bagehot had it) 'the age of discussion', but one in which thinkers, talkers, writers could feel that they had the chance to change the world. The playwright Charles Brookfield, looking back on his childhood home (his mother had become Thackeray's lover), noted that 'the society of the talented', not 'solitary grandeur', was the favoured environment.[17] The Athenaeum, in Pall Mall, having Sir Humphry Davy as its first Chairman and Faraday as its first

Secretary, used its premises to experiment with gas lighting, open-fire gas burners and electricity, Faraday inventing an apparatus specifically to deal with the dire effect gas burners had on leather-bound books. To an extent, in the second half of the 19th century, the division between Bentham's basic emphasis on utility and organizational efficiency, but essential blindness to the role played by the irrational and emotional in human affairs, was close at times to being reconciled with Coleridge's clerisy, rule by the learned seeking meaning. That did not imply consensus – disagreements, heated disagreements, lay in all directions – but for a while we can hear a bold confidence that all will be known about the universe and understood about the individuals and the societies that exist in it.

That mood was brief – the very range of discoveries made, knowledge uncovered and actions taken encouraged a new relativism that, in the 20th century, often threatened to create a vacuum, allowing those with power to close down debate entirely. Already the sheer amount of new knowledge at the middle of the 19th century made it impossible (so, as we have seen, George Cornewall Lewis argued in 1849) for any one person to be 'competent judge on all subjects'.[18] That was true, but it did not stop the intellectual community from connecting and stirring together social and political life, science, the study of the past, living in the present, making the future, using the literary imagination, belief, lack of belief, philosophy. The fragmented culture that came after the Victorians lived in a different universe and along the way lost or destroyed an important Victorian strength, what George Eliot called 'that idea of duty' – the 'recognition of something to be lived far beyond the mere satisfaction of self' – which a character in *Scenes of Clerical Life* says we owe to Evangelicalism.[19]

Might it be said that we are just talking about the incestuous gatherings of tiny numbers of people, probably living in London and removed from the reality of how life was for the vast majority? Matthew Arnold describing the Athenaeum as 'a place at which I enjoy something resembling beatitude'[20] might suggest so, though any social institution that elects Charles Dickens and Charles Darwin on the same day stands a chance of changing the world. If this was a conspiracy, it was a conspiracy of brilliant souls; they debated every conceivable subject, and to suggest they had homogeneity of expression would be absurd; they debated very often, and in each other's homes, implying social homogeneity, but accepting middle- or upper-class lifestyles did not confirm that you were born into them. The Athenaeum, founded in London in 1824, was rapidly joined by other Athenaeums, in Derby or Warwick or Brighton. In Manchester, where James Heywood was

President of its Athenaeum (1835), following his older brother Benjamin's foundation of the Manchester Mechanics' Institute ten years before, a target was the youthful self-help enthusiasm of the growing numbers introduced to commercial activities (an army of clerks, for example). Reading, learning, discussing was a key part of the energy of the age. Learning a trade remained important; using learning to transform a life became an enthusiasm. The Mechanics' Institute flourished and its building on Princess Street, opened in 1855, became the site of the inaugural meeting of the Trades Union Congress just thirteen years later.

Ideas didn't just live and die in Society drawing rooms. In Mallock's *New Republic*, Mr Stockton (John Tyndall), stresses the way the 'light of intellect' had moved on from laboratory or dissecting room to gild the dinner table or even the ballroom. In fact, Tyndall, from a humble background in County Carlow, Ireland, was one of those who were making it possible to shine in new urban environments. The real Tyndall was a member of the X Club, initiated by Huxley in 1864 and meeting in Albemarle Street in London. Here, those – Spencer was another – who wanted to explore how science ('untramelled by religious dogmas') affected everyday life and how public opinion was shaped in that context were focused on one thing: communication.

In the author's library is a long series of volumes of the monthly journal the *Nineteenth Century*, originally in the library of the Mechanics' Institute of the Royal Small Arms Manufactory, Enfield Lock. While the various serious weekly, fortnightly, monthly and quarterly journals of the Victorian period had their political biases and – without large circulations – depended on their much wider readership using libraries, the most striking thing about them was to demonstrate that this was a society interested in everything. The December 1850 *Quarterly Review* switched happily and earnestly from the latest views on animal breeding and rearing poultry to women in 18th-century France, from Imperial Rome to the sanitary conditions of the City of London, from the latest biography of Calvin to worries about 'the defenceless state of the country'.[21] Free speech could generate opprobrium, but compared to all previous history, as well as today in large parts of the world, transgressive opinions flourished among those 'stuffy Victorians' as liberalism grew ever stronger.

Viscount Amberley, when speaking to the Dialectical Society in 1868, the year of its foundation, on 'the principle of absolute liberty of thought and speech', appeared to be recommending abortion in some circumstances. The medical establishment gave an irate reaction to his 'Insult to the Medical Profession', shaming women and making them accomplices to unnatural crimes. We might observe that it remained common in the 19th century for women to be 'protected' by making them suffer, but the historical significance lay in the fact that Amberley had opened up the debate. When Queen Victoria was chloroformed giving birth in 1853, religious protesters could quote Genesis 3.16 – 'in pain you shall bring forth children'. Again, objections to change were common, but Victorians either made the future or set up agendas for it in every area of life. 'The stir and conflict in which we live' had barely begun, as Bagehot declared in an essay on 18th-century complacency. Even Trollope, more conservative than his own self-description in his autobiography as 'a conservative liberal' and well aware that politics is about practicality, allows Plantagenet Palliser to 'declare that equality is a dream' – but 'sometimes one likes to dream'.[22]

Of course, some of the time middle-class Victorian intellectuals debated in their own homes, far removed from the lives of the mass of the population. George Eliot gave an effective perspective on that, expressed in *George Eliot's Life*, edited by her husband, John Cross: 'She often thought it wisest not to raise too ambitious an ideal, especially for young people, but to impress on ordinary natures the immense possibilities of making a small home circle brighter and better.' All were born to that, even if few were suited to do the great work of the world. Besides, if every 'Home, Sweet Home' engaged in the exchange of ideas, the net result was a civilized nation. After *Adam Bede* was a great success – with congratulations from Dickens, Faraday, J.A. Froude,

46 Portraits – this one by Samuel Laurence from 1860 – were not kind to George Eliot. Henry James's encapsulating 'magnificently ugly' failed to capture the tenderness her face revealed to many others in person. Eliot's brilliance lay in the guileless strength, at its best expressed kindly, with which she tried to understand. In *Adam Bede* (Ch.52), she observes that 'the old world' was 'happy in his inability to know the causes of things, preferring the things themselves'. Victorians chose to find out.

Herbert Spencer ('quite an enthusiastic letter') and many others – her own opinions, in private and in public, are perpetually aired in a form of controlled ferment. She criticizes Darwin's *Origin of Species* when it is first published, 'not impressive, from want of luminous and orderly presentation', with a paucity of 'illustrative facts', 'but it will have a great effect on the scientific world, causing a thorough and open discussion of a question about which hitherto we have felt timid'. She may have seen herself as neither optimist or pessimist, but in the centre ground (her word was 'meliorist', the idea that the world does improve and that human agency can improve it the more), yet saw Darwin's ideas as a step 'towards brave clearness and honesty'.[23]

The very intensity of all this made it easy to caricature. Thomas Escott, who attended her salon with Robert Browning on a number of occasions, describes being ushered in with 'worshipping proprietorship' by her live-in partner George Lewes, giving something between a nod and a sigh to signify where to leave hats and umbrellas, and a nod towards a vase that Escott calls 'votive flowers to the goddess'. He thought it more like a religious ceremony than a social reunion, with Eliot at the centre of a little crowd of worshippers of whom only a few were permitted to hold conversation with her. The others, who included Darwin, were liable to a hush of rebuke from Lewes if speaking too loudly, or speaking at all when Eliot was speaking. All this was overdone. The novelist and poet Matilda Betham-Edwards found her subdued, but with a penetrating light shining from large dark eyes set against a white, marble-like complexion. Yes, it was Titania and Puck – she queen-like, effortless,

47 Great issues of literature, philosophy, science, together with belief in the unity of intellectual life, were made for the restless mind of George Henry Lewes, George Eliot's soulmate. Medicine, acting, business and experimental physiology were at one time or another his preoccupations; journalism, philosophy, writing fiction or biography, amateur but thoughtful scientific observations found fruition in his five-volume, very Victorian *The Problems of Life and Mind* (1874–79).

Lewes anticipating her behests here, there and everywhere – but no guests were neglected. But what guests! Poets, artists, men of letters, scientists, philosophers – she herself was introduced to 'Herr Liebreich, the discoverer of chloral'. That was not wholly true (Liebig had made the discovery in 1831), but Oscar Liebreich had developed its use as an anaesthetic and what Victorians called 'hypnotic'. According to Eliot's own account, in the 1850s the day's reading might include Spinoza's *Ethics*, Sydney Smith's *Letters*, Boswell, Whewell's *History of the Inductive Sciences*, the *Odyssey*, Heine's *Reisebilder*, all capped by a walk over Primrose Hill with George, discussing Plato and Aristotle.[24]

It would be wrong to see all this as irrelevant to everyday life. The German-born writer Mathilde Blind observed that though the young 'Miss Evans' had absorbed the social utopianism of St Simon and Proudhon when living near Geneva for eight months; 'she believed in progress only as the result of evolution, not revolution'. Her essay on 'The National History of German Life' focused on the 'notable failure of revolutionary attempts conducted from the point of view of abstract democratic and socialistic theories'. Her novel *Felix Holt* (1866) was set at the time of the Great Reform Act in 1832 and her subsequent – after the 1867 Reform Act – article in *Blackwood's Magazine*, 'Address to Working Men, by Felix Holt', emphasized that some ills were not curable, but others were, not by uprooting but by persistent cultivation of 'knowledge, industry, judgement, sobriety, and patience'. We might interpret that as 'education, and its accompanying values, creates a civilized society'.

Back in 1851, when the young Mary Ann Evans had come to live and work in the house at 142 Strand that John Chapman had leased, the prospectus for the *Westminster Review* declared that it was about 'fearlessness of investigation', yet recognized that 'truth' could be understood in different ways and that there should be an independent section for those who did not agree with the Editors. The prospectus spoke of 'the Law of Progress' and linked ideas of evolution, reform of social ills and meritocracy. John Stuart Mill actually criticized it for being too conservative, unconvincingly so, since it pushed for a national educational system, franchise extension, big reforms of the judiciary and courts, reforming and opening up the universities, constitutional government in the colonies. Talking shops – whether in magazines, public lectures and meetings, home salons, private letter exchanges, friends' conversation – provided goals, as well as methods, all linked to progress, for social change. Scholars debate the nature of Eliot's relationship with Lewes (married but living with her) and Cross (whom she married after Lewes died). But while that is not trivial, it is not the essence of Victorian intellectual life, nor revealing of how important it was to progressing society.[25]

When Benjamin Jowett died in 1893, a special train was laid on from Paddington to the Oxford funeral service for the man once described as 'mentor-in-chief' of the Victorian golden age. He had not taught a particular point of view, still less an ideology: the skills – of independent thinking and quick-thinking versatility in all situations – were intended for those of merit who would take them to the top of the professions and public service. This might mean a cacophony of voices, but a vigorous cacophony, and one held together by an overriding idea. J.A. Froude summed it up in December 1870: 'Amidst the varied reflections which the nineteenth century is in the habit of making on its condition and prospects, there is one common opinion on which all parties coincide – that we live in an era of progress.'[26]

In one respect, Jowett's ideas were rooted in Continental intellectual traditions that were to lead Europe into a very different direction in the 20th century. He responded to Hegel's and Kant's (and Plato's – Jowett translated Plato) idea that 'the state' was an agent of moral and social progress, and made three trips to Germany in the 1840s to explore the force of new German scholarship on biblical and Classical texts – 'German infidelity', as some labelled it. But he discerned that if you wanted the state to act for 'the common good', you help the brightest to become deeply committed to public service.

> My heart leaps up when I behold
> A rainbow over Balliol Hall,
> As though the Cosmos was controlled
> By Dr Jowett after all.[27]

There was nowhere closed to this small, apparently shy, connoisseur of silences that spoke volumes.

The challenges of specialization were invented by the Age of Progress – so much was discovered – but were left to the future to grapple with, or fail to grapple with, partly because cross-disciplinary collaboration became frowned upon by specialists, while ironically it had been one of the greatest strengths of intellectual communities in Victorian times. For now, though scientists were not totally secure in their status (unlike doctors, or lawyers or clerics, they had no institutional career structure), they could naturally form part of discussions involving politics, economics, social reform, theology, or philosophy, especially because scientific method was eagerly being adopted by disciplines other than science – economics or the study of society, for example. That was another legacy of the Age of Progress: could you sensibly analyse human behaviour via techniques scientists applied to inanimate objects?

Mallock's Mr Stockton, John Tyndall, the man who first explained why the sky is blue, turned that question around when addressing his students about 'the future culture of the world' by applauding the right the poet feels 'to look for that heightening and brightening of life which so many of us need…. Void of offence to science, he may freely deal with conceptions which science shuns'.[28] Not that he denied science's power to create a sense of wonder. To the contrary, he was keen to show that it could illuminate every aspect of the world; it was not something that should remain in isolation, rather be combined with all other efforts to better human lives. Early in his career, when teaching at the University of Marburg in Hesse-Cassel in 1850, he confided to his diary the regret that he had now to turn from Tennyson ('to whom I had appealed for inspiration') to the dry French mathematician Lefébure de Fourcy.[29] As he wrote to Tennyson's son, Hallam, after the poet's death, 'Your father's interest in science was profound, but not, I believe, unmingled with fear of its "materialistic" tendencies.' Effectively, in a wider context, he was suggesting that if poets followed science and scientists read poetry, the debates about progress would become the stronger. As a boy, Tyndall had read Carlyle's *Past and Present*, where he noted a line from Tennyson that not only sparked an interest in the poet, but also gave him the view that reading non-scientific literature acted as a spur to 'the pursuit of science'. A protégé of Faraday, who encouraged him to look after his health, he came to love both poetry and nature. We might imagine him declaiming the former aloud as he battled up Stye Head Pass in Cumberland in torrential rain (without heed to Faraday's advice).

History is neither kind nor fair in whom it remembers. John Tyndall was more famous, some have suggested, than Darwin in the second half of the 19th century, but only today's scientists still find traces of his presence everywhere: for example, in the greenhouse effect, sterilization of food ('tyndallisation'), understanding fibre optics and anaesthesia (how to monitor the breathing of the anaesthetized patient). Tyndall had become Professor of Natural Philosophy (in his case, effectively 'physics') at the Royal Institution in 1853. He helped T.H. Huxley run the science section of the *Westminster Review*; Tyndall and Huxley together paved the way for the publication of Darwin's *On the Origin of Species* at the end of the decade.

And why was the sky blue? Tyndall showed experimentally how small atmospheric dust and vapour particles scattered the blue components of sunlight to create the effect. Although it wasn't exactly what we would understand now, did it matter? Well, his work certainly did matter for lighthouses and fog signals. Not all answers were forthcoming, but the starting point was taking on the big questions scientifically, as Tyndall did when he explained the connection between brain and body and asked whether there was a definable molecular condition in the brain that related to an experience in our consciousness. What felt so exciting about this activity was that it wasn't conducted in opposition (or with disregard) to the humanities. The way Mallock presented Tyndall and Huxley presaged C.P. Snow's by then accurate identification of 'Two Cultures' in the 1950s, but in Victorian Britain that was not properly an issue. The Executive Director of today's Tyndall Centre for Climate Change at UEA, Asher Minns, notes that – like Tyndall himself – the Centre is interdisciplinary, something that might just have been called a rounded education by those who moved education on in Victorian times.

A guiding principle for Tyndall – not a bad one in a reforming society devoted to progress – was summed up in his sentence, 'The only question for any man to ask is this: "Is this true or is it false?"' *Vanity Fair* caricatured him as a preacher in 1872, perhaps exaggerating his beard to the extent that his face seemed entirely surrounded by ever-expanding grey hair. But if so, this was not someone who came to the Grosvenor Hotel meetings of the Metaphysical Society from a cloistered pulpit, or a cloistered anywhere; some years before, he led one of the first expeditions to climb the Matterhorn, while fitting in an *ad hoc* study of glaciers (two glaciers, in Chile and Colorado, are named after him, as are two mountains – one in Tasmania, one in California). No wonder he found it difficult to sleep; an accidental overdose of chloral hydrate for insomnia was what finally killed him in 1893.

Tyndall (and other Victorian scientists) were mostly unmotivated by commerce, but in any case, the making of money seemed less troubling to the church than the way science was explicitly embracing 'the whole domain of cosmological theory'. Where did that leave theology? The Victorian decades were full of practical aids of all kinds, but finding different methods for operating lighthouses was a different matter from threatening religion's hold on understanding the universe, or even putting forward social and political ideas, as Tyndall did.

His was the kind of perpetual curiosity that animated the Metaphysical discussions. Has a frog a soul? The arguments for a future life. Euthanasia. Utilitarianism. Animal rights (it was not just humans, but at least some animals who could feel a lot better as a result of the Age of Progress – the world's first animal charity, what became the RSPCA, began in a London coffee shop in the Strand in 1824). These were some of the topics debated. Of course, it was the nature of super-talented, argumentative human beings to make wry comments about each other in private. John Ruskin wrote to his American friend Charles Eliot Norton – patrician reformer, soon to be appointed Professor of Art History at Harvard – that he had gone to hear Huxley's paper on 'a Frog's soul – or appearances of soul' and wanted to change the frog to a toad and also say something about the eyes, but Huxley wouldn't let himself be taken 'beyond legs'. He came away complaining of 'the frivolous pugnacity of the world', whether it was 'the vain dispute over that table' or 'the campaign in France' (this was the time, 1870, of the Franco-Prussian War). Robert Lowe 'only made jokes' (which sounds most unlikely).[30] This was mostly mischief – and Ruskin came back to frogs and their souls in his own later lectures and writings.

Mallock's picture of Ruskin (Mr Herbert), which he claimed was closer to reality than some of his other characters, perhaps reflects the fact that the real man was such a brilliant caricature of himself that fiction was not up for the task. By all accounts, however, Mallock was accurate about his voice, 'that

48 John Everett Millais braved Scottish midges and Scottish rain in the Trossachs near Stirling over the two summers of 1853 and 1854 to paint John Ruskin. His Pre-Raphaelite 'truth to nature' was matched by his sitter's ability to understand nature by close observation and write about it with something close to genius. The painting of the portrait itself had a life-changing consequence for Ruskin: Millais fell in love with his wife, Effie, whom he was himself to marry in 1855.

singular voice...which would often hold all the theatre breathless.... There was something strange and aerial in its exquisite modulations that seemed as if it came from a disconsolate spirit, hovering over the waters of Babylon and remembering Zion.'

In Mallock, Mr Herbert calls for 'putting a stop to this progress'. Blow up Manchester, Birmingham, Liverpool, Leeds, Wolverhampton. Destroy every railway and nearly every steam engine. And things of a like sort to prepare for a better state of society. But these sort of wild statements, whether by the fictional or the real Ruskin, only show him as the extreme expression of the concerns raised by the materialism and effects of industrialization, which prompted diverse voices to call for the other planks of progress: new moral structures for society and the reform of its institutions. As we might say, perhaps without as much conviction, money isn't everything.

Matthew Arnold was probably right to observe that Ruskin was too febrile and too irritable to create perfect order out of what he studied and discussed, but nevertheless also said (of a passage in *Modern Painters*) that it was 'the highest point to which the art of prose can ever hope to reach'. He described Ruskin at a London dinner party in 1877 as looking 'very slight and very spiritual.... He gains much by evening dress, plain black and white and by his fancy being forbidden to range through the world of coloured cravats.'[31] Ruskin favoured plain blue. Here was a man who could display knowledge, as if he were a scientist, of clouds or rocks or trees or birds or snakes – but who could also describe a snake unforgettably as a 'running brook of horror on the ground'. He wrote about peasant weaving and naval architecture, English poetry and Austrian tyranny, Christian ethics and Greek coins. It says much for the Age of Progress that it could accommodate someone fiercely individualistic who still believed that the self could be perfected within society. That was a nourishing optimism that was to be destroyed for us by Freudian ideas of perfection of self from within, from which we can trace a line forward to the social media-induced evolution of individualism into narcissism of a dangerously authoritarian kind today.

We have a description of a paper given by Ruskin to the Metaphysical Society on miracles in a letter by the Bishop of Peterborough (and later Archbishop of York), William Connor Magee, to his wife in February 1873. He found the meeting calm, fair and, on the whole, reverent, something of an achievement since the company included an atheist and republican (Roden Nöel); the historian J.A. Froude (a Deist); Father Dalgairns, Roman Catholic priest at Brompton Oratory, and the spearhead of the Catholic revival, Archbishop Manning; Richard Hutton, Editor of *The Spectator*; two Scots

Freethinkers (the word 'secularism' had entered the language in the 1850s); James Knowles (by then, apparently, adopting the demeanour and manner of a country squire); another Deist, Lord Arthur Russell, nephew of the Liberal Prime Minister, Lord John Russell, and himself a Liberal MP who was notable for being one of the first to warn that Prussian militarism was going to be a threat to Liberal Democratic ideas. The only people missing, Magee observed, were a Jew and a Muslim.

It wasn't perfect. Sometimes the courtesy, though pleasant, was false; Ruskin later described Archbishop Manning as 'the most entirely complete representation of humbug we have in the world'. Manning in fact wrote to Ruskin in October 1873 with some empathy – to the effect that Ruskin was 'crying out of the depths of this material world', a world of 3 per cents, iron-clads, secularism and deified civil powers: 'You can now understand what we feel'. Unfortunately not. Ruskin and Manning might make common cause on some social realities, but faith as an answer had now been brought into question. Mallock's judgment on Manning was more subtle, a man of considerable presence; he described him 'solemnly gliding forward', a slight, emaciated figure in a long black cassock relieved only at the throat by 'one peeping patch of purple', surmounted by a face of 'delicate sternness' seemingly made of semi-transparent ivory. He visited him in his house in Westminster, where they discussed the philosophical, historical and scientific reasons that prevented 'the modern mind' from assenting to Roman Catholicism. Significantly, Manning spoke of Huxley and Tyndall without 'sarcastic anger or moral reprobation'. He spoke of their opinions not as moral anathemas or sins, but intellectual errors to be refuted by intellectual refutation.[32]

Progress had come a long way very quickly. Until Charles Lyell, another scientist who achieved great popularity, started to publish his *Principles of Geology* in 1830, questioning a literal reading of the Bible and describing geological change over millions of years and also using the word 'evolution', many still believed that the world was created at around 6pm on 22 October 4004 BC, a calculation of the Irish Archbishop James Ussher back in 1654.

Being self-critical people, the members of the Metaphysical Society blamed themselves when it was dissolved in 1880. 'After ten years of strenuous effort', said Tennyson, 'no one had succeeded in even defining the term "metaphysics".'

The best part of 40 years earlier, in *Locksley Hall*, Tennyson first expresses something close to self-pity in his regret at the loss of a childhood sweetheart, yet self-prescribes, in what was to become a very Victorian way, action and engagement: 'Forward, forward, let us range'. Looking to the future, he sees 'all the wonder that would be'. Writers and intellectuals of all periods, being human, have to cope with volatile temperaments. Tennyson could certainly be capricious, and in later life was pessimistic about progress. But at root, he comes back to the steadying principle that enabled Victorians slowly to build lasting social and political change: avoid the tyrannies both of reaction and revolution. 'Sudden change', he observed, 'means a house built on sand'. Ships, whether of the sea or the state, could be steered through safe and beneficial waters, but were not ultimately all-powerful. And it was not just Tyndall who was a fan of his; Huxley thought he was the first poet since Lucretius (who died in 55 BCE) who could comprehend where modern science was going.[33]

Moreover, science was not the whole story. There are many things that literary scholars might say about Tennyson's *The Princess*, published in 1847, but (on matters of progress) it begins with a visit to a festival at a country house, an account based on a feast held several years earlier at the Mechanics' Institute, Park House, near Maidstone, and also reflected Tennyson's views – coinciding with the opening of Queen's College, London, Britain's first college for women – on further education for the disadvantaged. While Tennyson retained the middle-class fear of 'violent, selfish, unreasoning democracy', Ruskin noted how strong was his sense of duty in devoting time to educating 'the poorer classes' when he lunched with him in the 1870s, with Tennyson as 'kind and courteous as ever'. The 'all-in-good-time' conservatism of the Victorians, often seen as hypocrisy, is from the perspective of many of them a well-judged approach to lasting change. Queen Victoria, who was not herself in favour of lasting change, invited her Poet Laureate to lunch in 1862. He came with some diffidence, supported by the ever-present Jowett, and impressed with his warm and genuine words about Prince Albert. The Queen recorded a rather accurate description of the poet: 'very peculiar looking, tall, dark, with a fine head, long black flowing hair and a beard – oddly dressed'.[34]

Victorians discussed social trivialities, but many of them – as we have seen – found endless time to discuss all that was seriously important to living and the question of how much to change society. Had it just been a talking shop? No. This was a country, like most countries, in which most of its people wanted to get on with their lives with a reasonable balance of change and tradition. Instead, it had to deal with massive change, economically, socially (in terms of population numbers), politically, scientifically, and in its belief system and moral structures, while wanting to hold on to traditions that were not only rooted in relation to power structures but also – often – loved. Unlike the 20th and 21st centuries, with humans feeling themselves marooned – at times – in a meaningless universe and increasingly concerned about the effects of out-of-control technology to which they are also addicted, the Age of Progress was intent on replacing one set of 'ultimate truths' with another related to the thrilling discoveries produced by reason and science. Politically, this was a moment in which the Western world had a choice of directions: the direction symbolized by Marx's expulsion from his country in 1849, the driving out of Victor Hugo from France in 1851, or Ibsen's self-exile in 1864; or the one summed up by John Stuart Mill in *On Liberty* in 1859: 'It is only by the collision of adverse opinions that the remainder of the truth has any chance of being supplied.' The former led to communism, fascism, technocratic autism, woke narcissism and other forms of authoritarianism. The latter was – at least some of the time – set to improve things for most people.

Poor Darwin, unlike the Continental exiles, was not expelled, though much harried. He denied atheism, accepted that not all had clarity, and (in a letter to the American botanist Asa Gray) could not see that 'brute force' was all there was in 'this wonderful universe'.[35] Clifford expressed the English way better: 'On the whole I feel confirmed that the English distrust of general principles is a very complex affair...and that for some time we must go blundering on, finding out by experience what things are to be left alone and what not.'[36] You could be passionate – Clifford certainly was – but you must be patient before you rush to the barricades.

CHAPTER 8

'ONE HALF OF ENGLISH SOULS THIS DAY'

THE CONDITION OF ENGLAND QUESTION

'Gander, the captain of the gang of boy crossing-sweepers, was a big lad of sixteen, with a face devoid of all expression, until he laughed, when the cheeks, mouth and forehead instantly became crumpled up with a wonderful quantity of lines and dimples. His hair was cut short, and stood up in all directions, like the bristles of a hearth-broom, and was a light dust tint, matching with the hue of his complexion, which also, from an absence of washing, had turned to a decided drab, or what house-painters term a stone colour.

'He spoke with a lisp, occasioned by the loss of two of his large front teeth, which allowed the tongue as he talked to appear through the opening in a round nob like a raspberry.

'The boy's clothing was in a shocking condition. He had no coat, and his blue-striped shirt was as dirty as a French polisher's rags, and so tattered, that the shoulder was completely bare, while the sleeve hung down over the hand like a big bag.

'From the fish-scales on the sleeves of his coat, it had evidently once belonged to some coster in the herring line. The nap was all worn off, so that the lines of the web were showing a coarse carpet; and instead of buttons, string had passed through holes pierced at the side.

'Of course he had no shoes on, and his black trousers, which, with the grease on them, were gradually assuming a tarpaulin look, were fastened over one shoulder by means of a brace and a bit of string....

'"To tell you the blessed truth, I can't say the last shilling I handled."

'"Don't you go a-believing on him," whispered another lad in my ear, while Gander's head was turned: "he took thirteen pence last night, he did".'[1]

Crossing the city street in the era just before motorized transport was a hazardous undertaking. Dirt and mud, litter, rubble, more or less anything might be in the road, but the one certainty – a challenge for those wearing skirts down to the ground – was the volume of horse dung. Mayhew's statistic was that a single horse excreted 38lbs of dung every day. Crossing-sweeping, sometimes a last resort before turning to begging, had the advantage that you just needed a brush and a patch, could reasonably expect a gratuity and, if working for any length of time in a particular neighbourhood, even a retainer.

When we imagine the poor in the 19th century, we are likely to be much influenced by the word-pictures of Dickens – by, for example, Jo, the crossing-sweeper in *Bleak House*, who dies in Chapter 47 mouthing a few words of the Lord's Prayer and would melt anyone's heart – as well as the several paintings of these 'juvenile highwaymen', as *Building News* unkindly called them in 1858, by Dickens's close friend, the realist artist William Powell Frith. Also influential were the works of investigative journalists, especially Henry Mayhew's *London Labour and the London Poor*, the first volumes of which were published as books in 1851 and included, along with many, many others, the story of Gander, the gang captain. Later in the century and early in the 20th century, such accounts were heavily reinforced by scientific

49 W.P. Frith's *The Crossing Sweeper* was modified by the artist a number of times after his first version in 1858, not least to update the clothes of the lady so that she was in fashion. Behind its artificiality was the boy's model – 'A low, dull Irish boy...one degree removed from a pig,' according to his reminiscences. The boy tried to rob him.

gathering of data, most famously in the work of Charles Booth, inspired by Auguste Comte, the inventor of modern sociology, beginning with *Life and Labour of the People in London*, the first volume of which – the first of seventeen – was published in 1889. Booth was not himself poor, a successful businessman in steam-shipping and leather and a Disraeli supporter, but one who acquired first-hand experience of Toxteth slums when canvassing door-to-door in the 1865 election and who also benefited greatly from his wife Mary, Macaulay's niece, practical, wise and organized, as so many unsung Victorian wives were. She became one of the distinguished Presidents of the Royal Statistical Society, founded a few years before Queen Victoria came to the throne. A common habit of subsequent generations – perfectly properly questioning the methods and character of their predecessors – completely fails to understand in Booth's case how much his research contributed to progress in understanding and progress in influencing public opinion. Not long after, Seebohm Rowntree went a stage further by attempting an actual definition of poverty and the minimum needed to maintain a healthy life, beginning with his first study of York in *Poverty: A Study of Town Life* (1901). Rowntree was also a businessman, from the Quaker Rowntree chocolate family. He did acknowledge the detrimental effect of alcohol on family life, but also introduced many progressive reforms in his own company – reducing working hours, starting a pension scheme and even, after the First World War, a psychology department. As ever, there is much to criticize about Victorians and the poor, but new methods and new attitudes were an undeniable legacy.

It matters less that the varied approaches different kinds of writer and investigator took to the poor can be (and have been) criticised for methodological reasons – and sometimes for accuracy – than that they focused attention on what, by any criteria, was a massive problem. How could it not have been? The UK population in 1750 is estimated to have been a bit under 11 million, more than half of which were in England. When Queen Victoria died in 1901, it was over 41 million. The great increase came in one century – the 19th – and that despite high mortality and a decline in Ireland as a result of famine and mass emigration. Independent of the absence of a modern welfare system, growth in population of that order (and for large parts of the Victorian period perhaps 40 per cent were under fourteen) would have taxed any society in need for housing, infrastructure to accommodate an explosion of urban living, and food to provide sustenance. As industrialization gathered pace, no wonder that Coleridge could speak (in 1819) of 'our poor little White-Slaves, the children in our cotton factories,' or William Blake a generation before of 'young Africans of our own growth' sweeping the chimneys.

First attempts at reform from the centre were wholly inadequate. In the early 1840s, you could not count on a life expectancy beyond your twenties in the disease-ridden, polluted new cities.[2] If the state was to acknowledge the problem, there were two essentials: get organized and provide resources; but first understand what being poor means. Despite a commission and the Poor Law Amendment Act (1834) in the wake of the 1832 Reform Act, it was to take the whole Victorian period to find a truly positive path. The Act set up a central Poor Law Commission with new local boards of guardians and a focus on the workhouse. In principle, that was more systematic than ever before, but cruelly and sometimes corruptly applied; it was generally hated by its beneficiaries (the 1830s and 1840s saw rioting against it) and widely criticized by middle-class commentators at the time and by many historians ever since. More fundamentally, however, what was 'poor'? The civil servant most associated with the poor and health reforms, Edwin Chadwick, determined and clear-headed, nevertheless managed to set up a bar to progress in an article in the *Edinburgh Review* in 1836. In this, he declared, accurately, that 'poverty' was the natural state of man. Wealth came from labour; poverty was simply an economic category. 'Pauperism', destitution, was something different: the result of a moral and social state, connected to criminality and a way of life that was unhealthy and untouched by education and religious values. Pauperism could be addressed, 'the proper object of Poor Laws', whereas 'all attempts to extirpate poverty have no effects but bad ones'.[3]

In a sense, the whole of the rest of the century went in resolving different methods of dealing with what Disraeli's *Sybil* (1845) put more simply than the Poor Law commissioners: the division between the rich and the poor. In its review, *The Athenaeum* acknowledged that there was now a change: the rich had more sympathy and the poor could expect to find amelioration of their misery.[4] Before the end of the century, as important, Booth's analyses decisively destroyed the idea that the poor were wholly responsible for bringing their troubles upon themselves.

Comparisons of the modern world with – even – the 18th century can only be very approximate in quantitative terms, but before the Industrial Revolution began, we might reasonably apply the word 'poor' or 'very poor' to at least 60 per cent of the population. The great achievement of the Age of Progress was not the conquest of poverty, but a change of attitude that moved the world on from all past history. It was awful, vile, almost indescribably horrible to be poor in the 19th century, even in the boom years of the 1850s. But so it had been anywhere at any time before that, especially since society as a whole had less wealth, and the poor were considered either incurably flawed, a danger to social order (and for that reason only needing some minimal amelioration of their condition), or – for some kind souls, far too few in number – deserving, to an extent, of support and understanding. What happened during the 19th century was a sea change: an increasing visibility of a social and political will towards improvement and a growing belief that, with the right methods, Jesus's assertion, 'The poor you will always have with you' (Matthew 26.11), might not be where the story ends.

There was one disastrous prequel to Victorian progress: Peterloo, when inexperienced, amateur cavalry charged at a large and predominantly non-violent crowd in St Peter's Fields, Manchester, in 1819. Although there were many demonstrations throughout the century (and another example of soldiers firing on workers, in Preston in 1842), Peterloo's main practical legacy was not to set the scene for revolution, but to bring home to those in authority that, in this new, urban society, continuing the old ways was not an option. Peel was heavily influenced by it in introducing a professional, unarmed police force in London in 1829. Large and expanding towns and cities were no place for rule by a handful of amateurs. The Municipal Corporation Act in 1835 came out of obvious need more than an ideological programme. By the time it came to the biggest demonstration – of the Chartists in London – no one was going to persuade the aged Duke of Wellington to find military solutions, even if troops were assembled just in case.

The Chartists did develop a mostly coherent and impressive set of ideas for dealing with working-class problems and rights, though their leaders were far too individualistic to agree for long – some wanted female suffrage, some didn't; some emphasized political aims, but not those mainly preoccupied by low wages; some favoured what became Victorian values, like Robert Lowery, the Newcastle delegate at the first Chartist Convention in 1839, who eventually joined the Liberal Party and became a temperance lecturer. Hostility to aristocrats with power did not in the main signal a rejection of property rights. While the 1840s was a difficult decade, the beginnings of government social and economic reform, especially Peel's abolition of the Corn Laws, defused some of the preoccupations with extending suffrage and political reform. Nevertheless, the six demands of the Chartists' first petition to Parliament in 1839 were all political, from universal male suffrage to paid MPs.

As we shall see, the programme subsequently written by William Lovett and John Collins from Warwick gaol also put considerable emphasis on state education, from infants to senior schoolchildren. That was highly discerning, though again it is hard to show a direct connection between working-class agitation and the reform that eventually came. And while there were women involved in Chartist organization and demonstrations, there is not much sign that they influenced either those in power to reform their own status (legally, economically, politically) or even Chartist men to change their own attitudes. It was still revealing about the British approach to politics that 'natural rights' were not centre stage; policies were informed by a sense of what was moral, but also what would be better in cost and other practical matters involved in doing away with the unnecessary complexities and unfairnesses that went with a system rooted in self-perpetuating oligarchy.[5]

A second petition, in 1842, like the first, was rejected. A third, in 1848, was moved directly by the Chartist leader Feargus O'Connor, who had originally become an MP for County Cork in 1832 as a supporter of Daniel O'Connell, one sign of many that what to do about Ireland preoccupied the 19th-century House of Commons and often seemed to be the most intractable problem of all – the Victorians failed. Each of the petitions had major support, the second one more than three million signatures and the third of the order of 5¾ million, though the signature of Queen Victoria on the second and other evidence suggests that these figures were inflated, probably greatly so. The numbers were certainly huge, yet this new expression of populism was still presented to Parliament; no one tried to burn the legislature down – that had happened by accident anyway. Those in power, however, did not respond with equanimity. As the Chartists prepared in large numbers – perhaps 50,000 in all – to meet on Kennington Common in 1848, they showed in some ways even more concern than the rulers of European countries whose regimes were to be toppled in that year of revolutions. Lord Malmesbury's diary for 5 April 1848 emphasized the strength of the alarm about the Chartists. Everybody expects the attack, he suggested, to be serious. All the troops within easy reach of London had been ordered there, even those at Windsor. General Lord de Ros says they are to be concealed as early as four in the morning of the 10th, near the Common. Officers would be present in plain clothes. Whoever said the Victorians made things dull?

Luckily, they did. Malmesbury's diary on the 10th tells a different story: 'The mob was not very considerable, and the best behaved I ever saw, and though there were very few police or special constables to keep order, there seemed to be no excitement, nothing but curiosity.' Just before 1pm, the chief officer of police, Richard Mayne, rode to the Common, with no soldiers in sight, only two policemen. Mayne summoned O'Connor, who was 'as pale as ashes, trembling from head to foot'.[6] The Chartists then dispersed. In some ways, O'Connor's achievement had been considerable, though his background – as an Irish landowner passionate about Irish rights – did not signal revolt from below. After losing his Irish seat, he had devoted himself to providing support for developing Chartism and providing it a mouthpiece in the *Northern Star*. In 1847, he became the only Chartist MP (for Nottingham) there was ever to be, but his oratory, powerful though it was, did not match the size of his ego, nor make up for his lack of management skills, most clearly seen in his failed plan to enfranchise working-class voters by raising money to give them smallholdings of sufficient size to give a voting qualification under the 1832 Act.[7] O'Connor's last, sad years were spent in an asylum before his death in 1855.

That was not quite the end of Chartism, though Ernest Jones, O'Connor's effective successor, also came from a landowning family. Not in doubt was his devotion to working-class rights, or his willingness to spend family money on the cause. But in the process, his personality did not help; this was a man who railed against everyone, not just aristocrats and businessmen, but middle-class reformers, many of his fellow Chartists and even trade unions. Still, 'extreme' was not to be the way for the English in general, or the working class in particular. Theodor Fontane noted in his diary in 1857 that the 'Hunger Parliament' had met in Smithfield Market, with a two-hour speech from Jones on 'the depravity of the Government' and 'the virtue of the people'. Then the gathering just melted away at 3pm, with no consequences, the whole affair being – he observed – greatly exaggerated in the Belgian and German newspapers.[8]

All this disguises the myriad ways in which working men did at least glimpse progress for themselves. The middle classes had not found their own way, economically or politically, by destroying the aristocrats; the reformers among them pointed an increasingly modern way forward: the Anti-Corn Law League had used door-to-door canvassing and targeted mailing. Thomas Cooper, the son of a Leicester dyer, at one point imprisoned in the 1840s for sedition, was not notable for falling out with O'Connor – many did that – but turned away from militant methods and captured a different mood in the early 1850s when the Duke of Wellington died: 'We all felt as if we lived, now he was dead, in a different England.' Engels, to his own annoyance, was exactly right: the English proletariat was becoming 'more and more bourgeois'. Later, Bertrand Russell was not entirely correct when he said universal and compulsory education resulted in the wage-earning classes reading not Tom Paine but the picture pages; but much working-class testimony suggests reasons for Engels' frustration. Edwin Lunn, from Huddersfield, summed it up perfectly in a letter to Robert Lowe: 'I am a working man, fifty-one years old, in good health and strength. I live in a £6 10s house. It is a clean, comfortable, and well-furnished cottage. I never received above 22 shillings per week in my life. I have brought up five children, and they can all read and write well.' He praised his 'careful and economical wife', 'worth more than 100 votes'. 'I have not a vote. I have not political power, but I have liberty. I can say what I like, I can go where I like, and I can do what I like, if I do not injure anybody else. I am lightly taxed.... There are no obstacles to my rise in life if I possess abilities and moral qualities essential to success.' He explicitly feared that he would lose these things if working-class majorities came to power.[9]

Of course, working-class experiences varied widely in all sorts of ways. Some were unskilled; some were moving up the ladder; some were already at the top of the lower-class ladder and ready for further improvement. A very small proportion of workers, even at the end of the Victorian period, worked for large organizations. Life was not all roses, but – judging by many contemporary commentators, many working-class voices and many economic historians – it seems valid to say that political quiescence was helped in the second half of the 19th century by rising real wages and reduction of working hours, and not only for the most skilled, the 'labour aristocracy'. Regional differences, family circumstances, economic cycles, rising and falling industries all conspire against the over-simplification of economic data. Disagreement and dissent never disappear, but the lives of many working people were touched for the better by the 'Age of Progress'.

That was not (yet) because of a benevolent state; it was not all because of self-help either, but there were plenty of role models, one reason for *British Workman* to have George Stephenson on its cover in January 1859. Sometimes, at least, from 'the humblest homes, in the depths of social life', it was possible to attain 'the summit of human greatness'. The idea was expressed in, and encouraged by, writers such as Mrs Gaskell, in *Mary Barton* (1848), in which Lancashire handloom weavers would keep open Newton's *Principia Mathematica* on their looms, with snatched looks during working hours, but 'revelled over' at mealtimes or at night. Equally, the novelist also provided abundant descriptions of appalling poverty.[10]

Self-help was often accompanied by mutual help. There were already hundreds and thousands of members of friendly societies by 1800, fuelled by the social consequences of the Industrial Revolution, but that had grown to millions by the 1850s, and grew again so that by the 1880s perhaps more than three-quarters of all workers had become members. Large and small, they provided help through member subscriptions in sickness or old age, ensured proper burials, arranged entertainment, encouraged savings and education, or compensated for a dead cow. The Co-operative Movement developed from similar principles. Edwin Waugh, who had been reduced to living in a cellar in Rochdale with his mother after his shoemaker father died, captured the excitement when he visited the Co-operative Store in Toad Lane at the end of June 1849: 'This association is creating a great sensation among the working people.... It is a healthy, independent enterprise.'[11] Rochdale is the place in which the Co-operative Movement had its symbolic beginning, but in fact it had developed earlier in response to the social changes of Industrial Revolution urbanization and a market economy for everyone's most basic need: food. Mistakes were made; private store owners resented the competition; fraud was not uncommon; and for a long time, an absent state failed to catch up with the need for regulation of the plethora of new societies, clubs and other working-class institutions. Yet the whole story is a remarkable testimony to many determined people. Progress came fast, to the extent of there being some 1,300 Co-operative Societies by the time of the movement's first congress in 1869.

Thomas Hughes, its first President, showed how those in the middle class – he was most famous as author of *Tom Brown's Schooldays* (1857), but was also an MP and social reformer – could act, in a characteristically earnest way, to provide time, money, expertise, organization to further working-class aspirations. Some people at the time, many more after the Victorians, ungenerously questioned its motives, suggesting that middle-class money-making and middle-class desires for control were at the heart of the story. They sometimes were. But once again the only relevant comparisons we can make are with how lives were conducted in all previous history and with how progress was now being made.

The Mechanics' Institutes opened up another avenue in which self-help was linked to the most important tool of all working-class progress: education. In these, the middle-class supporters were often accused of manipulating the workers towards their values, but – for that matter – as the decades passed, a new breed of tradesmen and clerks were not necessarily in harmony with factory toilers anxious to better themselves. Nevertheless, these places were unequivocally marvellous better-future-makers. In Swindon, great Victorian centre of locomotive engineering, workers based at Swindon railway works paid via subscription to find 'useful knowledge' and 'rational amusement'; they benefited from their institute's library, from lectures, from health services and, eventually, from a theatre. This was no backstreet building, but produced – mainly from limestone rubble – to the design of the London architect Edward Roberts in Gothic Revival style in the 1850s and expanded in the 1890s. At that point, its health facilities became accessible to other workers, to the extent that the founding genius of the NHS, Aneurin Bevan, was to refer to Swindon's 'complete health service': 'All we had to do was expand it to the country.'[12] Back in 1854, *The Builder* recorded that the Roberts building had a market for 32 shops and 30 stalls, a 'spacious' reading room, coffee room, dining hall with hot plates, hot and cold baths, and an air drain to expel stale air and gases.[13] Today, after years of assaults from vandals and arsonists, it speaks sadly of progress lost.

Of course, many Victorian workers died without leaving anything to memorialize. We cannot say that those who did find education in the Mechanics' Institutes were typical, but listen to the attitude of the 'Lancashire Burns', Edwin Waugh. He was already 30 when in November 1847 he recorded a resolve 'to begin immediately at the simple elements of Arithmetic and proceed steadily through the different departments of mathematical knowledge till I have mastered the most abstruse – I seldom grieve for the emptiness of my pockets when I meet with books, teachers and pictures.' He is happy later in the month, on a Saturday, to spend an hour with his Latin grammar, and on the following Monday he takes himself to one of Emerson's lectures (the American philosopher, abolitionist and poet toured Britain in 1847–48) – this one on 'The Superlative in Manners and Literature'. Not that everything was easy or well endowed. When he visits a bookshop in Shudehill, a rundown area of Manchester, with a friend, he finds 'a dirty little nook about two yards square'. The floor was broken in places; light came from two flickering candles (there were holes in the windows), one a rusty stick, the other held upright by a large potato.[14]

Not everyone was as sanguine about having as little money as Waugh. This was also the first great era of trade unions. They necessitated a willingness from both employees and employers to negotiate, rather than automatically engage in strikes (by the former) or lockouts (by the latter). From the 1850s on, bargaining became much commoner, though not without lockouts (of, for example, iron workers in 1866), and in the end it needed government political action to catch up with the realities of a different kind of economy and a huge increase in the numbers of urban workers. As late as 1825, a new Combination of Workmen Act banned collective bargaining and the right to strike. *The Times* half-signalled a change of mood in December 1853, acknowledging in its own way that 'there is such a thing as wholesome discontent'. Combination for increasing wages at least showed 'the workman has a taste for prosperity' and 'in the progress of mankind a phase of rashness and error'. Today that sounds patronising; then it showed an enormous leap forward, though a qualified one: the newspaper was in part commentating on what it called 'the noxious growth of northern disaffection'. In a strike that was to close the Preston cotton industry for seven months and spread to other Lancashire towns, the worker representatives George Cowell and Mortimer Grimshaw led a campaign that raised the astonishing amount of £100,000 and – thanks to the newly influential press – endowed them with celebrity. It ended badly for the workers. Blacklegs (otherwise known as 'Knobsticks') were brought in, though it was only when there was no money left that defeat came. In a comment that became a cliché in labour disputes ever after, *The Times* asserted that 'The present condition of the operatives has a direct tendency to stop...beneficial investment'.[15]

A transition from effectively no rights for workers to a modern world, the former being the historical norm, could hardly have happened quietly. In some ways, the fact that some Victorian employers behaved like Dickens's caricatures is less remarkable than the behaviour of others by mid-century. Anthony Mundella, himself from a poor home, consciously used machine advances in his Nottingham hosiery company not with riches in mind, but precisely to lift workers out of their previous 'serfdom'. Higher pay, better working conditions, bringing disputes to arbitration – these were his preoccupations before his later career as MP and member of Gladstone's Cabinets. And could it be imagined anywhere else in the world that an Amalgamated Society of Engineers could be formed (in 1851) with a stated policy of never doing anything 'illegally or indiscreetly'? Its members would seek to benefit themselves, but not with 'injury to others'.

This and other 'New Model Unions', beginning in the 1850s, consciously espoused a moderate approach, with a focus on prosperity and respectability. In fact, the history of the Engineers did not proceed anything like as smoothly as that. Even so, the distinctive British labour movements were noted from outside the country. Taine talked to Vincent, a young journeyman printer, representing the trade unions and speaking to worker audiences on union virtues. Vincent was happy because he could say what he wanted, except for making anti-Christian or anti-Queen Victoria remarks, for which the sanction – a metaphorical stoning – would come from his audience, not the state. The German economist von Schulze-Gaevernitz made a study of the trade union movement in England, *Social Peace*, first published in Leipzig in 1894 and edited for the English edition by the prominent Fabian Graham Wallas; it may have been called 'ponderously conscientious' by Sidney Webb in his review, but it was unequivocal that, unlike Germany or anywhere else, you

50 Skilled workers could show their power in 'New Model Unions'. This membership card for the Amalgamated Society of Journeymen & Cloggers (*c.*1873) proclaimed the idea that combination would lead to success and give justice to 'the Toilers'.

would not find in England 'the belief among the lower classes that salvation can only come through the overthrow and destruction of the existing order'.[16]

In fact, there was a change for the worse in worker-employer relationships towards the end of the century, but in the meantime – as in so many other areas of activity – the state engaged in reform. It did so, as usual, in an idiosyncratic way: Disraeli was responsible, in 1875, for an act that gave unions a freedom not to be found anywhere else on the planet; he did so using legislation already mapped out under Gladstone. Everyone was feeling their way. Gladstone's 1871 Trade Unions Act had prevented prosecution for conspiracies in restraint of trade, or – more plainly – trade unions had been made lawful, though it was followed by an Act that made picketing illegal. Disraeli specifically legalized peaceful picketing, and in other legislation in 1879, on the employer/working-man relationship, clarified that they were equal partners in a civil contract, and imprisonment could not be the sanction for a breach. That a new era had begun, to be followed by one step forward, one back, was further signalled not long after the end of the Victorian era in the 1906 Trade Disputes Act, extending worker immunity.

All this disguises an important reality: the division between skilled workers, for whom unions reinforced pride as well as having more concrete objectives, and the unskilled or semi-skilled. Partly because of the declining number of rural labourers transferring their work to towns and cities, the least privileged had a little more bargaining power, as well as less patience. The New Unionism, starting at the time of the London Dock Strike in 1889, encouraged the idea that there was more power if skilled and unskilled came together, and more to be gained from militancy. The level of violence, both by police and strikers, came to a head in the last years before the First World War, less an unhappy climax of the Victorian story shortly after its end than a signal that the 20th century needed to resolve – socially, economically and politically – how to deal with labour issues in vastly increased populations. Victorian middle-class gradualist reform had given way to the age of the masses.

One April evening in 1856, after a two-hour banquet of 'the choicest viands and condiments of the season' at the Bell Hotel in the Strand, Dr Marx rose to his feet to speak to 'the leading Democrats of England, France and Germany now in London'. He warned that the findings of the *Vehmgerichte* – a mysterious red cross applied to houses in medieval times as a sign of judgment and punishment – were ineluctably at work. History's executioner was to be the proletariat.[17] Marx's audience wasn't just revolutionary exiles from the Continent. In the chair were the Chartists Ernest Jones and James Finlen. All three men were to be disappointed. The British working class failed to follow the historical destiny Marx had carved out for it. Finlen fell out with Jones, was principally occupied with Irish republicanism, neglected his family (probably – he denied it), so that his children were taken to the workhouse and his wife to an asylum, and disappeared into obscurity with an assumed name. In later life, Jones returned to his practice as a barrister. His son Llewellyn had a long career as a Liberal MP, encouraging it – to little avail – to embrace the working class *en masse*; he became both KC and a judge.

You never can tell with technology. Both Chartists and communists predicted its effects on workers would be negative. Feargus O'Connor suggested machinery would have as bad a result for working people as the railways would have on the horse population, leaving the latter fit only for slaughter as meat. As it happened, for a while at least, the horses flourished: what else would carry the railway travellers to and from their station? Some years before the Strand meeting, Marx had given his readers in the *New York Daily Tribune* little room for doubt when he wrote about the Chartists. Tories, Whigs, Peelites belonged 'more or less' to the past (this in 1852). A straightforward power grab was going on to ensure 'the complete and undisguised ascendancy of the Bourgeoisie', the 'open, official subjection of society' under the rule of 'the directors of production'. The crown was of no use, nor the nobility, the army, the state church, the Chancery courts, nor – for that matter – wars (it was cheaper to exploit foreign nations if there was peace). Anyone who reads enough of Marx will find that it is not just the bourgeoisie and the old establishment to whom he is hostile. With Engels, he dismisses Mexicans because they would never progress anything, or Chinese because of inherited stupidity, though some US Negroes, he thought, can be – more or less – turned into Yankees, unlike those in Africa or Jamaica. Sometimes it is difficult to disentangle Marx the brilliant and prescient political ideologist from the man who bears everyone a grudge if they are not helpful to him. When he writes of 'The Jewish nigger Lassalle' in a letter to Engels in July 1862, it may not be outright racism and antisemitism so much as Fernand Lassalle's refusal to lend him money.[18]

Marx's sense of progress, sometimes misleadingly linked to Comte and Darwin, as well as with an inevitability about social evolution and change that neither of the latter had, is – surprisingly – connected to people. Without obstacles to progress towards a proletarian revolution, it will happen, but it requires help; it requires habits of thought unfolding within a painful process of class antagonism. If Marx had been in the House of Lords to hear the debate in January 1840, he might have picked up some clues about British society. True, the Bishop of Exeter had some extreme comments about the spread of the system 'denomined "Socialism"', which endangered morals, abolished private property, marriage and religion, and led to treason and sedition. The Marquess of Normanby, more circumspectly than the fiery cleric, believed in 'the good sense' of his fellow countrymen. There was no mass movement, and the small number of socialist adherents would fall out with each other. Lord Melbourne, then Prime Minister, tactfully suggested that 'the progress of the poison' should be watched, but unrest had much to do with the 'state of society' and 'the distress in which great numbers lived at present'. The Duke of Wellington wisely added that prosecutions were not desirable, and 'argument and reasoning' should be encouraged.[19]

So, should we view the Victorian working class contentedly peering out on their new world, navigating its opportunities, seeking education, valuing thrift, temperance and nonconformist community, as well as displaying pride in their country? Of course, that would be simplistic, but it may be significant that the founder of Britain's first fully socialist political party, Henry Hyndman, was the cricket-playing, antisemitic son of a rich businessman who popularized Marx's ideas and persuaded Marx's daughter Eleanor (though not Engels) to join his Social Democratic Federation, which had its inaugural meeting – when it was just called the Democratic Federation – in June 1881. Marx himself, who did not die until 1883, was not best pleased that Hyndman's *England for All* (1881) failed to mention him in its introduction. Hyndman, like Marx himself, was controlling by nature, and in what was to become a pattern for far-left parties – splits – showed itself when Hyndman refused to resign after a vote of no confidence in 1884. Eleanor, together with William Morris, left to form the Socialist League, which was split from the beginning between moderate Fabians, revolutionaries, Christian Socialists and anarchists. The anarchists eventually won. Evidently, despite Britain being predominantly working class, its working-class voices would not support extreme solutions.

George Burns, who was very briefly leader of the Labour Party in 1910–11, mentions in his autobiography that he attended an SDF meeting and reacted negatively to being 'so belaboured' with such words as 'exploitation', 'proletariat' and 'bourgeois' ('just imported from Germany') that he never went again. Mallock satirized Hyndman as Mr Foreman in his 1886 novel *The Old Order Changes* – 'Nine hundred vapid pages...relieved by a few venomous vomitings of weak spite', according to *The Commonweal*, the 'Official Journal of the Socialist League': Mallock's conservatism wasn't always applauded, or applaudable, but socialism veering towards Marxism was not a direction that ever found mass approval from British workers.[20]

The Fabians, founded in 1883–84, showed that clarity and careful analysis could be brought to political progress without adopting intolerant ideological certainties. They were over-optimistic in their assumption that central planning would be transformative, and perhaps the events and changes of the Victorian period suggested that the priority was first to achieve democratic power, then navigate what could be achieved practically. George Brodrick, historian and Warden of Merton College, Oxford, made a distinction in the *Nineteenth Century* in 1884 between democracy (for which the omens were good for various reasons, such as the spread of education) and socialism (which in its different forms made an assumption about the 'rights' and 'duties' of the wage-earning 'people').[21]

The leaders of the two great political parties before there was a Labour Party were sometimes deluded into thinking that, as the President of the Board of Trade, James Bryce, said, in the last days of Rosebery's 1894–95 administration, 'Socialistic ideas' would be contained by the existing parties and simply act as a stimulant to Parliament to deal with social reform and the improvement of the lot of the working classes. In fact, Keir Hardie, a key founder of the Labour Party and its parliamentary leader (1906–08), had decided that the working class needed its own party, beginning as an independent, succeeding in entering Parliament in 1892 and helping first to found the Independent Labour Party in 1893. His early career almost shouts 'self-help': the illegitimate son of a farm servant, sent out to work at the age of seven, then working in mines and quarries from the age of ten, practising his writing skills on slate in the pit and reading, reading, reading whenever he could. He did attend the conference of the Second Socialist International in 1889, but told Engels that the British were 'solid', 'very practical'. They didn't chase 'bubbles'.[22] In his head, he was helping – and did help – to create a 'Labour' Party, not a 'Socialist' Party.

As ever in Britain, a huge step forward that would create for the first time a successful political party did not begin with a bang, but some confusion: in 1892, he had variously been described as 'Independent', 'Labour' and even 'Liberal and Labour' (the Liberal Party in some sense contrived its own downfall by not putting up a candidate, though offering no help to Hardie against the Conservatives). Nevertheless, the cumulative changes of the Victorian period gifted the 20th century the possibility of an 'age of the masses' that did not mean a violent end to Britain's social structures.

There had been endless debate about 'the right methods' for change and no consensus. Fear of revolution could be a negative reason for change as a means of staving it off – and sometimes was. But though often making the most noise – noise by protestors, noise of a different kind by their conservative detractors – revolution was not one of the central motivations. The eminent French historian Jules Michelet, author of the monumental *Histoire de France*, arrived in Oxford and stayed with Benjamin Jowett at Balliol in 1848. He was confident that the Chartists would succeed. Not Jowett: 'It will be of little consequence.'[23] And so 1848 was – in Britain, though not in France – where the seesaws between constitutional monarchists and republicans, and between Bonapartists and both, lost Michelet all his public offices. As we saw in Chapter 1, another distinguished French historian and statesman, François Guizot, was sympathetic to British liberal opinion and wrote as the 1850s began a favourable comparison between Britain's Glorious Revolution in 1688 and the French Revolution, but he was too conservative for France's new progress towards revolution and ultimately permanent republicanism. He had spent a year in England after 1848 after the toppling of Louis Philippe, having briefly been Prime Minister in France.[24]

The 'different state of things' in relation to the poor, which was eventually to lead to Lloyd George's famous 'People's Budget' in 1909, declared to be

51 Disease and poverty created orphans. Thomas Barnado, after first training as a doctor, set up a ragged school in the East End of London while still in his twenties in the 1860s, shortly to be followed by the first of what became more than a hundred homes early in the 20th century. Fine distinctions between the deserving and the undeserving were ignored in an attempt to provide craft skills and give help in finding apprenticeships. The tough regime and the 'kidnapping' of children from abusive homes were often criticized by idealistic dreamers unable to understand the need for action.

a war budget against 'poverty and squalidness' and introducing old age pensions and higher taxes to fund social welfare, was created during the 19th century via multiple methods, though all were connected. Throughout the century, and despite the fact that the state was still in the process of learning its modern interventionist role and the funding that would entail, there was a great deal of legislation on everything from how factory work should be regulated to measures to improve public health. But though liberal opinion seemed the obvious focus for such activity, it was too often held up by deep-seated feelings that life was a matter of individual responsibility and moral choices, suggesting that the voluntary principle should not be lightly abandoned when it came to matters of social welfare and much else. For that reason, progress sometimes came from unlikely quarters. Disraeli's shrewd appreciation that newly enfranchised working men would be less interested in abstract ideas of political freedom (to them) than in improvements in the standard of living resulted in a raft of social and labour legislation during his second administration from 1874 to 1880, ranging from empowering new local sanitary authorities with power to provide hospitals from rates to giving local authorities power to purchase land for house building.

While the scale of poverty was daunting, it wasn't the case that 'working class' was synonymous with 'poor'. The earnest, 'respectable' working man was more than glimpsing a better world by the 1850s and certainly by the end of the century; he was better motivated to make it better still by applying himself rather than contemplating overthrowing the social, the economic and the political systems. In Booth's study of London, more than 50 per cent of the entire working population were 'working class comfortable'. Rowntree, in York, used 'comfortable' as a description of over 70 per cent of the population, including many who were working class. Piped water, water closets, gas lighting had become typical for the working classes by 1900. Cheaper food – corn from America, meat from New Zealand or Argentina – and tariff reductions for such basics as tea contributed.

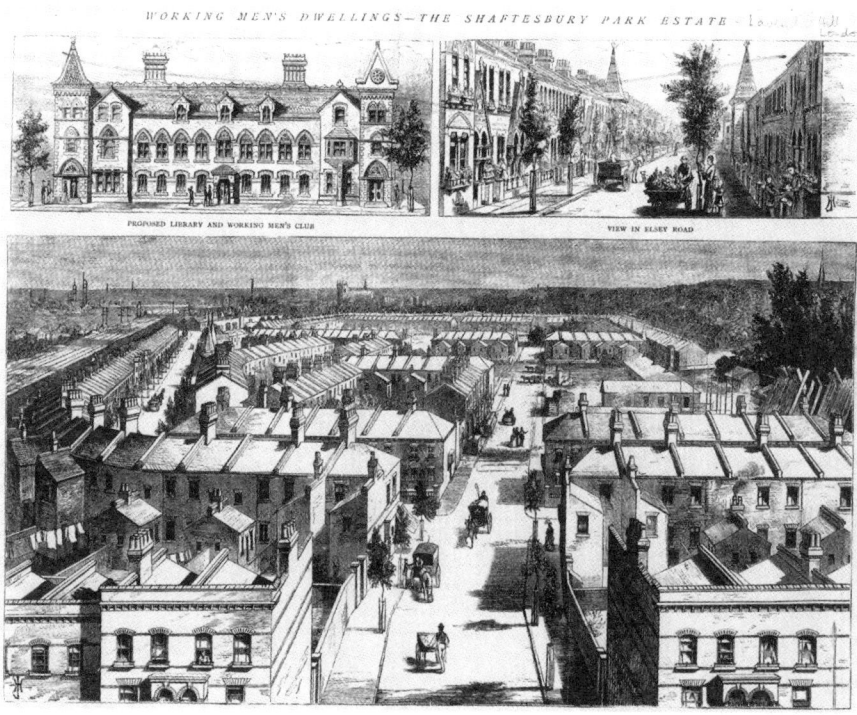

52 The speed of economic progress made Britain a global leader in slum creation; now it became a global leader in working-class homes. Promoted as 'the Workmen's City', the Shaftesbury Park Estate (1872–77) in south London was conceived by William Austin, a drain-laying contractor, and helped by Lord Shaftesbury. It was significant for two reasons: Disraeli, who opened part of what became a vast enterprise, signalled that henceforward governments could no longer treat the mass of the population at arm's length; and that housing the masses would lead to corruption and fraud. Money and morality: the unhappy twins of a modern world.

Victorian slums were irredeemably noisome places to live and die, but they were not the places where the great majority of the population lived. Thomas Escott compared the nearly 40 years between 1857 and 1896: the proportion of paupers to total population had dropped from 47 in every thousand to 24.[25] Their voices were mute; and because of their condition, it is almost beyond our ability to feel what it might have been like for them. Anyone spending their entire life in an environment of pain, hunger, disease, cold and death – both as children and adults – was marooned in a universe beyond the limits of our imagination. Novelists tried, but effectively only describe a life in which – as the writer and teacher Charles Rowcroft put it in a tale of 1846 – infancy was without nurture, childhood without sport, manhood without enjoyment, old age without sympathy.[26] Mayhew perhaps brings us closest.

The Commissioners responsible for organizing the Great Exhibition encouraged working-class committees to comment on its direction. In the end, there were 297 of them, keen to impress. Many working people took their first journey away from the district in which they had born – a first train journey also – to visit London and the Exhibition, there to have their cultural antennae alerted by examples of cutlery, or mirrors, or curtains: in retrospect, the moment when consumerism became more appetizing and at least within the realms of future possibility for those who were not members of the social elites. Post-Victorians through to the present day have poured scorn on what they feel is the cold impracticality of Samuel Smiles's 'self-help'. There is plenty of evidence of harshness. John Hollingshead, journalist and theatrical impresario, gave a terrible account of the poor in the winter of 1860–61 in the *Morning Post*, published as a book, *Ragged London in 1861*, yet apportioned blame to the underclass themselves: 'children produced without thought, set upon their feet without clothing, taught to walk, turned into the street without food or education, and left to the ragged school, the charitable public, or the devil'. Many looked 'to everyone to relieve them, but make few efforts to relieve themselves'.[27] The truth was that some found themselves unable to escape, some didn't try – and some did.

The serious-minded, earnest artisans who went to chapel, participated in temperance meetings, spent their evenings attending lectures and who provided the underpinning for socially transforming institutions such as trade unions and the Co-operative Movement have been written off in modern times as too po-faced, as humourless and as disapproving as their middle-class Victorian equivalents. It only requires a small amount of imagination to get back to the very different sense – of improvement – generated from below and inadequately encouraged from above, especially the state. The Co-operative Movement wasn't the only coming together of working people. The impact of the Friendly Societies brought recognition from Disraeli's Government in 1875, with a regulatory act. After Liverpool Victoria Friendly Society was founded in 1843, it became famous for its 'penny policies' collected by an army of agents and designed to ensure that its members would not have a pauper's burial. That was something to applaud – unlike the fate proposed by its Board in 2021 to demutualize it for a specious better future owned by an American private equity company.

Victorian Britain embraced the delights of learning to read in a way that cannot quite be replicated in societies taking that more for granted. Again, the state eventually learned from the experiences of those low down in the social hierarchy, and before the 19th century ended, education for under-14s had become compulsory. But much earlier than that there were the Mechanics' Institutes, the name reflecting the need for new skills in managing machinery as a result of the Industrial Revolution, but giving access to libraries, lectures, laboratories, courses. Wealthy benefactors did help enormously, and what had previously been a barren landscape of mostly closed opportunity for education was replaced by an efflorescence of Useful Knowledge Societies, Literary and Scientific Institutes, Reading Rooms, Athenaeums and Lyceums. Engels – of course – complained in 1850 that the Mechanics' Institutes just taught the Godlike properties of free competition and subservience to the existing political and social order. There were also many people who argued that education would produce only radicals. Sometimes they were right – but, for innumerable people, a conduit had been opened to a better future.

What happens if we see the process through particular eyes, the good and the not so good? Time and again, while we don't see one pattern in Victorian working-class stories, but many, and don't see at all the stories of those unable to deal with hardship in the absence of a benevolent state, we can see how progress is made. Joseph Gutteridge, who was born three years before Queen Victoria and died two years before the Queen did, had poor parents who could nevertheless read and write; Quaker benevolence started his schooling when he was only five. In his autobiography, he suggests that he was not typical, given that only one in ten had the basic skills (probably an underestimate and widely variable from place to place). Very early, he decides books are the answer, but too expensive for an artisan. Living in Coventry, he was apprenticed as a weaver at the factory where his father – a Waterloo veteran with no pension – worked. He did well at charity school, and his account shows how novelists' accounts were often too simplistic. Yes, it was a tough regime, with some boys struck so hard with a birch rod as to draw blood, but success in exams created possibilities. The school landscape was one of individual contrasts: a cruel master had a helpful, kindly wife; his successor lacked the skill to realize that boys' capacity for learning was as varied as their different characteristics; a new master was held in respect and esteem.

In the factory, there were 60 looms, half manned by journeymen, half by apprentices. Gutteridge's foreman had more appetite for drinking than teaching; the hours were long – fourteen hours a day in the summer, twelve or thirteen in the winter. He was always more interested in the mechanisms of the machines than the monotony of working them. There were moments of kindness; when his father was out of work for four months, he was sent off to the shop to get more credit. His basket was filled and, on Christmas Eve, the shopkeeper sent groceries and a quart of home-brewed ale. In the 1830s, a nearby factory owner named Joseph Beck, who introduced steam looms, enraged weavers by hiring female labour; machines were damaged and set on fire, the proprietor put on a donkey facing backwards. Three men were given death sentences, commuted to transportation for life. But nothing was easily predictable. One of them, Mr Toogood, later revisited from Australia, where he had obtained his independence and become 'comparatively rich'; there were now many more opportunities than ever before.

Gutteridge would not work for lower wages and was given an opportunity, as some were, to buy a loom in instalments. He 'would rather have died from sheer starvation than apply for poor relief'. For a time, he did odd-jobs as a carpenter, but had no savings when – back in a factory – the company suddenly went bankrupt. He found himself burning his own furniture at night to prevent his child from dying from exposure. Yet again it was not middle-class philanthropy that saved him; a publican he met in the street gave him money for bread. And yet again luck helped when he got work at the factory where he had been apprenticed. A constant focus, 'so dear to me', were 'the principles of self-help and individuality'. He reads Gibbon, but also Robert Owen, whose books were low-priced and whose experiments in improving the 'toiling classes' were expressed with 'intense earnestness' that appealed to him. He even studies Gray's 'Supplement to the Pharmacopoeia' when his son develops a serious eye condition in a bad reaction to a vaccination and the money for help at the eye infirmary runs out. What happens? He doesn't say, but later, and free of charge, he has developed enough medical knowledge to help friends and neighbours. He teaches himself about the use and structure of telescopes and microscopes, learning how to grind and polish lenses, and just manages to make a powerful chromatic telescope. He is also given a week to visit the Great Exhibition and uses it to find out more about botany, as well as finding it exhilarating.

The story this tells is of a particular kind of progress. A perpetual theme – when he is ill or out of work – is that 'our exchequer' becomes 'very low'. Yet there are the weekly meetings of the Mutual Improvement Society in winter 1857–58: social science, the physiology of digestion, propaganda and proselytism, the past, present and future of India. The future is always important: however great the achievements of modern science, 'the possibilities of the future are even greater'. In the present, the silk-weaving industry is by no means stable: silkworm disease in France and Italy hits supplies; the Cobden free trade treaty with France in 1860 increases French competitive imports, whereas the US Morrill Tariff Act of 1861, with tariffs as high as 40–60 per cent, effectively excludes British exports; and ribbon weaving goes out of fashion.

He is out of work for a year, though the landlord lets him live rent-free. There is no state social umbrella, yet many individual acts of kindness and some sources of help: he is promised funds to visit the Paris Exposition, then Lyon, Geneva and Basle, learning all the time. The funding does not arrive in time, and he is stuck in Paris unable to return to Coventry. He is lent money with the security only of 'the honour of an Englishman', though still has sixteen hours without food back to London Bridge and then another four from Euston to Coventry. Any reaction to Gutteridge's account should note that when he looked back in the 1890s, he focused on the visible signs of progress in his hometown: gas, water, sewage works; cemetery; market hall, hospitals, chapels; technical institute, free library, Wheatly Street Board Schools; new public baths. No previous generation would have been able to find equivalents; instead, they would only be able to match – and worse – the hardships Gutteridge had undoubtedly experienced.[28]

In the first year of the 19th century, William Lovett was born in Newlyn, Cornwall, not long after his fisherman father was drowned at sea. Access to education then very much depended on philanthropy and the Church, in his case enabling him to receive at least a little education in Penzance. He tried ropemaking as an apprentice, but came to his own conclusion that ropes were likely to be superseded by chains and turned to cabinetmaking, making for London when he was 21. More by chance than anything, a friend of his introduced him to a small literary association, 'The Liberals', mostly working class, who met in Gerrard Street, off Newport Street, near what is today Shaftesbury Avenue, and made a small weekly subscription towards forming a library for circulation to each other. It was the first time, he said, that he had ever heard what he called 'impromptu speaking', except from the pulpit – a good beginning to further Mechanics' Institute evening classes.

His first choice of direction was political. During the 1830s, he campaigned to draw working men together to lobby for universal suffrage, annual parliaments, secret ballots, an end to property qualifications for MPs. In June 1836, he was a founder of the London Working Men's Association, limited to 100 working men, with space for some honorary middle-class members, such as Radical MPs. This was not a career based on charisma; he was no orator, but rather, as an early historian of the Chartists put it in 1855, better than that: a 'clear and masterful intellect' who had 'great powers of application'. He was one of the six working men, joined by six MPs, who published in 1838 the *People's Charter*, which he co-wrote with Francis Place, who gives us a convincing picture of Lovett as a tall, thin, melancholy man.

Although he became the first Secretary of the Chartists, things did not go well. First, he was arrested for seditious libel after a speech in Birmingham in 1839 attacking the Metropolitan Police and spent an utterly grim time in prison. But then he encountered the classic dilemma for those who seek radical political change: should the method be more forceful, even veering towards violence, or should it rely on persuasion? Under attack, especially from Feargus O'Connor, who was much more confrontational and, as Lovett said, the exponent of 'the great "I am"', he retreated from politics to devote the rest of his life to furthering working-class education. That was the choice. A political route – or joining in the sunshine of the impending Age of Progress through education and prosperity. Of course, both were important, but when Lovett now formed a new National Association for Promoting the Political and Social Improvement of the People, his emphasis was on funding circulating libraries and encouraging educational missionaries. He opened a bookshop; he taught evening classes.

Looking back on his own life, he might have said – in fact, more or less did say – that it was the opposite of the Victorian dream. By his own account, he was 'a busy, restless, discontented fellow'. He had worked and worked, living frugally, struggling, not finding happiness and dying in poverty. Perhaps Marx, his fellow resident in perpetuity in Highgate Cemetery, would have said the same. But by espousing what the Victorian Scottish educational reformer William Hodgson called 'the noonday blaze of knowledge', it was Lovett who had most accurately shown that in the long term the disadvantaged would be better served by the constructive power of education than the destructive confidence trick of revolution.[29]

Three relatively unsung reforms that were radically to improve the lives of all classes of society were the abolition of duty on advertising in 1853, of newspaper stamp duty in 1855, and of paper excise duty in 1861. The brilliant Edward Lloyd, whose *Lloyd's Weekly News* was – a few years after his death – the only newspaper to reach a circulation of a million copies in the 19th century (which it did on what would have been his birthday, 16 February 1896), had begun with penny stories for working-class readers in the 1830s and 1840s, but the reforms encouraged him to invest in a Hoe rotary press in 1856 and a web press in 1873 – the first publisher to do so. Elites railed against his 'penny dreadfuls', *The Wild Boys of London* (1864–66), or *The Work Girls of London* (1865), but for innumerable school children, messengers, or clerks who read the 103 weekly instalments of *The Wild Boys*, there were incalculably large benefits in opening up horizons of understanding and potential betterment that were unavailable to previous generations. 'Penny dreadfuls' might not quite match an elite Classical education, but the reading habit carried with it the magic of imagining possibilities and also careers, rather than the insecurities of manual labour. Moreover, railway distribution ensured national distribution of the new publications for the army of new readers.

Lloyd was one of those who took himself to the London Mechanics' Institute. He had not found favour with Charles Dickens, who thought his work was being appropriated in Lloyd's early venture, *The Penny Pickwick*, and brought a failed court case. Nevertheless, in Lloyd's combination of thorough research, risk-taking and energy, he perfectly expressed the optimism of the age – you needed all those things if you were going to deal with paper demand by leasing 100,000 acres in Algeria to grow esparto grass (a low-cost alternative to rags in paper-making), and invest in the machinery and infrastructure to compress it, bale it, charter your own ships and sell on any surplus to other papers in the UK.[30]

Mayhew's first three volumes had made a distinction between 'Those That Will Work', 'Those That Can't Work' and 'Those That Will Not Work', with a fourth later devoted to 'Those Who Need Not Work'. In getting a sense of how far the aspirant working classes and the very poor had come by 1900, it would be right to identify philanthropy – enabling Shaftesbury's Ragged Schools, or Dr Barnardo's, or the National Society for Prevention of Cruelty to Children; it would be right to imagine the excitement generated by such early worker profit-sharing schemes as the one introduced by Henry

Briggs, albeit short-lived, in the mid-1860s at West Yorkshire's Whitwood Colliery, especially since it was a sign of moving on from his early aggressive management of his workers; and it would be right to put emphasis on the development, albeit not a smooth path, of trade unions (which were suspicious of profit-share as a mechanism for maintenance of owner control). There were key pieces of social legislation, and there was impressive working-class self-help; there was medical progress and there were reforms in local government.

But in the end, it may make most sense to observe just how much everything was changed by the spread of literacy and the printed word. How could the poor even acquire a perception of the possibilities of the world without the glimpses given by books, magazines and newspapers, the gleanings from them, all published on a scale and with an accessibility of price and distribution that could not even have been dreamed of before the 19th century. Equally, it was by the same mechanisms that the middle and upper classes – many of them – were informed and persuaded of the need for action. Government reports, of which there were many, were usually (though not always) conscientious attempts to record and define a situation and its remedies, but they perhaps could not persuade in the same way as a Dickens or a Mayhew. It was not of the essence that Mayhew was a journalist, with his own flaws, rather than a wholly scientific investigator.

As Thackeray said, what Mayhew showed was frequently only a hundred yards from 'our own front door', but we did not go to see. Mayhew did, first by visiting Jacob's Island in Southwark during a cholera epidemic. Back in Fleet Street, he persuaded the Editor of the *Morning Chronicle* to run a series of articles on the unknown, largely unseen, urban poor. Eventually, he was helped by numbers of other writers, hansom cabmen, office interviews and stenographers. Some of his subjects helped considerably by what we might call playing to the writer's camera. Equally, what later investigators had in abundance – the professional data-collecting and analytical skills of modern sociologists – left no room for Mayhew's human skills in encouraging people to talk frankly about themselves: the ham-sandwich seller who could describe his life as standing 'up to the ankles in snow till after midnight, and till I've wished I was snow myself, and could melt like it and have an end'. The guileless case for reform was more powerful than the pressure-group statistic. Nevertheless, not everything went smoothly, and the *Morning Chronicle* stopped its backing after an advertiser complained. The impecunious Mayhew retreated to Germany in the 1850s and wrote a variety of books, from travel literature to the very uncomplimentary *German Life and Manners*, in which he expressed his prejudice that the Germans had as much chance of joining the higher powers of Europe as 'a community of squirrels'. Being told by the Germans themselves 'very candidly' 'that Englishmen are ever foremost in all matters of progress', instead of diffidently demurring, he presaged later over-confident and over-bearing jingoism.

This was in itself revealing about the supreme confidence expressed in the Age of Progress. The English, Mayhew asserted, belonged to no one class of people, but the 'picked tribes of the world': ancient 'poetic' Britons, with an after-fusion of Welsh and Roman; the Saxons, from whom a love of liberty and justice was derived; the Scandinavians, infused with a spirit of maritime adventure and enterprise; and 'chivalrous' Normans, from whom the finest of 'the present day aristocracy' were descended. Germans were 'a century behind us in all the refinements of civilisation and the social and domestic improvements of progress'. While he was about it, he suggested the French were still in as corrupt and comfortless a state as Britain was in 1800; the Spanish lived a medieval, pre-Reformation life of 'intellectual darkness' and 'bigotry'; and the Russians had not evolved much by comparison with the feudal period after the Norman Conquest.

What had this got to do with the poor? Well, said Mayhew, 'English work people' were defined by 'how much better housed, better fed, better paid, better cared for, and better treated' they were than the labouring poor abroad. At that moment, the statement was in most respects a true one. In so far as it was a sweeping under the carpet of what his own researches had revealed about the London poor, it gives us a perspective lost by just focusing on the slums. The slums, and the suffering attached to them, were a colossal problem, but at least there was now an awareness of a need for action, rather than an acceptance that the poor had only themselves to blame and could not be saved.

As to Mayhew, one of the reasons he had gone to live in Germany was that the cost of living was lower and he could escape his debtors in London. Already, before his project on the London poor, he had almost become bankrupt in 1847. At times throughout his life, he withdrew into something close to indolence; at other times, he tried his manic hand at every type of writing, from fairy-tales to novels, as well as – without success – becoming a publisher himself. Everything failed in the end, and he had retreated into obscurity by the time of his death in 1887.[31]

Another Victorian dream that did not finish well. But, like Lovett and his sad career, Mayhew had started something enduring, something that could be referenced as progress was made. And it was made. When Booth and

Rowntree made their more scientifically based analyses of the poor in the late 19th and early 20th centuries, they were both clear that things were getting better. Yet, paradoxically, by shining more light on the whole scale of the problem at a time when the political world and the state had become much readier to play a much bigger role – both with funding and in social reform – they provided the evidence for action, a development that has continued through to the present day.

There had always been some philanthropy. It made a good excuse for the state to avoid responsibility; Peel told the House of Commons in March 1841 that 'he should abominate the Poor-Law if he thought it relieved the rich from alms-giving'. In fact, its scale grew ever larger even when the state began to be active in social reform: *The Times* reported in 1885 that just over 80 donors gave more than twice the annual revenues of the Swiss confederation to London charities. For many decades, books like *The Million-Peopled City* (1853), by the clerical secretary of the London Mission, stressed the urgent need to support the disadvantaged in a city containing 'all that is gorgeous in wealth, and all that is squalid in poverty'.[32] Mayhew, Booth and Rowntree all helped to reveal poverty to those who might help.

53 A midday porch meeting at the Rev. William Booth's 'We Welcome the Poor' People's Mission Hall, Whitechapel Road, *c.*1870. His East London Christian Mission was to become the Salvation Army in 1878. This was an 'army' that survived attacks on Booth for his authoritarian rigidity and literal attacks on its 'soldiers' from the alcohol lobby to become 150 years later one of the greatest humanitarian agencies ever created.

A surfeit of statistics lose their impact. Instead, we can share the reality of one attempt to help by action rather than just money: the so-called 'University settlements' in London's East End, beginning with the Oxford student – later an MP – Edward Denison's time in 49 Philpot Street, Whitechapel, in 1867. He gave talks to dock labourers, provided evening classes for workers, ran a school in John's Place, Stepney – and gave an example that encouraged others to spend at least part of their vacation helping. We are in what became Jack the Ripper territory 20 years later, though Denison gives a vivid glimpse in his journal not so much of extreme violence, but of the sheer hopelessness of the lives, 'the absence of anything more civilizing than a grinding organ to raise the ideas beyond the daily bread and beer, the utter want of education, the complete indifference of religion [that certainly wasn't true of St Jude's, Commercial Street, Whitechapel, where the Rev. Samuel Barnett became central to transformation] and the consequences: improvidence, dirt, crime, disease'.

Denison and others who followed could not offer immediate solutions, but they did offer a reason for living. In neighbourhoods where there might be fever just down the road, or a home being repossessed or stripped of its furniture, or houses that would have been unsuitable for cattle, you might see groups of adults and children waiting for admission to a well-kept house not by a servant but an earnest young man. Here they could be taught and could study, here they could provide ammunition to help their elite helpers to pressurize the authorities under the laws then existing but not necessarily enforced. Some could be taken off by railway omnibus to Putney or Hammersmith to learn about rowing, or introduced to cricket. The scale was insufficient to deal with the problem, but the effects were a lesson in how to make a small revolution without destruction.

The somewhat older Rev. Brooke Lambert, who became Vicar of St Mark's, Whitechapel, in 1865, was to stress that the point was not mission halls and philanthropy but a more basic activity: seek out the poor and help them. That's what he did when cholera hit Whitechapel shortly after he arrived, but he was also to apply the sort of statistical studies of what became known as 'the poverty threshold', similar to Booth's more elaborate investigations. Denison, Lambert and the historian J.R. Green met with Ruskin in 1867 to discuss the poor, with Brooke effectively pushing for the idea that the educated should 'colonize' where they lived, not as imperialists, but to enter the community in order to provide anchors for its troubles. None of them was in good health: Denison died at 29; Green in his forties with lung problems; Brooke lived longer, but after five years in Whitechapel, his health broke down and he never fully recovered.

Arnold Toynbee, whose nephew wrote the multi-volume *Study of History* in the next century and who was himself the first person to provide an analytical account of the machine culture created by the Industrial Revolution (see p. 50), the term he popularized, also died young, at 30, apparently from the complete exhaustion that resulted from constant work. Inspired by his work in Whitechapel, Samuel Barnett and his wife Henrietta founded a permanent base – 'settlement' – in Commercial Street, opened just after his death in 1883 and which they named Toynbee Hall. The objective was to provide lay education, but also to offer access to recreation and 'enjoyment' – just the use of that word was a victory for progress – for the people of London's poorer districts. All classes, creeds and opinions could come together to give East London 'the best gifts of the age'. Henrietta later took these principles to Hampstead and became a key figure in establishing the model garden community of Hampstead Garden suburb, as well as founding what became the girls' Henrietta Barnett School.

Hampstead Garden Suburb became more – if not exclusively – a middle-class haven, but Toynbee Hall continued to show what could be achieved in unpromising urban terrain. Among the early figures attached to it was Clement Attlee, who became secretary in 1910, and William Beveridge, perhaps Britian's greatest and most visionary social reformer. Part of the point was that the image of poverty planted in middle-class minds by Dickens was not the reality. Samuel Barnett, who visited Oxford – sometimes staying with Jowett – and later Cambridge to encourage students and graduates to live in rented houses in the East End for short or long periods, painted a different picture. People, he said, would visit after reading a story or some appeal and find it wasn't nearly as bad as they had supposed. There were terrible living conditions, but not everywhere and not something that it was impossible to change. The middle classes, some patronizing certainly, many not, just needed to supply the help that only they were able to give. That might explain why Jowett, according to Thomas Escott, had 'startled some of his hearers' by advising all young men, whatever their career, 'to make some of their friends among the poor'.[33]

Analysis and philanthropy – endowment or giving practical assistance – were increasingly supported by state social reform. The Liberal urge to prioritize liberty and economic progress, rather than equality and wealth redistribution, often in the genuine belief that the progress would benefit society as a whole, had held it back. Carlyle gave it short thrift ('liberty to starve' for the workers). An article in *Hogg's Weekly Instructor* – a magazine begun by the Scottish publisher James Hogg – in 1848, spoke of 'The cant of

Progress': 'the deluded mass' being told that they had only to struggle and strive a little longer and the 'good time' would arrive. Today, we need to make an imaginative leap to feel just how big a change it was for the state to take on social welfare, perhaps why what Beatrice Webb called 'this ministry of all the talents' – Gladstone's of 1880–85 – could not make up its mind whether it was individualistic or in favour of state intervention. Conservatives, meantime, rationalized the inertia of many of them by saying that reform needed to be 'wise, safe, and practical', not based on 'mere theory'.[34]

Nevertheless, numerous Factory Acts spanning the entire Victorian period, often inadequate or badly executed, were unequivocally transformative. The state was interfering with business and, for that matter, parental control. Ernst von Plenev, First Secretary at the Embassy for Austria-Hungary, published *The English Factory Legislation* (1873), written for a German public, and intended to 'remove the still prevalent disinclination' on the Continent to legislate to regulate working hours. He argued that the English government had 'done more for the improvement of the working classes than the Government of any other country'; there just wasn't the animosity between higher classes and workmen 'so noticeable on the other side of the Channel'.[35]

It had all begun with a factory Act in 1802, with a context of the spread of epidemic disease, and with a parliamentary inquiry into the condition of the factory population in 1815. Throughout the century, if all too slowly, reducing working hours, regulating child labour, legislating on particular industries – mines and printworks, textiles and paper, and glassworks and machine manufacturers – came under government scrutiny. Before the Industrial Revolution, almost all children had worked when jobs were available. To go from that to regulation and limitation on their employment and – still more – to full-time education up to a minimum age (albeit taking a century) altered the perceptions of children growing up and gave them a window into a wider world for ever. To go from the economist Nassau Senior telling the then President of the Board of Trade in 1837 that 'a ten-hour bill' would be 'utterly ruinous' because all the profit came from the last hour, to the Ten Hours Act a decade later was a good sign that the overthrow of vested interests had a chance of succeeding – and peacefully, too.

Behind these changes were many unsung heroes. Sir Arthur Helps (1813–75), an early advocate of animal rights and an authority on slavery, was singled out by Thomas Hughes for his contributions to the 'condition of England question' and 'every considerable social reform for a full generation'. In his early twenties, Helps wrote about the need for improvement in public governance, and then for four decades wrote discerning, constructive, thoughtful, practical essays and books, while having a variety of public service appointments and ultimately the Clerkship to the Privy Council. He had caught the excitement of living (this in 1859) when we were just beginning to understand 'the most potent elements in the universe', just beginning to investigate 'the laws of disease' in towns, just beginning to try to make the lives of the poor less squalid.[36] Like many Victorian intellectuals, his interest in character, morality or knowledge did not dissolve into losing sight of practical remedies; to the contrary, they enriched the ability of society to come up with the right solutions.

In the new world of the 20th century, there were also going to be many other challenges with which the 19th century did not have to wrestle (on which more below), and Victorians themselves had become beset as their era came to an end with doubts and pessimism. It was never again going to be possible to feel the kind of optimism *The Times* expressed in its reflective article towards the end of January 1859. *The Times*, of course, then as now, was not always right (though it would be going too far, as some do, to suggest that it was always wrong). The anonymous leader writer convincingly averred that there was nothing more difficult than arriving at a just comparison of one age with another. He was conscious that 'we of the 19th century' are accused of praising ourselves and perhaps 'we are guilty of this self-flattery'. Was that unusual? He didn't think it had ever happened before: 'All ages, as a matter of course, praise the ages before them, and call themselves degenerate; that is what has always been considered the proper thing to say.'

Today, we are used to the idea that, if you are old, you tend to remember 'the good old times'. Back in the 1850s, *The Times* suggested that the old did not offer reproof of 'the vanity of the present generation'. In the past, their refusal to say things had shown improvement 'was a good deal connected with the fact that there was none'. Now there was a general understanding 'on the subject of the facts of human want and misery'. Now we understood, and had resources, we could change things.

Of course, it was not true that everyone shared these sentiments, or – in the case of those below the poverty line – were even able to comprehend them. Yet, however much further there was to go, *The Times* was correct to identify a massive change and its accompanying optimism.[37]

The American political economist Henry George, best known for his *Progress and Poverty*, first published in 1879, pointed out that humans were the only animals whose desires increased as they were fed, the only animals whose desires are 'never satisfied'. As the seagulls circle the English Channel in Victorian times, they want no better food or lodging than the gulls who 'circled round the heels of Caesar's galleys'. (It took the visible gluttony of humans to teach the gulls at today's seaside human ways.) Humans were also unique in wanting quality, as well as quantity. Clothes were not just for comfort, but for adornment. Rude shelters became houses. And as power to gratify wants increases, so does aspiration.[38]

Did this just apply to what are now frequently described as the 'racist' makers of 'the white hegemony'? Charles Pearson, a British-born historian and academic, who eventually moved to South Australia to farm, published *National Life and Character* in 1893. That was used by proponents of a 'White Australia' policy because of its prediction of a day, 'perhaps...not far distant', in which the globe was 'girdled with a continuous zone of the black and yellow races'. No longer weak or under tutelage, self-governing and in command of their own economies and resources, they might 'even thrust aside' their former rulers. Regardless of whether Pearson's motive was to sound a racist panic button, it did accurately signal that what had been opened up by 19th-century progress would continue to have momentum. In July 2024, Britain's predominantly white electorate supported the election of 88 MPs that came from an ethnic minority, the number roughly proportionate to the size of population as a whole. The same election increased the percentage of women MPs to 40.[39] These things owe their origins to the Victorians.

Similarly, while far too many social ills continued, the principle that the state must act, and act after objective investigation, was firmly established, while (at least with hindsight) we can see that politically the application of the Continental European ideas of Comte, or Marx, or Hegel, or Gobineau and his theory of an Aryan master race, would evolve for the worse in the 20th century – but not in Britain, which was set on a non-utopian evolution of John Stuart Mill's or Herbert Spencer's 'progress', with a mixed message of material wealth, moral structure and individual liberty. The caveats should be many, but the opportunity to approach the poor and otherwise deprived sections of society in a new spirit was firmly on the table, as it had never – ever – been before.

CHAPTER 9

'EDUCATION FOR ALL'

EVEN WOMEN AND THE POOR?

So many of the speeches, the letters, the essays, the newspaper reports, the books – an avalanche of them – that survive from the Victorians, being written by males, leave a highly misleading image. There is a certain sad inevitability about it simply because men were the powerbrokers. The female inheritance from the past could hardly have been worse and applied across the classes. Blackstone's famous *Commentaries on the Laws of England* (1765–69) spelled it out with chilling accuracy: 'By marriage, the husband and wife are one person in law; that is, the very being or legal existence of the woman is suspended during her marriage or at least is incorporated or consolidated into that of her husband.'[1] Early in the Victorian period, *The Times* even observed that 'it seems to be considered one of the marital rights to kick and beat a wife to death, or to break her neck by flinging her downstairs without incurring the capital penalty', though the implicit objection was a sign that change – for the first time – was on the agenda.[2] Barbara Leigh-Smith, later Barbara Bodichon, and one of a remarkable band of middle-class women who were to push single-mindedly for women's rights, described in detail and 'in Plain Language' women's state in 1854. Her body belonged to her husband; any earnings 'belong absolutely to her husband'; all her assets or inheritances were his; he had custody of children; neither the common law nor equity had direct power to oblige a man to support his wife. It was nevertheless evidence of how deeply both men and women believed they were living in an era of progress that Bodichon used the argument that the violence to women in previous societies did give a reason for women to be 'protected', which was unnecessary now in a time of civilization.[3]

The challenges were legal, economic, political, but also psychological. Anthony Trollope's mother, Fanny, herself a prolific novelist but in an unhappy marriage, spoke of women believing 'not only that it was a wife's duty to obey, but that she should do nothing else, and think of nothing else from morning to night'.[4] Caroline Norton, granddaughter of the playwright

54 In the late 18th and 19th centuries, reform often ran in families. Barbara Bodichon's father, a Whig MP, was himself the son of the radical abolitionist William Smith, who was part of a group of social reformers, the Clapham Sect. Her father's sister was mother to Florence Nightingale. After she met George Eliot in 1852, they became lifelong friends; Eliot's characterization of the eponymous heroine of her novel *Romola*, with an 'expression of proud tenacity and latent impetuousness', seems perfect for Bodichon.

Richard Brinsley Sheridan, nevertheless demonstrated that in a situation of patriarchal control made worse by something close to indoctrination of girls when they were growing up, the state and public opinion could be pushed hard, if in a long battle. She left her husband George because of his behaviour (Lord Melbourne called him 'a stupid brute') in 1836; he then sued Melbourne, claiming that the two of them had engaged in 'criminal conversation', meaning adultery. The case was not proven, but Caroline vigorously protested that she effectively did not 'exist', not only unable to testify, not only losing access to her children, but unable to divorce, not even able to have income from 'my own copyrights' as a writer (George had gone to court when she tried to live off them). The fight continued into the 1850s when Caroline's mother died in 1851 and her inheritance became legally that of her husband. It took until his death in 1875 for her finally to be free.[5]

Caroline had a wildness that helped her determination. In 'A Letter to the Queen' at the time her campaigns and those of others led Parliament to debate marriage and divorce law in 1855, she spoke of 'the grotesque anomaly which ordains that married women shall be "non-existent" in a country governed by a female sovereign'. As it happens, Queen Victoria was herself not entirely consistent in what she said and did, but in 1860 she wrote to the Scottish biographer Theodore Martin's wife, Helena (Martin was subsequently entrusted by the Queen with writing a life of Prince Albert), enlisting the help of anyone who could speak or write against 'this mad wicked folly of Women's Rights, with all its attendant horrors'. The female campaigners were forgetting 'every sense of womanly feeling and propriety'. In fact, it was hardly surprising that the process of reform was full of noise and uncertainty, as well as both surprise – Caroline Norton had denied in *The Times* back in 1838 that she believed in the 'ridiculous doctrine of equality' – and predictability – Melbourne was not a supporter of her proposed changes to the law.[6]

Obviously, the story of the Victorian changes to women's status is a mixed one. Most of the voices and most of the campaigns were middle-class attempts to change the country's increasingly middle-class power structures towards recognition and equality. The concerns of the poorer female sections of society were necessarily more to do with improving their basic conditions of life. Some of the poor were able to describe and reflect upon their lives, in its way as special a step forward as a change to the law. Ellen Johnston (1835– c.1874), in Scotland, despite minimal education, probably being sexually abused by her stepfather and beginning her life in a textile mill in childhood, read and read whatever she could and became 'The Factory Girl' in her own poems, one of which was published in the *Glasgow Examiner* in 1854, followed by a stream in the *Penny Post*. She died in the workhouse a 'factory girl' while still in her thirties. It had hardly been a happy life; she had an illegitimate child along the way (the father appears to have deserted her), yet remained socially deferential in a way that annoyed her fellow workers. Her father, who had abandoned the family for America, committed suicide when he returned to find her mother had remarried. And she was not deferential enough to her employer, who blacklisted her from getting further work in Dundee after she sued for unfair dismissal. Terrible, terrible experiences – but the poetry survives, and that was a whisper of progress.[7]

Enthusiasm for books or religious belief, life at work, life at home, hardship – these tended to be the themes of the autobiographies and letters of working-class women. Middle-class women showed some of these preoccupations, some of them unsurprisingly expressed differently: the first magazine specifically devoted to their opinions and needs, *The English Woman's Journal*, asked in January 1860, 'what can Educated Women do?' It suggested that public opinion was now strongly in favour of 'increased avenues of employment' for women, yet the writer had received at least a hundred letters in the previous month in which everyone from Anne to Zora was asking how to get employment. Two particular problems were facing up to social hostility (women shouldn't have jobs) and the need to have a little money with which to begin. The 1851 Census showed only 7 per cent of middle-class women working, most of them limited to being a governess, a writer or an artist. The lower middle class was heavily influenced by a series of books about the female role by the Congregationalist Sarah Ellis, beginning with *The Women of England, Their Social Duties, and Domestic Habits* (1839). She also noted 'the degradation of what is vulgarly called *making their own living*' and put emphasis on seeking happiness 'only in the happiness of others', which included the privilege both of providing 'personal services' and of deference to husbands. Ellis acknowledged that teaching was 'considered lady-like', but noted also that out of the great increase in manufacturing, there might be some female occupations that were 'by no means polluting to the touch, or degrading to the mind', such as drawing patterns for calico printers, or engraving.[8]

By the end of the Victorian period, despite many setbacks, there was sufficient change or progress towards change, in all the main areas of concern – legal and political equality, education and access to employment – to suggest that there would never be a return to the degree of dominance (and in some matters absolute control) by males throughout history. It wasn't helped by Victorian ideas of what was appropriate, or by the males being so emotionally messed up by their education that – as a character in Edmund Yates's *Kissing the Rod* (1866) says – they had 'a horror of giving expression to or even indulging in any strong feelings'; or the women being emotionally messed up by being told – as Eliza Stephenson put it in *St. Olave's* (1863) – to 'cover the flame of their intellect', if they had one, 'with the ground-glass of humility and modesty'. Of course, Victorians, like all humans, didn't always behave as their society dictated, but it took the extraordinary tenacity of particular women to make progress.[9]

Caroline Norton had shown the way on the law. The first step removed divorce from the ecclesiastical courts and created a new civil Court of Divorce and Matrimonial Causes in 1857, nearly failing through the opposition of Gladstone (in favour of Church authority; the Prime Minister, Palmerston, was more pragmatic) and Darwin's subsequent foe, Bishop Wilberforce. Like all the legislation that followed, it was flawed, and a woman bringing a case had to prove not just her husband's adultery, but further offences, such as rape or desertion. From 1870, women could keep their own earnings or inheritances, extended to all property twelve years later. From 1873, women could be allowed custody of children, the main criterion being their needs, not the parents' rights. From 1884, women had the possibility of petitioning for divorce immediately after desertion and adultery. Cumulatively, these changes did make history. And in 1878, Frances Power Cobbe's essay in the *Contemporary Review* on 'Wife Torture', prompted in particular by working-class domestic abuse, had a powerful influence on an Act of the same year that empowered magistrates to grant separation and maintenance – though the problem with the law, then and now, was that divorce was usually too expensive.[10]

Frances Cobbe provided a key example of women's success, despite male opposition, in penetrating the world of the male professions – in her case, journalism. Her article in the *Fortnightly Review* in 1867, 'What is Progress, and Are We Progressing?', was notable for two reasons: it was rare for women to write for such a journal, but – ultimately more significant – she gives an almost gender-free analysis, despite herself being engaged in many feminist campaigns, supporting animal rights, or falling out with Darwin after encouraging him to read Kant's *Metaphysics of Ethics* and then writing a riposte to Darwin's *The Descent of Man* in her own *Darwinism in Morals*, with an emphasis on emotions – above all, sympathy.[11]

In writing about progress, she defines it as 'the progress both of the nation in its corporate capacity and of the individuals composing it', starting with the *Annus Mirabilis* of 1851, 'that era of bright dreams which opened with the first Great Exhibition'. Crime had decreased in a time of population increase; there was less cruelty to animals and most 'odious sports' stopped. Yet despite the failure of Overend Gurney (see p. 81), 'the "bears" pursue fresh games unpunished'. The ravages of 'a gang of Neapolitan banditti' would have seemed trifling by comparison to the 'stupendous swindles' found in the railway companies. Basic foods were adulterated; grocers, butchers, chandlers and bakers used false weights; sham medicinal drugs were sold; servants took a percentage from tradesmen. Overseas, where 'confidence in English probity' was once well-nigh unlimited, confidence had dwindled. The 'mischief' can 'of course' be attributed to 'the vast extension of commerce and industry'. Those caveats, it is true, might reflect the difference between female balance and males closing their eyes to awkward facts; they certainly showed the virtues of introducing a woman's voice into public debates.

However, Cobbe's view of commerce was also perhaps what might be expected from someone who came from a prominent Anglo-Irish landowning family. In other respects, she looked to a brighter future. Science could be used to spread 'nobler views of both God and destiny'. In that she was to be disappointed, but secular science – she also argued – would benefit public happiness and indirectly public virtue. Philanthropy was growing like mushrooms all over the country; a Social Science Congress came up with a thousand schemes of benevolence for sick and sound alike. Parents, without 'the old despotic authority', treated their sons and daughters as confidants. National legislation was limiting factory hours and banning transportation. Poverty, measured at 5.3 per cent of the population in 1851 was 4.6 per cent in 1865 (though of a larger population) – too high, but 'we are living under a system of continual amelioration'. If there was imperfection in law, we knew it could be improved – and that was happening. Expenditure on education increased by five times between 1850 and 1865, and we knew we had to go further. A huge range of practical inventions was transforming life.

Whatever else, the optimistic belief in progress (and, we might add, the misplaced new sense that statistics could always be believed) seems not to have been entirely a male invention, though Cobbe does keep including her reservation: 'the growth of commercial competition and dishonesty'. But if she had her differences with Darwin, there were other women who earnestly corresponded with him: in the case of Lydia Becker in Manchester, this lasted over fourteen years between 1863 and 1877, especially on the fertilization of plants and botanical subjects in general; she sent him her own *Botany for Novices* (1864). A great proponent of educating girls in science (as well as a leading member of the women's suffrage movement), Becker persuaded Darwin to send papers for her newly formed Manchester Ladies' Literary Society in 1866. Such open discourse in the pursuit of knowledge and making the future, with male and female together, jars with the post-Victorian characterization of its society as repressed, dreary and pompous.

Becker was even instrumental in securing a vote by a woman for the first time by taking Lily Maxwell, a shopkeeper included by mistake in the electoral roll in Chorlton, to the polling station in 1867. The vote was later ruled illegal, but faces were to the future. Not that everything was equally portentous: Charlotte Humphreys (1843–1925), another journalist, was given a platform by Henry Labouchere in *Truth* in the 1870s, but that was for a gossip column for women, with an audience stretching across the world via the Empire. And progress continued: her daughter Pearl became a journalist of a different kind, acting as a war correspondent in Paris in the First World War.

Other professions than journalism (though in law not until 1920 in Scotland, and 1922 in England and Wales) also slowly, slowly, slowly allowed women to participate. Jane Hughes, sister of the author of *Tom Brown's Schooldays*, and unhappily married to the unsuccessful barrister and son of the political economist Nassau Senior, did relief work for victims of war in an organization that was eventually to become the British Red Cross (in 1906). But it was after her work for pauper children that she became Britain's first female civil servant as an assistant inspector of workhouses. Was the appointment opposed by the Civil Service? Of course – it was entirely the result of support from a number of 19th-century middle-class politicians, in this case the estimable Sir James Stansfield, at the time President of the newly constituted Local Government Board. The report she produced on the lives of pauper girls also had a hostile reception, but Senior's continuing efforts led to the creation of several societies, essentially help given by the middle classes to young women whose previous lives had given them no information or benevolent structure to help them navigate life. Self-help could not function without a kick-start; middle-class women often helped enormously – and selflessly: an exhausted Jane Senior died at 48.

This was more than philanthropy (not that that should be dismissed – because of limited employment opportunities, though often also through a general social concern, there may have been more than half a million women in philanthropic work in the 1880s). Josephine Butler learned about life in the Liverpool workhouse while her husband was head of a large boys' school; she also saw the ravages of disease on the many prostitute 'incurables'. She was clear, as she explained to the Ladies' National Association in 1877, that the social pressures on women to conduct themselves unseen or strictly in a domestic context removed them from campaigning, leaving that by default to men. Although organization was not her strength, the passion, the energy and the determination she shared in rousing grassroots fervour about the laws governing the regulation of vice and spread of contagious diseases, mostly to the detriment of women (who were subject to compulsory checks and often to confinement) rather than the male users of prostitutes (who were ignored), was fundamental in achieving reform. She herself, in her reminiscences of the 'Great Crusade', described the prevailing attitude of the male MPs as (mostly) indifference before public opinion compelled attention. There was intrinsically a darker side to male middle-class social concern: the fear that criminality, working-class protest, working-class habits and lifestyles would overwhelm the very respectability for which the aspirational bourgeoisie had striven.

Florence Nightingale had been a big campaigner against the first of the Contagious Diseases Acts in 1864, basically penalizing women, and continued to give support to Josephine Butler, despite the fact that England's first female doctor, Elizabeth Garrett Anderson, supported the laws (though her Anglo-American rival for that title, Elizabeth Blackwell, spoke out against the ignoring of male responsibility). Women were inevitably hampered by not having a presence in Parliament, and while the growth of campaigning journalism helped, yet again James Stansfield was enormously influential in his efforts to secure repeal of the Acts, finally achieved in 1886. Along the way, Josephine Butler was set upon by hired thugs and had her life threatened.[12]

There were some things that women could do more quietly. Barbara Bodichon was probably the first to set out a rational case for *Women and*

Work (1857); she also provided financial help to get the *English Woman's Journal* off the ground. Josephine Butler, under her maiden name of Grey, published books on *The Education and Employment of Women* (1868) and *Woman's Work and Woman's Culture* (1869). The former calmly pointed out that 'the facts of the society have changed more rapidly than its conventions'. In the past, 'muscles did the business of the world, and the weak were protected by the strong; now brains do the business of the world, and the weak are protected by law.'[13] Yet scarcely a thousand women, without capital and 'by their own exertions', made £100 a year. The principal employments were governesses and teachers (just over 80,000 in 1861) and a large number in domestic service or sewing. Women just needed an opportunity. They had it, for example, when the School of Art in Newman Street, London, opened that year to give evening classes for females. More or less immediately, they improved the culture by working hard. Once admission was allowed to the Royal Academy, a woman won Gold Medal for best historical picture in 1867: 'Where there are equal facilities, the women are the most successful.'

The numbers in art school were tiny. But no one predicted just how many new jobs would shortly be invented by continuing economic progress, even if many were at the level of working in the department stores that proliferated towards century's end, or in the explosion of clerical labour in the same period. That left two further key routes to change: politics and education. On the former, we might admire the bravado of Louisa Bevington (1845–95), who anticipated rejection of the designations 'Miss' and 'Mrs' and, in 1879, discomfited Mallock with her essay 'Modern Atheism and Mr Mallock'. She is interesting not so much for being right, though she was accurate in predicting that socialism, at least of the communist kind, would never achieve the benevolent effects its adherents claimed (you could as easily turn the state into 'a benevolent public-spirited institution' as transform 'a wolf into a lamb'), but for expressing a different kind of over-optimistic Victorian progress – shared by a number of non-bomb-throwing anarchists, male and female: 'We shall be asked what we intend to put in the place of the State. We reply, "Nothing whatever!" The State is simply an obstacle to progress.'[14]

It won't do just to call this naïve. Women were living in an environment in which Matilda Betham-Edwards could be told by her friend Frederic Harrison, whom she calls 'last of the great Victorians' – he was certainly immensely learned – that 'Your words about Ireland show me how unfit the ablest and best women are for politics. They judge by their hearts, not their heads, and mistake vague ideals for observed facts.' Bagehot had put it even more rudely in *The English Constitution* (1867): 'The women – one half of the human race at least – care fifty times more for a marriage than a ministry.' Middle-class women, free from the financial cares of the working class, did in fact adopt a robust approach to campaigning for the franchise, unperturbed (some) or infuriated (many) by outright hostility or patronizing remarks – Gladstone for one feared that voting would 'trespass upon their delicacy, their purity, their refinement, the elevation of their whole nature'. Well, politics in any era can be a dirty business; he put it more delicately to Queen Victoria in February 1886, when female (and more male) voices were becoming more insistent: in the Cabinet, the Women's Suffrage Bill the following week should be 'what is termed an open question', but the Ministers generally were 'disinclined to the Bill, & disposed to vote accordingly'.[15] Interestingly, the Liberal MP Peter McLagan, a great supporter of female suffrage, was Scotland's first black member, his father from a slave-owning family, his mother from British Guiana.

The first mass political movement to include women was probably the Conservative Primrose League, formed in 1883 with at least a semblance of equality of status for men and women, while when the new Labour Party finally emerged in the early 20th century, it exuded a very male air, though an impressive group of Labour-supporting women did start the Women's Labour League in 1906 to push for female representation. There were local Women's Liberal Associations that first came together in 1887 as the Women's Liberal Federation at the initiative of Sophia Fry, wife of a Liberal MP; Catherine Gladstone, Gladstone's wife, became its first President and it grew rapidly. It didn't help that not all active members supported female suffrage; when William Gladstone himself reaffirmed his opposition in 1892, the Federation lost more than 50 of its member associations when it voted to support suffrage.

Outside the world of campaigning, often notable, but not often the key to unlocking change, most Victorian reforms of all kinds happened when the male controllers of institutions concluded that change was essential but would not completely undermine the status quo. That had the great benefit of securing grounded transitions and the great disadvantage of leaving social ills too long. In Mallock's house party, Mr Storks (T.H. Huxley) upsets Lady Grace (loosely based on Francis, the feminist wife of the Oxford intellectual Mark Pattison) by appearing to support an American physician arguing that 'the rights of woman must very probably be fatal to the existence of man'. Kate Amberley talks in her diary about a conversation she and Mrs Grote had with the real Huxley in May 1867, in which he criticizes the men who still want to keep women 'in the doll state', yet still does not believe they would ever be equal to men in power and capacity.[16]

55 John Stuart Mill in 1865: the momentous year of the end of the American Civil War and Lincon's assassination, but also – less portentously – the election of Mill to Parliament. In a painting in 1910 by Bertha Newcombe, of the Artists' Suffrage League, Mill was apocryphally presented by Emily Davies and Elizabeth Garrett Anderson with the first Women's Suffrage Petition outside Parliament. In fact, the super-thorough Davies had sent a printed copy to all the members of the Commons and the Lords.

The most powerful advocates for women's suffrage in the Victorian period were John Stuart Mill and, above all, his especially brilliant wife, Harriet Taylor, without whom, Mill suggests in his autobiography, he would not have understood how the effects of the inferior position of women 'intertwine themselves with all the evils of existing society and with all the difficulties of improvement'.[17] Although Harriet died in 1858, her daughter Helen Taylor – Mill's stepdaughter – took his side and, according to Mill in his autobiography, suggested he should write *The Subjection of Women* (1869);[18] she herself long campaigned, publishing *The Claim of Englishwomen to the Suffrage Constitutionally Considered* in 1867. If they were now beginning to have civil rights, why should political rights 'not accompany them'?[19] But it was Mill himself who was the one able (having become an MP in 1865) to put forward a motion. As Violet Effingham, in Trollope's *Phineas Finn*, responding to Finn's male desire to do 'something', says: 'a woman must be content to do nothing – unless Mr. Mill can pull us through'.[20]

Kate Amberley, in the Ladies' Gallery of the House of Commons with friends in May 1867, described Mill's speech. It began poorly, with a painful pause at the beginning, and for nearly two minutes he seemed 'quite lost', only his eyebrows working and that 'fearfully'. It later emerged that Lowe's learned-by-heart speech – Lowe had not only been opposed to the extension of the male franchise, but certainly to any talk of a female franchise – had made Mill think so hard that he lost his original text. He recovered, he was cheered, he continued with fluency – but to no avail. A hundred or more promises of vote turned into 73 at the count, with 196 against, despite Mill's simple proposal to change 'man' to 'person' in the draft Bill.[21]

That did not quieten women pushing for the vote – for the rest of the century, the impetus continued to grow, ready to explode at the time of the Edwardian Suffragettes. In 1885, Helen Taylor tried to stand for Camberwell North, only for the returning officer to refuse the nomination papers. It is hard to demonstrate a clear and direct line from agitation to legislation, even in the case of the Suffragettes and the limited franchise reform eventually made in 1918 and extended ten years later by the Equal Franchise Act. Yet arguably, the coming together of a small number of women of dazzling talent to discuss women's issues – the female equivalent of the Metaphysical Society, which achieved nothing practically – did have far-reaching consequences, above all in education.

Before Mill's intervention, several female members of the Kensington Society, formed in 1865, had worked on electoral reform: Elizabeth Garrett Anderson, Emily Davies, Barbara Bodichon and Jessie Boucherett, among them. Mill was used in 1866 to present a mass petition for suffrage to Parliament. There had already been a Langham Place Group, named after the address of *The English Woman's Journal*, formed in 1858 and providing a forum for discussion of women's rights, employment and higher education. Both societies, though short-lived, provided a forum for a new generation of mostly unmarried, determined, educated middle-class women to create a network that was to have little success with the franchise, but an enormous long-term influence on education – and the empowering that went with it – through the actions of individual members.

The Kensington Society met at the home of Charlotte Manning, who was to become the first Mistress of Girton College, Cambridge, and who after living with her first husband in India had published a scholarly study of *Life in Ancient India* in 1858. While there was unity about the main issues, there was plenty of falling out, too, some of it natural to any intellectual hothouse, some of it feeling suspiciously like the kind of power struggles, or passing on of blame when things went wrong, so common in male communities. During the preparation of the franchise petitions, Helen Taylor, who was not on the committee, appears to have undermined Emily Davies.[22] She complained to Clementia (Mentia) Taylor, wife of the MP for Leicester, that Davies had used the names of Kate Amberley and Mary Somerville ('the queen of science' – a designation that was another sign of the times – after whom Somerville College, Oxford was named) when they were just supportive, rather than signatories to the petition. That seemed to be untrue, at least in the case of Somerville, given that Mill himself had determined to ensure she was the first to sign. In any case, Clementia also complained because she felt she was being accused of being a dangerous revolutionary. Snide comments were made about her intellect, but – if so – she nevertheless had a phenomenal energy for liberal causes, and at Aubrey House in Holland Park, bought by her husband, Peter, in 1863, provided a library for continuing the education of the impoverished young, offered a focus for the movement to end slavery in America, and welcomed Mazzini and Garibaldi at receptions attracting other Continental European revolutionaries.

There was an outstanding success. By the end of the next decade, there were two women's colleges at Cambridge (albeit without degree-conferring powers). Josephine Butler was right to argue in her 1868 book on women's education that it was not just about 'intellectual progress', but of wider significance – especially the moral behaviour of society. Besides, there was nothing humorous or ironical about the attitude expressed in Anne Marsh-Caldwell's novel *Aubrey* (1854), in which Mama tells her child that 'Thinking

56 In 1892, the date of this cartoon, the lady cricketers want a team of their own. Gladstone holds the suffrage bat; that year, just before he became Prime Minister for the last time, he was hostile to the women's vote. Ironically, he was also against the 'invasion' of universities by female students, yet his youngest daughter, Helen, had just been appointed Vice-Principal of Newnham College, Cambridge.

is the worst thing in the world for your complexion.' If she couldn't sleep for thinking, 'Take a little laudanum.'[23]

Emily Davies, who had met Barbara Bodichon in 1858 in Algiers, in the midst of the tragedy in which three of her siblings had early deaths, despite the belief that the dry climate there would be good for weak lungs, had resolved to secure *The Higher Education of Women* (the title of a tract she published in 1866). The emphasis, entirely rational, lay in the practical consequences of success in the objective. To come to sound conclusions about how to help the poor (a mission to which women were naturally drawn) and to engage in unpaid work involved 'knowledge of almost everything a politician needs'. A 'warm heart' needed also 'a strong clear head' to tackle the organization of hospital management, workhouses, prisons, reformatories, charitable societies. Male MPs made codes, revised them, re-revised them, but were often dependent on women. How were the poor to be advised? Gushing benevolence was not a policy.[24]

In November 1867, George Eliot writes that 'There is a scheme on foot for a women's College, or rather University, to be built between London and Cambridge, and to be in connection with Cambridge University, – sharing its professors, examinations and degrees!' Two years later, 30 miles from Cambridge (a subject of complaint from male tutors who had to travel there), an unassuming women's college in Hitchin received its first five undergraduates. Barbara Bodichon's support for Emily Davies was essential, and it was the former's fund-raising that allowed a move to Cambridge itself, with her favourite architect, Alfred Waterhouse, designing Girton College. Emily headed it there between 1872 and 1875. Not that those conscious of a historic role, female or male, are always generous-spirited, and the semantics of 'founder' and 'originator', or 'one of the founders', led to disputes. Bodichon's friend Matilda Betham-Edwards observed tartly in 1916: 'No Girtonian has troubled herself about her benefactress.'[25]

Before these events, Emily had also successfully campaigned to ensure that girls' schools should be part of the remit of the government's commission to improve middle-class secondary education: the Taunton Commission, which was appointed in December 1864. No woman had previously been an expert witness for a royal commission, and Emily was joined by two other members of the remarkable Langham Place Group. Frances Buss, first headmistress of North London Collegiate School, took the view that girls should take the same competitive exams as boys, and that the best pupils from the lower middle class should not only be educated in a narrow sense, but encouraged to pursue or make opportunities. Her school had developed from another begun by her mother in Kentish Town and renamed in larger premises in April 1850; she was also to found Camden School for Girls to allow access to a good education for gifted girls from families that needed an affordable alternative. When Emily Davies was campaigning for girls to be allowed to participate in the tests provided by the University Local Exam Syndicates, North London ran a pilot.

For all the women in a close-knit group of future-makers, it was reading in childhood that was not just educative, but helped them to take on all the obstacles in the way of women's progress. Buss had herself studied with Dorothea Beale, another witness at the Taunton Commission, at the first college for women, Queen's College, Harley Street, founded in 1848. Beale, who became headmistress of Cheltenham Ladies' College in 1858, making it another beacon of female progress, was also to fund the foundation of St Hilda's College, Oxford in the 1890s. Curiously, it was a shy, sensitive, unflamboyant man who had been responsible for bringing Queen's College into existence: Frederick Maurice. Yet another significant Victorian intellectual, it was he and some of his colleagues at King's College, London, who provided the lectures. Still, it was one thing to help middle-class women, but what of the rest of the population? It was Maurice, with Charles Kingsley, who founded the Working Men's College in Bloomsbury in 1854 after he had been forced to resign his King's Professorship for refusing to accept that unrepentant sinners would be condemned to eternal punishment. Religion, too, was only slowly moving towards more tolerance – but it was moving. Later, he became a Professor at Cambridge, as well as returning to King's.

It took a little longer for there to be a Working Women's College. Frances Martin wrote about it in *Macmillan's Magazine* in 1879. The rationale was simple: women who earned their living had 'few opportunities for self-improvement'. Yet they could find it by 'remedying a defective education', or 'supplying the want of any education whatever'. Most important, tired after a day's week, you benefited from seeing 'the bright, kindly face of someone who is interested in you, and who makes the lesson cheerful'.[26] The College teachers were unpaid, making themselves available after their own day's work. Maurice's College had begun catering for women separately, then tried 'the experiment of mixed education'. Martin had been inspired by him, but wanted to help those working women who preferred a single-sex environment. She, too, had been a pupil at Queen's College. Her College for Working Women survived until 1966 when it merged with the Working Men's College. Ideas about education change and change again, but all these Victorian pioneers made immeasurable contributions to giving a new, modern, educated Britain a chance to make a better world.

Yet the shining lights of progress tell an incomplete story. By the end of the Victorian period, an enormous amount had been achieved educationally for the disadvantaged, as well as the elites. But for most of the 19th century, education was a mess. At the start of the Age of Progress, the differences between supporters of Anglican, nonconformist or secular control seemed irreconcilable, though all three were generally opposed to state control, and politicians felt the same. Victorians wanted to change the world, thought they were changing the world, did change the world – but often the processes were very inept because of an unwillingness to change the structures and shibboleths that underpinned their society. It was a great step forward to collect – mostly conscientiously – information (there were endless commissions and committees throughout the 19th century), but that raised an acute dilemma of all modern governments: how to move from understanding to action, and action with consensus.

The unprecedently rapid growth of population, combined with a new landscape of towns and cities like nothing before, cried out for a national policy to be operated on a local level. In the tiny hamlet of Thorne Coffin, Somerset, there had been thirteen people at the time of Domesday Book. Well over 700 years later, in 1811, there were 97 and never more than 110 throughout the 19th century. In 1818, there was a Sunday School in the parish, conducted by a curate, for ten boys and fifteen girls. The poor were 'very desirous' of having their children educated, but were 'deficient in the means'. The school was abandoned in 1833, then revived in 1847, held in the church, with eight boys and five girls, with a voluntary teacher and subscriptions.[27] When Jane Eyre, in Charlotte Brontë's 1847 novel, goes to Morton, there was no school ('the children of the poor were excluded from every hope of progress'). When she acquires 20 pupils, only three can read; none can write or do arithmetic.[28]

In the first half of the 19th century, there were dame schools, often run from the owner's home and teaching basic skills for a tiny fee – though sometimes in effect only offering childcare and closing when the villagers could not afford it. There were ragged schools for the poor and destitute, or outcast children, formed by philanthropists and given a boost in London in the 1840s by Lord Ashley's Ragged School Union (Ashley became Earl of Shaftesbury in 1851) to help coordination. There were factory schools, some enlightened, others like the one described by Robert Southey – a writer who travelled from republicanism to Toryism, though always supporting the underdog – in a letter to Ashley in February 1833: Sunday Schools attached

57 Destitute children were helped by Brook Street Ragged and Industrial School, Hampstead Road, London. John Pounds, crippled by a dock injury when he was fifteen, taught himself to read and later – as a shoemaker – started teaching homeless street children. The missing link to formal schools was provided by Lord Shaftesbury's philanthropy, alas only after Pounds' death in 1839. But the Scottish preacher, Thomas Guthrie, in his 1847 *Plea for Ragged Schools*, credits Pounds as the originator of the idea.

to factories were only there because the manufacturers knew they would be criticized if 'their little white slaves received no instruction'. There were some schools in prisons, as well as railway schools, colliery schools, agricultural schools. The 'system' offered pragmatic 'solutions', but was complicated by religious divides, and could be summed up as 'chaos'.[29]

The religious bodies were at the heart of it all, with the Church of England dominant and in many ways privileged. But the Education Census in 1851 showed just how variegated it was, with at least four types of Methodist, Baptists, varieties of Presbyterian, Roman Catholics, Jews, Quakers, Dissenters (without more precise definition) and many more. Religion enveloped everything. The ragged schools, for example, were very much the product of Evangelical Christianity; and religious schools of all kinds naturally prioritized religious instruction over education in any wider sense. Bagehot called it education as narcotic, with men of 'very great cultivation' attending 'minutely to the ecclesiastical state of the souls of their village', with no wider 'intellectual interests.... They have no anxiety to solve great problems, to busy themselves with the speculations of the age'.[30] There is no underestimating the trauma of change from a religious to a secular society. Sudden upheaval, Lord Salisbury argued in the House of Lords in 1870, 'dazzled and confused men's minds, and drove them in some cases from the landmarks of faith'; that had happened with the discovery of America and the invention of printing. Now 'the progress of physical science' and a greater knowledge of 'the modes of thought of the Eastern world' were propelling 'a violent movement towards unbelief' on the part of 'the most educated.'[31]

The fear of unbelief was accompanied by the battle of the faiths. As Dissenters gathered more and more economic and political power, the proposal to put factory schools under the control of Anglican clergy resulted in petitions (and not just from Dissenters – Catholics joined in). The provision was dropped, but the hostility remained. Ashley summed it up: 'Dissenters and the Church have each laid down their limits which they will not pass, and there is no power that can either force, persuade or delete them.' Even after 1870, when state elementary education was brought to most children, religion was often centre stage. The candidates in the Northern West Riding election in 1872 were divided: Mr Powell supported the act for giving religious equality but not for leaving our children 'to be educated like heathen'; Mr Holden was all for the disestablishment of the Church of England and a 'Godless education'. The local newspaper was not impressed: 'Everyone wants all due progress, political, social, and sanitary', but the paper was getting 'weary of all those advisors whose only idea of progress is destruction.'[32] That wasn't the view of the Liberal politician John Morley. In his *The Struggle for National Education*, he felt clear that 'There is not a single crisis in the growth of English liberties in which the state church has not been the champion of retrogression and obstruction.'[33]

Why did Victoria's reign nevertheless end with a record of considerable progress in providing education for all, another achievement made by no previous society? Morley's message was an obvious indicator: a society that allows free speech will not survive on a diet of inaction. A society with dramatically larger numbers of children in absolute terms, but also in the proportion of them living in poverty in ghetto-type conditions in towns and cities, cannot be ignored without risking social instability and an affront to the modern values Victorians effectively invented. The Minister responsible for the 1870 Education Act, W.E. Forster, without a great deal of encouragement from his Prime Minister, Gladstone, always himself using his faith in the Church of England as his reference point, put some emphasis on the urgent need to consider the relationship between industrial prosperity and competitiveness with education. Charles Parker, later to be an MP, noted in his 1867 *Popular Education* that the working class in general understood the value of education and the 'educated classes' had failed to provide it. Many middle-class people, reformers or not, also observed growing working-class power and saw education as defusing any trend towards revolution. That also connected with the franchise. Tennyson, delighted that the Forster bill passed, made up an epigram: 'No education, no franchise'. Lowe made the point less succinctly in the House of Commons, arguing that if you entrusted the masses with power, education was 'an absolute necessity'. He also made a decisive practical point: it had to be 'a national system'. These contexts also coincided with the wider development of changing the state's role from passive defender of social order and threat from invasion to active participant in facilitating progress.[34]

In the event, the poor had to wait for the universities to reform, and the biggest hurdle in Oxford and Cambridge was again the Church of England. First Oxford (1854), then Cambridge (1856) removed the need to sign the 39 Articles to matriculate, though 40 years later, Mallock was still bitter: the eponymous hero of his *Tristram Lacy*, exposed to the 'criticism and scientific thought of the day' about early Christianity at Oxford, even to be found at the pulpit in the College chapel, became a 'disbeliever of everything'.[35] Back in 1850, Lord John Russell had surprised the House of Commons by announcing a royal commission on the two universities. A *Times* leader suggested they had 'acquired the character of closed corporations' just when they needed to meet the expanding need for graduates to fill the liberal professions, magistracies, foreign missions, Indian and colonial administration. 'Science has advanced, but they have narrowed the circle of their teaching. Population has increased, but they have restricted the number of their pupils'.[36] As Catherine Gore had averred in her novel *The Banker's Wife* (1843), if all the time and brains expended upon Latin and Greek for the last 500 years had been applied to the sciences – key to 'the progress of mankind' – 'we shall have been millions of miles nearer the moon' and also been able to give the poor their coal 'this bitter winter...for sixpence the chaldron' or sold them 'their linsey-woolsey at two pence a yard'.[37] Pausing to note that the moon is less than a quarter of a million miles from Earth, we can still say that here is the origin of a lasting debate: should we study science and technology to make us prosperous, or should we study the humanities to learn about how there are other things than prosperity and destroying the planet?

The *Morning Post* was critical of Oxford's failure to take on board such issues as poor scholars, extending the professoriate or abolishing restrictions on fellowship and scholarship. But once started, the reforms had their own momentum.[38] True educators, like Mark Pattison – unkindly represented as Mr Casaubon in George Eliot's *Middlemarch* – saw education in a holistic sense, with elementary schools a priority like all else, but also – especially as Rector of Lincoln College, Oxford for well over 20 years (1861–84) – pushing reform, as did the historian John Seeley at Cambridge, helping to ensure the admission of women to the university. Jowett was there from the beginning, helping to get the original report on the two universities (1852) from discussion document to legislation.

Oxford and Cambridge were by no means the whole story. Scotland had had its own distinguished universities for centuries. King's College and University College were the founding colleges of the University of London in 1836. Civic colleges, to become the red-brick universities – Birmingham in 1900, Manchester and Liverpool in 1903 – disregarded religion at entry and focused on the kind of education that would prepare their students for working life. As ever, the effects of Lowe's sometimes annoying but always impressive single-mindedness showed themselves; back at the time of the 1850s reforms, he had urged in evidence the inclusion of 'physical sciences' in the curriculum. His experience in Australia had shown him how 'intimate acquaintance with remote events' left Oxford graduates in 'utter ignorance' of 'the laws of nature', accordingly disadvantaging them. Utterly relentless, when writing leaders for *The Times*, he argued, in March 1856, that the university was still casting a shadow of the Middle Ages far into the 19th century.[39] As ever, the changes that did come did not destroy everything. Taine found that the two universities still had a luxury place for Greek, Latin and pure mathematics, but sciences and modern ideas had 'infiltrated' and teaching widened (he mentioned Jowett in that context).

Whether it was the universities for elites or basic education for the poor, the instruments of change and operation included commissions of inquiry (sometimes using statistics to suggest that things were better than they were; for example, in relation to school attendance). In 1849, the Civil Service gave education (with around 50 civil servants) some prominence in the then tiny government machine; partly as a result of the untiring energy of James Kay-Shuttleworth, its decade-long Secretary, it evolved from being a committee of the Privy Council in his time to an Education Department in 1856, and eventually into a Board of Education in 1899, each evolution with more authority and responsibility.[40] There were also many pressure groups, whose effectiveness was often diminished by religious divisions. Joseph Chamberlain and other Birmingham nonconformists, however, pushed for elementary education for all children, without religious control, in what

58 Mr Punch tries to get John Bull as policeman to help the children denied an education by squabbles between Church of England, Roman Catholic and Dissenting Christians. *Punch*, 2 July 1870.

became the National Education League in 1869. The rival National Education Union (mainly Anglican, but with some Methodists and Roman Catholics) had a vested interest in continuing the existing system, in which most of the voluntary schools were under religious control.

When reform came in 1870, it was distinctly unrevolutionary; it is in retrospect that we can most easily see it as the signal that elementary education for all was destined to be both compulsory and free, but not just yet. William Forster, whose bill it was, had married Matthew Arnold's sister in 1850; not long after, George Eliot declared him to be 'a very earnest, independent thinker'. The Act did not abolish the existing schools, but created elective 'school boards' – this for England and Wales – to provide new and non-denominational schools where there was a need, as well as the teachers for them, paid for by levied rates and potentially able to pay for children most in need. As usual, there was little uniformity in practice; big cities could attract a Joseph Chamberlain (as Birmingham did) or a T.H. Huxley (as London did) onto the local board.[41]

Much further legislation followed: compulsory elementary education in 1880 (previously at the discretion of the local authority); the end of 'school pence' under Salisbury's Conservative government in 1891; a provision for technical schools and colleges for vocational training in 1889. The groundwork had been done for the more thorough-going reorganization that took place in 1902, including for the first time proper provision for secondary education. When James Saunders, a miller, observed the opportunities now available – he was writing in the late 1880s – it was clear that schools had changed much for the better; he confessed a little jealousy. Early 20th-century schools were no paradise, but flushing toilets, heating (up to a point) in the classroom, the tools and equipment of education, playgrounds – all were a sign that progress was not just about learning.[42]

There had been School Inspectors since 1839. At various times, their role and organization evolved. Jowett's influence was seen when his former pupil Ralph Lingen became Secretary to the Education Board in 1849; during his tenure, eight former Balliol men were appointed inspectors. Edmund Sneyd-Kinnersley gave a shrewd account of his life as an inspector after the 1870 Act (which, he correctly said, had gripped the public less than the Franco-Prussian War and the siege of Paris). Sent to meet the then Secretary of the Education Department, Sir Francis Sandford, at 11am, he was told by the porter that Sir Francis wasn't generally there until later. In his memoirs, he commented

59 *Mens Conscia*, an abridged version of 'a clear conscience', from the pupil asked by the School Inspector three times who signed Magna Carta: 'Please, Sir, 'Twasn't Me, Sir.' Charles Keene's cartoon dates from 1875.

on 'the intellectual numbness' of some of the Whitehall officials, with their 'positively Russian dread of individual opinion'. He was sympathetic to school managers dealing with the complexity of the notorious Form IX, with 'more traps to the square inch than are contained in any other nine pages in the world', and 'an army of clerks' in Whitehall 'to hunt for errors and omissions'. He had discovered the problem of modern government: the politicians often neglected the detail; the civil servants delighted in detail that didn't reflect the reality; the inspectors were adored neither by the teachers nor the civil servants; and the teachers varied from inspirational to incompetent. The children – some, at least – had 'an absorbing interest in the day's work' that 'was a constant reproach to me'. The problem with the school boards was that their members did not need to give 'proof of skill'; in one he encountered, none of the members could read or write.[43]

Robert Lowe, when Education Secretary, had a different view of the inspectors, at least according to the *Saturday Review* in 1864: he was like 'a brooding, resentful monster', unable to get his underlings to see things his way or report at his dictation. He wasn't 'the man to conceal his dislike of a bad smell'. Matthew Arnold, who was certainly well informed in all he wrote about education, was given a less than glowing review by the manager of a school in Westminster; after a shake of hands of managers and teachers and a few pleasantries, he walks through the classes between the desks, looking over the children's shoulders at some exercises, then departs. By then, Arnold had been an inspector for a long time. George Pegler, a headmaster in Huntingdon, was pleased to record that when Arnold (appointed in 1851) visited in March 1853, 'he found my boys better acquainted with History and Geography than any schools he inspects'. Pegler, like many headmasters, was no Wackford Squeers; rather, he started the year in 1850 with attendance at a lecture on electricity ('but the machine did not work well from the dampness of the room') and, shortly after, himself gives separate lectures on gravity and atmosphere (at the latter, two ladies were present; they 'appeared interested with what was advanced').[44] We should not assume that all Victorian education, formal and informal, was poor. Its organization improved only in fits and starts, but the sense of excitement about what was being discovered and the idea that education represented the key to advancement is palpable in the recorded experiences that have come down to us – 'the March of the Mind', as Bentham put it.

School logbooks were checked by inspectors. Introduced in 1862, they were to contain daily entries in bound volumes to exceed 500 pages. Entries were not to be deleted or changed. In St Clement's Boys School in Liverpool, a few pupils had to leave on 6 January 1863 rather than pay an extra penny. The following day, a teacher was disciplined for 'striking one of the scholars'. There were plenty of reasons for absence, from continuing gleaning (the harvest) to scarlet fever.[45] On the ground, such practical issues dominated, but Victorians also gave a great deal of thought to the basic questions: what is education for, and what should be on the curriculum?

On the curriculum, no one was in much doubt about what the Newcastle Commission in 1858 called 'the indispensable elements of knowledge, reading, writing and the primary rules of mathematics'. A *Punch* cartoon at the time of the 1870 Act had William Forster in front of a group of children (all unsmiling, one of the boys cheekily with hands in pockets). In 'The Three R's; or, Better, Late Than Never', Forster is happy to tell them that 'subject to a variety of restrictions, conscience clauses and the consent of your vestries', they may now learn to read. The Conservative MP Joseph Henley was one of many to argue – in a Commons debate in 1856 – that 'in educating a nation, the progress should be gradual, if it is desired to be certain and effective'. Try to add science or political economy, and a parent would respond by saying that they didn't know whether political economy was a good thing or bad, 'but I do understand the necessity of filling my boy's belly', so prefer him 'to work and help to maintain himself'.[46] Still, both schools and universities had widened their curriculum by the end of the century; it had been a struggle, but the consequences would be positive for ever.

On what education was for, the waters were muddied by religion and morality. Cardinal Newman, in *The Idea of a University* (1852), was firm that it was not about 'how to advance science, not how to make discoveries', but 'to form minds, religiously, morally, intellectually'. Ruskin went further: for children, it was not about teaching them 'to write or to cipher or to repeat catechism'; real education taught them about forming character, how to teach them to be clean, active, honest and useful. In fact, W.E. Forster himself was absolutely explicit in a lecture in Aberdeen in 1876: 'the law of humanity is progress'; the teaching of history not only proved this, but was an aid in ensuring that material progress would also lead to progress in virtue, which was not something to be taken for granted. In the public schools, as depicted in *Tom Brown's Schooldays* – its author, Thomas Hughes, had been a pupil of Thomas Arnold at Rugby – it became all about producing 'a brave, helpful, truth-telling Englishman, and a gentleman, and a Christian'. Of course, the best educators linked character-forming and widening the curriculum, and it became visible for the first time that education made society less violent and less crime-ridden. When Lord Malmesbury went to Eton in 1821 with his brother Edward, there were pitched battles – 'young Ashley, a most gallant boy, was killed'. In the last decade of the 20th century, Thomas Escott noted that the metropolitan mob had become the Sunday crowds around the Reformers Tree (the Hyde Park oak set alight by franchise protesters in 1866 and the predecessor of Speakers' Corner), the people indistinguishable from the weekday crowds in the Ladies' Mile in the park, except for the more affluent being better dressed.[47]

There were also new opportunities. F.J. Wild, the first boy from a board school to go to Balliol in 1880, was a magistrate in India's North-West province nine years later. An enormous amount had been said and done, but most importantly, markers had been laid down. Perhaps the best – and eventually to be the most convincing – document amongst the millions of words had been written by Lovett, the cabinetmaker, and Collins, the toolmaker, in Warwick gaol: *Chartism*, published in 1840. Just over a century later, it came educationally to fruition in the 1944 Education Act. Both Chartists and the makers of the 20th-century Act saw education as a right. Most Victorians came to think of it instead as the virtuous things that followed from having it. Joseph Fletcher, statistician, barrister and School Inspector, argued in 1847 that the right blend of moral and intellectual education would deal with unemployment, pauperism, crime, intemperance and disease.[48] He wasn't entirely wrong.

CHAPTER 10

'WHO OWNS PROGRESS?'

GREAT BRITAIN AND THE WORLD

On 12 June 1840, the first World Anti-Slavery Convention opened in Freemasons' Hall, London. 'These Delegates are extraordinary men in head, feature, & principle', observed the artist who memorialized the proceedings.[1] His comment omitted something key, however: the equally impressive women who attended. For nearly two weeks, 'the curse of Slavery' was dissected and analysed with passion and practicality before a concluding meeting in the even larger Exeter Hall. Throughout the Victorian period, one aspect of its support for progress was proclaimed in this building opposite the Savoy Hotel in the Strand. From its opening in 1831 to its demolition in 1907, the walls of Exeter Hall heard reforming voices on socially progressive issues. When it eventually made way for a hotel, that was perhaps an indication that the 20th century had learned Victorian materialism, but was starting to lose its passion for other forms of progress.

Invitations had been sent to 'friends of the slave of every nation and clime' the year before.[2] More than 500 delegates from the United States, France, Russia, Switzerland and Spain responded, Britain and its colonies providing the core. Delegates ranged from Saxe Bannister, first Attorney of New South Wales and author of *Humane Policy; or Justice to the Aborigines* (1830), and Adolphe Crémieux from Paris, Jewish advocate of tolerance and a free press, to Richard Musgrave from Antigua, who appears to have been brought to Britain as a domestic servant. Britain's role in influencing world opinion against slavery had been specifically acknowledged in America, with Daniel O'Connell, enabled at last to be an MP after Roman Catholic emancipation, asked by American delegates to petition Irish-American supporters of slavery; he gathered 60,000 signatures to that end. The response was not positive in the American South, where the whole convention was seen as an infuriating interference in American domestic affairs. In some sense – so the British lawyer John Witt later argued – the American South had 'a class without civil or political rights, devoted to labour', a situation, however, that was not unique to the US, but found across Europe; he quoted the British historian Henry Hallam – 'All the Polish nobles were equal in rights and were independent of each other; all who were less than noble were in servitude.'[3] Slavery had always been endemic across the globe; ending it was truly revolutionary.

On the first day of the convention, it was not difficult to agree the agendas. That day had a different significance: the changing attitude to women. An embarrassed George Stacey, a prominent Quaker abolitionist, had to speak against a proposal to admit women, the convention being that they were excluded from 'all matters of mere business'. The Congregational Rev. John Burnett politely suggested that the 'deepest respect' and 'most cordial welcome' the women should have did not make it desirable to 'clothe all the ladies with office in the general management of our social affairs'. Colonel Miller of Vermont observed that his state had never been troubled with 'the woman question'; women were 'our primeval abolitionists' who established 'a standard of liberty' that their husbands seconded.

The debate continued for hours, a delegate from Devizes saying that a decision must come 'the sooner the better'. The Chairman several times said he was ready to put the question, to no avail. He rebuked Samuel Jackman Prescod, soon to be the first person of African descent to be elected to the Parliament of Barbados, for reporting a private conversation when he quoted 'the ladies themselves' saying they had no high expectations.

The eventual decision – the debate went on and on and on – was to allow attendance but not official status. Elizabeth Cady Stanton, present with her delegate husband from Upstate New York and effectively attending the proceedings on her honeymoon (after omitting the word 'obey' from her marriage ceremony), and Lucretia Mott, a founder of the Philadelphia Female Anti-Slavery Society who bonded with Stanton, later – at least in Stanton's writings – explicitly suggested that this was where the women's suffrage movement in England and America began. William Lloyd Garrison, delayed by the weather – a common hazard for international conventions – arrived too late for the opening and insisted on sitting with the ladies in London. His career pointed to another challenge for movements arguing for progress; they split (he argued that the US constitution was pro-slavery, so Congress was not an option for an anti-slavery party); and they were not consistently benevolent (Garrison was antisemitic). For that matter, Joseph Sturge, who had been more single-minded and better informed than anyone in his fight 'against' slavery, also opposed women as delegates. He had ushered into the convention the 80-year-old Thomas Clarkson, whose 1779 Cambridge Latin essay arguing that it was unlawful to make humans slaves won a competition: quite a moment.

What a gathering. Not perfect, but such a wonderful symbolic moment in moving on many matters, not just slavery and women's rights, but raising questions about the role religion had played, despite perhaps a fifth of the delegates being church ministers. It was suggested that the Church had been a main support for American slavery and, after long, long debates, a resolution was passed that slavery was 'a sin against God'. As important, slavery was discussed globally: the Brazilian *fazendas* or the Indian cotton fields, or the indigenous people of Upper Canada, for example, not just the American South. The Rev. T. Scales spelled out the life of the Russian serf, who was 'deprived of all human rights; he has no property; the blood which flows in his veins belongs to his master; his toil and sweat only serve to satisfy his lord's disgraceful lusts; every hour of his existence must be devoted to the purpose of adding to his master's wealth'. This was a country where a young man swapped his cook for a friend's dog who 'pleases me'. The same applied in the Islamic world, despite – so argued Dr Bowing (after 'frequent interviews with distinguished men of the Mohammedan faith') – slavery being incompatible with the Koran.

Both in the USA and the UK, anti-slavery campaigns signalled greater power for populism. As William Jay wrote to James Birney in 1840 (both men contributing significantly to anti-slavery campaigns in America, if more conservatively than some radicals): 'This is an age in which Governments, as well as individuals, are amenable to PUBLIC OPINION, whether foreign or domestic.' It was also an age in which different reforms overlapped: after the World Anti-Slavery Convention ended, some hundreds met at the Crown and Anchor pub for less formal discussion on the Poor Laws, universal suffrage, women's rights, temperance. This book is not a history of those movements, or of Empire; instead, it tries to assess how Victorians felt about these matters, what changed and how that connected to progress. The two big changes that had happened earlier in the 19th century in Britain – the Act of 1807 prohibiting the slave trade in British possessions, and the Act of 1833 abolishing slavery itself in the colonies – were not perfect. There was bitter debate about compensation paid to slave owners and the provision for ex-slaves to be tied to the estates for five years in a period of transition.

When *The Times* correspondent William Clowes travelled in the American South later in the century and after the American Civil War, in the period between Reconstruction and codified Jim Crow laws enforcing segregation, he recorded in his 1881 book *Black America* that 'A white man may be ignorant, vicious, and poor. For him, in spite of all, the door is ever kept open. But the coloured man, no matter what his personal merits may be, is ruthlessly shut out.'[4] Whether it was America or Britain and Europe, Asia and Africa, it was implausible that slavery's immemorial practice, and the prejudices attached to it, would end just like that. It continues today in too many parts of the world.

There were happy stories. Ira Aldridge left America to escape race prejudice in the early 1820s; in the British census of 1851, he gave 'Africa' as his birthplace and in 1858 took the role of Othello at the Lyceum Theatre, more than 150 years before the 21st-century campaign to have black actors play black parts, though he did experience racist abuse. Howe Browne, Marquess of Sligo and a governor of Jamaica who was pushed out of office by the local assembly, used his compensation money to build schools and to begin to pay wages; eventually, he divided his land into smallholdings. Sarah Forbes Bonetta, presented to Queen Victoria as a child as if she was a chattel, was in fact enslaved in Africa, with her parents killed in the imperializing activities of the rich (rich largely through slavery) ruler of Dahomey. King Ghezo refused the British mission to get him to abandon slavery and refused to desist from the ancient practice of human sacrifice (it was African business); instead, he gave the little girl and other presents to Queen Victoria. There was a happy

60 Ira Aldridge as Aaron the Moor in Shakespeare's *Titus Andronicus, c.*1852. Was this a black actor delighting in making progressive performances on the London stage, or – as some argue now – should we instead focus on the role's self-incrimination in such lines as 'Aaron will have his soul black like his face'? Shakespeare's many villains are embroidered purely for dramatic effect, with natural characteristics that are not themselves villainous at all (Richard III being the most obvious example).

ending: the Queen had her educated; she married a black and prosperous African businessman who the British West African Squadron had freed from the Atlantic slave trade, and their daughter was sent to Cheltenham Ladies' College, one of the very earliest schools, opened in 1854, to provide a proper education for girls.[5]

Of course, such tales do not add up to a thesis of benevolence, and occupation of others' territories continued. But they are symbolic of the roots of change that would previously have been thought inconceivable. What was not symbolic were the efforts of the British to end the slave trade across the globe, especially using the Royal Navy, after Britain banned it in 1807 and for the rest of the century: in the Caribbean, where other European nations were still active; by blockading Brazil; using Cape Town as a base in the south; off West Africa; in the Indian Ocean, where Arabs sold slaves to the East. Some estimates suggest around 150,000 African slaves were freed; this was not a routine matter, and many British died in the process. Some historians today dispute the figures and criticize the activities and motives of the Navy, as if such an extraordinary step forward could ever have been perfect. As the century progressed, more and more much-needed attention was also paid to stopping the trade not just in Africa and west from Africa to the Americas, but east to Turks, Persians and Arabs. The Sultan of Zanzibar was forced to close the slave market in 1873, but that was not enough, since traders started increasing numbers down the Nile. The much-maligned General Gordon was almost as messianic in his desire to end slavery as the Mahdi was to continue it: 'noble failure' might not be a bad description of his efforts. There are not even descendant voices to memorialize in the case of many of the male slaves in the Eastern trade; because of the use of castration, the descendants often don't exist.

To understand how Victorians experienced the mad, bad, exhilarating, shocking, multifaceted globalization of the world in the 19th century, together with the deeply polarizing motives and consequences of imperialism – overwhelmingly significant and complex events – we need first to set aside interpretation and build a mental picture of the scope of the canvas. The maverick Laurence Oliphant – Mallock's Otho Laurence in *The New Republic* – was a child of empire, born in 1829 in Cape Colony. His father – from a family of Scottish landed gentry – was Attorney-General there, soon to move 5,000 miles to what was then called Ceylon as Chief Justice. Oliphant also spent some of his childhood in the old Scots castle of Condie, Perthshire; that was another long journey, more than 5,000 miles, with no steamships, let alone aeroplanes available.[6]

Britain's political and economic power opened up horizons for British influence, good and bad. In a frenetic 25 years before Mallock's book was published, we can find Oliphant everywhere. His first book, in 1852, memorializes *A Journey to Kathmandu*. On and off, he spends eight years as secretary to Lord Elgin, which takes him to Washington, where he helps negotiate a reciprocity treaty between Canada and the US, and also to China and to Japan. He happens to be on HMS *Furious* in Aden when it picks up the great explorer John Hanning Speke in 1859, on his way back to London after his expeditions and many misfortunes with his fierce rival, Richard Burton, in search of the source of the Nile; Oliphant, who knew Burton through Richard Monckton Milnes – brilliant literary patron, social reformer, politician – persuades Speke not to wait for the sick Burton, stuck in Aden, and on reaching London, to go to the President of the Royal Geographical Society and announce what he named Lake Victoria as the source of Nile.[7]

In Japan, in July 1861, he uses a whip against a two-handed sword when approximately fifteen xenophobic *ronin* attack the temporary British legation

61 5 July 1861: Laurence Oliphant had just arrived as First Secretary, but was in the thick of it in defending the British legation in Edo (Tokyo), headed by Sir Rutherford Alcock (1858–64), when it was attacked by supporters of the isolationist, virulently anti-Western Mito fiefdom. As he rose from his bed, Alcock described the arrival of Oliphant, streaming blood from 'a great gash in his arm and a wound in his neck'.

at Tozenjin in Edo. Quite badly wounded, en route home, he comes across a Russian force lurking in a secluded bay on the Nagasaki Tsushima Island and somehow gets it to withdraw. He was with Elgin in China after the Chinese seized the *Arrow* – flying the British flag, but Chinese-owned – in Canton harbour in 1856, and gives an account of how they hunted Chinese in creeks and burned villages 'not, it must be confessed, in a manner calculated to increase their terror for our arms, or their respect for our civilization'.

The Chinese, then as now, had their own views about civilization. George Wingrove Cooke, *The Times* correspondent in China just after this (1857–58), gave praise to 'the greatest Chinaman of the present day', Ye Ming-ch'en, Commissioner in Canton and the man who had seized the boat. Cooke gave special mention of the Chinese cultural link between cookery and civilization, and the barbaric habit of the English of doing the work of the slaughterhouse on their dinner tables with knives and forks.[8] Whatever happened, China would not forget its certainty that it was the true home of civilization in every sense.

Containing Russian expansionist aims, especially towards the ailing Ottoman Empire and China, was always a key British foreign policy aim in the 19th century. Ironically, given the alliance of Russia and China today, the Chinese Emperor – under duress – ceded 230,000 square miles of territory to Russia in 1858 at the Treaty of Aigun; it remains Russian to this day. Just before that, Oliphant managed to endear himself to the British army when, in the Crimean War, he was able to advise on request from Lord Raglan about the Russian defences at Sevastopol, which finally fell in summer 1855. It helped that he had explored Russia and the Crimea earlier in the 1850s and was there again briefly during the siege. Oliphant appears in northern Europe again, this time in Poland, sent as an observer when there was a Polish revolt against Russia in January 1863; denied entry later in the year, he travels to Moldavia and takes time to observe something of the second Schleswig-Holstein War, in which Prussia, supported by Austria, defeated Denmark. Nationalism was beginning to create havoc in the many parts of Europe with ethnically mixed populations and complicated histories.

But you could not describe Oliphant as a shadowy figure, even if he was sent by Palmerston or Lord John Russell on secret missions into central and eastern Europe. To the contrary, he became an MP (for Stirling Burghs in 1865) and showed a taste for a while of being a society figure. Kate Amberley, in a letter to her brother Lyulph in 1861, doesn't think 'Mr Oliphant' is as conceited as her sister Blanche does, and notes that Blanche tries to get her to confide in him while abusing him behind his back.[9] No wonder that

62 Child of Empire: whether playing a central role in W.H. Mallock's house party, or depicted – as here – by the caricaturist 'Dicky' Doyle in his own novel *Piccadilly*, Laurence Oliphant symbolised a world in which old certainties had been destroyed and restlessness struggled almost desperately to find a new home, in the process disrupting the lives of millions.

society did not satisfy Oliphant for long, though long enough to join friends in starting a political journal, *Owl* – mostly gossip – and write the novel *Piccadilly*, first published in *Blackwood's Magazine* in 1865, and as a book that was to influence Mallock in 1870, though with a disclaimer that none of the characters was intended to represent a real person.

The central character, Lord Frank Vanecourt, rents a house overlooking Green Park after many travels. As he dresses before going out, he contemplates writing the 'history' of civilisation – you could not call it 'the progress of civilisation', so perhaps he should 'do the Gibbon business' and make it 'the decline and fall of civilisation'. He paints (in a picture that might well be recognized today) a money-dominated society replacing a love of ease with the lust of gain, expediency replacing principle.[10]

This disillusion was to lead Oliphant himself in another direction that would be recognizable today, especially on social media: he joined the cult of self-proclaimed prophet Thomas Lake Harris, in Brocton, New York, adjoining Lake Erie, and later in Santa Rosa, California. Harris was in fact born in Buckinghamshire and returned across the Atlantic on a number of occasions after his parents emigrated. Everyone seemed to be on the move in a world becoming not just global in its horizons (and the more so when there was steam transport), but accompanied by a great restlessness. Economic development and opportunity, spiritual unease, and confused and often upsetting clashes of cultures, as well as ever-greater Western technological dominance, all played out against the often violent competitiveness generated by nationalism. Harris's cults – he led a series of them – were based on a classic mix of misunderstood philosophy and science. Oliphant provided financial support and accepted, with his first wife and his mother, both of whom joined, the familiar restraints of cult leaders. These he later recorded in his novel *Massollam* (1886), in which Harris is characterized as an idealist who turned to avarice and demanded absolute obedience.

When they fell out (though not before Queen Victoria invited Oliphant to Balmoral to discuss his experiences), Oliphant re-directed his energies towards establishing a home for Jews in northern Palestine. The Russo-Turkish War (1877–78) – all the European powers were keenly attuned to the decay of the Ottoman Empire – helped to prompt the idea of a mission to Constantinople. With letters of recommendation from Disraeli and his Foreign Secretary, Salisbury, and support from George Eliot (whose novel *Daniel Deronda* in 1876 showed British antisemitism but also its eponymous hero's interest in a Jewish homeland), he managed to get some support from the Turkish leadership, but not from the Sultan, distrustful as he was of British motives.

The story of British Christian Zionists, while not ultimately influential (that had to wait for Jewish Zionist momentum leading to Theodor Herzel's World Zionist Organization and its first Congress in 1897), fitted the overall context of the many piecemeal Victorian reforms – Jews received legal equality in Britain in 1856 – but was also the result of the greater awareness of world issues attached to globalization and, in particular, Russia's extreme violence towards Jewish communities in Eastern Europe.

The sad little story of Mary Seddon from Wigston, near Leicester, who set off for Jerusalem with English Jews and a white donkey in 1823, was in some sense a signpost to the future. Her companions appear to have abandoned her when they reached France, and her husband, highlighting the increasingly questioned powers of a husband over a wife, committed her to an asylum for the next 50 years. Two formidable granddaughters of hers, Georgina Meinertzhagen and Beatrice Webb, had begun to reap some of the benefits of the progress made in women's rights by the time they met in Mary's old age; they found her to be remarkable, if not entirely balanced about her own personal mission to lead the Jews back to Jerusalem.[11]

There were other, more prominent figures who supported Zionism: the social reformer Lord Ashley was instrumental in getting Britain to open a consulate in Jerusalem in 1838 and encouraged his stepfather, Palmerston, to support Jewish colonies in Palestine (not that everyone agreed: the sharp-tongued Florence Nightingale suggested that if Ashley hadn't tried to reform asylums, he should have been in one). Disraeli, son of a Jewish convert to Christianity, predicted that half a century later (he was writing in 1877) there would be a million Jews in Palestine – shepherded by the British.[12]

The shepherding points to a key feature of Britain's interaction in the 'Age of Progress': the skilled mixing of motives. That did not necessarily mean idealism was guileful. Oliphant was genuinely moved by the Russian pogroms and spent his last years in a religious community in Haifa, among his friends Naftali Imber, poet and author of the Zionist anthem *Hatikvah* ('The Hope'), who acted as his secretary after travelling from what was then Austrian Poland. They fell out eventually, and Imber moved to England and the United States.

Oliphant's own plan for 'The Land of Gilead' envisaged a rail link from the Mediterranean to what is now northwestern Jordan; it would develop the economic potential of the region, to the benefit of Europeans and Ottomans; it would hold back Russian imperial expansion; and it would provide settlers on the east side of the Suez Canal that felt supportive to Britain. Here was a mix of economics, politics, cultural exploration, scientific exploration – the underpinning of formal and informal imperialism, usually adjudged now just as exploitation. After Oliphant's death in 1888, the newspaper *Havatzelet* reported in May 1890 that 'His Highness the Sultan (May His Glory Be Exalted)' had granted a concession to build a railway to a Christian Arab from Beirut named Yusuf Elias. The finance was to come from the English entrepreneur J.R. Pilling, 'the head of a rich company in Great Britain which has deposited ten thousand pounds sterling with the treasury to carry out the project'.[13]

The project seemed rational. It took 75 hours by camel to take grain from the Bashara Valley to port in Akko and Haifa; the train would take seven. Was it an easy return for the investor? Apparently not: the plan failed and eventually Abdul Hamid II decided on Ottoman control with the German engineer Heinrich August Meissner. Opening up the world had become, almost suddenly, competitive. Pilling bankrupted himself, though managed to involve himself in ever-more dubious ventures, including a promise to Lloyd George during the First World War that he could get the Turks to cede Syria (including Palestine) to England. Lloyd George was unimpressed.

Oliphant's career does not support the idea that 'Britishness' is a parochial and inward-looking identity, though the British usually displayed their Britishness wherever they went in the world. Photographs of quintessentially

British rituals – tea on the lawn – tend to show that distance, climate, local culture and environment made little difference. When not being oppressive or exploring or making money, you might say they were a little dull. Ruskin, fully acknowledging the strength of the aspirations, the desire for excitement, the purity of the passions, the wildness of the dreams of continental Europeans, suggested they lacked 'the calmer flow' – 'the stillness of the domestic peace, and the pleasures of the humble hearth, consisting in every-day duties performed, and every-day mercies received'.[14] Revolutions were not suited to tea parties – but tea parties could be held in the Arctic or exploring for the source of the Nile.

In one respect, however, Europeans (including Britain), although often divided among themselves, were in agreement. They saw themselves as the heirs of Greece and Rome, creators of Christian civilization, with the view that the barbarian rest of the world would benefit from their values, their beliefs and – in the Age of Progress – their prosperity. The British, the world leader in economic development and political stability for several decades in the 19th century, and with a merchant marine to transport people, ideas and goods to the ends of the earth, were almost predestined imperialists. Benevolent imperialism (not all of it was reprehensible) tended to insist that the imperialized changed to their benefit, though of course that word 'benefit' is highly subjective. The distinguished sinologist Robert Douglas, in his biography of the Chinese 'Bismarck', statesman and diplomat Li Hung-Chang (1823–1907), despite acknowledging his many achievements (if often made using cruelty and treachery), criticized him for being 'hopelessly out of touch with modern ideas of progress'. China could not achieve Western superiority without 'remodelling her institutions and social life in accordance with the ideas of liberty and progress which are common to all enlightened nations'.[15] The Western sense of superiority could not comprehend why others might not want to join the club using similar methods. The Chinese took more than a century, but then found their own idea of success.

It often seemed, through British eyes, that while Britain was engaged in trying to create a global economy based on free trade, the Continental European nations were either parochially occupied with maintaining political stability in their own countries or taking every opportunity to disrupt the balance of power in a Europe of competing nationalisms. British foreign policy, under leaders of all political complexions, was firmly opposed to involvement in any European conflict without very good reason, usually to ensure that Britain itself was not going to be threatened. There were some exceptions. Palmerston's response to an antisemitic attack in Athens on Don Pacifico

63 Palmerston became Prime Minister for the first time in 1855 (the date of this portrait) when he was 70, the oldest to take that office and over 45 years after becoming Secretary of War in 1809. Prime Minister again in 1859, he went on to increase his majority in 1865 and died in office later that year at 80. He tends to be underrated, except for his oratory and philandering, but was the ideal figure to lead the country at a time of newfound power and prosperity, while politics made a transition to the new, professional, party-based politics.

– born in Britain's Gibraltar – in 1850 was to send the Navy to blockade Greek ports. When censured by a motion more preoccupied by damage to Britain's relationship with France than with Don Pacifico's well-being, Palmerston spoke of the rights of a British citizen (in fact, he used English and British as if they were the same in his brilliant, very long, very eloquent and way over-the-top speech in the House of Commons on 25 June). A British citizen, 'in whatever land he may be, shall feel confident that the watchful eye and the strong arm of England will protect him against injustice and wrong'.[16] It remained true that conceited national pride was a very different thing from a desire to acquire territory through aggressive nationalist expansionism. When *The Times*, in reporting on Queen Victoria's coronation in June 1838, suggested foreigners were astonished at 'the manifest possession of the comforts of life to a degree far more abundant than any other nation' and the power of the people 'over the Government which nominally and ostensibly rule them', its worse sin was vanity, not inaccuracy.[17]

There is always hypocrisy, but increasingly the moral underpinning of foreign policy for Europe was the idea of independent nations peacefully co-existing. It was well-expressed by Gladstone in 1879 as something not to be embodied in a supra-European body, but an acceptance of 'a new law of nations' which 'frowns upon aggression', settles disputes peacefully and applies 'the general judgment of civilized mankind'.[18] With hindsight, we may say it was naïve or pernicious in its use of 'civilized', but throughout this book, the concern is to convey what Victorians thought they were doing, did do, and why.

The immediate obstacles genuinely did not come from Britain. They precisely related to a Continental desire to continue expanding borders, especially from Russia, and a growing wish for independence from many European peoples still tied to the expansive behaviour of nations in the past. Italy was a central case. Napoleon had become king of Italy (at least, northern and central Italy). After the Congress of Vienna, Austrian hegemony, direct or indirect control, and papal secular power were effectively confirmed, if in a political map of impracticable complexity. Mazzini's 'Young Italy' movement in the 1830s pointed to the future, but self-determination hit many obstacles (Mazzini himself spent the 1840s and much of the 1850s in safe England), not least that Napoleon III had his own expansionist motives for supporting those who wanted to liberate the country from Austria.

Debates in the House of Commons were detailed and animated. Austen Layard, twice Under-Secretary for Foreign Affairs, spoke the year after the foundation of modern Italy in 1861 of the conditions in southern Italy: corruption of the grossest kind prevailed; there was no law, no justice, no roads, no commerce, no agriculture, no education, 'no attempt whatever to raise and improve the moral and physical condition of the people'. In the north, there had been some progress in education and public works, a free press and trial by jury. Palmerston added that posterity would judge those who championed and defended everything corrupt, tyrannical and oppressive in the former institutions of Italy. Gladstone had been a slow convert, partly because he believed, at least in 1851, that Italian unity was an abstract idea (and 'if there are two things on earth that John Bull hates, they are absolute propositions, and the Pope'). Evidently – and especially under the influence of Italian exiles – things changed. His six year-old son (in 1860) summed it all up perfectly: his mother had explained that Garibaldi was 'good' – 'And I want the King of Naples to go because he is so wicked and shuts up people.'[19]

Lord Houghton, champion of Tennyson and himself a poet as well as a politician, was probably more accurate when he humorously told friends in Paris what England really wanted: for the Austrians 'to beat you French thoroughly', for the Italians 'to be free' and then 'very grateful to us for doing nothing towards it.'[20] The English were not saints – but a lot of the time they managed to be both practical and hard-headed, as well as earnestly idealistic, within a society by no means of perfect freedom, but much freer than it was in other countries.

None of the four main Continental European powers were natural partners for Britain, though alliance was a necessity when the balance of power needed to be restored. Mayhew's investigations into the London poor had no effect on his view that Russian villeinage and serfdom were the kind of thing England had experienced 800 years before, at the time of the Norman conquest. At the same time, 19th-century Russia was firmly intent on expansion, beginning with the annexation of Georgia in 1801 and the acquisition of Finland in 1809. Little wonder that nearly 80 years later, a Yorkshire newspaper could say that Finland's Parliament was 'hardly abreast of modern ideas of progress',[21] or that the *Morning Post*, reporting in 1862 on the retirement of Count Panine, the Russian Minister of Justice, commented drily that he had not sought 'to represent the cause of progress and of liberal ideas'.[22] And by the end of the 1850s, Russia had completed the conquest of the Caucasus; Russia seemed a threat, as Britain saw it, both within Europe and in its constant desire to spread further. In 1860, the gains from China that Russia had made at the Treaty of Aigun were confirmed at the Convention of Peking, quickly followed by development of Vladivostok as an official port. As early as the Crimean War, General Alexander Duhamel had prepared plans for Tsar Nicholas I to invade British-ruled India.

Nor did the German states seem liberal, at least to the writer Seth Russell Whitney in his 1868 novel *Mortimer's Money*, in which the possibility of rising socially for those with talent and an intellect in Germany seemed relatable only to a strict emphasis on birth and genealogy, very similar to India's caste system. Worse, George Eliot had shrunk from seeing '300,000 puppets in uniform' on Prussian streets.[23] Even if the German path to the future was as an industrial giant, it was a giant that wanted tariff-supported self-sufficiency, not free trade, and one that overcame its strong regional differences when, on the back of no less than three Prussian victories in seven years – against Denmark, the Habsburg monarchy and France – it became an Empire in 1871, with Bismarckian and Prussian values dominant.

Yet in the following decades, British concern had less to do with militarism than economic competitiveness. The title page of Ernest Williams's *Made in Germany* (1896) quoted Lord Rosebery esteeming Germans for their industry, their systematic and scientific approach, but concerned that they were now far ahead of England in technical and commercial education. Mayhew's book *German Life and Manners* (1864) had asked a question in its last chapter, 'Why is Germany so poor?' But that was misleading. The fruits of German emphasis on education, going back at least to Wilhelm von

Humboldt's work at the Prussian department of education in 1809–10, were helping in transforming German economic power.[24]

France was Britain's traditional enemy; a Frenchman, to Ruskin, seemed to have a continuing 'thirst for "gloire" to be gained by agonised effort to become something he is not', while an Englishman had a 'silently conscious pride in what he *is*'. England gave a place of safety to both Louis Philippe and Louis Napoleon; both left on exactly the same day (in 1830 and 1846 respectively), with the former returning after his forced abdication in 1848 and the latter returning to live out his days as a deposed Emperor after the disastrous Battle of Sedan in 1870 in a war against Prussia he had initiated. From a French point of view, Napoleon III had enabled France to modernize itself – in the rebuilding of Paris, the building of the railway network, and the putting in place of a new financial system. Yet France seemed perpetually unstable, unable to decide between Bourbons or Bonapartists or middle-class republicans, or taking to the streets with the Communards, while the Roman Catholic Church managed to maintain a seemingly malign influence under all the regimes. The Italian who tried to assassinate Napoleon III in 1858, the revolutionary Felice Orsini, had been received in England in 1856 as a fighter for freedom and even returned the following year to have his bomb made by a British gunsmith, just as the British government were to refuse to extradite Communards who had become refugees in England. Jacob Tillett, Liberal MP for Norwich, contrasted 'the progress of popular ideas and popular measures in England as compared with their corresponding progress in France'. France, he said, had known a monarchy, a republic, an empire, then another republic, amidst violence, in 40 years; when the English remodelled their constitution, 'they never went back'.[25]

That was not necessarily how the British or French behaved diplomatically (and the French were earlier than the British to have manhood suffrage). When Lord Lytton presented his credentials as Ambassador to President Carnot in 1887, Carnot responded by suggesting 'the best guarantee for the triumph of progress, peace, and liberties' was friendship.[26] But the way the 'Age of Progress' had developed in Britain – from practice to an idea, rather than the other way round – was very different from the view expressed in Balzac's *Lost Illusions* (1837–43), in which a cynical journalist advises a colleague: 'Demolish your previous argument showing that we're in advance of the 18th century. Invent *Progress* – a delightful hoax to play on the bourgeois.'[27]

Britain's overwhelming preoccupations were free trade and business, liberal values and keeping the peace domestically and internationally, with the latter allowing violent methods only if there was no alternative. This went deep into society: as we have seen, the diary of the medical student Shephard Taylor in 1859 shows him totally won over by Alexander Kingslake's argument that the English had been foolishly dragged into the Crimean War by Napoleon III in order 'to bolster up his ill-gotten power'.[28] As so often in history, facts are less important to understanding than what people believed happened; Taylor may have been influenced by a persistent invasion scare centred on Napoleon III's intentions towards Britain. As it happens, Richard Cobden, who was to be instrumental in negotiating a free-trade agreement with France in 1860, had given the French view of that in the House of Commons before the Crimean War; he began by quoting the French magazine *Le Constitutionel* in the House of Commons: 'The sight of an armed brig in the distance, or even the appearance of a foreign fishing-boat on the horizon, is instantly metamorphosed into another Armada.' In the same debate, Disraeli – despite Napoleon III terminating the parliamentary constitution and abrogating the liberty of the press – advised that if commerce and political relationships were alive, we shouldn't involve ourselves with French 'domestic concerns'.[29]

Time and again, Victorian ideas of the right way to achieve progress privileged trade and commerce, not conquest. Military action would only follow if those were threatened by the power and aggression of other states, with an additional emphasis on liberal values and treaty obligations. Bagehot, for example, thought it 'not improbable' that somehow or other, 'on some wolf-and-the-lamb pretext', Napoleon III might invade Belgium 'to restore to the French the "natural limit" of the Rhine'.[30] King Leopold had a British guarantee. In that circumstance, Britain would be bound to honour it, and, if necessary, wage war to defend itself. But in general, after John Bright conceived the idea of a commercial treaty with France, Cobden worked on Gladstone, and against some Cabinet opposition, free trade or limited tariffs were agreed in 1860. The American diplomat Benjamin Moran described John Bull no longer talking of 'a French invasion of his Island' and 'arming himself with muslin, sugar, and British goods generally for his own invasion of "la Belle France"'.[31]

How did Britain seem to Americans by mid-century? The two countries were in some ways far apart; after all, one of them had been born not so long before of a rebellion from the other, and 'family' quarrels are sometimes especially bitter. Nevertheless, many ties were relatively recent. Moran, who became Secretary to the US Legation in London in January 1857, had been born in Pennsylvania in 1820, but his father had only emigrated from England less than two decades before. Evidently, while it turned out to be true that the fledgling USA was a place of almost unlimited opportunity, that didn't guarantee success, and the cotton mills his father established did not bring riches.[32]

Benjamin himself lived in England at the beginning of the 1850s, resulting in a book, *Wanderings of an American in Great Britain*, and he also acted as a correspondent for the US press. When he arrived at the Legation – there was no Ambassador until 1893 – the Minister was George M. Dallas, whose mother had been born in Devon and whose father had been educated in Edinburgh. In a New World, things happened fast, and the family quickly became involved in Pennsylvania and federal politics. Dallas himself had a long political career, including four years as the 11th Vice-President (from 1845). While the fluidity of American political parties in the first half of the 19th century was in some ways comparable to British politics, the new Secretary at the Legation was in an interesting position, being a supporter of Dallas's political rival, James Buchanan.

Buchanan, himself with relatives in the British aristocracy, was in fact Dallas's immediate predecessor as Minister, and had given young Moran unofficial work in the consulate and legation when the latter came back to England in 1853. More to the point, James Buchanan became the 15th President of the United States the year after Benjamin formally joined the London Legation. We have in Moran's diary a window into how Americans with British roots, also heavily involved in the divisions in America's evolving politics, both domestic and international, felt about Great Britain. He was to remain until May 1865, and for four of those years his Minister, Dallas's successor, represented a sure sign that America was quickly developing its own aristocracy – of sorts. Grandson of America's second President, John Adams, and with a father who became sixth President, Charles Francis Adams had entered the US Congress for his father's old district in 1858 and was given the posting after the Republican victory two years later. Diplomacy had not yet conquered distance, or conflict at home, and the month or more that it took to get a response from Washington to anything was not a help in the period immediately before the outbreak of the American Civil War.

Moran's own office life certainly did not start in a glamorous environment. Like many others in a light-starved 1850s, with just a candle to try to affront the thick fog outside his window, he was also located in a basement full of miscellaneous Legation junk gathering dust. While there were many organizational and administrative tasks in running a legation, recognizable within an embassy today, Moran was not averse to helping his income by supporting his friend James McHenry – another American in London – in his highly dubious bond-issuing activities in support of the ill-fated Atlantic and Great Western Railway. The London capital markets were a key source of money for the ever-expanding US economy.

This was not just a period encouraging speculation across the globe, in which the British had a central role. An expanding free press – better printing technology, better distribution and a better-educated population – was becoming more influential at a gallop, and Moran saw a dubious way of exploiting it when he acquired in secret – with McHenry and via a nominee – *The Spectator*, partly to help Buchanan and oppose the prevailing anti-slavery stance of the British press. Under the long editorship of its founder Robert Rintoul (1828–58), that influential journal had acquired the reputation defined by *The Newspaper Press Directory* in 1857 as 'impartial' and 'fair'. Moran and McHenry also had a commercial motive for their acquisition, but the marriage of ideology and trade went badly for them. In 1861, *The Spectator* was sold again for a very low price to the journalist Meredith Townsend, soon joined by Richard Holt Hutton.[33]

America was not alone in deciding that the British press could be useful. The nominee used by Moran and McHenry, who also acted as Editor, was Thornton Hunt, also joint editor of the *Daily Telegraph*. During his tenure, there have been suggestions that the court of Napoleon III provided finance (the French Emperor was even more unpopular in the British press than American supporters of slavery). In fact, Napoleon already had form. In the first half of the 1850s, it appears that he negotiated with the then owner of the *Morning Chronicle*, Sergeant Glover, to pay for favourable treatment. This resulted not only in Glover needing to take suits in the French courts for non-fulfilment of contracts, but also in the financial collapse of the paper, leading to its sale and then ceasing publication in 1862, first temporarily, then for good. Controlling the media entered public agendas as an objective; in Britain, the audience wasn't necessarily willing to be manipulated by propaganda – yet.

Just for a historical moment, the power relationship between the new country and the old was symbolized by Moran's annoyance that the American diplomatic presence in the UK did not match the scale of British overseas representation. He reflected upon it in July 1857: Britain had 420 Consuls and Commercial Agents around the world, 24 in the US itself. The British Minister in the US was paid the vast sum (for then) of £4,500 a year. The British either owned property abroad, as in France or Turkey, for the Minister's use, or paid the Minister's rent; the US Government did not.

Moreover, with both countries finding their way to spectacular economic growth, there was a fine mix of commerce, politics and national pride. At first, British and American governments were happy to collaborate on a transatlantic telegraph cable. Moran, with a financial as well as a diplomatic stake, recorded in July 1858 that Americans were now seen as Britain's 'neighbors, their natural allies, their proper friends', while Napoleon III, appearing to threaten England, became for Moran a 'French thief', a 'brute and liar'. It did not take much for patriotism to alter those opinions. A month later, after the *Morning Herald* claimed the cable was entirely an English idea, supported by English development and execution, Moran was quick to assert that it was American in concept, an American project, with stock procured by an American when the English failed, and with American machinery.

This general rivalry was hardly surprising. Both countries liked being in the forefront of material progress, and both countries were making a section of their populations very rich. In 1853, the *New York Daily Tribune* gave an admiring description of a tobacco pressing machine, just one of which – it was suggested – might 'press as much Tobacco in a day as all mankind ought to chew from this hour to the final conflagration of the world'. In his book *America and Europe* (1857), Adam G. de Gurowski, an exiled Polish aristocrat who had plotted to bring Poland into the Russian Empire, suggested that the US would have the edge on the British; in America, millions would ignore a work of the Fine Arts, but be brought to a state of 'feverish excitement' by 'an industrial and mechanical invention'. Invention to respond to demand was a US 'speciality'.[34]

There were plentiful signs. In Maryland, the first locomotive was put in service on the Baltimore Ohio track between Baltimore and Ellicott's Mills as early as 1829. By 1850 there were perhaps 9,000 miles of track, with as much as 20,000 more to come in the succeeding ten years. Samuel F.B. Morse operated the first practical telegraph in January 1836; two decades later, the lines were linked to form Western Union (it came naturally to Americans in a vast country that thinking big was the right direction). The speed of printing machines was transformed by Richard M. Hoe's rotary printing press in the 1840s (Josiah Warren had been the true inventor in 1832, but Hoe patented his; Americans quickly understood the way successful commerce worked). And this vast land quickly brought machines to agriculture: John Deere's first steam plough dated from 1837, a year after he moved to Illinois to escape bankruptcy (Americans also understood that you didn't give up). Long before that, Americans, like the British, often used the word 'improvement' to describe the positive making of the future. James Fenimore Cooper's *The Spy*, set during the American Revolution and published in 1821, records 'the improvements which had been made in cultivation' and defines 'improvements' as 'every degree of change in converting land from its state of wildness to that of cultivation'.[35]

Progress connected to wealth creation. Moses Yale Beach, entrepreneur and proprietor of the *New York Sun*, showed the practical implications by compiling a guidebook to credit and marriage in New York. This had already gone through ten editions in 1846, two years after its first publication, identifying 850 names with $400,000, 28 with $500,000 to $750,000, three with $750,000 to $1 million, and five millionaires. The latter included William Backhouse (with $30 million, originally from the fur trade), Isaac Bronson, the banker, and Henry Brevoort, Jr (speculation in city land, playing the fast-developing market, with support from a rich Southern wife).[36]

Both America and Britain had rapidly increasing credit needs, and both had numerous crises while creating a modern financial system. Many American bonds were floated in London, high interest rates attracting British money (and more than a little was lost as a result). The US had 691 banks in 1843 and 1,416 by 1857, but the process of development was not smooth, with multiple crashes and plentiful scope for feverish excitement – the California Gold Rush, for example, generated over $40 million in 1849, and reached a high point of $65 million in 1853.[37]

Both America and Britain also made progress towards modern democracy, if more slowly than the economic development. With a US population of approximately 15 million in 1836, 1.6 million voted that year; by 1840, with around 17 million people, 2.4 million voted. Both America and Britain went forward with a broadbrush liberal ethos, by no means the same in the two countries, but considerably closer than the very reactionary (in many respects) rest of the world. Family and, more especially, intellectual ties reinforced the practical connections of commerce and finance.

Could it be said, then, that there was more to unite the two countries than to divide them? Count Gurowski, who emigrated to the US in 1849, suggested that 'The mental dependence upon England is so wide-embracing, that even in the judgment of the most cultivated American, familiar with the literature of other European nations, as well as with their development, march, and history, England still represents the whole of Europe.' Matthew Arnold, from an English perspective, suggested that Anglo-American culture was 'not a having and a resting, but a growing and a becoming'.[38]

There were family ties (which had not prevented American Independence or, for that matter, the War of 1812), trading ties (which easily became rivalries) and liberal values (which corresponded in a joint wish for widening democracy, a faith in progress, and a belief in justice and the rule of law, but which were expressed through competitive nationalism and in neither case earned the word 'liberal' by progressing beyond then global practices, common to all races, tribes and nations, of discrimination against each other). Nevertheless, we are at the beginning of something new. America quickly became intent on making its own future, an ever-enlarging Union spreading across a Continent: Louisiana in 1812, Illinois in 1818, Missouri in 1821, through to Washington, North and South Dakota, and Montana in 1898, and vast acquisitions of territory, especially after war with Mexico in the 1840s, in between.

In 1836, the Hon. Julian Verplanck, who had successively been elected to the New York State Assembly and to the US House of Representatives, set the agenda when speaking to the young men of Union College, Schenectady, during its great period before the Civil War, ranking with Harvard, Yale and Princeton, when it quickly adapted to the new world by introducing science and engineering to join Latin and Greek in the curriculum. Verplanck confidently asserted that America's vast extent of fertile territory was the context for a new system of federated sovereignties carrying out principles of republican democracy that the boldest theories of the British Harringtons, Sidneys and Lockes had never envisaged.[39]

It was this polity, he proclaimed, that would be responsive to matters of social and domestic concern; it would allow unconstrained freedom of opinion, of speech and of press; it would be characterized by lack of serious inequalities of wealth and rank; it would respect religious division by toleration and foster evangelical zeal. It did have the advantage of intimate connection to the old world, but also a 'quick and keen sense of self-interest', giving 'energy and sagacity to the business operations of the country'.

In this account, Britain got off lightly. But the very pride in a new nation was bound to produce more strident voices in considering an old nation. In 1844, America's first literary magazine, the *North American Review* (founded in 1815), defined the British population as divided into masters and serfs, aristocracy and people. The former were illegitimate descendants of marauding tribes who had conquered the country, the latter the present-day representatives of the barbarous, ignorant races the marauders had subjugated. Neither warranted approval – the higher class showed 'insufferable arrogance and haughtiness', the lower 'cringing senility'.[40]

To an extent, such views were a reflection of clashing political and commercial interests and, increasingly, one major difference on what constituted 'liberal': slavery. Verplanck did not mention it (at a time when the British, having abolished their slave trade in 1807, had recently abolished the thing itself, in 1833, though not without compensation for loss of 'property'). But by the 1850s, when just seventeen days after John Brown was hanged by the State of Virginia for inciting insurrection, President Buchanan reported on the state of the nation with the words, 'Prosperity smiles throughout the land', the two countries had moved far apart.[41]

It was in fact William Edmondstoune Aytoun (1813–65), the Scottish poet, lawyer, academic and writer, who suggested in his three-volume novel *Norman Sinclair* that the British were hypocritical. The Yankee character, Mr Jefferson J. Ewins, describes Manchester Liberals 'thrashing round like short-tailed bulls in fly-time' at any suggestion that the British poor were worse off than the American slaves. Every one of them 'has made his pile by caving up white girls in their factories like birds in a pigeon-roost' and 'if they don't work double tides, treating them to a touch of the billy-roller'. 'We manage things very differently in the States, I can tell you', Mr Ewins asserts.[42]

Both countries, like all would-be and actual democracies, struggled with how to reconcile democratic egalitarianism with individual rights, and still do. In the case of slavery, disputes were frequent, both before the Civil War and in the war itself. Even though Congress had forbidden further import of slaves from the beginning of 1808, there was plentiful smuggling and plentiful Anglo-American disagreement. Benjamin Moran, in his diary in May 1858, notes the anti-slave ship patrolling of the British Navy in the Gulf of Mexico and in the coastal waters of the US and Cuba. When the British gunboat *Forward* encountered a slave trader bearing (illegally) the American flag, it allowed the captain to escape, sold his boat and took the proceeds. Suppression of the slave trade, Moran suggests, is 'money getting by any means', which is the object of 'the pinks of humanity, and very gentlemanly fellows, the British naval forces'. The British also captured the *Cortez* and, after investigating, found it Spanish-owned and certainly not entitled to American papers. Moran says they were then 'beastly drunk' for days, while the crew stole the shoes from the captured crew.

While the US and the British, at the Treaty of Ghent (1814), agreed to help enforcement, the Americans neither had the naval resources, nor perhaps – having declared slave trading as piracy and piracy a capital offence – the will (no trader was hanged until 1862). When the traffic expanded in the 1850s, especially because of Cuba and its sugar, the British were accused by the Americans of using searches to eliminate commercial rivalries. The fact of the matter was that both moral and economic progress were features of the era; sometimes commerce won.

As Minister at the US Legation in London, Charles Francis Adams sent frequent protests to the Foreign Office because of British shipyards building vessels for the Southern states. The *Alabama*, designed in secret in Birkenhead as an armed vessel (albeit under British neutrality law not provided with armaments), slipped out to the Azores in July 1862 and was to destroy 65 Northern vessels in the two years before it was finally sunk. As it happened, 'progress' resulted this time in the development of international law, since an arbitration commission later awarded the US considerable compensation (if not a handover of Canada, as some optimistic Americans proposed) for the activities of the *Alabama* and other British-fitted ships.

There were plentiful opportunities for diplomatic incidents between the two countries. In the House of Commons in June 1862, Sir John Walsh (1798– 1881) referred to 'so extraordinary a proclamation, so utterly repugnant to the spirit of the 19th century and the whole usages of civilized warfare'. What Palmerston, the Prime Minister, called 'the outrage' of General Butler took place when Union troops occupied New Orleans and their commander proclaimed that 'when any female shall by word, gesture, or movement, insult or show contempt for any officer or soldier of the United States army, she shall be held liable to be treated as a woman of the town plying her avocation'.

Walsh insisted that he wasn't questioning 'impartial and strict neutrality' in the war. Another Member, Mr Gregory, insisted on the right of the House of Commons and the Government to remonstrate about acts of inhumanity anywhere in the world. Here was Britain reflecting both its moral self-esteem (which was by no means always to be scorned) and its then global power (which was, if not unlimited, a reality). Not that the US acquiesced to such criticism. Although the often flamboyantly bellicose Palmerston did complain, resulting in a protest by Adams to the British Foreign Minister, Lord John Russell, for this 'unprecedented attack', the matter was not pushed further.[43] Honour was perhaps satisfied by changes made to her guestlists by Lady Palmerston.

Moral protest was one thing. More difficult was that both countries were in expansionary mode. The US also in some senses believed in its unqualified virtue, which was bound to create especial conflict in geographical areas adjacent to it, especially Central America and Canada. There had been British settlers in Belize since the 17th century; it was to become a Crown Colony as British Honduras in 1862. The Mosquito Coast of Honduras and Nicaragua had in fact become a British Protectorate in 1820, with a nominal indigenous king subject to Britain. For its part, the US – after the Gold Rush in 1849 – wanted a transit route from east and west across Central America. Territories adjoining became a focus for concessions or control. Both sides argued what became enshrined in the Clayton-Bulwer Treaty in 1850 – that their concern was safety and neutrality, not imperial expansion. But disputes continued, to the extent that when Buchanan was Minister in London, he briefed Washington in 1853 that, without a conclusive settlement, war was likely.

There was no war, but the issues only reached some kind of eventual resolution when Britain effectively removed itself from Central America (with the exception of Belize). It might be noted how often, in the tortuous negotiations over a long period, the British emphasized the importance of preventing slavery in the region: the moral stance was genuine, though commercial objectives were also a constant. Nevertheless, it cannot be said that a moral stance by the British was much in evidence at the outset of the Civil War. A year after the launch of the *Alabama*, Laird was constructing two more fighting vessels for the 'Emperor of China', a very British, drily humorous, synonym for the Southern States.

While it would be true that, as in any era, the entrepreneurs and the men of action could be completely unreflective about anything but the pursuit of success, it remains true that a central theme of Victorian progress was how to reconcile materialism with moral development. John Laird (1805–74), son of the founder of what became in a matter of decades one of the great engineering companies of the modern world, had a younger brother, Macgregor (1808–61), who also established a shipyard. As a byproduct of his shipbuilding, Macgregor became interested in the sea routes to West Africa and rivers into the interior. We might think now that his enthusiasm for opening up contact inland was purely self-interested, but that was certainly not how it struck him. Despite British efforts to use the Navy to blockade the slave-traders, many smuggled their ships out. A man of strong humanitarian and evangelical beliefs, Macgregor firmly believed that legitimate and honest trade would act as an antidote to slavery.

In attitudes to the American Civil War, it has to be observed that it took Lincoln's Emancipation Proclamation at the beginning of 1863 for British public opinion to begin fully to associate the Unionists with morality and right on their side. Britain remained officially neutral, but Liberals, nonconformists, working-class activists and middle-class reformers made their feelings increasingly clear inside chapel and church, and outside in public meetings.

In Jules Verne's novel *The Adventures of Captain Hatteras* (1864), British and American members of a polar expedition are both aiming to claim the newly discovered island of New America (the relevant chapter is entitled 'John Bull and Jonathan'). There is much more to be said about the evolving relationship of Britain and the United States in the remaining decades of the 19th century, and much began to change in the balance of power between them. Until now, the old nation, certain in the reality of its global economic dominance, unwilling to involve itself unless absolutely necessary in Continental European quarrels, and with a belief in a civilizing mission, could make its peculiarly British way forward with a confidence accompanied by questioning and self-doubt. The United States could also look forward with confidence to what the future would bring, unmoved by any disdain from the other side of the Atlantic, but for the moment still preoccupied by nation-building and finding a satisfactory form of union for what it was building.

A certain ambivalence was bound to be at the centre of a relationship between the two countries throughout its history and the changing fortunes of the old and the new. Benjamin Moran, from the American standpoint, could complain in his diary in September 1859 that 'as usual John Bull abuses Jonathan, and attributes all kinds of bad motives to him'. And yet, though he left England to take up an appointment as US Minister in Portugal in 1875, he chose the land of John Bull for his retirement, there to die at the Tudor Bocking Hall in Essex, his gravestone comfortably resting in the nearby Church of St Mary and St Christopher, Panfield. The church was built at about the same time as Columbus sailed West. The continuities of British history helped ensure that prosperity four centuries later provided the basis for its restoration in 1858. What would happen next was unknown to both John Bull and Jonathan, though both had plenty of opinions about that, mostly optimistic in a way that we perhaps now find difficult.

Empires, taking many different forms but with some common characteristics, have occupied the human landscape for at least 4,000 years, beginning with the Assyrians. Those who suffered from being conquered (or understandably did not welcome rulers from outside, as well as their descendants) often – though not always – resisted, heavily limited by inequality of power. After historical change and the passage of time, the depredations of European and American imperialism tend to be the focus today; what the Chinese, or the Mughals, or – for that matter – the Comanche and the Asante did is less remembered. Today, alongside continuing imperialism, we have a new form of colonization – the colonization of minds, surrendered without a fight to tech companies – which among many other consequences makes the writing of history much harder.

In the case of the British Empire, examining how and why it developed within the context of its own time is a necessary beginning to understanding why imperialism is ubiquitous – and much more complex than is popularly supposed. There had never been an empire that was quite so ethnically diverse, with such a variety of belief systems, climates, territorial sizes, languages and systems of governance, nor one on such a huge scale that evolved so unsystematically or – for much of the time – with such little eagerness from annexation-hostile governments back home. Nevertheless, by the time a small island off the north-west coast of France – a description of Britain once given to French schoolchildren – had reached control of at least a quarter of the world's population (just before the First World War), as well as an influence close to control over a whole lot more, with for the first time widespread support from a large proportion of the domestic population, it was already finding that even the predominantly white dominions wanted a degree of independence, with the other colonies showing signs of the same – small to begin with, but changing an empire into a historical memory in little more than half a century. Joseph Chamberlain, whose short-lived Imperial Federation League gathered delegates from colonies worldwide for Queen Victoria's Golden Jubilee in 1887, suggested that it gave 'security, peace, and comparative prosperity to lands that had never seen them before'.[44] That was true to a limited and greatly varying extent, but it does not dent today's consensus that it was a plundering and racist evil.

What were the motives? In the 19th century, Britain had fast-increasing capital surpluses, which was not true of the rest of Europe for much of the century. It pioneered making free trade global, using mechanized shipping, mastery of the seas, availability of finance, as well as the expertise of new professional classes. Its domestic industries wanted access to raw materials wherever there was a shortage in Britain or just no availability. William Lever, later Lord Leverhulme, built Port Sunlight for his soap-making business, a vast experiment in creating a materially pleasant environment for the workers; 'nice homes, comfortable homes, and healthy recreation', he said. But expansion greatly increased the need for palm oil, and his treaty with the Belgian government in 1911 led to using the utterly brutal methods of the Belgian colonial authorities in the Congo with forced labour. The end of slavery did not mean the end of slave-like working conditions.

Exports were equally a motive; already by 1870 perhaps 20 per cent of Britain's gigantic textile exports went to India. J.A. Hobson's influential *Imperialism: A Study* (1902) put commerce right at the centre of imperial motivation and became a key text for Lenin. It also offered disdain for 'colonial primitive peoples' and was close to genocidal in its attitude to 'unprogressive races', as well as antisemitic in its comments about the financiers of empire. As ever, the supposedly very 'international' communist movement, which in practice only supported Western workers' rights (Hobson himself had a more general hostility to capitalist greed), had some common ground with extreme imperialists.

The tragedy of racism in the 19th century – in the West, very little related to political differences (anyone who reads Engels' account of perhaps the cruellest of all colonial wars, the French conquest of Algeria, will not doubt the racism of socialists) – was that it was an implicit assumption because Western civilization had become so very 'successful'. It was not helped by the traditional practices of many of the colonized – human sacrifice in Dahomey, by the Asante and other tribes in West Africa, as well as widespread slavery, first practised long before Europeans arrived and continued long after the British abolished it and tried to stamp it out in Africa. Many of the British – at least, more than most Europeans – associated colonialism with bringing progress. Just as Charles Kingsley's 1855 historical novel *Westward Ho!* strongly celebrates the activities of the Elizabethan privateers against the Spanish, their values and their furtherance of Roman Catholic domination, so the train of thought could be transferred to 19th-century colonialism, with Britain bringing – the argument went – the moral and material values of its embodiment of progress (for Kingsley, Protestant progress). One of the dedicatees of the book was Sir James Brooke, who was granted what became Sarawak by the Sultan of Brunei in 1841 for his help both with piracy and in suppressing local revolts.

There was a clear difference between racists who argued that races were essentially the same but had very varying patterns of development (the English hadn't always been prosperous and free) and racists who identified a permanent inferiority, largely immune to progress. For the former, progress was possible; for example, Herbert Spencer encouraged the idea of US emigrants marrying indigenous Americans. Mary Seacole, daughter of a free black woman in Jamaica and with a British army officer as a father, effectively supported the idea by taking herself to the Crimean War as a nurse. For the latter, unreflective and widespread acknowledgment of European superiority became, for some, outright racism.

That was very different from the approach taken by Thomas Arnold, famous as the reforming headmaster of Rugby school from 1828 to his death in 1842. He suggested 'distinctions of moral breed' are natural, 'just as those of skin or of arbitrary caste are wrong': convicts tended to breed convicts, but people whose skin was not white were not automatically tainted. In fact, when Sir John Franklin (eventually to disappear into the ice on his final expedition to find the Northwest Passage between the Atlantic and the

Pacific) was Governor of Van Diemen's Land (Tasmania), Arnold wrote to him from his Lake District summer house in July 1836 mentioning that, if the Government were to make him principal of a college or a bishop, he might be tempted to emigrate: 'There can be, I think, no more useful or more sacred task, than forming the moral and intellectual character of a new society...the surest and best kind of missionary labour'. Equally, he had a good sense that Van Diemen's was not the place to bring up a family, a colony founded in 1803 as a penal settlement and one where the Aboriginal population was treated with extreme brutality and responded in like manner.[45]

William Arnold, one of Thomas's sons and Matthew's brother, left England intent on escaping doctrinal disputes in the Church of England, wanting to bring religion into everyday life and thereby help the development of the Empire. In the Punjab, in 1855, he succeeded in separating Church and state in public education; Hindus were not obliged to study Christianity or for that matter the Koran. He took the view that all Europeans in Asia should adopt a 'civilizing' approach. There were many variants, rather than undifferentiated colonial oppression; in 1861, John Henning Speke, in Buganda (part of what became Uganda), tried to persuade the Bantu monarch Rumanyika that the Bible was superior to the Koran, the key to becoming prosperous. The Kabaka, or King of Buganda itself, Muteesa I, violently aggressive, cruel and imperialistic, nevertheless saw advantage in allowing Christian missionaries (in 1877) and using the British as an ally, as well as a source of modern weaponry.[46]

Victorian explorers, once much loved, are now viewed as racist imperialists, exploitative of people and places. It would be hard to apply that description to Charles Kingsley's niece Mary, who aimed at 'Fair Commerce' (the name given to an organization formed just after her death) of a collaborative kind and in effect made the point that Western males were a problem because they did not want to end their historical dominance, whether of English women or African tribespeople. Travelling without male company after her father's death, she dealt with innumerable dangers from predators, human and animal, encountered cannibals, and thought nothing of tackling swamps or unforgiving terrain. This super-strong personality, who died of typhoid at age 37 after helping Boer prisoners of war, was not in favour of Boer female suffrage, but fiercely opposed to the idea of 'a natural race hatred'. She felt sure that 'the majority of Anglo-Saxons are good men', so 'equally that the majority of the true Negroes are good men'. Neither had as many perfect angels and calm scientific minds as we would like, but the two need to understand each other and certainly not interfere with each other's institutions.

64 For once, the word 'extraordinary' is unarguable: after a quiet first 30 years in England, Mary Kingsley packed more into the less than ten years before she died than most men or women could manage in several lifetimes. She was the epitome of a Victorian woman not concerned about her 'rights' but just about finding out. The first European to explore parts of Gabon, she nearly died on numerous occasions in her empirical researches – books were 'worthless or wanting' – in West and Equatorial Africa, exploring natural history and studying empathetically every aspect of tribal societies: legal, political, social, religious.

Christianity wasn't a guarantee of anything good, as you could see in the histories of the Dutch or the Spanish, the Italians or the Germans. Instead, we had to aim for a world in which 'all races, all colours, all religions, can live, worship, trade, labour, or live quietly…live as freemen, whether rich or poor, white or black, cultured or uncultured, ambitious or unambitious'. Her version of imperialism was open to anyone – Celt, Slav, Asiatic, African – with protection by law and participation in freedom. It did require *Oberhoheit* (overlordship), but to use power to ensure peace, secure communications, help trade, provide an ultimate court of appeal. All that without stealing of *Landeshoheit* (territorial rule). Regions of Central Africa were like a neglected garden: you could pull everything up or cut up everything, have a bonfire and the resulting tidiness would be 'the Abomination of desolation'; or you could take the wild garden, weed it, plant it, prune it into a beautiful thing. The French Revolutionary notion of 'Liberty, Equality, Fraternity' was 'an unworkable thing because not in touch with the facts': you have to come through with what you offer.[47]

This remarkable woman, whose father had criticized the treatment of indigenous Americans (and missed being with Custer at the Little Big Horn because of freak weather), was a great example of Victorian self-education (her father's library) and empirical investigation. In no way was she typical of the British in Africa, but rather a sign – shown in so many ways by Victorians – that there could be a better approach to life, society and politics than just transferring the immemorial patterns of behaviour from Europe on to a global stage. Europeans (and Asians and Africans and Americans) had always been – many of them – cruel and violent. Now it was time for a change.

Sir John Pope Hennessy was an MP first (from 1859) and then made his career in colonial service. He acquired many European enemies while serving as Governor of British possessions across the world, from the West Indies to West Africa to Hong Kong (where he was dubbed 'Number One Good Friend' by the Chinese). While Henry Drummond, in his account of Nyasaland (1890, today Malawi) and H.M. Stanley, in *In Darkest Africa* (1890), pushed hard for policies of colonial annexation, regardless of climate or health (although Stanley is not given credit for his energetic assistance in ending African slavery in East Africa), Pope Hennessy asked the question, 'How is this to affect indigenous peoples?'. Pope Hennessy's dispatch, sent to the then Secretary State for the Colonies Lord Kimberley in 1873, when he was Governor of Sierra Leone, sums up an attitude that would have been virtually unthinkable without the Victorians. He goes into the interior to Kambia, the only European there. The whole area was governed by locals. 'It was admirably governed. I never saw a happier population': cheerful, contented, industrious, very good agriculturists in their own way. 'What a contrast between the smiling faces to be seen in the crowded streets...and the careworn faces of Cheapside.'[48]

Amidst huge variety (and of course with exceptions), the British attitude to colonies was different from that of Continental Europeans, who were often focused on exporting the conflicts of their nation-states to other parts of the world. It took a modern Nigerian writer, Chinua Achebe, very much opposed to colonialism and writing about the Biafra Civil War, to refer to the 'considerable care' with which the British ruled his country and the ways in which British colonies were 'more or less, expertly run'.[49] The 'more or less' was accurate and high praise compared with Portugal, where – according to *Pall Mall Magazine* in August 1899 – 'The average Portuguese cannot understand ideas of progress, or why a sensible man should exert himself seriously in a broiling climate.' 'Disdain' and 'apathy', it was argued, was at variance with British 'push'.[50] Similarly, while the Boers of the Transvaal understandably wanted to keep their independence and, in the subsequent war, were often appallingly treated by the British, the view from Aberdeen in 1896 – that Boer rule was a curse to the natives of South Africa – or from Bristol in the same year – that settlers were needed who 'will carry with them ideas of progress, political and social' – was precisely what people in those cities felt.[51]

Such beliefs became common because, as the many books by William Hughes in the decades after 1850 suggested, any 'progress and improvement'

Asia and Africa were making was because of the 'skill, intelligence and wealth' that came from outside, supplemented by 'energy'. That doesn't excuse the economic exploitation or unjustified acquisition of territory that often accompanied these activities, but it is left to today's generation to debate whether bringing town and city infrastructure, railroads, irrigation schemes and other engineering projects on a massive scale – and the profits that followed for the white populations – would nevertheless be ultimately helpful to regions of the world that had never known anything but poverty, wretched governance and slavery. At the least, there were an increasing number of voices that shared Kipling's view that if rulers did not behave better than their subjects, they lost the moral justification for their rule. As Pope Hennessy wrote, in their homes, native inhabitants were 'in certain important and vital respects superior of the European'. That was a long way from Karl Marx telling his readers in the *New York Daily Tribune* that England was not to be questioned for conquering India: it was necessary to 'annihilate' the old Asiatic society and lay foundations for Western society in Asia. Historical destiny was always more important for him than human beings. For Engels, slavery was just a necessary stage in the development of capitalism.[52]

Unlike the French, who tended to offer no alternative for indigenous people to learning how to be French, the British often used existing power structures to function. You could say that was just a Machiavellian method of ruling vast territories with minimal resources, but it certainly also reflected the very deep-seated British cultural sense that you don't make a solid future simply by destroying what is already there. In India, some of the existing princely states were larger than many European nations; at Independence in the next century, the Nizam of Hyderabad still tried to maintain his rule over what then had become 16 million people. In the film that survives of the parade of the Maharajahs to celebrate Edward VII's accession in 1902, the British use of Mughal ceremonial forms – elephants, for example – was not typical of other colonial powers in their approach to such events.

In Africa, indirect rule, from Buganda to the Islamic emirates in northern Nigeria, enabled old political institutions to continue. That worked less well where there was no tradition of centralized rule – in the Igbo region of eastern Nigeria, for example – and the British tried to construct it by giving warrants to indigenous representatives. Still, the whole of Uganda, made a protectorate in 1894, had around 25 British officials in the last decade of Victoria's reign. Eventually, the underpinning ideas were developed by the very experienced Lord Lugard in *The Dual Mandate in British Tropical Africa* (1929): Africans should be helped to be ready to navigate the modern world; in return, the helper should have access to natural resources. Sometimes, there were objections from past imperialists – the Chinese, said Colonel Thomas Lewin after returning from India in 1879, didn't want British trade between British India and Tibet, which would involve 'troublesome ideas of progress'.[53]

In India, there was no one reason for the rebellion that began in 1857. In this vast, vast territory, by no means yet 'a nation' whomever claimed to rule, Muslims, Hindus, local rulers of widely varying powers, Indians with aspirations, the armies of the poor, all could object to Britain's proxy rulers: the East India Company. James Mill's *The History of British India*, first published in 1817 and widely influential, made the case for bringing Benthamite rational utilitarianism and Western technology to India. Absurdly, he had not been to India and had no knowledge of its languages; it would have helped if he adopted the approach he dismissed as unnecessary – a long period of using eyes and ears in the country about which he was writing. Little wonder that 'great engines of social improvement', as the reforming governor Dalhousie (1848–56) called them, were not welcomed. Railways, a modern postal system and the telegraph were benefits, but in the end, many human

"NEW CROWNS FOR OLD ONES!"

(ALADDIN *adapted.*)

65 In 1876, Disraeli's Royal Titles Bill made Queen Victoria Empress of India. The largely unconsulted Liberal opposition and other critics presented the move as un-English and despotic. The Queen was pleased; Disraeli received the worst antisemitic abuse of his career. Tenniel's cartoon in *Punch*, 15 April 1876, portrays the Prime Minister as Aladdin's wicked uncle, Abanazar.

beings in any country – not unreasonably – resent (and still do) imposed modernity.

The revolt was very bloody on both sides, but out of it there did come some progress. The British government removed control by the East India Company and appointed a Secretary of State, with a Viceroy, as head of government in India. Thereafter, Indians joined the Civil Service; some Indian rulers and those of higher castes joined the government. The British brought the first modern universities to India, keeping step – or even going faster – than educational reform back home. That wasn't to say that colonial affairs were well handled from Britain in any territory. There had been a Secretary for the Colonies from 1828, but little continuity and sometimes little interest from its incumbents in the following decades. As the Permanent Under-Secretary from 1836 to 1847, Sir James Stephen was a shining exception, highly efficient and diligent, but certainly not someone pushing for or against aggressive imperialism, more highly motivated to support the kind of work done by the Church Missionary Society. As the century developed, that organization's astonishing geographical range, often in extremely hostile conditions – of climate, accessibility, political instability – is one of history's great stories, albeit without the questioning of its entitlement to proselytize for Anglicanism in places that had their own belief systems.

It was in what eventually became the Dominions, including Canada, Australia and New Zealand, that issues of self-government developed earliest. All had a dishonourable record in relation to indigenous peoples, but all became a logical experiment – given the extent of white emigration to them – in whether British values and institutions could be transported overseas. It is easy to see why – removed from political and moral questions of who rules whom – emigration might have seemed exciting. It is often forgotten that Mr Micawber in *David Copperfield* did eventually prove that 'something will turn up' by becoming Port Middlebay District Magistrate in Australia. And in *Great Expectations*, Magwitch even manages, after transportation as a convict, to make money from sheep farming and become Pip's benefactor. There were many opportunities in Victorian Britain, but there seemed to be many more in distant places without centuries of aristocratic rule and restraints that seemed irrelevant if you were prospecting for gold or building or farming or engineering; professionals in education, or finance, or medicine soon followed.

The sea voyage to Australia took at least eleven or twelve weeks, even on the magnificent steam-powered *Great Britain*, but compared to travel before its first voyage as an emigrant ship in 1853, and with the abundant opportunities to make a new life, it was appealing enough to take 16,000 people in the years that followed. Many emigrants didn't flourish, but expectations were high and given support by the press and by books. In Aberdeen, the *Journal* enthusiastically gave space to the ideas of Charles Marshall's *The Canadian Dominion* (1871). Science, 'saving time and annihilating space', would keep Greater Britain in touch. Railroads would save 1,200 miles between the Atlantic and the Pacific. There were plentiful coal deposits at either end. 'Progress' was phenomenal in trade and areas under cultivation, with a population that had more than quadrupled to 4.5 million in 30 years.[54]

There were political opportunities, too. Robert Lowe spent nearly ten years in Australia in the 1840s. 'Who is Mr Lowe?', asked the *Sydney Morning Herald* in November 1843 after he joined the New South Wales Legislative Council. His wife Georgiana wrote to her mother that month: 'Now, my dearest mother, does not Robert overcome every obstacle and impediment?' He did; there was a need for his knowledge of education, finance and law, skilfully communicated by his speeches. In a portent for the future, he used an after-dinner speech in January 1846 to paint a devastating picture of Downing Street bungling: 'all meddling interference in matters of a domestic nature should be utterly and for ever renounced.... England herself is but a part of the Empire.' The apparent inability of London to help constructively, far from embodying an imperialism that wanted to annex to territory at all costs, had quite a lot to do with thinking of colonies either as a nuisance, or a necessity if trade or strategic considerations appeared to make them essential. Besides, as the *Quarterly Review* said in 1860, 'England cannot expect to retain for ever as dependencies colonies that have grown into populous, rich, and self-supporting commonwealths.' Walter Besant, well remembered for his work and writing about the fate of the poor in city life, added another perspective. Colonies and home country were falling apart because change had accelerated in England after decades of momentum: 'What is wild Radicalism one day is mild Liberalism the next.' Not so in the colonies.[55]

Were there thoughtful and earnest exponents of colonialism before the argument for empire became temporarily unarguable amidst the fiercely competitive nationalisms of the European powers towards the end of the century? As ever, that was more a question of a small number of individuals than either a political or populist movement. A key figure was Edward Gibbon Wakefield (1796–1862), Secretary to Lord Durham in 1838 in Canada (where there had been colonial unrest) and a major proponent of colonies in Australia and New Zealand. In the strange way that history happens, he first became involved in prison, following not one but two elopements with heiresses.

66 Miss Canada denies to Mrs Britannia that she is giving Cousin Jonathan (not yet Uncle Sam) encouragement, 1869. Some politicians in the northern USA wanted annexation after the Civil War. In 1868, Benjamin Mills Peirce had also recommended that the US should purchase Greenland and Iceland, partly to ward off the power of the British Navy: the 'special relationship' had to await Churchill's use of the phrase nearly 80 years later.

In Newgate, he studied penal reform and colonial policies, subsequently acquiring a reputation for his writings, kept anonymous because of his uneasy social status after the elopements. In a very modern way, fearing that the government would bury the Durham Report, which recommended uniting Upper and Lower Canada with one legislature and a responsible government, and knowing that few MPs wanted to be bothered with distant colonies, let alone acquire more, he released it to *The Times* prematurely.[56]

In his (fictitious but highly informed) *Letters Between a Statesman and a Colonist* (1849), Wakefield's definition of 'colonization' was strictly the process of emigration and settlement of the emigrants 'in a country wholly or partially unoccupied'. The colonies came from the mother country, but they could be independent sovereign states (as in the case of the Ancient Greeks in Asia Minor and Sicily). It was not necessary for them to be dependent (just as the USA was not). The positives might be finding a new home for excess population, sourcing food and raw materials, spreading national pride in language, religion, laws, institutions. But as it was in 1849, they all seemed to get into 'a state of disorder and disaffection': Ceylon (Sri Lanka), for example, with its 'uproarious' government and native insurrection; New Zealand with its 'deadly feud between colonists and natives'.

Colonization was not yet widely popular: the Colonization Society, formed in 1830, mostly with young men, had been greeted with hostility or indifference. All this was quite peculiar. Colonies were hardly a recent invention, any more than tribal imperialism. In the past, migration and colonization had peopled Earth; founded countries, sometimes new empires; stimulated economic activity; promoted manufacture and commerce; contributed to increasing the wealth and population of the world. Sometimes those movements went into unpeopled lands; often they did not. This apparently natural (or at least characteristic) behaviour by human beings, however undesirable, was bound to have winners and losers. In Britain, landowners, producers, suppliers of finance were the main beneficiaries; in the colonies, taxation helped government, businesspeople had the chance to flourish – and so to an extent did those finding employment. Yet the acid test of the British bourgeoisie – would you want to meet a colonist in your friend's home? – was generally answered disdainfully.

Unlike the French and the Spanish, the British way had always been to allow local ('municipal') rule, limited mainly in curbing local laws repugnant to the laws of England, reserving a Crown veto, with appointed officials. Britain, Wakefield argued, had lost the American colonies because it attempted to deprive them of 'their dearest municipal rights'. It wasn't that he was arguing, in the back-and-forth dialogue of the letters, that colonies were irrelevant to the mother country, rather that there needed to be a much stronger focus on defining the relationship between the two, with full account of local issues. Lord Durham himself had been too progressive in his emphasis on local conditions in Canada, which were difficult enough without obstruction or lack of understanding in London: there were not just differences between Europeans and indigenous peoples, but a deep clash of cultures between French and British Canadians. Durham resigned on his return, prior to submitting his report.

How complicated it was – quite apart from moral considerations – to be an imperialist country. One view – and sometimes many views – on the spot, with inconsistency and incoherence back in Britain. If you wanted colonies, at least for trade, how did you induce imperial unity? Wakefield had a few talented, sometimes moodily wayward, fellow spirits, Charles Buller and Sir William Molesworth in particular, but Durham, Buller and Molesworth all died in their forties and Wakefield had disappeared into insignificance by the time he died.

Yet something – and something literally big – happened: the British Empire quadrupled in size in a few decades after 1870. The Liberal John

Morley recalled being asked what he meant by 'Jingo'; his answer was 'men who held that territory was territory, and all territory was worth acquiring without regard to cost'.[57] The word's origin seems to lie in a 17th-century euphemistic oath, used instead of 'by Jesus', but it became heavily politicized after an anti-Russian music-hall song at the time of Russia's war with Turkey in 1877–78 was used by George Holyoake, a true radical who earlier in his life had been one of the last people to be convicted of blasphemy (in a Mechanics' Institute lecture) and also coined the term 'secularism'.

Was British imperialism motivated by naked aggression? Much of Europe had conscription; Britain did not. The military forces of the great powers dwarfed those of Britain. You could enter Britain as an immigrant simply because it operated what we would call an open-door policy (until the next century). You could get away from Britain without a passport (until the First World War). Did Britain's wealth and influence come from her colonies? Some of it, but the facts don't support that position. The context for increased imperial activity in the last decades of the 19th century was rampant, aggressive nationalisms ambitious to boost their own stature and, outside Europe, Africa offered the most scope for action. There was copper in what became Zambia; there were diamonds in South Africa. Yet 96 per cent of Britain's trade at the end of Queen Victoria's reign was not with Africa.[58] The momentum behind the 'scramble' for Africa was apparent in practice before the Conference called by Bismarck in Berlin in 1884, when delegates from fourteen countries tried to define rules for expanding into Africa (including anti-slavery policies, given the number of continuing African-owned slaves).

The Conference provided a symbolic signal, but each country pursued it in its own way. In Britain, the journalist Edward Dicey, a prolific writer on foreign affairs, advised that any British expansion should be confined to 'profitable' extensions of the British Empire; if that made him 'a jingo', he said, he was certainly not a supporter of the kind of policies proposed by Stanley in central Africa, from which there would be no trade benefit or strategic gain against European rivals. Victorians always displayed and – in the second half of the 19th century – gradually accommodated very different views. Today, we see militant Islam as a threat in Africa; Dicey said it was not represented by 'mere gangs of slave-dealers', but was 'a powerful instrument of civilisation'; he had another view of why central African expansion was unwise – that it was like 'some crazy architect' putting the top stories of a building on foundations barely commenced.[59]

Some historians have argued that the 'scramble' was a reaction to Islam attaching itself to a form of nationalism. When Colonel Urabi's nationalist revolt in Egypt – nominally Ottoman – injured the British Consul, massacred perhaps 50 foreigners and directed guns at the Royal Navy in June 1882, Gladstone would not have minded if another European power responded, especially because of the threat to the Anglo-French Suez Canal. They didn't. So Britain occupied Egypt, then indirectly controlled it and finally made it a protectorate in 1914. Disraeli had predicted that economic considerations would lead to political control; they usually did. Britain was Egypt's dominant trading partner, both for imports and for exports, as well as holder of perhaps a third of the country's public debt.[60] But while the defeat of Urabi generated some politically liberal Islam, it also encouraged something much more aggressive: the radical nationalism of Abd al-Aziz Jawis, and in some sense set in train the history of the 20th century.

Similarly, while the British had refused to send an army to Sudan, seized by the Mahdi, self-appointed redeemer of Islam, it instead sent General Gordon to Khartoum to arrange evacuation. Gordon believed the Mahdi would move on to attempt to control Egypt; Gladstone did not. Gordon died with the Khartoum garrison and perhaps 4,000 townspeople. Gladstone had even argued that the Sudanese were a people struggling to be free of colonialism – Egyptian colonialism. The eventual result, fourteen years later, originally entirely unintended, was the Battle of Omdurman and Kitchener's victory over the Mahdists. Effectively, Sudan was then governed as a British possession, with sovereignty shared with Egypt. As so often, jingoism was not jingoism at all, but unintended consequences of muddle, increasingly followed by unpleasant triumphalism.

Despite all this complexity, there was a change in the British mood about empire in society as a whole. In the Queen's speech that closed a parliamentary session that had seen an enormous extension of British territory in 1890, in that unique way official Britain says nothing but tells all, the monarch's only comment about Africa was that the expansion was 'for the purpose of avoiding the inconveniences of possible conflicts with European powers'. When Lord Salisbury had left the Foreign Office in 1880, 'nobody thought about Africa'. Back in office five years later, he could not understand the change in public feeling; he never fully did. The message about empire, not sent by anyone in particular, was perfect for populism. What was not to like about being top dog, your country ruling so much of the world? The explorer, botanist, linguist and eventually colonial administrator Harry Johnston called it 'the newly developed zeal suddenly displayed by the British public for the possession and exploitation of African countries'.[61] The popular press, especially the *Daily Mail* and, from 1900, the *Daily Express*, exemplified populist uncritical praise for empire. Anti-imperialism existed, but it did not fully find its mouthpiece in the fast-developing new Labour Party, whose existence reflected the improvements in the life of many working people over the Victorian period.

As we have seen, the motives for empire were diverse, with a strong economic and balance of power core, as well as, for some, a belief – sometimes hypocritical in practice – that they were bringing civilized values. Those values were Western, so not necessarily received warmly or accepted. Many people felt – if they reflected at all, for those who control the dialogue for or against always greatly overestimate the number of those like them – that what had happened was a natural result of the British 'Age of Progress'. The colonized, including their rulers, did not always revolt against their fate, and not just because it was difficult to defeat an occupier with superior technology, if usually limited numbers, but because they had always known poverty, experienced cruelty from their elites, or attacks by invaders or neighbouring tribes, from all of which there was no escape. But we should forgive without qualification the distant heirs of the colonized today if they prefer to see colonialism as irredeemable. What people feel has always been a more powerful force in history than the complexity of reality. We should respect that.

There were many other countries and empires that Britain encouraged to modernize, but did not colonize, Persia and the Ottomans among them. When the Shah of Persia visited Britain in the summer of 1889, the view from Aberdeen was that despite being shown 'the beneficent effects of free institutions on the commercial and industrial advancement of a nation', the 'King of Kings' would not change and would spend the remainder of his days 'in his old luxurious Oriental fashion'.[62] Existing power structures rarely accept their own demise; they certainly didn't in Continental Europe without revolution. Only in Britain did monarchy and aristocracy go peacefully, if not always gracefully, into the future.

CHAPTER ELEVEN

'What Happened Next?'

CONNECTING VICTORIANS TO US

Everything has an ending. Not many years after Queen Victoria died, a car came across a ruined house, 'its cracked windows opaque with immemorial dirt', a 'for sale' board outside, all askew. The board described a Classical villa with magnificent gardens and replete with Latin and Greek inscriptions, literary associations and fully matured Oxford allusions. 'Apply to the owner': Mr W.H. Mallock, author of *The New Republic*.

The car's occupants enter and see 'the decaying, rat-disordered ruins of the scene before which Jenkinson who was Jowett, and Herbert who was Ruskin, preached'. The aged custodian suggests that Mr Laurence was 'Mr Mallup 'imself', who was also sometimes Mr Leslie and Miss Merton. Wasn't young Laurence in love with her? 'They was all Mr Mallup.' And the gentlemen that pretended they were Mr 'uxley and Mr Tyndall were in fact Bill Smithers, the chemist's assistant, and the chap that used to write and print the *Margate Advertiser*.[1]

67 As the Victorian era ended, W.H. Mallock became increasingly embittered by what he saw as the movement towards socialism. This photograph, from the American magazine *The World's Work*, founded in 1900, was a sign that the US appreciated him more. In a visit to Harvard, Mallock met US President Theodore Roosevelt, a great reader who told him what a deep impact Mallock's recent book *Veil of the Temple* (1904) had had on him. The book was a denial that faith was in any way irrational.

This story from H.G. Wells's post-Victorian novel *Boon* was published in 1915, though it was not until later that he acknowledged authorship. For Mallock was still alive during the First World War, the combined wit and earnestness of his youthful perceptions lost in his own case to embittered hostility towards socialism and the new world that had replaced that of *The New Republic*. In the century and more that has since passed, the Victorians have often been ridiculed, their achievements been thought boring, their behaviour despised, but also – and mistakenly – thought irrelevant to lives that came after.

For the Victorians themselves, the price of success was often worry. Even in 1851, when *Fraser's Magazine* provided an over-the-top testimonial to the achievements of the previous 50 years, bringing about changes that the sluggish past had failed to make for centuries, there was still a question: did the country still have the energy and talents that had raised it to 'such an unexampled pitch of greatness' to continue and avoid 'that degeneracy which history records as having been, sooner or later, the fate of all great and powerful empires'?[2] For the next 50 years, times of depression apart, many people would have complacently answered 'yes', or been too busy making the future to stop to reflect. Yet there were always doubters – especially on the question of whether moral values were in an appropriate relationship with materialism, and the question of whether the pace of change was sufficient to benefit all sections of society.

At the end of the Victorian era, certainly, much had been achieved. Solid progress had been made towards democracy; the operation of the State had been reformed; the legislature had introduced laws that would have previously never have been contemplated on the protection of employees and of women within marriage, the regulation of companies, public health, education for all, reform and expansion of universities, local government. There had been reports, commissions, debates – serious, detailed and with statistical evidence – on innumerable subjects of public concern. The population had become an urban one, but mechanization had also come to the countryside. Communications of all kinds in themselves would have made the country unrecognizable to anyone who had died a century earlier.

To call all this 'a revolution' would be facile, especially since it was achieved through a better mix of new and old than a revolutionary would recognize. The Canadian Grant Allen, writing in the *Westminster Gazette* in 1893, argued that there had not been a battle between 'the Haves and the Have-nots', but 'the selfish hares on the one side, and the unselfish hares who wish to see something done for the Have-nots on the other'.[3] Permanent changes were made, and – most of them – with strong foundations, and often applied locally. Glance around in 1871 and you could find out about the Llandudno Improvement Commission, the Truro River Improvement, the Chester City Walls Improvement, the Aberdeen Association for the Improvement of the Poor, the Bitterne and Westend Gardeners' Mutual Improvement Society, Hampshire, the Rhyl Improvement Commission, and so on. These were solid gains, not imposed ideologies, and not undertaken without discussion; in Tipperary, Mr Michael Mullaly asserted that 'they would rather die in Tipperary than submit to the extra taxation which the Towns' Improvement Act would be sure to impose upon them'. Mr O'Connor half-saved the day by proposing 'amid uproarious applause' a ten-year moratorium. His motion passed, though Clonmel and Dungarren regretted the decision.[4]

Many of the pleasures of life in wider society had been greatly enhanced just as Progress was losing its ineluctability. The population as a whole was better educated, more prosperous and had been introduced to leisure, with the growth of sporting activities, the statutory provision of holidays and, from the 1850s, excursions to the countryside and the seaside. The beginnings of mass culture and consumption were widely visible. There was no perfect meritocracy in 1900, any more than there was in 2000, or will be in 2100, but social standing, money and the Established Church no longer had a stranglehold on preferment. There were new office jobs, servants, yes, but acquiring bourgeois values, ever more powerful trade unions and a Labour Party poised to move forward. Patriotism was often over-strident, but it could also display finer characteristics than naked nationalism.

And yet towards the end there appeared to be an unease that had not been visible in the middle decades of the 19th century. It wasn't mysterious, but you could feel it symbolically. Lurking in Tennyson's paean to Queen Victoria's reign in 1887 were the lines – some said added at the Queen's suggestion – 'Are there thunders moaning in the distance? / Are there spectres moving in the darkness?' In Kipling's 'Recessional', a poem written by him ten years later for the Queen's Diamond Jubilee, it is more explicit: 'Judge of the Nations, spare us yet', even if 'drunk with sight of power, we loose / Wild tongues that have not Thee in awe'. Britain's 'pomp' and greatness could fade away to nothing, like the ancient civilizations of the past, Nineveh and Tyre. The poem was not published until after the official celebrations were over, but was plainly at odds with their spirit. Kipling felt the Jubilee expressed 'a certain optimism that scared me'; he had seen the naval review at Spithead, with a display of such power that he seems to have been overwhelmed. It acted, he said in his autobiography, 'in the nature of a *nuzzur-wattu* [a remedy for

68 Even the weather seemed to be signalling a downturn in Britain's fortunes, especially if photography could use its symbolic power: February 1895 was the coldest on record. Shipping came to a halt in both the Thames and the Manchester Shipping Canal. Here, below Limehouse, human life disappeared, leaving only starving seagulls on floating ice blocks.

warding off bad things]'.[5] There had been many times in Queen Victoria's reign when the Queen, the country's elites and the mass of the population had shown signs of being over-confident, but when 'the idea of Progress' had been at its height, the belief that power and responsibility belonged together was almost universally accepted, if sometimes hypocritically. Perhaps that was no longer so.

Moreover, there was also a sense that the power was on the wane. Not everyone would have suggested that, if so, it was because vanity had overcome the victor, and before the end of the first decade, Lloyd George went further than any previous Chancellor in his People's Budget – not, to say the least, that it had an easy progress through Parliament. But there were plentiful concerns, other than moral behaviour, to create an unease. They began with the economy. The return to tariffs and protectionism towards the end of the 19th century could not but impinge on the world's biggest trader; Britain's share of world trade dropped from nearly a quarter to roughly 17 per cent in the 30 years from 1880 to 1910. In industry, just as the United States

69 'Unfair Trade Winds', *Punch*, 20 December 1884. Britain had opened up the world for trade; now its competitors sent their own goods to its shores, increasing unemployment. Chamberlain's emotive campaign for tariff reform two decades later – 'Why benefit the foreigner and starve the British working man?' – was a complete electoral failure. Competition took no prisoners in a Darwinian modern world.

and Germany were in the ascendancy, British investment in heavy industry at home fell; many of the newly rich preferred the delights of society to the grimness of the factory and industrial landscape – their sons, with a better education than the entrepreneurs, were drawn to finance, the professions or government administration. Trade unions became more militant as they became more powerful.

The political landscape was not reassuring either. 'It is the age of international stress,' said the *Morning Post* in August 1897, which, it added correctly, 'may possibly end in international storm.' The newspaper suggested that, in such an age, the public instinct was not for legislation and constitutional change but strong leadership to deal with 'other nations' crowding around or against Britain. While the cockpit of 'international stress' might remain close at hand – Europe – all the powers of Europe (the USA and Turkey also participated) embarked on imperial expansion after the Conference of Berlin. Bismarck excluded questions of sovereignty in his opening statement; the Conference also excluded African voices. The West African *Lagos Observer* suggested as it was closing in February 1885 that 'the world had, perhaps, never witnessed a robbery on so large a scale'. Looking back, six years later, another Lagos Editor noted that forcible possession of land had simply taken the place of forcible possession of people in the era of slavery.[6] At its height, European imperialism was often just a byproduct of power struggles among the European nations.

Anxiety about competing, as well as arrogance, therefore replaced a relative unwillingness to acquire colonial possessions unless absolutely necessary. With militant rivals in every direction, John Ruskin had already argued in 1870 that England must compete 'or perish'; 'she must found colonies as fast and as far as she is able' (though that was no good if she remained a materialistic 'heap of cinders').[7] But quite independent of the moral issues involved, in any even medium-term view it was bound to end badly. The underrated Ford Madox Ford expressed the point thoughtfully in his 1907 *The Spirit of the People*. In this, he suggests that the matter is not a matter of race 'but quite simply of place – of place and of spirit, the spirit being born of the environment'.[8] How could an insular nation even define, let alone defend or reform, the complex of possessions that had resulted from imperial expansion? The Emperor Napoleon's task was much easier by comparison. Even those who went off to displace local populations with much larger ones from home soon began to distance themselves from the motherland. For the moment, jingoism was a rousing call in response to survival of the fittest, but those who had always argued that if trade was not manageable without political interference, best to avoid creating a problem, were vindicated.

There was another aspect of this. The proponents of the idea of Progress in its heyday emphasized both material prosperity and the spread of civilizing values. When conflict arose in an imperial situation, prejudice went in the opponents' direction, regardless of whether the opponent was white or black. The Blackburn *Weekly Standard and Express* (provincial newspapers by no means confined themselves to local issues) on the last day of the year in 1898 complained that the Boer mind was 'closed to all ideas of progress' and monopolized 'all the power of the State'.[9] Earlier that year, the Rev. Thomas Gray, a Welsh Presbyterian, went out as a Welsh Liberal full of sympathy for the Boers (so it was reported in Middlesborough's *North-Eastern Daily Gazette*) and found they were 'too ignorant to understand modern ideas of progress', were incorrigibly lazy and that their President, Paul Kruger, was to blame.[10] Yet the resulting war severely damaged the idea of Britain as the world's liberalizing and progressive catalyst. Images of thousands dying behind barbed wire enclosing their encampments as prisoners were a chilling premonition of what was to happen later in the century.

The shadow of loss of high ground also manifested itself culturally. The leading proponents of connecting morality to art and literature in the decades following mid-century were most obviously Matthew Arnold and John Ruskin. When we first met Walter Pater and the other two in 1876 in the Prologue of this book, Pater already had a considerable reputation for art for art's sake, a belief that was to lead to a decadent end to the 19th century: an egotistical, sometimes perverse and artificial, if curious, mood as it was described by its first interpreter, Holbrook Jackson. Aesthetes rejected the idea that ethics had anything to do with creative activity. Oscar Wilde, by effectively making himself an artwork, seemed the antithesis of the high-mindedness of the era of Progress. Moral earnestness, or even hard work, were absent from the 'new and beautiful and interesting disease' described by the poet Arthur Symons in the essay 'The Decadent Movement in Literature' (1893). Whether the privileging of fantasy and hedonism over logic and the natural world was fairly labelled 'cultural pessimism' might be disputed. But it was no longer the 'Progress' that the Victorians had recognized.

In 1880, supreme optimism had not yet died. Describing the 19th century in April 1882, Frederic Harrison was able to assert that 'We all feel a-tiptoe with hope and confidence. We are on the threshold of a great time.... In science, in religion, in social organization, we all know what great things are in the air...our children and our children's children will see it.' Just twenty years later, there were many objections to the idea of an 'age of great expectation and unwearied striving after better things'.[11]

Charles Trevelyan, then a young Liberal politician (but eventually to become the last surviving member of the first Labour Cabinet), spoke at a Liberal Association meeting in Sheffield in March 1896. He outlined a problem. The great difficulty of modern progress was that 'Peace, freedom and democracy had not brought happiness in their train.' Socialists had discovered a truth as old as the hills – most people had a poor time of it on Earth. The solution for them was surely a different type of society that would bring the millennium. Trevelyan dismissed that naivety. Of course, abuses should be rectified, but human nature could never guarantee an administration that would always avoid dishonesty, or things that were not practical, or tyranny, or lack of intelligence.[12]

Trevelyan's solution was the perfectly sensible one of slow amelioration, leaving each generation one degree happier, one degree more civilized. But that signalled the end of the era of Progress, of unstoppably bold and optimistic ambition. Unfortunately, the genie had been let out of the bottle: the 20th and 21st centuries lost the optimism, but demanded perfectability, and quickly.

The 20th century began with an old confusion: when do new centuries start? The *Daily Mail*, the new voice of mass newspaper readership, in celebrating its dawn on 31 December 1900, commented that the old century had been around for a long time – '100 years at least, perhaps 101?' Experts were asked to define the previous century's greatest achievements. H.M. Stanley noted progress in every form of knowledge and every field of action, but focused on electricity. In the future, it would purge impurities in the atmosphere, making streets and underground cleaner and more wholesome; it would provide, by countless methods, for common needs, as well as create luxuries previously enjoyed only by the wealthiest; it would create energy from power inherent in water, from the wild Mosi-oa-Tunya (Victoria Falls) of the Zambezi to the White Nile. The artist Sir William Richmond agreed that 'Science has truly made The Mark', but did identify progress in art because of its entering of daily life with new vitality, as well as singling out journalism (which had done wonders, though also some harm), archaeology and writing history. The Liberal politician Sir Arthur Arnold focused on 'the representation of the people' in local and central government. Oscar Browning, who contributed greatly to professional teacher-training, suggested the Forster Education Act, with more priority to secondary education now a greater need than anything.

Most of this was convincing, though the colonial administrator Sir Richard Temple was less accurate in his prediction that two international power structures would dominate the world going forward – the English-speaking, including Britain and its colonies and the USA, and the Russian or Slavic. An Asian century seemed inconceivable. The effects of applied science were the dominant choice of the contributors for what had been achieved. As for the people who 'had no history because men did not wish them to have any', they – women – now had rights of education, travel, public office, professional positions; they also numbered mountaineers and golfers among them.[13]

Victorian culture was infused with values, whether applied practically or explored philosophically: acceptance of a hierarchical or class-based society, religious belief and moral structure, plus a developing identity for Englishness (a highly provocative 'synonym' for Britishness), recognizable but usually not tightly defined. The odd thing is that these Conservative attitudes and beliefs were all complicated by a massive influx of materialism, yet this 'Progress' did not lead to collapse into the arms of revolution. Instead, the most historically significant feature of the period was the way it mapped out – as we can see in retrospect – a series of routes for what has transpired ever since.

That is not at all how Victorians were perceived by the generations that came immediately after, still less how they are viewed by popular culture today. Nor did any of the three values survive in substantive form: secularization effectively replaced a state religion, and while moral structures continued to be navigated when faith declined, we can see the ways in which they became threatened, especially in the amoral digital era, by strident voices replacing understanding with intolerance and tech-induced behaviour that has no meaningful engagement with anything but mindless money-making and power; and 'gentleman' (or 'gentlewoman') became pejorative terms, to be replaced not by equality but by display of wealth and celebrity; in addition, 'Britishness' was battered by (relative) economic decline, desires for independence in the UK's constituent countries and loss of Empire, surviving primarily in the far-right and more positively in sport or in response to direct threats, notably of war.

The immediate mood as the 20th century began included some thoughtful voices. The year before Queen Victoria died, the young Desmond MacCarthy (who made a distinguished career as literary critic and lived until the 1950s) suggested to his friends in the secret Cambridge society of intellectuals, the Apostles, that 'all institutions, the family, the state, laws of honour, etc., which have a claim on the individual' had 'failed to produce convincing proofs of their authority'. People put more trust 'in their immediate judgment'.[14] It was a wise thought that the age of the masses was also to be the age of individualism. But the liberating effects of removal of social controls were eventually to evolve into a basic political problem: where does authority lie?

The most influential of the early anti-Victorian voices, Lytton Strachey in *Eminent Victorians*, seems frivolous by comparison. In private, he told John Maynard Keynes that nearly all the great Victorian luminaries – Arnold, Jowett, Ruskin among them – were physically impotent. At least the Victorians themselves, while given to triumphalist outbursts and smugness, also owned up to anxiety, a fear of loss of earnestness, a fear of loss of faith, yet still managed optimistically to see the excitement of finding the source of the Nile and exploring the world, and of trying to take their society forward, politically, economically and morally. Strachey, with the avowed intent to be objective, was happy making things up (Matthew Arnold's legs were not 'shorter than they should have been'). It took the working-class son of a jobbing gardener, Howard Spring, to put Strachey in his place (in 1941) as a 'dry, desiccated, juiceless, cynical man whose very contact is enough to freeze all generous emotion and immobilize all noble endeavour'. But of course, such intemperate debates arising from one age's view of another, or one person's view of another, are not very meaningful. We can note that the new supplement to the *Oxford English Dictionary* in 1931 defined 'Victorian' as 'prudish, strict, old-fashioned, out-dated', but that is no more significant than saying their happier legacies included the creation of the football league or consumer magazines or modern shopping.[15] We may safely take it that disparaging Victorians has been the national sport ever since.

What continuities were there from the Victorian period? In an imperfect world, pragmatism remained a strength, if itself applied imperfectly. Between the wars, the two main Prime Ministers, Baldwin and MacDonald, did not come from the same political traditions, but most of the time provided relative stability, despite dealing with the appalling problems created by the First World War. It did not always feel like that, with the General Strike in 1926 and MacDonald as first Labour Prime Minister, then leader of a Conservative-dominated national government – but it certainly had nothing to do with the vicious authoritarians of right and left plotting their expansionist designs elsewhere. There was too much consensus for some: a Labour Party manifesto in 1934 was clear that there was no halfway house between societies based on private and on public ownership, while Oswald Mosley's British Union of Fascists had more adherents than many have been comfortable to admit. But politics has often seemed as if it is a natural extension of what was determined in the 19th century. In so far as the objective of achieving full employment and enabling a welfare state within a capitalist system was achieved via the ideas of John Maynard Keynes and William Beveridge, they were both Liberals. But just as Conservative administrations passed many of the Victorian social reforms, it was a Labour Government that, to an extent, gave an increased role for the state after the Second World War. Victorians established a 'British' way of politics in which opinions from all sections of society (except the extremes) were accepted. Moreover, well over 50 years after the end of the Victorian period – half a century in which an enormous amount had happened – it was still possible to say that Victorian values of hard work, public and civic duty continued (if qualified by some of the same hypocrisy), while the widening of educational opportunity and an increase in meritocracy followed the Victorians' own trajectory of change.

What eventually influenced such matters was the inability of any political party to arrest economic decline, with a resulting clash with the much-enhanced expectations of a modern consumer society. Thus when Mrs Thatcher, in 1983, proudly spoke of coming from a tradition in which you were taught to work 'jolly hard', self-reliance, self-respect, getting on, then helping others to create prosperity, taking pride in your country, and called them Victorian values, as well as perennial values, she evoked a passionate hostility from those sections of society that were suffering from the country's economic decline, and suffered the more from what her administration applied as remedies.[16] Even so, she won three elections. It has only been in the 21st century that the country properly threw off its Victorian inheritance,

Develop the Power
that is within you

Get ahead. Books are free
at your Public Library

70 In the nearly 80 years after Queen Victoria died before Margaret Thatcher became Prime Minister, perhaps the Victorians' greatest gift – libraries free to everyone and the cultural encouragement to read both for pleasure and to get on in the world – flourished. The evidence from the years since, as these policies have been abandoned, appears to be a legacy of unreasoning polarization and the now rapid decline of mental wellbeing. In this 1921 poster, books unleashed power.

but not with happy consequences. It has suffered from a very rapid increase in income inequality, with elites apparently more out of touch with the reality of most people's lives than, surprisingly, they were in Victorian times and yet constantly under public gaze revealed to have a more or less complete lack of moral structure in their conduct. In addition, with nearly everyone exposed to the polarizations exhibited on social media and (many argue) orchestrated by its mind-colonizing owners, we have entered a different political landscape. Economic decline was followed by political decline.

In a world context, there seems to be a clear line from the Victorian era of Progress to more or less all of the greatest challenges of this century. Progress, at its most fundamental level, was underpinned by scientific and technological discovery. The discoveries, plainly, have resulted in astonishing benefits, not all spread throughout society, but by the standards of any pre-modern society transforming more lives than could ever have been previously conceived. Yet, while the Victorians felt themselves in an era of great change, their inability to predict the consequences of what science and technology were doing to their society was less troublesome to them than it is for us. Science and technology are like compound interest: an ever-worsening trap for the unwary.

The most obvious way in which this has been apparent lies in technology's destructiveness. The First World War was the first major reminder of the scale of the problem. There were many reasons why that war might have happened, and many reasons for it being prolonged, but they all in the end come back to technology, which can never be neutral when it encounters either living beings or inanimate matter. Each side could batter the other more or less indefinitely, with terrible consequences, but no victory. The lesson was not learned. Instead, ever since the desire has been the search for successively more powerful weaponry, to the extent that today the planet could easily be destroyed by the pressing of a button. What made the difference in the First World War? The destructive power of tanks, the British alone having hundreds in action as the war progressed; mortars, for Britain in 1915 able to fire 22 3" shells a minute over 1,200 yards; machine guns developed from Hiram Maxim's design of 1884, firing 450–600 rounds a minute; better designed artillery, with a longer range; submarines; aircraft (a good example of unintended consequences, first used for reconnaissance before bombing capacity was realized); poison gas. These were the weapons built on the idea of technological progress. They had their own vulnerabilities, so the lesson was to strive to make them more reliably destructive.

Warfare was not the only beneficiary of technology. There was also a new ability, mostly not foreseen, though obvious to anyone who cared to think, to exploit the natural resources of the planet until the issue ceased to be just damage to humans and animals but the destruction of the planet itself (actually, as we have noted, it was Disraeli whose government passed the first Rivers Pollution Prevention Act in 1876). Added to this were the largely unforeseen consequences of encouraging urbanization and creating the transport systems allowing urban populations to be mobile on a global basis, thereby creating a lifestyle ideal for the spread of pandemics. An unwillingness to do anything but marvel at the wonders of modern medicine, thus distracting from a focus on what might unexpectedly happen once humans started meddling with the basic building blocks of life, creates another faultline. There was a certain inevitability about all this because of a human strength – curiosity – but it was all made possible by unleashing the capacity, in Victorian times, for humans to start behaving like Gods, ironically just as some of them were losing their belief in God.

In a perceptive review of J.B. Bury's book *The Idea of Progress* in May 1920, the *Manchester Guardian* suggested that Progress 'belongs to the same order of ideas as Providence or personal immortality. It is true or it is false, and, like them, it cannot be proved either true or false. Belief in it is an act of faith.' Materialists, intent on money-making, have – not necessarily consciously – accepted that 'act of faith', just as the makers of the Industrial Revolution and the modern banking system in Victorian times did. But while Victorians kept working on reconciling prosperity with other human needs, by the time the First World War was over, the picture seemed considerably bleaker, and not just because of the technological destructiveness of the war. Science had its consequences also. What were humans to make of the astronomer Arthur Eddington's plain statement in 1928 that the universe was 'no more than a fortuitous concourse of atoms'? His own Quaker faith was no protection for the bombshell this created for the rest of us. Victorians had also embraced science and their scientists – Faraday, Tyndall, Huxley – were very successful at popularizing it. The Scottish novelist Robert Louis Stevenson, who died in 1894, nevertheless wondered where it might take humans – perhaps to 'zones of speculation' that were not a 'habitable city for the mind of men'. That way lay modern depression. As Michael Ignatieff has said, 'We eat well, we live well, but we do not have good dreams.'[17]

The development of sociology in the 19th century didn't help. It looked as if there were big benefits from the scientific analysis of society, but one of the consequences was to make people feel like ciphers, with no agency in making change. Freud reinforced that sense while thinking he was increasing understanding. His introductory lectures on psychoanalysis, delivered during the First World War, were translated into English in 1920. There had already been 'two great outrages' upon humanity's 'naïve self-love'. One went back to Copernicus in the 16th century, when 'home' for humans stopped being the centre of the universe; instead, it was just a speck in an apparently limitless universe. More recently, Darwin had 'robbed man of his peculiar privilege of being specially created'. And now, thanks to applying science to psychology, it was plain that we did not even know our deepest motives; we just had 'scraps of information' about what was really going on inside us.[18] Those who had survived the high-tech weaponry of a world war were now robbed of their self-esteem.

Of course, none of this was to suggest that understanding is anything other than an extraordinary human attribute. But it did result in what the American Hoxie Fairchild called 'Hollow men eating their Naked Lunches in the wasteland while awaiting Godot.'[19] Aldous Huxley (no fan of the

Victorians) veered wildly from dystopia in *Brave New World* (1932) to utopianism in his last novel, *Island* (1962), a route that has been common in the post-Victorian world, though usually taking the opposite direction as utopian ideas turn out to be dystopian. 'Being Victorian' had been felt much more strongly across Victorian society than the fragmentation that began with the modern, continued with the postmodern, and collapsed into narcissism in the era of social media and identity politics.

Freud himself had warned during the First World War that there had never been so destructive an event. Character sometimes overrode *zeitgeist*. H.G. Wells, whose parents were domestic servants, had escaped to a different life – as many upwardly mobile Victorians did – and by the time Queen Victoria died when he was 34, he was optimistically happy to look forward to enjoying a greater freedom from Victorian social constraints, though influenced also by the more pessimistic 1890s. His own belief in social progress, expressed in such books as *A Modern Utopia* (1905), took a severe knock in the First World War, but as he turned more to the virtues of education and science as a long-term means of making social progress by adapting better to change, he managed an optimistic end to his *A Short History of the World* (1922), at least in its first edition, which Einstein recommended for its use of history to interpret progress in civilization. Could we doubt that 'presently our race will more than realize our boldest imaginations', with unity and peace?[20]

The destructive effects of science and technology, countered to an extent by using them to increase prosperity, thereby making possible the explosion of consumerism after the Second World War – a window of prosperity without consequences now ended – was not the only fundamental legacy of the Victorians. On the face of it, a very surprising acceptance by the ruling elite that steps must be taken towards democracy, for the first time in history, seemed wholly good and certainly 'progress'. Accompanying it was an equally surprising acceptance (in an era of laissez-faire) that the state was needed to play a much bigger role than its function hitherto. There could be complaints that improvements were happening too slowly, though some were conscious that real, long-lasting change can only be absorbed comfortably bit by bit. One other historically fundamental principle, enunciated in the Enlightenment but now viewable in practice – that human beings had rights – gathered pace, though Victorians were quick to emphasise that duties and responsibilities were attached to rights. These aspects of 19th-century progress evolved into the democracy that we know today.

But there was a different evolution that the same trends unleashed. The ever-wise Alexis de Tocqueville, originally sent to the United States by the

French Government to study the prison system in 1831, later produced his two volumes entitled *Democracy in America* (1835 & 1840). In these, while finding plenty to applaud, he suggested that there could be dangers of a new form of tyranny: the tyranny of the majority. Karl Marx, in exile in England, didn't think of it like that, but his authoritarian heirs were able to exploit the bogus right to paradise – Tocqueville had warned that social reform fomented social discontent – by replacing democracy with authoritarian rule by the few ostensibly expressing the will of the many. Progress presented by populist ideologues as absolute belief in ideas of welfare, justice and freedom was often more appealing than the limitations inherent in democracy. So here was another unintended consequence of 19th-century Progress. Marx took advantage of the freedom of speech and other freedoms available to him in Britain. The British themselves rejected his message, but there were many other countries providing better opportunities.

The mantle of 'Progress' passed into different hands in the 20th century, with terrible consequences. Marx's belief in progress, in accordance with the laws of development of history, came to fruition in a society responsible for more deaths in the 20th century – Stalin's Russia and Hitler's Germany not excepted – than any other: Mao's China. The Victorians, after the first big strides towards industrialization, asked questions about the balance between materialism and morality. That legacy helped their successors to enlarge the power of education, to enable organized working-class representation, to use the state to help the weak, to increase the standard of living, and to become more meritocratic. But the possibilities they unleashed through embracing technological change and a more ambitious form of government mutated into something completely different. Democracy was not the only political choice.

Does the arrival of the digital age make what happened in Victorian Britain irrelevant? Computers tend to destroy any sense of linear development, which strikes at the heart of what history is: an account showing that one thing happened after another, with consequences. Authoritarian societies remain very aware of the power of history; they respect it, though manipulate it by re-writing it. Victorians also wrote their own narrative of the past – no one can be completely objective about either their own past or that of their society – but they applied themselves conscientiously to detailed study and research in a way that came to be seen as modern and professional. Many of them were also much better than we are today in acknowledging imperfection (the Internet encourages the idea that only 'perfect' counts, yet also enables fake perfection). The radical journalist John Wade, once a wool-sorter, whose multi-edition *Black Book* (first published in 1820) exposed corruption, correctly described England in 1856 as 'progressive' but 'imperfect'.[21]

Would Victorians have welcomed social media? They would certainly have wanted to experiment with it; some would have become addicted because it is addictive; but as observers, many would have had at least three objections. The most obvious is the absence of true debate as people shout over each other's heads, not at all what John Stuart Mill meant in *On Liberty* (1859), in which he links free speech to utility, not human rights. 'Collision of adverse opinions' by people listening to each other was essential, so that a more mature truth would result and provide the opportunity for improving things for most people. There was no agreement about votes for women, but that did not stop Mill from seeking an amendment to the 1867 Reform Act and arguing the case, even if he failed. Victorians would also have found it difficult to understand the way social media appeared to trap people in webs of hatred, without having the redemptive possibility of understanding how we came from the past to the present and what we discovered in the process that provides positive values. And most obviously, they would feel what Solzhenitsyn identified before the Internet was invented, but which has been so magnified by social media's relentless scrutiny – scrutiny for which it is never apparent whether fact or lie or just gross simplification has been revealed. That would show Victorians a loss of faith in society's own values, not a collapse of power but of its opposite – authority. A loss of faith in authority tends to be catastrophic for a society, given that it is an essential underpinning of everything; without it, there is permanent instability and no genuine protection for either liberty or creativity.

Such generalizations, and those used throughout this book, are of course no more than partial truths, as all attempts to describe complexity are. But we can perhaps safely say that Victorians learned more tolerance and enjoyed more Progress than any previous society, but that their legacy allowed for two choices.

The first choice was to consider the consequences and unintended consequences of applying technological power with ever-greater care and continue making steady forward steps in prosperity, social welfare, education, freedom for all, while addressing new problems, including the loss of 'home' created by imperialism, nationalism, a global economy and the no man's land of the digital universe. Ironically (because at the time, he felt education was a necessity before extending the franchise further), it was Robert Lowe in 1865 who defined the only view of government – then and now – that enables democracy to flourish: 'the true view of the science of government is that it is not an exact science, that it is not capable of *à priori* demonstration, that it rests upon an experiment, and that its conclusions ought to be carefully scanned, modified, and altered so as to be adapted to different states of society, or the same state of society at different times'.[22]

The second choice comes out of the journey taken by the world since the Enlightenment. The Enlightenment emphasized reason, learning and study, with – as yet – little effect on the material world. It was followed, in the first half of the 19th century, with gigantic, highly visible changes enabled by machine technology, which provided a basis for ideas of progress and improvement. So all-encompassing were these that, as the 19th century proceeded, in some places they took on the characteristics of a fixed preconception, an ideology, which morphed in the 20th century into perfectability – an idea easily exploited by demagogues able to manipulate its emotional appeal. Thus, the second choice left by the Victorians – one that, however much they disagreed with each other, they would not have taken – is to seek absolute 'progress' by revolutionary or tech-induced populist means and accept the violence, the abandonment of tolerance, the totalitarianism, the fundamentalism, the narcissism necessary for getting on the fast-track to the delusional paradise that is everyone's 'right'.

NOTES

After first mention, titles are identified by author and publication date. Where it is convenient, some references have been brought together under one note number.

Prologue: 'A Weekend by the Sea'

1 W.H. Mallock *The New Republic* 1877 (reprinted with intro. by John Lucas, 1975). Quotations are from this edition

2 Bertrand and Patricia Russell (eds) *The Amberley Papers* 1937 (vol. 2, reprinted 1966), p. 35

3 George Eliot, 'Art and Belles Lettres: Review of *Modern Painters III*', *Westminster Review*, April 1856 (vol. LXV), p. 626; Matthew Sweet *Inventing the Victorians* 2001, p. 195

4 G.K. Chesterton *The Victorian Age in Literature* 1913, p. 69

5 Quoted in Asa Briggs *The Age of Improvement* 1959 (reprinted 1960), p. 475

6 *Encyclopedia of the Victorian Era* 2004 (vol. 2), p. 323

7 *Morning Post*, 11 April 1874

8 *Saturday Review*, 5 May 1874

9 W.H. Mallock *Memoirs of Life and Literature* 1920 (reprinted 2014), p. 208

10 George Saintsbury *A Second Scrap-Book* 1923, p. 180

11 T.H.S. Escott *Great Victorians* 1916, p. 288

12 Review of 'W.H. Mallock *A Critical Examination of Socialism*', *Journal of Education*, 22 August 1907

1. 'Wonderful Discoveries of a Wonderful Age'

1 Walter Benjamin *The Work of Art in the Age of Mechanical Reproduction* 1935

2 *The Times*, 10 October 2020

3 Quoted in Kelly J. Mays, 'Looking Backward, Looking Forward: The Victorians in the Rearview of History', *Victorian Studies*, Spring 2011, pp. 445–56

4 *The Times*, 24 January 1859

5 Sweet 2001, p. 107

6 David Newsome *The Victorian World Picture* 1997, p. 6

7 Michael Ignatieff *Prospect Magazine*, 20 October 1999

8 William Johnston *England As It Is* 1851 (vol. 1), p. 64

9 William Thackeray, 'De Juventute' 1860, quoted in Walter E. Houghton *The Victorian Frame of Mind* 1957, p. 3

10 George Eliot *Adam Bede* 1859, Ch. 52

11 Thomas Carlyle *Chartism* 1839, p. 83

12 Quoted in E.T. Cook and A. Wedderburn (eds) *The Library Edition of the Works of John Ruskin* 1903–12 (vol. 36), p. xcv

13 Quoted in Bruce McPherson *Between Two Worlds: Victorian Ambivalence about Progress* 1983, pp. 21, 23

14 *Ibid.*, p. 9

15 James Aitken (ed.) *English Letters of the XIX Century* 1946, p. 104

16 Benjamin Kidd *Social Evolution* 1893 (reprinted 1920), pp. 29–30

17 Charlotte Riddell *Far Above Rubies* 1867 (vol. 1), p. 202

18 Edward Hamley *Lady Lee's Widowhood* 1854 (vol. 1), p. 152

19 H.G. Wells, 'A Story of the Days to Come', *Pall Mall Magazine*, Mays 2011, p. 448

20 Sebastian Faulks *Paris Echo* 2018 (pb 2019), p. 122

21 Robert Kemp Philip *The History of Progress* 1859, p. 6

22 *Ibid.*, pp. 64, 272

23 *Quarterly Review*, December 1849–March 1851 (vol. 86), p. 526

24 Hippolyte Taine *Notes on England* 1872, p. 373

25 Quoted in Myron F. Brightfield *England and Its Novels 1840-70* 1971: William Pickersgill *The Belle of the Ball* 1865 (vol. 1), p. 15

26 Briggs 1960, p. 437

27 Taine 1872, p. 325

28 Houghton 1957, p. 27

29 Brightfield 1971: Mrs Henry Wood *The Shadow of Ashlydyat* 1863 (vol. 1), p. 92

30 H.G. Wells *A Short History of the World* 1922 (reprinted 1929), p. 318

31 Quoted in David Reynolds, 'The return of big history', *New Statesman*, 23–29 January 2015

2. 'The Peculiar Pride of the Present Age'

1 Martin J. Wiener *English Culture and the Decline of the Industrial Spirit 1850-1980* 1985, p. 14

2 Jonathan Clark (ed.) *A World by Itself: A History of the British Isles* 2010, Essay by William D. Rubinstein, pp. 468–9

3 Quoted in Wiener 1985, p. 84

4 *Leeds Mercury*, 21 December 1865

5 Taine 1872, p. 174

6 T.H.S. Escott *Social Transformations of the Victorian Age* 1897, p. 112

7 Caroline Norton *Letters to the Mob* 1848, p. 15

8 Brightfield 1971: Charles James *The Bramleighs of Bishop's Folly* 1868, p. 21

9 *Ibid.*; John Saunders *Hirrell* 1869 (vol. 2), p. 185

10 Esmé Wingfield-Stratford *The Victorian Tragedy* 1930, p. 100

11 *The Gentleman's Magazine*, January–June 1850 (vol. 33)

12 Patrick Brantlinger *The Spirit of Reform: British Literature and Politics 1832–1867* 1977, pp. 119–20

13 Charlotte Bowen *How a Farthing Made a Fortune* (n.d.), p. 96

14 Ian Inkster (ed.) *The Golden Age: Essays in British Social and Economic History, 1850-1870* 2000, Essay by Kim Stevenson, p. 273

15 Ross McKibbin *The Ideologies of Class Social Relations in Britain 1880–1950* 1990, p. 14

16 J.M. Golby (ed.) *Culture and Society in Britain 1850–1890* 1986, pp. 229–30

17 *Sheffield and Rotherham Independent*, 30 March 1889

18 Letter from Engels in Manchester to Marx in London, dated 7 October 1858, in *Marx and Engels: Works* 1929 (Moscow, vol. 40), p. 343

19 J.W. Cross *George Eliot's Life* 1885 (vol. 1), p. 210

20 Gordon S. Haight *George Eliot and John Chapman* 1969 (2nd edn), p. 48

21 *Pall Mall Gazette*, 26 April 1890

22 Cook and Wedderburn 1903–12 (vol. 37), p. 479

23 John Morley *Recollections* 1917 (vol. 1), p. 112

24 *Bristol Mercury and Daily Post*, 24 October 1878

25 Quoted in Robert Nisbet *History of the Idea of Progress* 1980, p. 186

26 Quoted in J. Buzzard, J.W. Childers and E. Gillooly (eds) *Victorian Prism: Refractions of the Crystal Palace* 2007, pp. 1, 129

27 *Ibid.*, p. 4

28 George Sala *The Seven Sons of Mammon* 1862, p. 43

29 Margaret Oliphant *The Athelings* 1857, p. 663

30 Buzzard, Childers and Gillooly 2007, pp. 236–44

31 Cook and Wedderburn 1903–12 (vol. 34), p. 249

32 *Glasgow Herald Advertisements and Notices*, 12 June 1872

33 *The Examiner*, 4 August 1877; *Pall Mall Gazette*, 4 December 1877 (review of Sully)

34 Catherine Gore *Progress and Prejudice* 1854 (vol. 1), p. 12

35 *Aberdeen Weekly Journal*, 19 December 1884

36 Laurence Oliphant *Piccadilly* 1870 (Part II)

37 Cook and Wedderburn 1903–12 (vol. 22), p. 507

38 Review in *Daily News*, 7 July 1859

39 *The Midland Progressionist* 1848 (vol. 1)

40 *Berrow's Worcester Journal*, 31 October 1874

41 J.H. Newman *Historical Sketches* 1873 (vol. 1), p. 187

42 *Morning Post*, 11 March 1852

43 *Glasgow Herald*, 17 September 1864

44 Wiener 1985, p. 37

45 H.H. Asquith, 'Some Aspects of the Victorian Age', Romanes Lecture, University of Oxford (1918)

46 Quoted in C. Harvie, G. Martin and A. Scharf (eds) *Industrialization and Culture 1830–1919* 1970, p. 153

3. 'Triumph Over All Inanimate Matter'

1 T.B. Fontane *Journeys to England in Victoria's Early Days, 1844–59* 1939 (trans. Dorothy Harrison), pp. 127ff

2 Taine 1872, pp. 273ff

3 Newsome 1997, p. 22

4 Letter to *Daily News*, 18 September 1851

5 Newsome 1997, p. 21

6 *Quarterly Review*, January–April 1860 (vol. 107)

7 Quoted in Christine MacLeod *Heroes of Invention* 2007, p. 102

8 Lord Byron, Canto 1 of *Don Juan*, st. CXXX11

9 MacLeod 2007, p. 142

10 *Idem*

11 Adam Hart-Davis *What the Victorians Did for Us* 2001, p. 132

12 At the time of writing, the historian and current head of the UK-based Entrepreneurs Network, Anton Howes, is writing a book on this theme

13 Aitken 1946, p. 122

14 Elizabeth Gaskell *North and South* 1854, Ch. 20

15 Samuel Smiles *The Life of George Stephenson and of His Son Robert Stephenson* 1857 (rev. edn 1867), Preface

16 Robin Smith, '"Catch Me Who Can?" [the name of a Trevithick engine], Richard Trevithick and George Stephenson', *The Historian*, 2009, p. 102

17 Chris Williams (ed.) *A Companion to Nineteenth-Century Britain* 2004, Essay by William J. Ashworth, p. 228

18 MacLeod 2007, p. 7

19 Williams 2004, p. 230

20 *The Athenaeum*, 17 January 1852

21 James Vernon *Distant Strangers: How Britain Became Modern* 2014, p. 13

22 Johnston 1851, pp. 260–61

23 Brightfield 1971: Lord William Pitt *Percy Hamilton* 1851 (vol. 1), p. 101

24 *Pearson's Magazine*, January–June 1896 (vol. 1)

25 Escott 1897, pp. 28, 37

26 Arthur Patchett Martin *Life and Letters of the Right Honourable Robert Lowe* 1893 (vol. 1), p. 19

27 E.F. Benson *As We Were* 1930 (pb 1938), p. 107

28 Vernon 2014, p. 32

29 James Grant *The Life and Times of the Greatest Victorian* 2019, p. 27

30 Emma Robinson *The Gold-Worshippers; Or, The Days We Live In* 1851, p. 274

31 *Birmingham Daily Post*, 16 June 1864

32 Unpublished lecture by Stephen Halliday on the early history of the Underground

33 Matilda Betham-Edwards *Mid-Victorian Memories* 1919, p. 167

34 Inkster 2000, Essay by Colin Griffin, p. 30

35 Quoted in Wiener 1985, p. 43
36 Taine 1872, p. 261
37 *Morning Post*, 13 January 1897
38 *The Annual Register: A Review of Public Events at Home and Abroad* 1870, p. 319
39 *Le Temps*, quoted in *Dundee Courier and Argus*, 2 August 1866
40 S.A. Wallace and F.E. Gillespie (eds) *The Journal of Benjamin Moran 1857–65* 1948, p. 115
41 Inkster 2000, Essay by Gillian Cookson, pp. 78–9
42 Johnston 1851, p. 252
43 Hart-Davis 2001, p. 99
44 *Nineteenth Century*, January–June 1884 (vol. XV), p. 10
45 *The Times*, 7 November 1857
46 Robert Vaughan *The Age of Great Cities* 1843, p. 102
47 *Leeds Mercury*, 20 October 1872
48 *Bradford Observer*, 12 January 1871; *Liverpool Mercury*, 19 January 1871; *Birmingham Daily Post*, 25 January 1871; *Manchester Times*, 28 January 1871
49 *Ipswich Journal*, 18 February 1871
50 Simon Szveter, 'A Central Role for Local Government. The Example of Victorian Britain', *History and Policy*, 2 May 2002
51 Martin Daunton (ed.) *The Cambridge Urban History of Britain* 2000 (vol. 3), Essay by John Davis, p. 261
52 *Charity Organization Review*, September 1889 (vol. 5), pp. 368–71
53 *Ipswich Journal*, 24 August 1886
54 Szveter 2002
55 Shephard T. Taylor *The Diary of a Medical Student during the Mid-Victorian Period 1860–64* 1930, pp. 16 (5 December 1860), 17 (17 December 1860), 20 (10 January 1861), 99 (23 June 1862)
56 Quoted in Daunton 2000, Essay by Richard Dennis, p. 95
57 Fyodor Dostoevsky *Winter Notes on Summer Impressions, Vremya (Time)* 1863 (trans. David Patterson, 1997)
58 For these changes in detail, see Roy Porter *London: A Social History* 1994
59 James Hole *Lectures in Social Science and the Organisation of Labour* 1851
60 Francis Wey *A Frenchman Sees the English in the 'Fifties'*, adapted Valerie Pirie, 1935
61 Charles Collins *Singed Moths* 1864 (vol. 1), p. 260
62 James Hatton *Club-land, London and Provincial* 1890, p. 68
63 *The Times*, 9 October 1852
64 Williams 2004, Essay by Anthony Hare, p. 1
65 *Caledonian Mercury and Daily Express*, 5 December 1859
66 A.D. Harvey, 'Painted Advertisements on Houses', *The Historian*, Summer 1997, pp. 14–15
67 Anthony Trollope *The Struggles of Brown, Jones, and Robinson* 1870, Preface

68 Thomas Richards *The Commodity Culture of Victorian England* 1991, pp. 3, 21, 87
69 The account of the City is largely drawn from David Morier Evans's *City Men and Manners* 1852; *Speculative Notes and Notes on Speculation, Ideal and Real* 1864; and his various writings on financial crises between the 1840s and 1860s. He himself died bankrupt in 1874
70 *The Times*, 26 January 1870
71 *Pearson's Magazine*, January–June 1896 (vol. 1), pp. 146–50
72 Karl Marx, *New York Daily Tribune*, 21 August 1852–February 1861; available from 'Marxists Internet Archive' online
73 Grant 2019, p. 138
74 *Ibid.*, p. 165
75 Newsome 1997, p. 79
76 *The Bankers' Magazine and Journal of the Money Market*, June 1866
77 Grant 2019, p. 141
78 Quoted Herbert F. Tucker (ed.) *A New Companion to Victorian Culture and Literature* 2014, Essay by Christian Crosby, p. 230
79 Rothschild was immortalized as Adrian Neuchatel in Disraeli's 1880 novel *Endymion*; see M.C. Rintoul *Dictionary of Real People and Places in Fiction* 1993

4. 'A New World Under Scrutiny'

1 Joseph Hatton *Journalistic London* 1882, p. 64
2 Robert Surtees *Ask Mamma* 1858, p. 342
3 Hatton 1882, p. 240
4 Brantlinger 1977, p. 22
5 P. Appleman, W.A. Madden and M. Wolff (eds) *1859: Entering an Age of Crisis* 1959, p. 226
6 Frederick Knight Hunt *The Fourth Estate* 1850 (vol. 2), pp. 221, 240
7 Hatton 1882, pp. 1, 5
8 *Ibid.*, p. 246
9 Hunt 1850 (vol. 2), pp. 196, 216
10 Escott 1897, p. 380
11 Hatton 1882, p. 118
12 Hunt 1850 (vol. 1), p. 1
13 Arthur Lysiak, 'T.H. Escott, Victorian Journalist', unpublished dissertation, Loyola University, 1970, pp. 7–8
14 Taine 1872, p. 220
15 Hatton 1882, p. 96
16 *Ibid.*, pp. 42–3, 240
17 Fontane 1939, p. 186 (13 May 1857)
18 Wallace and Gillespie 1948, p. 612 (3 December 1859)
19 Hunt 1850 (vol. 2), pp. 242, 263, 280, 292
20 Anthony Trollope *The Warden* 1855 (reprinted 1913), pp. 186–7
21 Brantlinger 1977, p. 206
22 Fontane 1939, p. 112 (11 September 1855)
23 Wallace and Gillespie 1948, pp. 291–2 (6 April 1858)
24 Quoted in Wiener 1985, p. 33

25 Quoted in Elaine Hadley *Living Liberalism: Practical Citizenship in Mid-Victorian Britain* 2010, p. 41

26 Chesterton 1913, p. 105

27 Sir Edward Clarke *Memories of My Life* 1918

28 Amy Cruse *The Victorians and their Reading* 1935, p. 320; Betham-Edwards 1919, p. 151

29 J. Burnett, D. Vincent and D. Mayall (eds) *The Autobiography of the Working Classes 1790-1900* 1984, pp. 3, 9–10, 36; B. Hollingworth (ed.) *The Diary of Edwin Waugh* 2008; Ian Bradley *The Optimists* 1980, p. 150

30 Cruse 1935, p. 154; Leslie Stephen *George Eliot* 1902, pp. 67–8; Richards 1991, p. 118

31 Cruse 1935, p. 333

32 Brantlinger 1977, p. 28; 'Turing Institute report', *The Times*, 14 October 2019

33 Escott 1897, pp. 368, 370

34 Johnston 1851 (vol. 1), pp. 244, 250; Bernard Lightman *Victorian Popularizers of Science* 2007, p. 3

35 J. Paradis and T. Postlewait *Victorian Science and Victorian Values: Literary Perspectives* 1981, p. 161

36 Taylor 1930, p. 22

37 Paradis and Postlewait 1981, p. 3

38 Richard Yeo, 'Science and Intellectual Authority in Mid-Nineteenth Century Britain', *Victorian Studies*, Autumn 1984 (vol. 1), pp. 7, 25

39 Walter Bagehot, 'Count your enemies and economize your expenditure', May 1862

40 Escott 1897, p. 248

41 Cross 1885 (vol. 3), p. 351 (7 December 1865); Lightman 2007, p. 8; *The Athenaeum*, 3 January 1852; *The Times*, 22 September 1854

42 Lightman 2007, pp. 353–4, 363; *The Athenaeum*, 28 February 1852

43 John Canning (ed.) *Great Nineteenth-Century Lives* 1983, Essay by Laurence Wilson, p. 147; *The Athenaeum*, 28 February 1855; Lightman 2007, pp. 29, 99, 103; G.W.E. Russell *Letters of Matthew Arnold 1848-1888* 1895, p. 313

44 Paradis and Postlewait 1981, p. 115; Russell 1895, p. 388 (22 February 1868); J.B. Bullen (ed.) *Writing and Victorianism* 1997, Essay by Patricia O'Neill, p. 105

45 *Nineteenth Century* January–June 1884 (vol. XV)

46 Oliphant 1870, Part 1

47 Margaret Barton and Osbert Sitwell *Victoriana: A Symposium of Victorian Wisdom* 1931, p. 66; Arthur Ponsonby *English Diaries: A Review of English Diaries from the Sixteenth to the Twentieth Century* 1923, p. 388; Saintsbury 1923, p. 300; Hansard, 15 March 1870 (vol. 199, col. 2065)

48 B.I. Coleman *The Church of England in the Mid-Nineteenth Century: A Social Geography* 1980, p. 8

49 Brightfield 1971: Catherine Spence *The Author's Daughter* 1868 (vol. 2), p. 188

50 John Morley *The Struggle for National Education* 1874 (3rd edn), p. 3

51 *Annual Register 1870*

52 Brightfield 1971: Shirley Brooks *Sooner or Later* 1868, p. 141; *Ideas and Beliefs of the Victorians* 1949, p. 199

53 Peter Bowler *The Invention of Progress: The Victorians and the Past* 1989, p. 139

54 Newsome 1997, p. 206; Golby 1986, p. 46; Lucy Walford *Memories of Victorian London* 1912, p. 223

5. 'Nobody Dares Resist It'

1 Patrick Cormack, 'The Great Fire of Westminster 1834', *The Historian*, Autumn 1984

2 J.C. Ingham, 'Liberalism against democracy: A study of the life, thought and works of Robert Lowe, to 1867', unpublished PhD thesis, University of Leeds, 2006, p. 169

3 Edward J. Gillin *The Victorian Palace of Science: Scientific Knowledge and the Building of the Houses of Parliament* 2007, p. 1

4 *Ibid.*, pp. 118, 265

5 Hansard, 24 May 1850 (vol. 111, cols 328–59); Taine 1872, p. 197

6 Fontane 1939, pp. 191–2; Martin 1893 (vol. 2), p. 349

7 Martin Hewitt (ed.) *An Age of Equipoise? Reassessing Mid-Victorian Britain* 2000, p. 114; Angus Hawkins *Victorian Political Culture* 2015, p. 99

8 Betham-Edwards 1919, pp. 92, 96

9 *Quarterly Review*, July–October 1860 (vol. 108)

10 Escott 1916, p. 231; Earl of Malmesbury *Memoirs of an Ex-minister* 1884 (vol. 1), p. 434

11 Russell 1895, p. 221 (28 January 1864)

12 Horace B. Samuel *Modernities* 1913, pp. 66, 68

13 Grant 2019, p. 203

14 Hawkins 2015, p. 264

15 Philip Magnus *Gladstone* 1954 (pb 2001), p. 174

16 Bradley 1980, p. 162; Martin 1893 (vol. 2), p. 153

17 John Stuart Mill, 'On the Extension of the Suffrage', *Representative Government* 1861, Ch. 8

18 Russell 1895, p. 352 (2 March 1867); Ingham 2006, p. 12; Malmesbury 1884 (vol. 2), p. 371; Martin 1893 (vol. 2), p. 309

19 Hansard, 18 February 1853 (vol. 124, cols 280–1)

20 Quoted in Briggs 1960, p. 492

21 W.F. Moneypenny and G.E. Buckle *The Life of Benjamin Disraeli* 6 vols 1910–20 (rev. vol. 2; 1929), pp. 286, 289, 291

22 Quoted in Gertrude Himmelfarb *Victorian Minds* 1968, p. 344

23 'The Leadership of the Opposition', *The Economist*, 14 March 1874

24 Frederick Lascelles (Wraxall) *Married in Haste* 1863, p. 14; H.J. Hanham (ed.) *The Nineteenth-Century Constitution* 1969, pp. 12–13; Hawkins 2015, p. 15; quoted Tucker 2014, p. 9

25 Malmesbury 1884 (vol. 2), p. 66; Miles Taylor *The Decline of British Radicalism* 1995, p. 22

26 Mallock 2014, p. 189

27 Charles Dickens *Bleak House* 1853, Ch. 12 ('On the Watch')

28 *Manchester Times*, 25 April 1857

29 Bowler 1989, p. 5; Taylor 1995, pp. 6, 24

30 Hadley 2010, p. 1

31 *Morning Post*, 19 October 1878; *Leicester Chronicle and the Leicestershire Mercury*, 1 February 1879; *Pall Mall Gazette*, 5 January 1882; Robert Blake *Disraeli* 1966 (reprinted 1998), p. 342

32 David Cannadine *Victorian Century: The United Kingdom, 1800–1906* 2017, pp. 150–56

33 *Nottinghamshire Guardian*, 14 November 1873; *Glasgow Herald*, 25 April 1884; *Western Mail*, Cardiff, 29 November 1893

34 *Bristol Mercury*, 6 September 1862; *Bristol Mercury and Post*, 4 November 1885

35 *Pall Mall Gazette*, 27 July 1872

36 *Freeman's Journal and Daily Commercial Advertiser*, Dublin, 6 January 1883

37 Sydney C. Buxton *A Handbook of Political Questions of the Day* 1880 (2nd edn), pp. 40–41

38 Hole 1851, *passim*

39 Bradley 1980, p. 66

40 *Morning Post*, 14 April 1873

41 Cross 1885 (vol. 1), p. 146 (February 1848)

42 *Morning Post*, 27 March 1867

43 Wallace and Gillespie 1948, p. 76 (12 June 1857); Ponsonby 1923, p. 395; John Wade *England's Greatness* 1856, p. 783

44 Martin 1893 (vol. 2), p. 243; Escott 1916, p. 219; *Annual Register 1870* (Henry Lytton-Bulwer *Life of Henry John Temple, Viscount Palmerston* 1870)

45 Escott 1916, p. 279; Martin 1893 (vol. 1), p. 36 and (vol. 2), p. 392

46 For Lowe, see especially Martin 1893, Ingham 2006 *passim*

47 Grant 2019, p. 526

48 Blake 1998, pp. 570, 606–07; Magnus 2001, p. 217; Benson 1938, pp. 95, 97

49 Magnus 2001, p. 21

50 *Ibid.*, pp. 98, 112, 149, 292

51 *Ibid.*, p. 257, *Punch*, 13 December 1879 (reproduced p. 256)

52 Magnus 2001, p. 176

53 Moneypenny and Buckle 1929 (vol. 2), p. 534 (24 June 1872)

54 Blake 1998, pp. 543, 555; *Nineteenth Century*, July–December 1890 (vol. XXVII) (review by T.E. Kebbel), pp. 988–92

55 Hawkins 2015, p. 54; Moneypenny and Buckle 1929 (vol. 2), p. 838 (14 August 1876); Bradley 1980, p. 253

6. 'The Sound Common Sense of the Country'

1 For Elizabeth Blackwell, see her *Pioneer Work in Opening the Medical Profession to Women: Autobiographical Sketches* 1895; Julia Boyd, 'Florence Nightingale and Elizabeth Blackwell', *The Lancet*, 2 May 2009; Canning 1983, Essay by E. Royston Pike, pp. 422–7; J. Boyd *The Excellent Dr Blackwell: The Life of the First Female Physician* 2005

2 Lytton Strachey *Florence Nightingale* 1938, pp. 66–8

3 Sarah A. Tooley *The Life of Florence Nightingale* 1905, p. 241

4 Michael Warboys, 'British Medicine and Its Past at Queen Victoria's Jubilees and the 1900 Centennial', *Medical History*, 2001 (vol. 45), pp. 461–82; Thomas Humphrey Ward *The Reign of Queen Victoria: A Survey of Fifty Years of Progress* 1887 (vol. 2), pp. 388–444

5 Warboys 2001, p. 472

6 Heather Creaton (ed.) *Victorian Diaries* 2001; first published in St Thomas's Hospital house journal, *Circle*, 1972

7 *Quarterly Review*, December 1850–March 1851 (vol. 88)

8 Oliver MacDonagh *Early Victorian Government 1830–1870* 1977, p. 149

9 Rick Rylance *Victorian Psychology* 2000, p. 204

10 Malmesbury 1884 (vol. 1), p. 39

11 Annie Challice *The Sister of Charity* 1857, p. 112

12 *Annual Register 1851*, pp. 422ff

13 Warboys 2001, p. 469

14 Taylor 1930 *passim*

15 *Quarterly Review*, June-September 1850 (vol. 87)

16 Henry Thompson *Diet in Relation to Age and Activity* 1886

17 Edward Hughes, 'Civil Service Reform 1853–5', *History*, June 1942 (vol. 27, no.105), pp. 51–83; Herbert Spencer *The Proper Sphere of Government* 1843; David Roberts *Victorian Origins of the Welfare State* 1960 (reprinted 1969), p. 13; David Morse *High Victorian Culture* 1993, p. 4

18 Charlotte Riddell *The World in the Church* 1862, p. 117

19 MacDonagh 1977, p. 199

20 Escott 1916, p. 226

21 Martin 1893 (vol. 2), pp. 81–2 (20 February 1855)

22 Hughes 1942; *Quarterly Review*, July–October 1860 (vol. 108); MacDonagh 1977, p. 198

23 Roberts 1969, p. 119

24 Mary Poovey *Making a Social Body: British Cultural Formation, 1830–1864* 1995, p. 108; Morse 1993, p. 4

25 Hughes 1942

26 *Idem*

27 H.D. Traill *Central Government* 1881, p. 155

28 *Hampshire Telegraph and Sussex Chronicle*, 7 January 1865

29 Kenneth Poole, 'The Origins of the Local Government Service', *The Historian*, 2001 (no. 72), pp. 12–19

30 J. Toulmin Smith *Local Self-Government Un-Mystified* 1857; *The Times*, 15 December 1856; *The Times*, 21 October 1857; Daunton 2000, Essay by John Davis, p. 264

31 Porter 1991, p. 242; Roberts 1969, pp. 10–11; Taine 1872, p. 299; Szreter 2002

32 *British Medical Journal*, 18 June 1870 (vol. 1, no. 494), p. 634

33 Poole 2001

34 Bradley 1980, p. 210

35 Martin 1893 (vol. 2), p. 29

36 Fontane 1939, p. 114

37 J.G. Witt *Life in the Law* 1900 (reprinted 1906), p. 218; Escott 1897, p. 426

38 Taine1872, p. 262

39 Willis B. Perkins *Michigan Law Review*, February 1914 (vol. 12, no. 4), pp. 277–92

40 J.B. Atlay *The Victorian Chancellors* 1906–08 (vol. 2), pp. 392, 402

41 *Ibid.* (vol. 1), p. 4; Spy, *Vanity Fair*, March 1898

42 Witt 1906, pp. 25, 65–6, 68

43 *Ibid.*, pp. 98, 107

44 *Ibid.*, pp. 184, 189, 195

45 John Hollams *Jottings of an Old Solicitor* 1906, pp. 10, 82–3, 151

46 Henry Maine *Ancient Law: Its Connection with the Early History of Society and its Relations to Modern Ideas* 1861, pp. 8, 22, 169, 184

47 Escott 1897, p. 422; Clive Emsley *Crime and the Victorians* (available from: www.bbc.co.uk/history/british/victorians/crime 01.shtml)

48 Wallace and Gillespie 1948, p. 49 (24 June 1857); *The Times*, 31 October 1854, quoted in Ben Wilson *Britain and the Birth of the Modern World* 2016, p. 171; *Pictorial History of the Russian War* 1856, pp. 318–20, 387, 389

49 Spencer 1843, Letter 5; *The Times*, 27 October 1859

50 Hansard, 5 June 1856 (vol. 142, cols 980–1001, 1020–23, Wellington quoted by Sidney Herbert); *Morning Post*, 26 May 1868; Gwyn Harries-Jenkins *The Army in Victorian Society* 1977, pp. 220, 259

51 *Leeds Mercury*, 4 April 1894; Harries-Jenkins 1977, pp. 137, 271; Cardwell quoted in Simon Heffer *High Minds: The Victorians and the Birth of Modern Britain* 2013, p. 490

52 Harries-Jenkins 1977, pp. 2, 106

53 Hansard, 5 June 1856 (see note 50); Hansard, 18 February 1853 (vol. 124, cols 280–81; Disraeli)

54 Escott 1916, p. 129; Escott 1897, p. 298

55 Escott 1897, p. 296

56 *Ibid.*, p. 311; Harries-Jenkins 1977, p. 209

57 Williams 2004, Essay by Edward M. Spiers, p. 85; *Annual Register 1860*, p. 326; Charles Lever *Charles O'Malley: The Irish Dragoon* 1841, p. 147

58 *The Gentleman's Magazine*, January-June 1860 (vol. 208); cartoon reproduced in OPCS SPOTLIGHT 13, *150 Years of Population and Medical Statistics* 1987

59 Bradley 1980, p. 63; *Ideas and Beliefs* 1950, Essay by H.G. Nicolas, pp. 132–3; Inkster 2000, Essay by Sarah Wilson, p. 211

60 Fontane 1939, p. 58

7. 'The March of Intellect'

1 Mallock 2014, pp. 219–20

2 For the Metaphysical Society, see R.H. Hutton, 'The Metaphysical Society: a Reminiscence', *Nineteenth Century,* July-December 1885 (vol. XIX); Alan Willard Brown *The Metaphysical Society: Victorian Minds in Crisis, 1869–1880* 1947; Catherine Hajdenko-Marshall, Bernard V. Lightman and Richard England (eds) *The Papers of the Metaphysical Society,1869-80: A critical edition* 2015; Catherine Hajdenko-Marshall *Believing After Darwin: The Debates of the Metaphysical Society (1869–80)* 2012

3 Morley 1917 (vol. 1), p. 124

4 Quoted in Richard Altick *Victorian People and Ideas* 1973, p. 110; quoted in Alan Bullock *The Humanist Tradition in the West* 1985, p. 109; Chesterton 1913, p. 78

5 Quoted in Macpherson 1983, pp. 42, 46

6 Matthew Arnold *Culture and Anarchy* 1869, Ch. 2 ('Doing As One Likes')

7 Morley 1917 (vol. 1), p. 125; Asquith 1919

8 W.H. Mallock *Atheism and the Value of Life* 1884, p. 14

9 Leslie Stephen and Frederick Pollock *Lectures and Essays by the Late William Kingdon Clifford* 1879 (reprinted 1901, vol. 1), pp. 7, 12; W.K. Clifford obituary, *Nature*, 1879 (vol. 19), pp. 443–4

10 Stephen and Pollock 1901 (vol. 1), p. 4

11 *Fortnightly Review*, December 1874 (vol. 22); *Ideas and Beliefs 1950*, Essay by J. Bronowski, p. 165

12 Fyodor Dostoevsky *The Brothers Karamazov* 1880, Part 4, Book 11

13 Mallock 1884, pp. 24, 74

14 Daniel Bivona, 'W.K. Clifford and the *Ethics of Belief*, BRANCH: Britain, Representation and Nineteenth-Century History (ed. Dino Franco Felliga), n.d.

15 Cook and Wedderburn 1903–12 (vol. 24), p. 448; Brown 1947, p. 90

16 Stephen and Pollock 1901 (vol. 1), p. 36; Lindsay Wilhelm, 'The Utopian Evolutionary Aestheticism of W.K. Clifford, Walter Pater and Mathilde Blind', *Victorian Studies*, Autumn 2016 (vol. 59, no. 1)

17 Henry Sidgwick, 'The Prophet of Culture', *Macmillan's Magazine*, August 1867 (vol. 16), pp. 271–80; Newsome 1997, p. 156

18 George Cornewall Lewis *An Essay on the Influence of Authority in Matters of Opinion* 1849

19 George Eliot *Scenes of Clerical Life* 1858, Ch. 10

20 Russell 1895, p. 50 (31 March 1856)

21 *Quarterly Review*, December 1850 (vol. 88)

22 Russell and Russell 1966 (vol. 2), p. 173; Bagehot quoted in Newsome 1997, p. 2; Anthony Trollope *The Prime Minister* 1876 (reprinted 1991), p. 573

23 Cross 1885 (vol. 3), p. 377; Cross 1885 (vol. 2), pp. 99 (26 July 1859), 118 (23 November 1859), 122–3 (5 December 1859)

24 T.H.S. Escott *Politics and Letters; A Personal Retrospect* 1886, p. 258; Betham-Edwards 1919, pp. 38–44; Ponsonby 1923, pp. 405–06 (24 January 1851)

25 Mathilde Blind *George Eliot* 1883, pp. 52, 175; Haight 1969, pp. 29–34

26 J.A. Froude, 'On Progress', *Fraser's Magazine*, December 1870

27 D.R. Thorpe (ed.) *Who's In, Who's Out: The Journals of Kenneth Rose 1944–79* 2018 (vol. 1), p. 121

28 John Tyndall, 'An Address to Students', *Fragments of Science* 1892 (vol. 2), p. 99; for Tyndall, see Roland Jackson *The Ascent of John Tyndall: Victorian Scientist, Mountaineer, and Public Intellectual* 2018

29 Hallam Tennyson *Alfred Lord Tennyson, A Memoir by his Son* 1897, pp. 470–71 (Tyndall's diary, 19 October 1850)

30 Printing of some of Ruskin's writings 1905 (vol. 2, eds E.T. Cook and A. Wedderburn), p. 208 (11 November 1870)

31 Russell 1895, p. 141 (December 1877)

32 Cook and Wedderburn 1905–12 (vol. 36), p. lxxxvi (21 October 1873); Mallock 2019, p. 241

33 Tennyson 1897, p. 339; Bullen 1997, Essay by Patricia O'Neill, p. 110

34 Tennyson 1897, pp. 108, 338; Queen Victoria's description of Tennyson (quoted in Christopher Hibbert *Queen Victoria: A Personal History* 2000, p. 481)

35 Golby 1986, p. 46 (22 May 1860)

36 Stephen and Pollock 1901 (vol. 1), p. 48

8. 'One Half of English Souls This Day'

1 Henry Mayhew *London Labour and the London Poor* 1851 (vol. 2)

2 Cannadine 2017, p. 203

3 *Edinburgh Review*, 1836 (vol. 63)

4 Cruse 1935, p. 139

5 Hawkins, 2015, p. 141; T.C. Smart *Victorian Values* 1992, Essay by Anne Digby, p. 199

6 Malmesbury 1884 (vol. 1), pp. 224–5

7 Peter Searby, 'Chartism', *The Historian*, Spring 1986 (no. 10)

8 Fontane 1939, p. 185 (20 February 1857)

9 Quoted in McKibbin 1990, p. 124; Inkster 2000, Essay by Jeff Hall, p. 144; *Ideas and Beliefs* 1950, p. 21; Martin 1893 (vol. 2), p. 314

10 McKibbin 1990, p. 295; Altick 1973, p. 256

11 W.G. Runciman *Very Different, But Much the Same: The Evolution of English Society Since 1914* 2015, p. 72; Jonathan Rose *The Intellectual Life of the British Working Classes* 2001, p. 58; Hollingworth 2008, p. 103 (30 June 1849)

12 Quoted in Victorian Society 'Endangered Buildings' appeal

13 *The Builder*, 1 July 1854

14 Hollingworth 2008, pp. 18 (4 November 1847), 22 (27 November 1847), 23 (29 November 1847), 52–3

15 *The Times*, 10 December 1853

16 Asa Briggs *Victorian People* 1955 (reprinted 1990), p. 28; Taine 1872, p. 218; Gerhart von Schulze-Gaevernitz, *Social Peace: A Study of the Trade Union Movement in England* 1893, reviewed

by Sidney Webb, *The Economist*, March 1894, pp. 84–6

17 *The People's Paper*, 19 April 1856, reprinted in Marx/Engels *Selected Works* 1969 (vol. 1), p. 500

18 MacLeod 2017, p. 160; *New York Daily Tribune*, 25 August 1852; Carlos Moore, 'Were Marx and Engels White Racists?', *Berkeley Journal of Sociology*, 1974–5 (vol. 19), pp. 125–56

19 Discussed in detail in John Plamenatz *Man and Society: Hegel, Marx and Engels and the Idea of Progress*, 1963 (vol. 3, revised M.E. Plamenatz and Robert Wohler, 1992); Hansard, 24 January 1840 (vol. 51, cols 510–46)

20 Quoted in Rose 2001, p. 306; *The Commonweal*, 16 October 1886 (vol. 2, no. 40)

21 George C. Brodrick, 'Democracy and Socialism', *Nineteenth Century*, January–June 1884 (vol. XV)

22 *The Standard*, 7 June 1895; Hardie quoted in Canning 1983, Essay by Lawrence Wilson, p. 143

23 Quoted in Newsome 1997, p. 45

24 *Quarterly Review*, December 1849–March 1851 (vol. 86)

25 Escott 1897, p. 44

26 Charles Rowcroft *Fanny, the Little Milliner; or the Rich and the Poor* 1846, p. 21

27 John Hollingshead *Ragged London in 1861* 1861, p. 241

28 Valerie E. Chancellor (ed.) *Master and Artisan in Victorian England. The Diary of William Andrews and the Autobiography of Joseph Gutteridge* 1969; Joseph Gutteridge *Lights and Shadows in the Life of an Artisan* 1893

29 William Lovett *The Life and Struggles of William Lovett in His Pursuit of Bread, Knowledge, and Freedom* 1876

30 John Springhall, 'The Penny Dreadful', *The Historian*, 2009 (no. 103), pp. 14–18; Hatton 1882, pp. 156–7, 189, 193–4

31 Christopher Hibbert, 'Introduction', in *London Characters and Crooks* 1996; Henry Mayhew *German Life and Manners*, 1864 (vol. 1), pp. viii, ix, 210

32 Smart 1992, Essay by M. Crowther, p. 193; John Garwood *The Million-Peopled City; or, One Half of the People of London made known to the other half* 1853

33 On the 'University' settlements, see Escott 1897, pp. 115ff.; G.A.C. Ginn, 'Answering the "Bitter Cry"', University of Queensland doctoral thesis, 2001; G.S. Reaney, 'Outcast London', *Fortnightly Review*, December 1886, pp. 688ff.; Baldwyn Leighton (ed.) *Letters and other writings of the late Edward Denison, M.P. for Newark* 1872; S.A. Barnett *Perils of Wealth and Poverty* (ed. V.A. Boyle, 1920); Rev. Brooke Lambert, *Contemporary Review*, December 1885, pp. 916–23

34 McPherson 1983, p. 44 (*Sartor Resartus*, written 1831, published later); Brantlinger 1977, p. 4; Bradley 1980, p. 211; *Quarterly Review*, January–April 1860 (vol. 107)

35 Ernst von Plenev *The English Factory Legislation* 1873, p. xxi
36 Hewitt 2000, Essay by Stephen L. Keck, pp. 168–70, 172; *Fraser's Magazine*, March 1859 (vol. 59), p. 260
37 *The Times*, 24 January 1859
38 Kidd 1920, p. 263
39 *Ibid.*, p. 317; *The Times*, 6 July 2024

9. 'Education for All'

1 *Commentaries on the Laws of England* 1765 (vol. 1), 'The Rights of Persons'
2 *The Times*, 31 August 1846
3 Barbara Leigh Smith (Bodichon) *A Brief Summary in Plain Language of the Most Important Laws Concerning Women* 1854, p. 17
4 Frances Trollope *One Fault* 1840 (vol. 2), p. 52
5 Oliver Livesay (ed.) *Victorian Social Activists' Novels* 2011, pp. 3–6
6 'A Letter to the Queen on Lord Cranforth's Marriage and Divorce Bill', 1855; Cruse 1935, p. 338; Laurence Stone *Road to Divorce: England 1530–1987* 1990, p. 263
7 For Johnston, see Christopher A. Whatley *DNB*; Susan Brown *et al.*, 'Ellen Johnston', *Orlando* (available from: orlando.cambridge.org)
8 *The English Woman's Journal*, 1 January 1860 (vol. 4, no. 23); Tucker 2014, p. 31; Sarah Stickley Ellis *The Women of England, Their Social Duties, and Domestic Habits* 1839, pp. 91, 345, 347
9 Brightfield 1971: Edmund Yates *Kissing the Rod* 1866, p. 133; Eliza Stephenson *St Olaves* 1863 (vol. 1), p. 274
10 *Contemporary Review*, April 1878 (vol. 32), pp. 155–87
11 Hadley 2010; *Fortnightly Review*, 1867 (vol. 7, no. 3), pp. 357–70
12 Canning 1983, Essay by E. Royston Pike, pp. 422–7; Josephine Butler *Personal Reminiscences of a Great Crusade* 1896, pp. 13, 408; Jane Jordan *Josephine Butler* 2001; Smart 1992, Essay by Anne Digby, p. 200
13 Josephine Grey (Butler) *The Education and Employment of Women* 1868, pp. 4, 11, 17, 24
14 Louisa Bevington *An Anarchist Manifesto* 1895, pp. 8, 9, 15
15 Betham-Edwards 1919, p. 26; Bagehot quoted in Dorothy Thompson, *The Historian*, Spring 1997 (no. 53); *Ideas and Beliefs* 1950, Essay by Viola Klein, p. 267; Golby 1986, p. 277
16 Russell and Russell 1966 (vol. 2), p. 35 (14 May 1867)
17 Mill quoted in Heffer 2013, p. 568
18 J.S. Mill *Autobiography* 1873 (reprinted 1944), p. 186
19 Helen Taylor *The Claim of Englishwomen to the Suffrage Constitutionally Considered* 1867, p. 11
20 Anthony Trollope *Phineas Finn: The Irish Member* 1869 (reprinted 1989), Ch. 59, p. 488
21 Russell and Russell 1966 (vol. 2), p. 31 (20 May 1867)
22 Andrew Rosen, 'Emily Davies and the Women's Movement, 1862–67', *Journal of British Studies*, Autumn 1979 (vol. 19, no. 1), pp. 101–221. Rosen draws on Emily Davies's *Family Chronicle* (Girton College, Cambridge)
23 Grey 1868, p. 11; Anne Marsh Caldwell *Aubrey* 1854, p. 100
24 Emily Davies *The Higher Education of Women* 1866, pp. 63, 78–9
25 Cross 1885 (vol. 3), p. 320 (22 November 1867); Betham-Edwards 1919, p. 38. For Bodichon, see Jane Robinson *Trailblazer: Barbara Leigh Smith Bodichon, the First Feminist to Change Our World* 2024
26 Frances Martin, 'A College for Working Women', *Macmillan's Magazine*, reprinted as a pamphlet October 1879
27 A.P. Baggs, R.J.E. Bush and M. Tomlinson, 'Parishes: Thorne', *A History of the County of Somerset* (ed. R.W. Dunning) 1974 (vol. 3)
28 Charlotte Brontë *Jane Eyre* 1847
29 Colin R. Chapman *The Growth of British Education and its Records* 1992 (2nd edn), pp. 40, 45; Aitken 1946, p. 148 (7 February 1833)
30 Chapman 1992, p. 45
31 Hansard, 14 July 1870 (vol. 203, col. 206)
32 *Huddersfield Chronicle and West Yorkshire Advertiser*, 3 February 1872
33 Gillian Sutherland *Elementary Education in the Nineteenth Century* 1971, p. 17; Morley 1870, p. 3
34 Brantlinger 1977, p. 243; Tennyson 1897, p. 108; Lowe quoted Heffer 2013, p. 412
35 W.H. Mallock *Tristram Lacy, or The Individualist* 1899, pp. 11, 71–2
36 *The Times*, 24 April 1850
37 Catherine Gore *The Banker's Wife* 1843, p. 60
38 *Lloyd's Weekly Newspaper*, 26 February 1854, reporting on the *Morning Post* discussion of the Oxford Reform Bill
39 Ingham 2006, pp. 47, 138
40 Anne Digby and Peter Searby *Children, School and Society in Nineteenth-Century England* 1981, pp. 6–7; Chapman 1992, p. 51
41 Cross 1885 (vol. 1), p. 242 (1 February 1853); Sutherland 1971, p. 32
42 Rose 2001, p. 151
43 E.M. Sneyd-Kinnersley *H.M.I.: Some Passages in the Life of One of H.M. Inspectors of Schools* 1908 (reprinted 1913), pp. 2, 123, 135
44 'Mr Lowe's Latest Blunders', *Saturday Review*, 9 April 1864; Sneyd-Kinnersley 1913, pp. 156–7; Creaton 2001, pp. 11, 19
45 Pamela Horn *School Log Books* 1993, 'Short Guide to Records, No.44'
46 Hansard, 6 March 1856 (vol. 140, cols 1983–4)
47 Newman quoted in Harries-Jenkins 1977, p. 112; Cook and Wedderburn 1903–12 (vol. 37), p. 496; Forster quoted in Valerie E. Chancellor *History for the Masters: Opinion in the English History Textbook 1800–1919* 1970, p. 45; Thomas Hughes *Tom Brown's Schooldays* 1857, Ch. 4, pp. 73–4;

Malmesbury 1884 (vol. 1), p. 15; Escott 1897, pp. 154–5

48 Roberts 1969, p. 185

10. 'Who Owns Progress?'

1 Richard Ormond *Early Victorian Portraits* 1973 gives an extended account of Benjamin Haydon's *The Anti-Slavery Convention* 1840, drawing on Haydon's published journals and autobiography

2 *Proceedings of the General Anti-slavery Convention: Called by the Committee of the British and Foreign Anti-slavery Society* 1841 *passim*. See also: Douglas H. Maynard, 'The World's Anti-Slavery Convention of 1840', *Mississippi Valley Historical Review*, December 1960 (vol. 47, no. 3), pp. 452–71 *passim*

3 Witt 1906, pp. 156–7

4 W. Laird Clowes *Black America* 1881, p. 87

5 Keshia N. Abraham and John Woolf *Black Victorians: Hidden in History* 2022 discuss Aldridge and Bonetta. Kathleen Chater *Untold Histories: Black People in England and Wales during the Period of the British Slave trade, c. 1660–1807* 2011 uses primary sources to show how the black population, often thought to be entirely living in abject poverty, also included those who acquired various professional roles

6 For Oliphant, see Margaret Oliphant *Memoir of the Life of Laurence Oliphant and of Alice Oliphant, his wife* 1891; Anne Taylor *Laurence Oliphant, 1829–88* 1982. Oliphant's own books include: *A Journey to Kathmandu* 1852; *Narratives of the Earl of Elgin's Mission to China and Japan* 1860; *Episodes in a Life of Adventure; or, Moss from a Rolling Stone* 1887

7 Fawn M. Brodie *The Devil Drives* 1967 (pb 1971), pp. 207–08

8 George Wingrove Cooke *China: Being the 'Times' Special Correspondence from China in the Years 1857–8* 1858

9 Russell and Russell 1966, p. 133 (5 March 1861)

10 Oliphant 1870

11 Eilan Bar-Yosef, *Israel Studies*, Summer 2003 (vol. 8, no. 2), pp. 18–49; Alan R. Taylor, 'Zionism and Jewish History', *Journal of Palestine Studies*, Winter 1972 (vol. 1, no. 2), pp. 35–51

12 Benjamin Disraeli *The Jewish Question is the Oriental Quest* 1877

13 Yair Safran and Tamir Goven *Middle Eastern Studies*, September 2010 (vol. 46, no. 5)

14 John Ruskin *The Poetry of Architecture* 1893 (first published in *Architectural Magazine*, 1837–8)

15 Reviewed in *Leeds Mercury*, 8 July 1895

16 Hansard, 25 June 1850 (vol. 112, cols 380–444)

17 *The Times*, 29 June 1838

18 Quoted in Bradley 1980, pp. 145–6

19 Hansard, 11 April 1862 (vol. 166, cols 859–970); Magnus 2001, pp. 100, 144

20 Quoted Cook and Wedderburn 1903–12 (vol. 18), p. xxiii

21 *Huddersfield Chronicle and West Yorkshire Advertiser*, 2 June 1888

22 *Morning Post*, 10 November 1862

23 Eliot quoted in Peter Pulzer, 'Special Paths or Main Roads', *Proceedings of the British Academy*, 2002 (vol. 121), p. 219

24 Bullock 1985, p. 99

25 Cook and Wedderburn 1903–12 (vol. 35), p. 206; Bradley 1980, p. 92; *Daily News*, 19 January 1884, reporting Jacob Tillett's speech

26 *Pall Mall Gazette*, 30 December 1887

27 Honoré Balzac *Lost Illusions* 1837–43; thanks to Peter Conrad for this reference

28 Taylor 1930 (29 April 1859)

29 Hansard, 18 February 1853 (vol. 124, cols 246–311)

30 Walter Bagehot, 'Letters to *The Inquirer*', January–February 1852, Letter 5, Paris

31 Wallace and Gillespie 1948, p. 631 (18 January 1860)

32 Wallace and Gillespie 1948 provide a contextual introduction to Moran

33 *The Yearbook of English Studies,* 'Breaking the Code of Anonymity', *Literary Periodicals* Special Number, 1986, pp. 187–96; Richard Fulton, '*The Spectator* in Alien Hands', *Victorian Periodical Review*, Winter 1999 (vol. 24, no. 4), pp. 187–96

34 Carl Bode (ed.) *Midcentury America: Life in the 1850s* 1972, pp. 33, 102

35 E. Douglas Branch *The Sentimental Years 1836-60* 1934, pp. 12–14; James Fenimore Cooper *The Spy* 1821 (reprinted 1924), p. 4

36 Moses Yale Beach *The Wealth and Biography of the Wealthy Citizens of the City of New York* 1846 (10th edn); Branch 1934, pp. 45–6

37 Branch 1934, pp. 21, 31

38 Bode 1972, p. 100; Leslie Butler *Critical Americans: Victorian Intellectuals and Transatlantic Liberal Reform* 2007, p. 7 (from *Culture and Anarchy*)

39 Branch 1934, pp. 10–11

40 *Ibid.*, p. 99

41 James Buchanan, 'Third Annual Message to Congress on the State of the Union', 19 December 1859

42 W.E. Aytoun *Norman Sinclair* 1861 (vol. 2), p. 115

43 Hansard, 13 June 1862 (vol. 167, cols 612–17)

44 Morley 1917 (vol. 2), p. 79

45 Aitken 1946, pp. 162–3 (20 July 1836)

46 Morse 1993, pp. 266–7

47 Hart-Davis 2001, p. 88; Mary Kingsley *Travels in West Africa* 1897 and *West African Studies* 1899 (2nd edn, 1901), *passim*

48 John Pope Hennessy, 'The African Bubble', *Nineteenth Century*, July-December 1890 (vol. XXVII), pp. 1–4. This volume also includes rejoinders to Pope Hennessy and his response under the title 'Is Central Africa Worth Having?', pp. 478–87

49 Chinua Achebe *There was a Country* 2012

50 *Pall Mall Magazine*, 22 August 1899

51 *Aberdeen Weekly Journal*, 2 January 1896; *Bristol Mercury and Daily Post*, 31 December 1896

52 William Hughes *The Treasury of Geography*, quoted in Morse 1993, p. 36; M.E. Chamberlain *The*

New Imperialism 1970, p. 39; Pope Hennessy 1890, p. 2; *New York Daily Tribune*, 8 August 1853

53 Williams 2004, Essay by Douglas M. Peers, p. 74; Chamberlain 1970, p. 41; *Huddersfield Daily Chronicle*, 25 August 1879

54 *Aberdeen Journal*, 30 August 1871

55 Martin 1893 (vol. 1), pp. 186–7, 291; *Quarterly Review*, January–April 1860 (vol. 107); Walter Besant *All in a Garden Fair* 1883; *Trewman's Exeter Flying Post*, 25 July 1883

56 For Wakefield, see Edward Gibbon Wakefield *A View of the Art of Colonisation*, in *Letters Between a Statesman and Colonist* 1849; Robert J. Schultz, 'Edward Gibbon Wakefield and the Development of his Theory of "Systematic Colonization"', University of Nebraska at Omaha thesis, 1965

57 Morley 1917 (vol. 2), p. 80

58 Clark 2010, Essay by W.D. Rubinstein, p. 492; Williams 2004, Essay by Douglas M. Piers, p. 60

59 Edward Dicey, 'Is Central Africa Worth Having?' (Part 2), *Nineteenth Century*, July–December 1890 (vol. XXVIII), pp. 488–500

60 Magnus 2001, p. 287; Cannadine 2017, p. 415

61 Pope Hennessy 1890, p. 487; Chamberlain 1970, p. 37; H.H. Johnston, 'The Value of Africa', *Nineteenth Century*, July–December 1890 (vol. XXVIII), p. 170

62 *Aberdeen Weekly Journal*, 7 August 1889

11. 'What Happened Next?'

1 H.G. Wells *Boon* 1915, pp. 69–70, 74, 76, 77–8

2 *Fraser's Magazine*, 'The First Half of the Nineteenth Century', 1851 (no. 43), pp. 1–15

3 *Westminster Gazette*, 26 April 1893

4 *Belfast News-Letter*, 7 September 1871

5 Rudyard Kipling *Something of Myself: The Autobiography of Rudyard Kipling* 1937, pp. 147–8

6 *Morning Post*, 21 August 1897; *Lagos Observer*, 19 February 1885; G.N. Uzoigwe, 'Reflections on the Berlin West Africa Conference, 1884–1885', *Journal of the Historical Society of Nigeria*, December 1984–June 1985 (vol. 12, nos 3–4), pp. 9–22

7 Cook and Wedderburn 1903–12 (vol. 20), pp. 42–3

8 Quoted in Ian Baucom *Englishness, Empire, and the Locations of Identity* 1999, p. 1

9 *Weekly Standard and Express*, 31 December 1898

10 *North-Eastern Daily Gazette*, 16 August 1899

11 Frederic Harrison, 'A Few Words about the Nineteenth Century', *Fortnightly Review*, 1 April 1882 (vol. 31, no. 184), pp. 411–26

12 'Modern Ideas of Progress', *Sheffield and Rotherham Independent*, 17 March 1896

13 'The Dawn of the Twentieth Century', *Daily Mail*, 31 December 1900

14 Clark 2010, Essay by Robert Skidelsky, p. 600

15 Michael Holroyd *Lytton Strachey: A Biography*, pb 1971, p. 312; Sweet 2001, p. xvi; Spring quoted in John Gardiner *The Victorians: An Age in Retrospect* 2002, p. 42; *OED ibid.*, p. 3

16 Radio interview with Peter Allen for IRN programme, 'The Decision Makers', broadcast 15 April 1983

17 *Manchester Guardian*, 14 May 1920; Arthur Eddington *The Nature of the Physical World* 1928; Stevenson quoted in Paradis and Postlewait 1981, p. ix; Ignatieff 1999

18 Sigmund Freud *A General Introduction to Psychoanalysis* 1920

19 Quoted in Nisbet 1980, p. 328

20 H.G. Wells *A Short History of the World* 1922, p. 427

21 Wade 1856, Preface

22 Martin 1893 (vol. 2), p. 253

Captions

Captions are identified by illustration number. Books already included in the Notes on the main text are identified by author's name and date of publication.

1 Jowett on education: Evelyn Abbott and Lewis Campbell *Letters of Benjamin Jowett, M.A.* 1899, p. 242

2 Froude on the portrait: J.A.Froude *Thomas Carlyle: A History of his Life in London, 1834–81*, vol.2, 1884, p. 461

9 Jowett on Spencer: Abbott and Campbell, 1899, p. 195 (30 March 1875)

16 Thomas Carlyle *Latter-Day Pamphlets* 1850, Ch. VII 'Hudson's Statue'

18 Brunel quote: written on the back of the original photograph

25 William Whewell *History of the Inductive Sciences* 1859, p. 133

28 Justin McCarthy *A Short History of Our Own Times 1837–1880*, p. 405

34 Jowett on Disraeli: Abbott and Campbell, 1899, p. 103 (23 December 1878)

37 Moneypenny and Buckle, 1929, vol.2, p. 507; Magnus 2001, p. 220

44 Jowett on Arnold: Abbott and Campbell, p. 223 (11 May 1888)

49 W.P. Frith *My Autobiography and Reminiscences*, 1887, vol.1, p. 296; vol. 2, pp. 215–19

60 William Shakespeare *Titus Andronicus* Act 3, Scene 1

61 Sir Rutherford Alcock *The Capital of the Tycoon* 1863, vol. 2, p. 147

LIST OF ILLUSTRATIONS

Frontispiece Private Collection; **1** *Vanity Fair*, 26 February 1876; **2** National Portrait Gallery, London. NPG 968; **3** *Vanity Fair*, 28 January 1871. Smithsonian Libraries and Archives; **4** Private Collection; **5** London Borough of Tower Hamlets; **6** The Dickens Fellowship; **7** The Dickens Fellowship; **8** The Mercer Gallery, Harrogate. HARAG 46; **9** Private Collection; **10** *Illustrated London News* 20 September 1851; **11** *Vanity Fair* 24 July 1869. National Gallery of Victoria, Melbourne. Gift of Edward Cole, 1958. 42.19.5; **12** Private Collection; **13** Sketch by Erasmus Darwin for *The Botanic Garden* (1789–91); **14** John Phillimore Collection; **15** *Punch* 11 October 1845; **16** Ironbridge Gorge Memorial Trust; **17** Private Collection; **18** Metropolitan Museum of Art, New York. Gilman Collection, Purchase, Harriet and Noel Levine Gift, 2005. 2005.100.11; **19** National Portrait Gallery, London. NPG 2829; **20** *Illustrated London News* 17 September 1881; **21** The British Museum, London. 1862, 0614.226; **22** Port of London Authority; **23** *Illustrated London News* 14 November 1863; **24** *The Times* 1866; **25** National Portrait Gallery, London. NPG195725; **26** The Royal Institution, London; **27** Wellcome Collection. V0027281; **28** Frontispiece, George Barrett Smith *The Life and Times of William Ewart Gladstone c.*1875; **29** *Vanity Fair* 30 September 1871; **30** The British Museum, London. 1983, 0127; **31** National Portrait Gallery, London. NPG 4893; **32** *Vanity Fair* 27 February 1869. CCNY Libraries; **33** John Leech, *Punch*, vol.19, July 1850, p. 157; **34** National Portrait Gallery, London. NPG 3093; **35** Private Collection; **36** Tariff Reform League pamphlet, 1903; **37** H.Peirera Mendes *The Earl of Beaconsfield K.G.* 1904; **38** Wellcome Collection. V0026055; **39** The British Museum, London. 1859, 1210.1019; **40** Imperial War Museum. Q71597; **41** Private Collection; **42** *Building News* 21 September 1860; **43** *Illustrated London News* 7 July 1860; **44** Private Collection; **45** *Popular Science Monthly*, vol.15, 1879; **46** John C. Fant Memorial Library; **47** The British Museum, London. 1906, 0419.2728; **48** Accepted by HM Government in lieu of Inheritance Tax and allocated to the Ashmolean Museum, 2013. WA2013.67; **49** Wellcome Collection. 32011i; **50** Private Collection; **51** Private Collection; **52** *The Graphic* 28 November 1874; **53** The Salvation Army; **54** Girton College, University of Cambridge; **55** National Portrait Gallery, London. p. 46; **56** *Punch* 28 May 1892; **57** *Illustrated London News* 17 December 1853; **58** *Punch* 2 July 1870; **59** *Punch* 24 April 1875; **60** From a daguerreotype by William Paine, Islington. Library of Congress; **61** *Illustrated London News* 12 October 1861; **62** Frontispiece, Laurence Oliphant *Piccadilly* 1870. Illustration by Richard ('Dickie') Doyle; **63** National Portrait Gallery, London. NPG 3953; **64** Frontispiece, Mary Kingsley *West African Studies*, 2nd ed., 1901; **65** *Punch* 15 April 1876; **66** 'A Pertinent Question'. *Canadian Illustrated News*, 1869; **67** *The World's Work*, vol. XIV, no.1, May 1907; **68** Private Collection; **69** *Punch* 20 December 1884; **70** Private Collection. With thanks to Eugenia Font and Domniki Papadimitriou for their assistance with illustrations.

AUTHOR ACKNOWLEDGEMENTS

At Unicorn, grateful thanks to Lucy Duckworth for her skilful, courteous, calm and efficient help in taking this book through the press, and to Michael Eckhardt (for his editorial skills), Ramona Lamport (for her eagle eye), Nick and George Newton (for their design of the book) and Felicity Price-Smith (for the jacket design): a great team.

INDEX

Locators in *italics* refer to illustrations.
Additional information for concepts may be
found under the individuals mentioned in the
index.

Aberdeen, Lord 122, 132
Aberdeen Journal/Weekly Journal 39, 282
abortion 181
accessibility 217
activists 272
Adam Bede 15
adaptability 22
administration 72, 156
adultery 228
advertising 38, 72–3, 80, 216
aesthetics 14, 294
Africa 279, 285
Age of Great Cities, The 62
Age of Progress 22, 239; England's condition
    196, 200, 215, 218; Progress 258–9, 263,
    287; reason and faith 185–7, 189, 192
agency 300
agricultural machines 267
Alan Turing Institute 94
Albert, Prince *12*, 37, 171
Aldridge, Ira 252
alienation 24
All the Year Round 10
Allen, Grant 289
alliances 262
Amalgamated Society of Engineers 203
Amalgamated Society of Journeymen &
    Cloggers *204*
Amberley, Kate (Viscountess Amberley) 2,
    234, 235, 255
Amberley, Viscount 181–2
amelioration 17, 51, 178, 196–7, 230, 294
America 46, 51, 71, 79, 264–9, 284; *see also*
    United States of America (America)
anaesthesia 142–3, 150
Analytical Engine 48

animal rights (cruelty) 222, 229
Annual Register 12, 150
Anson, Sir William 159
Ansted, David 99
Anti-Corn Law League 120, 199
antisemitism 206, 257
arbitration 203
aristocracy 26, 53, 73, 137, 197
Arkwright, Richard 47
armies 165
Arnold, Matthew 3, 6, 17, 54, 114, 148, 172,
    178, 246, 268, 293; governance 113, 116;
    Progress 29, 42–3; reason and faith
    174–6, 179–80, 189; under scrutiny 84,
    88, 100–1
Arnold, Sir Arthur 295
Arnold, Thomas 275–6
Arnold, William 276
Arrol, Sir William 58
art schools 232
artificial intelligence (AI) 25
artillery 167; *see also* weaponry
artisans 46, 211, 295
artists 86
Ashanti Empire 85
Ashby, Joseph 92
aspiration 224
Asquith, Herbert 43, 128, 169, 176
Athenaeum Club 47, 99, 179, 180
Athenaeum, The 11, 52, 88, 93, 100, 196
Atlantic and Great Western Railway 265–6
Aubrey House 236
authorities, local 159
authority 296, 303
Aytoun, William Edmondstoune 270

Babbage, Charles 45, 48
Backhouse, Edward 49
Bacon, Francis 34
Bagehot, Walter 173, 182, 232, 240; global
    economic dominance 80–1; governance

114, 120–1; reason and faith 83; under scrutiny 91, 98
ballots 118
Bank Charter Act 79
Bank of England 74–5, 76, 79–80
Bankers Magazine and Journal of the Money Market, The 82
banking systems (bankers) 19, 28, 75, 81, 83, 268
Bankruptcy Act 1883 162
bargaining, collective *see* collective bargaining
Barings Bank 78
Barnardo, Thomas *209*, 216
Barnett, Samuel & Henrietta 221
Bazalgette, Joseph 69, 122
Beach, Moses Yale 268
Beale, Dorothea 238
Becker, Lydia 230
Beckett (Denison), Sir Edward 110
Belgravia 16
belief systems 24, 287
Belle of the Ball, The 21
benefactors 212
Besant, Walter 282
Bessemer, Henry 57
Betham-Edwards, Matilda 112, 183, 232
Beveridge, William 221, 297
Bevington, Louisa 232
Birkbeck, George 94
Birmingham Daily Post 63
Black Friday 81
Blackstone, Sir William 160, 225
Blackwell, Elizabeth 142, 143, 144, *145*, 146, 147, 231
Blackwood's Magazine 88, 184, 256
Blair, Tony 25
Blind, Mathilde 184
blockades, naval 169, 260, 272
Bodichon, Barbara 225, 226, 231, 237
bonds 268
Bonetta, Sarah Forbes 252–3
books 168, 227; England's condition 212–13, 217; under scrutiny 84, 94, 96
bookstalls, railway 85, 92
Booth, Charles 196, 210, 218–19; *Life and Labour of the People in London* 195
Booth, Mary 195
boroughs, metropolitan 68
boundaries, testing of 22
Bowen, Charlotte 30
Bramleighs of Bishops Folly, The 27

Brassey, Thomas 54
Bray, Charles 94
Brewster, David *95*
bribery 135
bribes 82
Bright, John 71, 103–4, 115, 126, 127, 264
Bristol Mercury 127
British Honduras 271
British Medical Register 147
British Museum 104
British Red Cross 230
British Union of Fascists 297
British Workman 200
Britishness 258–9, 296
Brontë, Charlotte 92, 103, 239
Brooks, Shirley 104
Brougham, Henry 51, 149, 154, 161
Broughton, Rhoda 93
Browne, Howe, Marquess of Sligo 252
Brunel, Isambard Kingdom 58–9, 83, 109, 165
Buchanan, James 60, 265, 270, 272
Builder, The 202
Burgoyne, Sir John 167
Burns, George 207
Bury, J.B. 34, 40, 65, 300
Buss, Frances 237–8
Butler (Grey), Josephine 231, 232, 236
Byron, Lord 46, 135

cables, submarine telegraphic 59–60, 83, 267
Caledonian Mercury and Daily Express 71
campaigners 119, 226
campaigns 233, 251
canals 57
Canary Wharf *14*
capital 51, 54, 94, 274
capitalism 23, 81, 279
Cardwell, Lord 166
Carlyle, Thomas 5, 16–17, 38, 114, 138, 175, 176, 186, 221
Carter, Robert Brudenell 147, 150
Cecil, Robert 115–16; *see also* Salisbury, 3rd Marquess of
celebrities 91, 95, 100, 203, 296
censuses 143, 153, 169; 1851 227
Central Government 156
Chadwick, Sir Edwin 93, 112, 155, 196
Challice, Annie 149
Chamberlain, Joseph 65, 88, 128, 138, 139, 159, 162, 243–4, 274, 292

Chambers, Robert 105
Chambers, William 86
charities 64
Charity Organization Review 64
Chartism (Chartists) 16, 20, 93, 205, 208,
    248; England's condition 197–9, 215;
    governance 112, 130
chauvinism 148
Chesterton, G.K. 3, 26, 91
Chichester, Frederick 93
children 222; custody of 228
China 255, 259, 262
chloroform 13
cholera 149, 150, 220
Church of England 134; *see also* religion
    (churches)
Churchill, Randolph, Lord 128
cities 18, 197, 239; global economic
    dominance 50–1, 62, 64, 66;
    professionalization 157–9
City Corporation 68
City of London 73–4, 76, 78
citizens, British 260
civic pride 63, 65, 96, 149, 159
civil registration 153
Civil Service 131, 152–6, 230, 243
civilization, Christian 259
Clarke, Sir Edward 91–2
Clarkson, Thomas 250
Clayton-Bulwer Treaty 271
Clifford, W.K. 4, 8, 9, 176–8, 179, 192
Clowes, William 251–2
clubs 31, 51
co-operation 47
Co-operative Movement 201, 212
coal 49, 51
coalitions 125, 138, 156
Cobbe, Frances Power 228–9, 230
Cobden, Richard 26, 71, 264
codification 160
coffeehouses 77
collaborations 122, 185, 266
collective bargaining 202
colleges 236, 237
colleges, civic 243
Collins, Charles 70
Collins, John 197, 248
Collyer, Robert 92
Colonial Society 284
colonialism 275, 278, 282, 287

colonies 168, 274, 282, 284, 285, 293
colonization 273, 283–4
Combination of Workingmen Act 202
Commentaries on the Laws of England 225
commerce 99, 187, 229; governance 119, 136;
    progress 264, 266, 268, 270, 272
common law 161
common sense 18, 59, 98; governance 112,
    121, 132, 141; professionalization 158, 165
communications 18–19, 181, 289; global
    economic dominance 47, 52, 59; under
    scrutiny 91, 98
communism 274
Communist Manifesto 20
communities (community spirit) 63, 157
compensation 251, 252
competition 39, 63, 230, 257, 262
complacency 121
conscription 285
consensus 112, 180, 208, 239, 297
consequences, unintended 303
Conservative Party 124, 126, 127, 128
Conservative Primrose League 233
consumerism 72, 93, 301
consumption 290
Contagious Diseases Acts 231
Contemporary Review 172, 178, 228
contexts 10, 45
contracts, construction 55
Cook, Thomas 171
Cooke, William 60, 61
Cooper, Thomas 199
copyright 86
Corn Laws 71, 120, 130, 197
correspondents 87
corruption 129
cost of living 218
costs, property 66
cotton industry 203
councils, local 157
Court of Appeal 161
Court of Chancery 160
Court of Divorce and Matrimonial Causes 228
Covid 23, 111
Cowen, Joseph 86–7
Craik, Dinah 30
credit 268
Crewe 62–3
Crimean War 122, *146*, 147, 151, 156, 164–6,
    255, 264

Crimean wounded *164*
crimes (criminality) 154, 157, 196, 229
crises, banking 80, 268
Croker, John Wilson 47
Crompton, Samuel 46
Cross, Richard 140, 182, 184
Crossing Sweeper, The *194*
cross-sweepers 194
cults 256
cultures 51, 179, 257, 268; mass 290; *see also*
    popular culture
currency 80
curricula 247
customs 160

Daily Mail 62, 294
Daily News 84, 87, 89, 91, 153
Daily Review 84
Daily Telegraph 29, 87, 88, 266
Dallas, George M. 265
Darwin, Charles 2, 55, 97, 100, 106, 133, 174,
    179, 180, 183, 186, 192, 216, 229, 230; *On
    the Origin of Species* 105
Darwin, Erasmus 47, *47*
data 94, 112, 169, 195, 200; *see also*
    information
Davies, Emily *234*, 235, 237, 238
Davy, Sir Humphry 46, 47, 96, 99, 142, 179
debates 33, 229, 289, 296; governance 115,
    125; Progress 251, 261; reason and faith
    173–5, 179, 186; under scrutiny 90, 103,
    107, 173–5, 179, 186
decline, economic 297, 298
Delane, J.T. 87–8, 89, 134
democracies, liberal 23, 24
democracy 111, 122, 124, 268–9, 289, 301–3
demonstrations 119, 197
Denison, Edward 220
department stores 73
deprivation 64
Derby, 14th Earl of 26, 112, *113*, 116, 122, 123,
    125–6
Derby, 15th Earl of *113*, 125–6
desertion 228
devolution 64
Dicey, Edward 285
Dickens, Charles 10, 15, 17, 29, 65, 74, 108,
    143, 149, 154, 180, 182; *Bleak House* 123,
    194; *Hard Times* 102, 169; *Nicholas
    Nickleby* 72; scrutiny 90–1, 94

dictatorships 24
diets 152, 168
digitalization 25
Dilke, Sir Charles 129
diplomacy 72
discoveries, scientific 22–4, 40, 109, 192, 298;
    under scrutiny 95, 97, 105
discussions 181
diseases 143, 153, 154, 222, 231
dishonesty 230
Disraeli, Benjamin 5, 7, 19, 37, 53, 65, 80, 83,
    87, 93, 113–14, 126, 128, 131, 133, 134,
    135, 138–41, 196, 204, 209, 264, 280, 286,
    299; under scrutiny 89, 102–3; *see also*
    governance
Dissenters 241
distribution 86, 216, 217
diversity 274
division of labour 50
divorce 228
docks, London *14*, 70
doctors 147
domestic abuse 228
domination 45
Dostoevsky, Fyodor 67–8, 178
Douglas, Robert 259
drinking water 143
duties 301

East India Company 280, 281
eccentricity 162
economic dominance 45, 58, 273
economics 51
economies 14; global 24, 61, 83
Economist, The 88, 120, 155
Edinburgh Journal 86
Edinburgh Review 54, 88, 90, 101, 135
Edmundson, Thomas 47
education 228, 247–8, 289, 292, 295, 301–3;
    elementary 241–4; England's condition
    196, 198–9, 201, 212, 215; expenditure
    230; global economic dominance 46,
    62; higher (further) 173, 191, 202, 235;
    governance 130–1; Kensington Society
    235; mass 20; professionalization 143,
    147, 170; Progress 29, 34, 43, 253, 261–3,
    276; reason and faith 175–6, 179; religious
    240–1; under scrutiny 99–100; women
    34, 103, 143, 238–9; working-class 88; *see
    also* knowledge; state-funded education

Education Act 1870 101
Education Act 1944 248
Edwards, Edward Watkin 81
efficiency 21, 64
Egypt 286
electricity 61–2, 295
Eliot, George 15, 32, 99, 131, 149, 179, *226*, 237, 244, 257, 262; *Adam Bede* 15, 182; reason and faith 183–4; *Scenes of Clerical Life* 21, 180
elites 20, 176, 216, 298, 301; governance 112, 122; professionalization 147, 170
Ellis, Sarah 227–8
elopements 282–3
Emancipation Bill 126
emigration (emigrants) 143, 281–2, 283
empires 273
employees 289
employment 297; female 61, 227, 228, 232
energy 157
enforcement 66
Engels, Friedrich 20, 119, 199, 206, 208, 212, 275, 279; global economic dominance 62, 80; Progress 31, 40
Engineering 57
engineering (engineers) 56–8, 69, 167
England As It Is 14
England: Its People 88
English Woman's Journal, The 227
Enlightenment 15, 18, 34, 304
enthusiasm 52
entrepreneurs 50, 57, 272
environments 18, 77
Equal Franchise Act 235
equality 28, 32, 122, 221, 296; education 227–8, 233
equity 160
Escott, Thomas 88, 95, 98, 167, 183, 211, 248
ethics 14, 294
Ethics of Belief, The 178
Evans, David Morier 75, 82
Evans, Marian *see* Eliot, George
evolution 105, 179, 190
Ewart, William 94
excursions 171, 290
exiles 67
expectations 282, 297
experience, practical 158
experts 34, 98, 158, 237, 274, 294

exploitation 19, 24, 276, 279, 299, 304
exports 71, 79–80, 274

Fabians 207
factories 13; education 240; England's condition 195; global economic dominance 51, 71; governance 124; Progress 28, 270; under scrutiny 86
Factory Acts 222
facts 169, 177
failures 50
Fairchild, Hoxie 300
fairness 107, 131, 160
faith 174, 190; *see also* religion (churches)
famine fever 143
fantasy 294
Far Above Rubies 18
Faraday, Michael *95*, 96, *97*, 99, 100, 179–80, 182, 186
Farr, William 69, 159
fashions 99
Faulks, Sebastian 19
females 225; *see also* employment
feminism 229
Fifteen Decisive Battles of the World 168
financial systems 82, 268, 292; global economic dominance 54–5, 57, 61, 73, 79
Finlen, James 205
First World War 23, 34, 131, 297, 299, 300
fishermen 39
Fletcher, Joseph 248
Fontane, Theodor 44, 89, 91, 110, 159, 171, 199
food 195, 201, 229
Ford, Ford Madox 293
foreign policy, British 259–60
Forster, W.E. (William) 162, 241, 244, 247, 295
Fortnightly Review 88, 99, 229
France (Paris) 21, 78, 144–5, 262, 263
franchise extension 124, 125, 129, 184
Fraser's Magazine 22, 88, 289
free speech 181, 303
free trade 71, 136–7, 165, 259, 263–4, 274
freedom, individual 21, 23, 269, 302
freight, rail 57
friendly societies (Friendly Societies) 200, 212
Frith, William Powell *28*, *194*
Froude, Isy 1, 6, 7
Froude, J.A. 5, 16, 122, 140, 182, 185, 189

Fuchs, Dr C.J. 71
Fukuyama, Francis 22
fundamentalism 24
funding 66

Galton Report 60
Garrison, William Lloyd 250
Gaskell, Mrs 50; *Cranford* 53; *Mary Barton* 200
General Board of Health 150
General Elections 129
General Medical Council 142
Gentleman's Magazine, The 29, 169
Geological Society 97
geology 104
George, Henry 223–4
George, Lloyd 208 9, 258
Germany 52, 78, 185, 203, 262, 292; England's condition 217–18
Girton College 237
Gladstone, Catherine 233
Gladstone, William 80, 93, 101, 113, 125, 131, 133, 134–8, *140*, 141, 166, 173, 204, 228, 233, 236, 241, 260–1, 264, 286; *see also* governance
Glasgow Examiner 227
Glasgow Herald 41
Gleig, George 125
globalization 71, 79, 253, 257
gold standard 79
Gordon, General 286
Gore, Catherine 38, 242
Goschen, Viscount 82
governance 21, 68
government programmes 156
governments, central 63, 131, 140, 157–8, 295
governments, local 63, 131, 156–7, 217, 289; Progress 27, 34
Grant, James 72
Gray, Asa 106, 192
Gray, Thomas 293
Great Exhibition 97, 130, 229; England's condition 211, 214; global economic dominance 68, 72; Progress 35–7
Great Reform Act: 1832 111, 114, 118, 119, 124; 1867 118
Great Stink 122
greed 24, 39, 82
green fields 69
Gresham Street 77

Greville, Charles 154
Grosvenor Hotel 172–3
Grote, George 33
Grove, Sir George 167
growth, economic 112
Guizot, François 20, 21, 208
gunpowder 15
Gurney, Samuel 81
Gutteridge, Joseph 212–14

Hamley, Sir Edward 19
Hampstead Garden Suburb 221
Handbook of Political Questions of the Day 129
Harcourt, Sir William 141
Hard Times 17
Hardie, Keir 207
Hargreaves, James 47
Harris, Thomas Lake 256–7
Harrison, Frederic 294
Harvard Mark 1 48
Hatton, Joseph 71
health, public *see* public health
hedonism 294
Helps, Sir Arthur 222–3
Herbert, George 4, 167
Herbert, Sidney 167
heroes 46, 49, 50
Heron, Sir Joseph 158
High Court 161
hindsight 23
Hirrell 27
History of Progress in Great Britain 39
History of Progress, The 20
History of the Inductive Sciences 97
Hodgskin, Thomas 45
Hole, James 69, 130
Hollams, Sir John 162
Hollingshead, John 211
home working 51
horses 110–11, 194
hospitals 19, 143, 144, 148, 157, 158–9, 165
House of Commons debates 89–90
household suffrage 161
Houses of Parliament 108, *109*, 110
housing 19, 153, 195
How a Farthing Made a Fortune 30
Howard, George 132
Hudson, George 55–6
Hughes (Senior), Jane 230

Hughes, Thomas 104, 201, 222, 247
human behaviour 186
human rights 301, 303
humanitarianism 29
humanities 179, 242
humour (funny) 21, 57
Humphreys, Charlotte 230
Hunt, Frederick Knight 84, 88, 90
Hunt, Thornton 266
Huxley, Aldous 300–1
Huxley, T.H. 2, *8*, 9, *95*, 99–100, 148, 151,
    173–4, 176, 181, 186, 190, 191, 233, 244
Hyndman, Henry 206–7
hypocrisy 72, 260, 270

Idea of Progress, The 34, 40
identity politics 301
Ignatieff, Michael 14, 300
Illustrated London News 85–6
imperfections 302–3
imperialism 18, 24–5, 85, 253, 292–3;
    education 258–9; Progress 273, 276, 282,
    284–5
improvements 35, 278, 304; social 197
income taxes 29
independence 274
Independent Labour Party 208
India 279, 280, 281
indigenous peoples 281
individualism 64, 296
Industrial Revolution 19, 103, 121–2;
    England's condition 196, 200, 212, 221–2;
    global economic dominance 48, 50, 57;
    professionalization 143, 152, 157
industrialization 17, 189, 195, 302; global
    economic dominance 44, 51; Progress 33,
    39, 43
industries 119
inequalities 269, 273
influence, unfair 129
information 61, 83, 88, 153, 169, 239; *see also*
    data
infrastructure 77, 195; public 158
Ingram, Herbert 85
inheritance 228
Inns of Court 159
inoculations 134
inspectors 154, 245–6
Institute of Civil Engineers 58
Institute of Mining Engineers 58

institutions 31, 72, 129, 233
institutions, professional 29
integrity, media 89
intellectuals 67
interdisciplinary 187
international cricket team *170*
inventors 45, 46, 48, 49, 50, 51
investors 54, 55
Ireland 195
irony 89
isolation 18
Italy 78, 137, 261

James, Charles 27
James, Henry 66
Jay, William 251
Jews 257–8
Jingo (jingoism) 285, 286, 293
Johnson, Joseph 30
Johnston, Ellen 227
Johnston, Harry 286
Johnston, William 14, 52, 61, 96, 121
Jones, Ernest 199, 205
journalism (journalists) 84, 87, 89, 229, 295;
    investigative 89, 194
journals 86
Jowett, Benjamin 2, *3*, 6, 7, 9, 32, 93, 133, 135,
    147, 155, 166, 172, 174, *175*, 185, 191, 208,
    221, 243
judges 163
Judicature Acts, 1873 & 1875 160
justice 302

Kay-Shuttleworth, James 243
Kell, Sir John 172
Kensington Society 235
Keynes, John Maynard 79, 297
Khartoum 286
Kidd, Benjamin 17, 18
Kingsley, Charles 22, 93, 149, 238, 275, 276
Kingsley, Mary 276–7
Kipling, Rudyard 59, 279, 290
knowledge 14, 133, 223, 295; education 230,
    241; Progress 34–5; reason and faith 178,
    180; scrutiny 93, 95
Knowles, James 172, 173, 178, 190
Knox, Isa 34

Labouchere, Henry 89, 230
labour 50, 94, 121, 130, 196

labour movements 203
Labour Party 128, 130, 207, 208, 233, 287, 290, 297
Lady Lee's Widowhood 19
Lagos Observer 292
Laird, Macgregor 272
Lambert, Brooke 220
Lancet, The 149
Langham Place Group 34, 235, 237
Law and Custom of the Constitution, The 159–60
law 159–64, 271
lawnmowers 170
Lawson, Edward Levy 88
Layard, Austen 261
leadership 24, 138, 292
learning 181, 245
Lecky, William 124
lectures 96, 99, 212
Lectures on the Industrial Revolution 50
Leeds Mercury 62, 166
legal system 161
legislation 27, 118, 289; education 229, 244; England's condition 209, 217; global economic dominance 79, 81; professionalization 159–60; under scrutiny 94, 96
Leigh-Smith, Barbara *see* Bodichon, Barbara
leisure 170, 290
lenders 81
Lennox, Lord William 53
Lever, William 274
Levy, Moses 88
Lewes, George Henry 32, 149, 183–4
Lewis, George Cornewall 98, 155, 180
Liberal Party 124, 127, 128, 130
liberty 39, 111, 122, 124, 221
libraries 130, *298*; England's condition 212, 215; professionalization 159, 169; under scrutiny 92, 94–5
life expectancy 196
life, quality of 15
lighting 157
Limited Liability Act 81
List, Georg Friedrich 71
literacy 86, 105, 217
Literary and Scientific Institutes 212
Liverpool 71
Liverpool and Manchester Railway 49
Liverpool Mercury 63

Liverpool Victoria Friendly Society 212
Lives of the Engineers 58
living conditions (standards) 128, 227, 302; England's condition 209, 221; global economic dominance 51, 62
living costs 218
Living to Purpose; or Making the Best of Life 30
Lloyd, Edward 216
Lloyd's Coffee House 77
Locksley Hall 54
logbooks, school 246–7
London 66–8, 87, 158
London County Council 68
London Dock Strike 205
London Working Men's Association 114, 215
Lovelace, Ada 48
Lovett, William 197, 214–16, 248
Lowe, Robert 54, *104*, 111, 161, 173, 188, 234, 282, 303; education 242, 246; global economic dominance 80–1; governance 115–17, 125, 132–4; professionalization 150, 154, 159; scrutiny 101–2
Lowery, Robert 197
Lunar Society 47
Lunn, Edwin 199–200
Lyell, Charles 98; *Principles of Geology* 190

Macaulay, Thomas Babington 74, 90, 101, 120, 135, 195
MacCarthy, Desmond 296
machines, agricultural 267
Macmillan's Magazine 88
magazines 27, 217
Maine, Sir Henry 111; *Ancient Law* 163
maintenance, child 228
males 228
Mallock, W.H. 2, 5, 7, 8, 39, 172, 176, 178, 181, 188, 189, 190, 200, 207, 232, 233, 242, 252, 253, 288–9
Malmesbury, Lord 122, 149, 198, 247
Manchester 44–5, 120, 158–9, 180–1
Manchester Daily Chronicle 87
Manchester Examiner 92
Manchester Guardian 37, 86, 300
Manchester Times 63, 104, 124
Manning, Cardinal 173, 189, 190
Manning, Charlotte 235
manufacturers 28
maritime technologies 71

markets, commodity & financial 61, 79, 83
marriages 27
Martin, Frances 230
Martin, Helena 226
Marx, Karl 20, 31, 40, 67, 88, 119, 130, 176,
    279, 302; England's condition 205–7;
    global economic dominance 79–80
materialism 16, 19, 21, 289, 295, 302; Progress
    39, 272; reason and faith 189
Maurice, Frederick 238
May, Erskine 140, 158
Mayhew, Henry 36, 89, 211, 216–18; *German
    Life and Manners* 262; *London Labour
    and the London Poor* 194
McHenry, James 54–5, 265–6
McLagan, Peter 233
Mechanics' Institute 5, 31, 94, 130, 181, 201–2,
    211, 212
Mechanics Magazine 45
mechanization 50, 289
media control 266
medicine 23, 147, 299; specialized 148
Melbourne, Lord 125, 206, 226
memoirs 161
memorialization 51
Mens Conscia 245
mental health 52
merchants 28
meritocracy 81
Metaphysical Society 173–4, 176, 178, 187,
    189, 190
Metropolitan Board of Works 68–9
Metropolitan line 57
Michael Armstrong: Factory Boy 42
Michelet, Jules 208
middle classes 26–8, 39, 67, 137, 199, 201
Middlesbrough 54
Midland Progressionist, The 40
migration 284
Mill, James 280
Mill, John Stuart 13, 33, 55, 71, 93, 224, *233*,
    303; education 234–6; governance 123,
    125; professionalization 146, 160, 169;
    reason and faith 176, 184; *Representative
    Government* 115; *The Subjection of
    Women* 116
misinformation 82
missionaries 276
modernization 80, 102
money 170

money printing 80
morality 170, 247, 289, 293–4, 298, 302;
    discoveries 19, 21, 24; England's condition
    198, 209, 223; global economic dominance
    63, 72; governance 126, 132, 135–6;
    Progress 30, 34, 39, 260, 270–2, 279;
    reason and faith 174, 178; under scrutiny
    105, 107
Moran, Benjamin 264–7, 270, 273
Moran, Caitlin 10
Morley, John 114–15, 173, 174, 176, 241,
    284–5
Morley, Samuel 35, 153, 285
Morning Chronicle 27, 89, 104, 217, 266
Morning Herald 267
Morning Post 41, 53, 89, 90, 131, 165, 211, 242,
    262, 292
Morris, William 38, 207
Morse, Samuel F.B. 267
mortality rates 143, 195
Mosquito Coast of Honduras and Nicaragua
    271
Mott, Lucretia 250
Mudie, Charles 92, 93, 127
Mundella, Anthony 203
Municipal Corporation Act 1835 157, 197
museums 96
music halls 171
Mutual Improvement Society 214

Napoleon III 31, 89, 151, 261, 262, 263–4,
    266–7
National Association for Promoting the
    Political and Social Improvement of the
    People 215
National Association for the Promotion of
    Social Science 34
National Education League 244
National Education Union 244
National Gallery of Practical Science 46
national improvement 131; *see also*
    improvements
National Liberal Federation 128
national pride 266; *see also* civic pride
National Review 80
National Union of Conservative and
    Constitutional Associations 128, 139
nationalism 25, 71, 137, 285; Progress 255,
    257, 259, 268
nations 25

Natural History Museum 96
natural resources 299
natural rights 198
natural selection 178, 179
NatWest bank 76
naval resources 270
navy (Royal Navy) 168–9; *see also* Royal Navy
negotiations 72
neutrality 271, 272
New Model Unions 203, *204*
New South Wales 134
New Unionism 205
New York Daily Tribune 79, 205, 267, 279
Newcastle Daily Chronicle 86, 87
Newman, Cardinal 6, 41, 101, 174, 175, 247
news 61, 87
Newspaper Press Directory, The 266
newspapers 84, 88, 216, 217, 294
Nichols, Peter 151
Nightingale, Florence 146, 147, *164*, 231, 247, 258
Nineteenth Century 181, 207
nonconformists 41–2, 63, 103
North American Review 269
North and South 50
North and South America Coffee House 77
Northcote, Sir Stafford *113*, 155
Northern Star 93, 199
Norton, Caroline 27, 225–6, 228
Nottinghamshire Guardian 127
novels 16, 22, 30

O'Connell, Daniel 126, 198, 249
O'Connor, Feargus 20, 198–9, 205, 215
officers 166
old age pensions 209
Oliphant, Laurence 1, 4, 9, 37, 253–8;
    Piccadilly 7, 39, 101
Oliphant, Margaret 37
opportunities 58, 213, 248, 281–2
oppression 276
optimism 223
Order in Council 156
organizations 64, 114; religious 31
Origin of Species 183
orphans *209*
Outlines of English History 46
overcrowding 150
Overend Gurney 81–2, 229
Oxford English Dictionary (OED) 91, 296

Palestine 258
Pall Mall Gazette 32, 129
Pall Mall Magazine 278
Palmerston, Lord 89, 122–3, 132, 134, 136, 167, 255, 257, 259–60, 261, 271
paper 216
Paris Echo 19
parks, public 159
Parliament, Houses of 108–10
parliamentary reports 90
Past and Present 16, 38
Pater, Walter 1, 2, 293
patients 148
patriotism 267, 290
patronage 162
Pattison, Francis 6, 129, 233
Pattison, Mark 243
paupers *see* poverty
Paxton, Joseph 37
peace, maintenance of 79, 263
Pearson, Charles 224
Pease, Edward 49
Peel, Sir Robert 48, 79, 91, 102, 110, 119–20, 123, 126, 132, 152, 197, 219
penny dreadfuls 86, 216
'penny policies' 212
people, colonial 274; *see also* indigenous peoples
People's Mission Hall meeting *219*
perfection (perfectibility) 23, 24, 103, 189, 294, 304
periodicals 84
Pessimism 38
Peterloo 197
petitions 198
philanthropy 15, 64, 216, 219–21, 229, 231
Philharmonic Hall, Islington *171*
Philip (Philp), Robert Kemp 20, 39, 70, 71
philosophers 69
Pickersgill, William 21
picketing, peaceful 204
pioneers 167
planning (planners) 68, *76*; *see also* town planning
Plenev, Ernst von 222
Plevins, Charles 144
poetry 186, 227, 290
poisons 134
police forces 168, 170, 197
politeness 73

political decline 298
political parties 121, 122
politics 14, 112, 128, 232, 266; media 89; professionalization 147, 152; relationship with press 89
Pollock, Frederick 177
pollution 65
Poor Law Amendment Act 1834 196
Poor Law Commission 154, 196
Pope Hennessy, Sir John 278–9
popular culture 72
popularization 105
populations 86, 153, 239, 293; England's condition 195, 205; global economic dominance 50, 65; urban 117
populism 198, 302, 304; governance 114, 119; Progress 251, 286–7
postal systems 280
poverty 42, 45, 121, 229; England's condition 195–6, 209–10, 219–21; professionalization 150, 157
power 227, 291, 296; abuse of 162; governance 111, 138; international 295; professionalization 157, 170; sharing 137; see also Progress
practices, traditional 275
pragmatism 297
prejudice 34
press 19, 21, 25, 40, 56, 43, 168, 203; governance 127, 129; Progress 266, 286; relationship with politics 89; under scrutiny 84–90, 95–6, 98–100, 102, 104, 107
prestige 46
Preston 203
pride 29
Primrose League 128, 129
Principles of Biology 33
printing 15, 61, 217, 266; scrutiny 84, 92, 97
privilege 43
professional institutions 29
professionalization 147, 156, 161, 169
professionals 149
professions 98, 142, 170, 230, 292
profit-sharing 216–17
Progress 8, 35, 90, 282, 293, 298, 300, 303–4; discoveries 10–16, 19–20, 22–5; economic 221, 229, 278; global economic dominance 47, 58; governance 116, 118, 127; global 36

Progress and Prejudice 38
propaganda 266
prosperity 19, 290, 293, 300–1; England's condition 203, 215; global economic dominance 51; governance 123, 132; professionalization 157; Progress 270; under scrutiny 86, 94, 97
pseudoscience 98
psychoanalysis 300
psychology 18, 38
public duty 153
public health 34, 139, 149, 158, 209, 289
Public Health Act 139, 150; 1848 155
Public Libraries Act 94
public opinion 88, 166, 181, 195; education 227, 231; governance 119–20, 130; Progress 251, 272
public spirit 170
publishing 100
Punch 53, 66, 76, 137, 244, 247; 'New Crowns for Old Ones' 280; 'Unfair Trade Winds' 292
Punch's Monument to Peel: CHEAP BREAD 120

quantitative easing 79
Quarterly Review 20, 45, 88, 112, 149, 151, 154, 181, 282
Queen's College (school) 191

racism 206, 224, 275, 276
railways (railroads) 12, 15, 170, 172, 201, 229; global economic dominance 47, 49–50, 52–7, 66; Progress 258, 267, 280, 282; under scrutiny 84, 97
reading 63, 168, 181, 216, 238; see also literacy
Reading Rooms 212
reality 25
reason 14, 17, 106, 192, 304
records 78
recruitment 156
Reform Act: 1867 80, 138, 303; see also Great Reform Act
Reform Bills 108; 1867 117, 119; 1884 124
reforms (reformers) 19, 21–2, 68, 102–3, 136; England's condition 196–7, 216; governance 112, 129; political 131; Progress 29, 39, 272
regionalism 103

regulation 23, 66, 71, 201, 289
relationships 27; worker-employer 204
religion (churches) 14, 196; education 227, 240–1, 243–4, 247; Progress 39–41, 251, 269, 276; reason and faith 178, 182, 187; under scrutiny 96, 100–7
reports 93
repression 24, 122
reputations 21
resources 223; naval 270
respectability 203
responsibilities 155, 291, 301; individual 209
retail *see* shopping
Reuleaux, Franz 52
revolutions 20, 21, 119, 121; political 46
Richmond, Sir William 295
Riddell, Charlotte 18, 152–3
riots 13
rivalries 60, 267
roads 57, 157
Robins, Arthur 127
Rochdale 201
Roman Catholicism 101, 126; *see also* religion (churches)
Rosebery, Lord 27, 125–6, 207, 262
Rothschild Bank 78
Rothschild, Lionel de 83
Rothschild, Nathan Mayer 74
Rothschild, Nathaniel de 113
Rowntree, Seebohm 210, 219; *Poverty: A Study of Town Life* 195
Royal Academy 232
Royal Commission 150, 157
Royal Commission on Noxious Vapours 65
Royal Exchange 78
Royal Free Hospital 148
Royal Institution 96, 109
Royal Navy 79, 253
Royal Society 99, 109
Ruskin, John 2, 9, 16, 42, 91, 136, 172, 179, 220, 247, 259, 293; Progress 31, 33, 37, 38; reason and faith 179, 188–91
Russell, Bertrand 2, 199
Russell, Lord John 112, 127, 131, 136, 153, 190, 242, 255, 271
Russia 257, 262
Russo-Turkish War 1878 257

Salisbury, 3rd Marquess of 241, 245, 286
Salomons, David 75–6

Salomons, Levi 75
Salt, Titus 28
Salvation Army *219*
Samuel, Horace 122
Sanitary Condition of the Labouring Population of Great Britain, The 155
sanitation 19, 29, 150
satire 90
Saturday Review 88, 99, 100, 246
Saunders, John 27
scandals 56
scholarship programmes 31
School Inspectors 245–6
School of Art, London 232
schools 19, 134, 212, 239–40, 241, 247; professionalization 143, 158; *see also* education
science 14, 50, 96, 282, 295, 299–301; education 229, 242; reason and faith 177–9, 181, 186, 191–2
Science Museum 96
scientific discoveries 40
scientific methods 111
scientists 51, *95*, 98, 108, 185
Scrope, Poulett 98
Second World War 297
secularization 102
Seddon, Mary 257
Seeley, John 52, 243
segregation 251
Selborne, Lord 161
self-esteem 73, 300
self-government 281
self-help 46, 64, 73; England's condition 200–1, 208, 211, 213, 231
Self-Help 29–30
self-improvement 30
self-respect 73, 137
selfishness 33
Selfridge, Harry Gordon 76
Senior, Nassau 222, 230–1
separation 228
sewerage systems 122
sewers 68, 69
Shadow of Ashlydyat, The 22–3
Shaftesbury, 7th Earl of (Lord Ashley) 239, 240, 241, 257
Shaftesbury Park Estate *210*
shipbuilding (shipyards) 270, 272
shipping 274

shopping 73
Sidgwick, Henry 173, 179
Simon, Sir John 148, 150
Singleton, Mary (Violet Fane) 5, 6, 7
skills 168, 212; technical 158
slavery *47*, 143, 153–4, 222, 249, 279; *see also* colonialism; imperialism; Progress
Slavery Abolition Bill 153
slums 67, 211, 218
Smiles, Samuel 29–30, 31, 46, 50, 58, 74, 170, 211
Smith, Adam 123
Smith, George 104–5
Smith, Thomas 73
Smith, W.H. 84–5
Smith, William 73
smoke 153
Snow, John 150
social behaviour 31
social classes (structures) 27, 31, 208
Social Darwinism 33
Social Evolution 18
social improvement (change) 31, 86, 280
social media 31, 94, 256, 298, 301, 303; discoveries 18, 25
social mobility (climbing) 29, 93
social networks 47
social order 197
social problems 132
social progress 301
social reforms 40, 42, 131, 156
social responsibility 149
social welfare 209, 222
social wellbeing 94
Socialism in England 64
Socialist League 207
societies 30, 33, 51, 231
sociology 32
soft power 60
soldiers 169
Somerville, Mary 235
specialization 185
Spectator, The 127, 189, 266
Spence, Catherine 103
Spencer, Herbert *32*, 33, 101, 152, 183, 224; *Nineteenth Century* 61; *Principles of Psychology* 179; *The Proper Sphere of Government* 165
Spirit of the Age, The 13
sport 170, 290

Spring, Howard 296
SS *Great Britain* 59, 73, 281
SS *Great Eastern* 59, 83
St Mary's Hospital 143
St Peter's Fields 197
St Thomas's Hospital 144
stability 38, 297
Stanley, H.M. 285, 295, 298
Stansfield, Sr James 230, 231
Stanton, Elizabeth Cady 250
state-funded 31, 43, 130–1, 134, 198–9, 244–5; England's condition 212, 214
Statesman, Liverpool 46
steam looms 213
steam power 49, 169
steam transport 50
steamships 59
Stephen, Sir James Fitzjames 91
Stephen, Sir Leslie 93
Stephen, Sir James 153–4, 281
Stephenson, George 46–7, 48, 49–50, 52, 53, 200
Stephenson, Robert *36*, 47, 49–50, 58–9, 60
Stock Companies Act 81
Stock Exchange 78
stockbrokers 74, 78
Stockton and Darlington railway 49, 54
Strachey, Lytton 146, 296
strikes 202–3
Struggles of Brown, Jones, and Robinson, The 73
students, medical 151
Sturge, Joseph 250
subscriptions 200
suffering 15
suffrage 197; household 161
suffrage, female 115, 128, 130, 234, 235, 236
Suffragettes 235
Sully, James 38
Sunday Schools 42
superiority 121, 275
Supreme Court of Judicature 161
Surrey docks *70*
Surtees, Robert 84
Swan, Henry 31
Swindon 201–2

Taine, Hippolyte 21, 26, 30, 88–9, 110, 158, 160, 203, 243; global economic dominance 44, 58

Tariff Reform League *139*
tariffs 71, 78, 123, 264, 291
Taunton Commission 237
taxation 29, 84, 119, 130, 131, 209
Taylor, Clementia (Mentia) 235–6
Taylor, Harriet 116, 234
Taylor, Helen 234–5
Taylor, Henry 154
Taylor, Shephard 65, 66, 98, 151, 152, 264
Taylor, W. Cooke 45
technologies 296, 299, 301, 303–4; discoveries 23, 25; England's condition 205, 242; global economic dominance 82; governance 110, 122; Progress 257; reason and faith 192; under scrutiny 86, 92, 96
telegrams 60
telegraph system 165; discoveries 13, 19; global economic dominance 60–1, 83; Progress 267, 280; under scrutiny 84, 97
Temple Bar 163–4
Temple, Sir Richard 295
Temps, Le 60
Tennyson, Alfred 54, 101, 173, 186, 190–1, 242, 290
territorial acquisitions 279
Thackeray, William M. 15, 95, 166, 217; *Pendennis* 84
Thatcher, Margaret 297
Thompson, Sir William 152
Thomson, William (Baron Kelvin) 61
Thorne Coffin, Somerset 239
Thornton, Richard 74
Thrift 30
time, global 82–3
Times, The: discoveries 11, 15, 99; education 227, 242, 243; England's condition 152, 202, 203, 219, 223, 225, 250, 283; global economic dominance 57, 61, 71, 82; professionalization 157, 165; Progress 38, 255, 260; under scrutiny 82, 84, *85*, 87–9, 90
Tocqueville, Alexis de 301–2
toleration (tolerance) 102, 303, 304
Toulmin Smith, Joshua 157
Tower Bridge 58
town arms, Crewe 62–3
Town Improvement Act 68
town planning 62
towns 64, 158, 197, 239; industrial 65, 157

Toynbee, Arnold 50, 221
Toynbee Hall 221
trade 13, 136, 291, 293; global economic dominance 66, 71–2, 77; international 51, 83, 160; Progress 264, 282
Trade Disputes Act 1906 204
trade unions 202, 203, 204, 217, 290, 292
Trade Unions Act 1871 204
traditions 191; *see also* practices, traditional
trains 14; *see also* railways (railroads)
transport 18, 49, 299
travel 53, 171, 281
Treaty of Aigun 255, 262
Treaty of Balta Liman 72
Treaty of Ghent 270
Tremenheere, Simon 154–5
Trevelyan, Sir Charles 155, 294
Trevithick, Robert 50
tribes 25, 178
Trollope, Anthony 39, *42*, 90, 182, 234
Trollope, Fanny *42*, 225
Truth 89, 230
truth (truthfulness) 25, 73, 179, 184, 192
Tyndall Centre for Climate Change 187
Tyndall, John 4, 9, *95*, 99, 101, 173, 181, 186, 187, 190
typewriters 133
typhoid 143

Underground Railway 57; London *67*
understanding 34
United States of America (America) 249, 272–3, 291; *see also* America
universities 94, 242, 243, 247, 289
University College Hospital 143
University settlements 220
urban living 195
urbanization 62, 86, 103, 121, 299
Useful Knowledge Societies 212
USS *Alabama* 270–1
utilitarianism 17
utilities 158
Utopia, Limited, or, The Flowers of Progress 81

vaccinations 148
value systems 24, 34, 295
Vanity Fair 166, 187
Vaughan, Robert 62
Verplanck, Julian 269

Victoria, Queen 11, *12*, 22, 43, 44, 46, 60, 128, 130, 149, 182, 191, 252, 257, *280*, 291; education 226, 233; governance 101, 114, 118; professionalization 154, 159, 164, 168
violence 24, 119, 205, 225, 263, 304
visitors 171
vocational training 245
voters 111, 118; working-class 128
voting (votes) 117, 124, 230, 233, 235

Wade, John 132, 303
wages 200, 202
Wakefield, Edward Gibbon 282–4
Walsh, Sir John 271
Walter III, John 85, 89
Ward, Mary 100
Ward, Thomas 148
warfare 299
wars 54
waste 153
water power 51
water supplies 134, 150, 153, 157, 169
waterways 57
Watkin, Sir Edward 57
Watt, James 47
Waugh, Edwin 92, 201–2
wealth 221, 268, 296
weaponry 299
Webb, Beatrice 64, 222, 257
Webb, Sidney 64, 203
Webster, James 38
Wedgwood, Josiah *47*
welfare state 297, 302
wellbeing 35
Wellington, Duke of 49, 165, 167, 197, 199, 206
Wells, H.G. 64, 301; *Boon* 289; *Pall Mall Magazine* 19; *Short History of the World* 24, 301
Welsh, Jane *17*
Westminster Review 184, 186
Wey, François 69–70
Wheatstone, Charles 60, *95*
Whewell, William 36, 97, 108, 177
Whitehouse, Edward 'Wildman' 61
Wilberforce, Samuel, Bishop *41*, 101, 228
Winchester 156
Wingfield-Stratford, Esmé 27
Witt, John 161–2
women 21, 32, 198, 289, 295, 303; education 229, 231–3; governance 116, 124–5,

128–30; professionalization 142, 145, 147–8; Progress 250, 271; reason and faith 181–2, 191; under scrutiny 93, 100, 103; *see also* suffrage, female
Women's Labour League 233
Women's Liberal Associations 233
Women's Liberal Federation 233
women's rights 34, 225, 257
Women's Suffrage Bill 233
Wood, Henry, Mrs 22–3
work ethic 29
workers 93, 121, 128, 203, 205
working classes 15, 231; England's condition 200, 206, 210; global economic dominance 62, 67; governance 115, 137; Progress 26, 29, 31, 39–40
working, home 51
working hours (conditions) 200, 203, 222
working men 136, 209
Working Women's College 238
World Anti-Slavery Convention 49, 249
Wraxall, Sir Frederick 121

Zionism 257